Lecture Notes in Computer Science 2944

Edited by G. Goos, J. Hartmanis, and J. van Leeuwen

Springer

Berlin
Heidelberg
New York
Hong Kong
London
Milan
Paris
Tokyo

Karl Aberer   Manolis Koubarakis
Vana Kalogeraki (Eds.)

Databases, Information Systems, and Peer-to-Peer Computing

First International Workshop, DBISP2P 2003
Berlin, Germany, September 7 – 8, 2003
Revised Papers

Springer

Volume Editors

Karl Aberer
Swiss Federal Institute of Technology (EPFL)
Distributed Information Systems Laboratory
School of Computer and Communication Sciences
1015 Lausanne, Switzerland
E-mail: karl.aberer@epfl.ch

Manolis Koubarakis
Technical University of Crete
Dept. of Electronic and Computer Engineering
Chania 73100 Crete, Greece
E-mail: manolis@intelligence.tuc.gr

Vana Kalogeraki
University of California, Riverside
Dept. of Computer Science and Engineering
Riverside, CA 92521, USA
E-mail: vana@cs.ucr.edu

Cataloging-in-Publication Data applied for

A catalog record for this book is available from the Library of Congress.

Bibliographic information published by Die Deutsche Bibliothek
Die Deutsche Bibliothek lists this publication in the Deutsche Nationalbibliografie;
detailed bibliographic data is available in the Internet at <http://dnb.ddb.de>.

CR Subject Classification (1998): H.2, H.3, H.4, C.2, I.2.11, D.2.12, D.4.3, E.1

ISSN 0302-9743
ISBN 3-540-20968-9 Springer-Verlag Berlin Heidelberg New York

Springer-Verlag is a part of Springer Science+Business Media

springeronline.com

© Springer-Verlag Berlin Heidelberg 2004
Printed in Germany

Typesetting: Camera-ready by author, data conversion by PTP-Berlin, Protago-TeX-Production GmbH
Printed on acid-free paper   SPIN: 10982693   06/3142   5 4 3 2 1 0

Preface

Peer-to-peer (P2P) computing is currently attracting enormous media attention, spurred by the popularity of file sharing systems such as Napster, Gnutella and Morpheus. In P2P systems a very large number of autonomous computing nodes (the peers) pool together their resources and rely on each other for data and services.

The wealth of business opportunities promised by P2P networks has generated much industrial interest recently, and has resulted in the creation of various industrial projects, startup companies, and special interest groups. Researchers from distributed computing, networks, agents and databases have also become excited about the P2P vision, and papers tackling open problems in this area have started appearing in high-quality conferences and workshops.

Much of the recent research on P2P systems seems to be carried out by research groups with a primary interest in distributed computation and networks. This workshop concentrated on the impact that current database research can have on P2P computing and vice versa. Although researchers in distributed data structures and databases have been working on related issues for a long time, the developed techniques are simply not adequate for the new paradigm. P2P computing introduces the paradigm of decentralization going hand in hand with an increasing self-organization of highly autonomous peers, thus departing from the classical client-server computing paradigm. This new paradigm bears the potential to realize computing systems that scale to very large numbers of participating nodes. Taking advantage of this potential for the area of data management is a challenge that the database community itself is asked to face. The realization of the P2P computing vision is however a Herculean task, fraught with immense technical difficulties. As a result, it offers database theoreticians and system developers a new set of exciting open problems.

We believe that database research has much to contribute to the P2P grand challenge through its wealth of techniques for sophisticated semantics-based data models, clever indexing algorithms and efficient data placement, query processing techniques and transaction processing. The database community could benefit from the P2P computing vision by developing loosely coupled federations of databases where databases can join and leave the network at will; a single global schema is not a possibility, and answers need not be complete but should be best effort.

Database technologies in the new information age will form the crucial components of the first generation of complex adaptive information systems. These are an emerging kind of information systems that are very dynamic, self-organize continously and adapt to new circumstances, they are locally but not globally optimized, and form a whole which is greater than the sum of its parts. These new information systems support highly dynamic, ever-changing, autonomous social organizations and can no longer be developed using traditional analysis, design and implementation techniques. This workshop also concentrated on complex adaptive information systems, their impact on current database technologies and their relation to emerging industrial technologies such as IBM's autonomic computing initiative.

This workshop, collocated with VLDB, the major international database and information systems conference, brought together key researchers from all over the world working on databases and P2P computing with the intention of strengthening this connection. Also researchers from other related areas such as distributed systems, networks, multiagent systems and complex systems participated.

The workshop was jointly organized with the AP2PC workshop which is part of the AAMAS conference and is under the responsibility of the same steering committee. Together these two workshops address both the agent and the database communities and thus take account of the interdisciplinary nature of P2P computing.

The DBISP2P workshop received 32 submissions that entered the review process. All submissions underwent a rigorous review that was completed by an online PC discussion for making the final selection of 16 papers. The organizers would like to thank at this point all program committee members for their excellent work. The program was completed by a keynote speech and a panel. The keynote speech with the title "Design Issues and Challenges for RDF- and Schema-Based Peer-to-Peer Systems" was presented by Wolfgang Nejdl from the University of Hannover. Aris Ouksel organized a panel on the topic "P2P Computing and Database Technologies: Convergence of Technologies and Socioeconomic Characteristics on the Web, Benefits and Technical Challenges in Database Applications" with the goal to explore the promise of P2P to offer exciting new possibilities in distributed information processing.

The organizers would particularly like to thank Klemens Böhm from the University of Magdeburg for his excellent work in taking care of the local arrangements, the VLDB organization for their valuable support of the workshop organization, and the steering committee for the opportunity to set up this workshop and for their continuing support.

September 2003   Karl Aberer, Manolis Koubarakis, Vana Kalogeraki

Organization

The 1st International Workshop on Databases, Information Systems and Peer-to-Peer Computing took place at Humboldt University, Berlin, Germany on September 7–8, 2003, collocated with VLDB 2003.

Workshop Chairs

Program Chairs   Karl Aberer (EPFL, Lausanne, Switzerland)
                        Manolis Koubarakis (Technical University of
                        Crete, Greece)
                        Vana Kalogeraki (University of California,
                        Riverside, USA)

Panel Chair   Aris Ouksel (University of Illinois, Chicago, USA)

Organization Chair   Klemens Böhm (University of Magdeburg, Germany)

Steering Committee

Karl Aberer (EPFL, Lausanne, Switzerland)
Sonia Bergamaschi (University of Modena and Reggio-Emilia, Italy)
Manolis Koubarakis (Technical University of Crete)
Paul Marrow (BTexact Technologies,UK)
Gianluca Moro (University of Bologna, Cesena, Italy)
Aris M. Ouksel (University of Illinois, Chicago, USA)
Claudio Sartori (CNR-CSITE, University of Bologna, Italy)
Munindar P. Singh (North Carolina State University, USA)

Program Committee

Ozalp Babaoglu, University of Bologna, Italy
Klemens Böhm, University of Magdeburg, Germany
Beng Chin Ooi, National University of Singapore, Singapore
Partha Dasgupta, Arizona State University, USA
Alex Delis, Polytechnic University, USA
Fausto Giunchiglia, University of Trento, Italy
Zachary G. Ives, University of Washington, USA
Carole Goble, University of Manchester, UK
Oliver Guenther, Humboldt University, Germany
Dimitris Gunopoulos, University of California at Riverside, USA
Manfred Hauswirth, EPFL, Switzerland
Achilles D. Kameas, Computer Technology Institute, Greece
Yannis Labrou, Fujitsu Labs of America, USA
Witold Litwin, University of Paris 6, France
Ling Liu, Georgia Institute of Technology, USA
Peri Loucopoulos, UMIST, Manchester, UK
Dejan Milojicic, Hewlett-Packard Labs, USA
Alberto Montresor, University of Bologna, Italy
Jean-Henry Morin, University of Geneva, Switzerland
John Mylopoulos, University of Toronto, Canada
Wolfgang Nejdl, Learning Lab Lower Saxony, Germany
Dimitris Papadias, Hong Kong University of Science and Technology, China
Mike Papazoglou, Tilburg University, Netherlands
Evaggelia Pitoura, University of Ioannina, Greece
Dimitris Plexousakis, Institute of Computer Science, FORTH, Greece
Onn Shehory, IBM Haifa, Israel
Spiros Skiadopoulos, National Technical University of Athens, Greece
Katia Sycara, Robotics Institute, Carnegie Mellon University, USA
Peter Triantafillou, University of Patras, Greece
Martin Wolpers, Learning Lab Lower Saxony, Germany

Referees

W. Black
Claus Boyens
David Buttler
James Caverlee
Eleni Christopoulou
Matthias Fischmann
Christos Goumopoulos
Tasos Gounaris
Verena Kantere

Mujtaba Khambatti
Georgia Koloniari
Bin Liu
Nikolaos Ntarmos
Themis Palpanas
Michel Pawlak
I. Petrounias
Theoni Pitoura
Th. Schwarz

Table of Contents

Data Streams and Publish/Subscribe

Data Structures and Query Processing

Design Issues and Challenges for RDF- and Schema-Based Peer-to-Peer Systems

Wolfgang Nejdl

Learning Lab Lower Saxony and University of Hannover, 30539 Hannover
nejdl@learninglab.de

Abstract. Databases have employed a schema-based approach to store and retrieve structured data for decades. For peer-to-peer (P2P) networks, similar approaches are just beginning to emerge. While quite a few database techniques can be re-used in this new context, a P2P data management infrastructure poses additional challenges which have to be solved before schema-based P2P networks become as common as schema-based databases. We will describe some of these challenges and discuss approaches to solve them, basing our discussion on the design decisions we have employed in our Edutella infrastructure, a schema-based P2P network based on RDF and RDF schemas.

K. Aberer et al. (Eds.): VLDB 2003 Ws DBISP2P, LNCS 2944, p. 1, 2004.
© Springer-Verlag Berlin Heidelberg 2004

SIL: Modeling and Measuring Scalable Peer-to-Peer Search Networks*

Brian F. Cooper and Hector Garcia-Molina

Department of Computer Science
Stanford University
Stanford, CA 94305 USA
{cooperb,hector}@db.Stanford.EDU

Abstract. The popularity of peer-to-peer search networks continues to grow, even as the limitations to the scalability of existing systems become apparent. We propose a simple model for search networks, called the *Search/Index Links* (SIL) model. The SIL model describes existing networks while also yielding organizations not previously studied. Using analytical and simulation results, we argue that one new organization, *parallel search clusters*, is superior to existing supernode networks in many cases.

1 Introduction

Peer-to-peer search networks have become very popular as a way to effectively search huge, distributed data repositories. On a typical day, systems such as Kazaa support several million simultaneous users, allowing them to search hundreds of millions of digital objects totaling multiple petabytes of data. These search networks take advantage of the large aggregate processing power of many hosts, while leveraging the distributed nature of the system to enhance robustness. Despite the popularity of peer-to-peer search networks, they still suffer from many problems: nodes quickly become overloaded as the network grows, and users can become frustrated with long search latencies or service degradation due to node failures. These issues limit the usefulness of existing peer-to-peer networks for new data management applications beyond multimedia file sharing.

We wish to develop techniques for improving the efficiency and fault tolerance of search in networks of autonomous data repositories. Our approach is to study how we can place indexes in a peer-to-peer network to reduce system load by avoiding the need to query all nodes. The scale and dynamism of the system, as large numbers of nodes constantly join and leave, requires us to re-examine index replication and query forwarding techniques.

However, the space of options to consider is complex and difficult to analyze, given the bewildering array of options for search network topologies, query routing and processing techniques, index and content replication, and so on. In

---

* This material is based upon work supported by the National Science Foundation under Award 9811992.

K. Aberer et al. (Eds.): VLDB 2003 Ws DBISP2P, LNCS 2944, pp. 2–16, 2004.

order to make our exploration more manageable, we separate the process into two phases. In the first phase, we construct a coarse-grained *architectural model* that describes the topology of the connections between distributed nodes, and models the basic query flow properties and index placement strategies within this topology. In the second phase, we use the insights gained from the architectural model to develop a finer-grained *operational model*, which describes at a lower level the actual processing in the system. The operational model allows us to study alternatives for building and maintaining the topology as nodes join and leave, directing queries to nodes (for example, using flooding, random walks or routing indices), parallel versus sequential query submission to different parts of the network, and so on.

Our focus in this paper is on the first phase architectural model. We have developed the Search/Index Link (SIL) model for representing and visualizing peer-to-peer search networks at the architectural level. The SIL model helps us to understand the inherent properties of many existing network architectures, and to design and evaluate novel architectures that are more robust and efficient. Once we understand which architectures are promising, ongoing work can examine operational issues. For example, in [4], we examine the operational question of how the architectures described here might be constructed. In this paper, we first present and analyze the SIL model, and show how it can lead to new search network architectures. Then, using analytical and simulation results, we show that our new organizations can be superior to existing P2P networks in several important cases, in terms of both efficiency and fault tolerance.

2   The Search/Index Link Model

A *peer-to-peer search network* is a set of peers that store, search for, and transfer digital documents. We consider here content-based searches, such as keyword searches, metadata searches, and so on. This distinguishes a peer-to-peer search network from a distributed hash table [14,11], where queries are to locate a specific document with a specific identifier (see Section 5 for more discussion about SIL versus DHTs). Each peer in the network maintains an index over its content (such as an inverted list of the words in each document) to assist in processing searches. We assume that the index is sufficient to answer searches, even though it does not contain the whole content of the indexed documents.

The search network forms an *overlay* on top of a fully-connected underlying network infrastructure. The topology of the overlay determines where indexes are placed in the network, and how queries reach either a data repository or an index over that repository's content. Peers that are neighbors in the overlay are connected by network links that are logically persistent, though they may be implemented as connection-oriented or connectionless.

The Search/Index Link (SIL) model allows us to describe and visualize the overlay topology. In the SIL model, there are four kinds of network links, distinguished by the types of messages that are sent, and whether a peer receiving a message forwards the message after processing it:

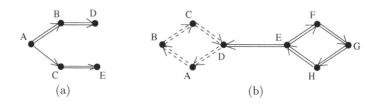

Fig. 1. Networks: (a) with search links, (b) with search and index links.

- A *non-forwarding search link* (NSL) carries search messages a single hop in the overlay from their origin. For example, a search generated at one peer A will be sent to another peer B, but not forwarded beyond B. Peer B processes each search message and returns results to A.

- A *forwarding search link* (FSL) carries search messages from A to B. Peer B will process each search message, return search results to A, and forward the message along any other forwarding search links originating at B. If A is not the originator of the query, it should forward any search results received from B (and any other nodes) along the FSL on which A received the query.

- A *non-forwarding index link* (NIL) carries index update messages one hop in the overlay from their origin. That is, updates occurring at A will be sent to B, but not forwarded. Peer B adds A's index entries to its own index, and then effectively has a copy of A's index. Peer B need not have a full copy of A's content.

- A *forwarding index link* (FIL) carries index update messages from A to B, as with non-forwarding index links, but then B forwards the update message along any other forwarding index links originating at B.

For FSLs and FILs, messages should have unique ids, and a peer should discard duplicate messages without processing or forwarding them. This avoids infinite propagation of messages if the network has cycles.

Network links are directed communications channels. A link from peer A to peer B indicates that A sends messages to B, but B only sends messages to A if there is also a separate link from B to A. Modeling links as directed channels makes the model more general. An undirected channel can be modeled as a pair of directed links going in opposite directions. For example, the links in Gnutella can be modeled as a pair of FSLs, one in each direction. Although forwarding links may at first glance seem more useful, we will see how non-forwarding links can be used in Section 3.

Figure 1a shows an example network containing search links. Non-forwarding search links are represented as single arrows ($\longrightarrow$) while forwarding search links are represented as double arrows ($\Longrightarrow$). Imagine that a user submits a query to peer A. Peer A will first process the query and return any search results it finds to the user. Node A will then send this query to both B and C, who will also process the query. Node B will forward the query to D. Node C will not forward the query, since it received the query along an NSL. The user's query will not reach E at all, and E's content will not be searched for this query.

A peer uses an *index link* to send copies of index entries to its neighbors. These index entries allow the content to be searched by the neighbors without the neighbors having to store the peer's actual content. For example, consider a peer A that has an index link to a peer B. When B processes a query, it will return search results both for its own content as well as for the content stored at A. Peer A need not process the query at all. We say that B is *searched directly* in this case, while A is *searched indirectly*.

Whenever a peer creates a new index entry or modifies an existing entry, it should send a message indicating the change along all of its outgoing index links. A peer might create an index over all of its locally stored documents when it first starts up, and should send all of the index entries to each of its index link neighbors. Similarly, if a node deletes a document, it would remove the corresponding entries from its own index as well as notifying its index link neighbors to do the same.

Figure 1b shows a network that contains both search and index links. Index links are represented as dashed lines, single ($\dashrightarrow$) for non-forwarding index links and double ($\Rrightarrow$) for forwarding index links. (Note that Figure 1b contains only FILs.) Nodes A, B, C and D are connected by a "ring" of FILs. An index update occurring at peer A will thus be forwarded to B, C, D and back to A (A will not forward the update again). In fact, all four of the nodes $A...D$ will have complete copies of the indexes at the other three nodes in the index "ring". Nodes E, F, G and H are connected by FSLs, and a search originating at any peer $E...H$ will reach, and be processed by, the three other nodes on the search "ring." Notice that there is also an FSL between E and D. Any query that is processed by E will be forwarded to D, who will also process the query. Since D has a copy of the indexes from $A...C$, this means that any query generated at E, F, G and H will effectively search the content of all eight nodes in the network. In contrast, a query generated at nodes $A...D$ will be processed at the node generating the query, and will only search the indexes of the nodes $A...D$.

A search path from X to Y indicates that queries submitted to X will eventually be forwarded to Y, either through a sequence of FSLs or by a single NSL. For example, in Figure 1b there is a search path from F to D but not from D to F. There is (trivially) a search path from a node to itself. Similarly, an *index path* from X to Y is a sequence of FILs from X to Y, or one NIL from X to Y. In this case, X's index updates will be sent to Y, and Y will have a copy of X's index.

2.1 "Good" Networks

The network links we have discussed above are not by themselves new. Forwarding search links are present in Gnutella, forwarding index links are used in publish/subscribe systems, non-forwarding index links are used in supernode networks, and so on. However, different link types tend to be used in isolation or for narrowly specific purposes, and are rarely combined into a single, general model. Our graphical representation allows us to consider new combinations. In fact, the number of search networks of n nodes that can be constructed under the SIL model is exponential in n^2. Only a small fraction of these networks will allow users to search the content of most or all the peers in the network, and an even smaller fraction will also have desirable scalability, efficiency or fault tolerance properties. We want to use the SIL model to find and study "good" networks, and this of course requires defining what we mean by "good."

First, we observe that a search network only meets users' needs if it allows them to find content. Since content may be located anywhere in the network, a user must be able to effectively search as many content repositories as possible, either directly or indirectly. We can quantify this goal by defining the concept of *coverage*: the fraction of peers in the network that can be searched, either directly or indirectly, by a query generated by a peer p. Ideal networks would have *full coverage*: all peers have *coverage* $= 1$, and if content exists anywhere in the network, users can find it. It may be necessary to reduce coverage in order to improve network efficiency.

Even a network that has full coverage may not necessarily be "good." Good networks should also be efficient, in the sense that peers are not overloaded with work answering queries. One important way to improve the efficiency of a network is to reduce or eliminate redundant work. If peers are duplicating each other's processing, then they are doing unnecessary work.

Definition 1. *A search network N has* redundancy *if there exists a network link in N that can be removed without reducing the coverage for any peer.*

Intuitively, redundancy results in messages being sent to and processed by peers, even when such processing does not add to the network's ability to answer queries.

Redundancy can manifest in search networks in four ways:

- *Search/search redundancy* occurs when the same peer P processes the same query from the same user multiple times.
- *Update/update redundancy* occurs when the same peer P processes the same update multiple times.
- *Search/index redundancy* means a peer A processes a query even though another peer B has a copy of A's index and processes the same query.
- *Index/index redundancy* is where two different peers B and C both process a search over a copy of a third peer A's index.

In each of these cases, a node is doing work that is unnecessary to achieve high or full coverage.

Note that redundancy may actually be useful to improve the fault tolerance of the system, since if one node fails another can perform its processing. Moreover, redundancy may be useful to reduce the time a user must wait for search results, if a node near the user can process the user's search even when this processing is redundant. However, fault tolerance and search latency tradeoff with efficiency, since redundancy results in extra work for peers.

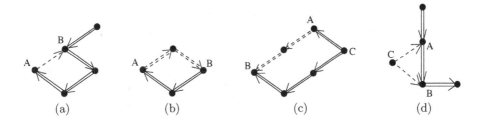

Fig. 2. Networks: a. with search/index redundancy, b. no search/index redundancy, c. search-fork, and d. index-fork

2.2 Topological Features of Networks with Redundancy

The concept of "redundancy" and even the subconcepts like search/index redundancy are quite general. Rather than avoiding generalized redundancy when designing a peer-to-peer search network, it is easier to identify specific features of network topologies that lead to redundancy, and avoid those features.

A feature that causes search/index redundancy is a specific type of cycle called a *one-cycle*. A *one-index-cycle* is a version of a one-cycle:

- A *one-index-cycle* is when a node A has an index link to another node B, and B has a search path to A.

An example is shown in Figure 2a. This construct leads to redundant processing, since B will answer queries over A's index, and yet these queries will be forwarded to A who will also answer them over A's index. More formally, a one-index-cycle fits our definition of *redundancy* because at least one link in the cycle can be removed without affecting coverage: the index link from A to B. Another version of a one-cycle is a *one-search-cycle*:

- A *one-search-cycle* is when a node A has an search link to another node B, and B has an index path to A.

While *one-cycles* (one-index-cycles and one-search-cycles) cause redundancy, not all cycles do. Consider the cycle in Figure 2b. This cycle may seem to introduce redundancy in the same way as a one-cycle, except that none of the links can be removed without reducing coverage for some node.

Another feature that causes search/index redundancy is a *fork*.

- A *search-fork* is when a node C has a search link to A and a search path to B that does not include A, and there is an index path from A to B.

An example of a search-fork is shown in Figure 2c. Again, A will process any searches from C unnecessarily, since B can process the queries for A. The redundant link in this example is the link $C \Longrightarrow A$. We specify that there is a search path from C to B that does not include A because if the only path from C to B included A there would be no link that could be removed without reducing coverage. The analog of a search-fork is an *index-fork*; an example is shown in Figure 2d.

- An *index-fork* is when a node C has an index link to A and an index path to B that does not include A, and there is a search path from A to B.

The third feature that causes redundancy is a *loop*:

- A *search-loop* is when a node A has an search link l_s to another node B, and also another search path to B that does not include l_s.

- An *index-loop* is when a node A has an index link l_i to another node B, and also another index path to B that does not include l_i.

Avoiding all of these topological features is sufficient to avoid the general property of redundancy in a network.

Theorem 1. *If a network has no one-cycles, forks or loops, then it has no redundancy.*

Proof. The proof is straightforward: a redundant edge implies one of the named features. The full proof is available in the extended version of this paper [5]. □

3   Network Archetypes

We can now identify some archetypical network organizations described by the SIL model. Each archetype is a family of topologies that share a common general architecture. We restrict our attention to somewhat idealized networks, that is, non-redundant networks with full coverage, in order to understand the inherent advantages and disadvantages of various architectures. We do not claim to examine the entire design space of peer-to-peer topologies. Instead, by looking at some representative archetypes of a particular design point, that is, non-redundant full-coverage networks, we can both understand that design point clearly and also illustrate the value of SIL as a design tool.

We consider only the static topologies described by the SIL architectural model, in order to determine which topologies have efficiency or fault tolerance benefits and are worth examining further. If a particular archetype is selected for a given application, there are then operational decisions that must be made. For example, if a supernode archetype (described fully below) is chosen as desirable, there must be a way to form peers into a supernode topology as they join the system. One way to form such a network is to use a central coordinator that selects which nodes are supernodes and assigns them responsibility for non-supernodes. Alternatively, nodes could decide on their own whether to be supernodes or not, and then advertise their supernode status to connect to other, non-supernode peers. This dynamic process of forming a specific topology is outside the scope of this paper, as we wish to focus for now on which topology archetype is most desirable under various circumstances. For a discussion on how a topology can be constructed dynamically, see [4,16].

Also, we focus on networks with no search/index or index/index redundancy. The impact of search/search and update/update redundancies is mitigated by the fact that a node processes only one copy of a duplicate search or update message and discards the rest (see Section 2). In contrast, search/index and index/index redundancies involve unnecessary work being done at two different peers, and it is difficult for those peers to coordinate and discover that their work is redundant. Therefore, in order to reduce load it is important to design networks that do not have search/index and index/index redundancies. To do this, we consider networks that do not have one-cycles or forks.

First, there are two basic network archetypes that can trivially meet the conditions of no search/index or index/index redundancy while providing full coverage:

- *Pure search networks*: strongly connected networks with only search links.
- *Pure index networks*: strongly connected networks with only index links.

In graph theory, a *strongly connected directed graph* is one in which there is a directed path from every node to every other node. Recall from Section 2 that in our SIL model, a path is either a sequence of forwarding links or a single non-forwarding link. When we say "strongly connected" in the definitions above (and below), we mean "strongly connected" using this definition of search and index paths.

In these basic topologies, there cannot be search/index or index/index redundancies since index links and search links do not co-exist in the same network. However, these networks are not really "efficient," since nodes are heavily loaded. In a pure search network, every node processes every search, while in a pure index network, every node processes every index update. These topologies may be useful in extreme cases; for example, a pure search network is not too cumbersome if there are very few searches. A well known example of a pure search network is the Gnutella network.

Other archetypes combine search links and index links to reduce the load on nodes. We have studied four topology archetypes that are described by the SIL model, have full coverage and no search/index or index/index redundancy:

- Supernode networks
- Global index networks
- Parallel search cluster networks
- Parallel index cluster networks

As we discuss in more detail below, each different topology is useful for different situations. Some of these topologies are not new, and exist in networked systems today. Supernode networks are typified by the FastTrack network of Kazaa, while the global index network is similar to the organization of Netnews with a central indexing cluster (like DejaNews). However, the parallel search and index clusters have not been previously examined. While these four archetypes are just a sample of the topologies that can be described by SIL, they illustrate how SIL can be used to model a variety of networks with different characteristics.

A *supernode network* is a network where some nodes are designated as "supernodes," and the other nodes ("normal nodes") send both their indexes and searches to supernodes. The supernodes are linked by a strongly connected pure search network. A supernode network can be represented in our SIL model by

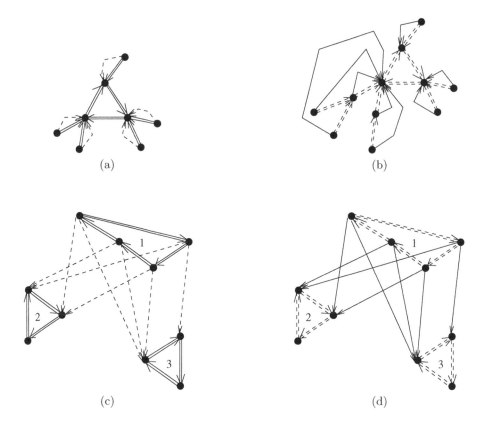

Fig. 3. Topology archetypes: a. Supernodes, b. Global index, c. Parallel search clusters, and d. Parallel index clusters. Some inter-cluster links are omitted in networks c and d for clarity.

having normal nodes point to supernodes with one FSL and one NIL, while supernodes point to each other using FSLs. An example is shown in Figure 3a. Each supernode therefore has the copies of several normal nodes' indexes. Supernodes process searches before forwarding them to other supernodes. Normal nodes only have to process searches that they themselves generate. Thus, supernodes networks result in much less load on an average peer than a pure search network. A disadvantage is that as the network grows, the search load on supernodes grows as well, and ultimately scalability is limited by the processing capacity of supernodes. This disadvantage exists even though there is unused processing capacity in the network at the normal nodes. These normal nodes cannot contribute this spare capacity to reduce the search load on supernodes, because even if a normal node is promoted to a supernode, every supernode must still process all the queries in the network. Supernode networks are most useful when search load is low and when there are nodes in the network powerful enough to serve as supernodes.

An organization similar to supernodes is a *global index network*, as illustrated in Figure 3b. In this organization, some nodes are designated as global indexing nodes, and all index updates in the system flow to these nodes. A normal node sends its queries to one of these global indexing nodes. The global indexing nodes themselves are connected by a strongly connected pure index network. Under our model, normal nodes have a FIL to another normal node or to a global index node, and normal nodes also have NSLs to global index nodes. In this example, the normal nodes form a tree of index paths rooted at a global index node. Index updates flow from the normal nodes to form a complete set of global indexes at each of the global index nodes. Note that a similar tree-like structure could be constructed in the supernode network, where normal nodes would form a tree of search paths rooted at a supernode, while each normal node would have an index link directly to a supernode.

The advantages of global index networks are similar to those of supernode networks. Most nodes process only index updates and their own searches, while leaving the processing of all other searches to the global index nodes. Moreover, there are multiple nodes that have a complete set of indexes, so the network can recover from the failure of one node. However, the load on the global index nodes is high; each global index peer must process all the index updates in the system and a significant fraction of the searches. Global index networks are most useful when update load is low and when there are nodes in the network powerful enough to serve as index nodes.

A third organization is called *parallel search clusters*. In this network, nodes are organized into clusters of strongly connected pure search networks (consisting of FSLs), and clusters are connected to other clusters by NIL index links. An example is shown in Figure 3c. In this figure, the cluster "1" has outgoing NILs to the other clusters "2" and "3". Clusters "2" and "3" would also have outgoing NILs to the other clusters, but we have omitted them in this figure for clarity. The nodes in each cluster collectively have a copy of the indexes of every node outside the cluster, so full coverage is achieved even though queries are only forwarded within a cluster. Unlike in a supernode topology, there are no nodes that must handle all of the queries in the network. Nodes only handle queries that are generated within their own cluster. Moreover, all of the search processing resources in the system are utilized, since every node processes some queries. A disadvantage of this topology is that nodes must ship their index updates to every other cluster in the network. If the update rate is high, this will generate a large amount of update load. In [5], we discuss how to tune the cluster network to minimize the update load. Parallel search clusters are most useful when the network is relatively homogeneous (in terms of node capabilities), and when the update rate is low.

Finally, the fourth organization is *parallel index clusters*. In this organization, clusters of strongly connected pure FIL index networks are connected by NSL search links. As a result, nodes in one cluster send their searches to one node of each of the other clusters. An example is shown in Figure 3d. (Again, some inter-cluster links are omitted in this figure.) Parallel index clusters have advantages and disadvantages similar to parallel search cluster networks: no node handles all index updates or all searches, and all resources in the system are utilized, while inter-cluster links may be cumbersome to maintain and may generate a large amount of load. Index cluster networks are useful for relatively homogeneous networks where the search rate is low.

These topology archetypes can be varied or combined in various ways. For example, a variation of the supernode topology is to allow a normal node to have an FSL pointing to one supernode and an NIL pointing to another. Another example is to vary parallel cluster search networks by allowing the search clusters to be constructed as mini-supernode networks instead of (or in addition to) clusters that are pure search networks. These and other variations are useful in certain cases. Allowing a mini-supernode network as a search cluster in a parallel search cluster network is useful if the nodes in that cluster are heterogeneous, and some nodes have much higher capacities than the others. Moreover, pure index and pure search networks are special cases of our four topology archetypes. For example, a supernode network where all nodes are supernodes and a parallel search cluster network with only one cluster are both pure search networks.

Note that our restriction of no redundancy can be relaxed to improve the fault tolerance or search latency of the system at the cost of higher load. For example, in a supernode network, a normal node could have an NIL/FSL pair to two different supernodes. This introduces, at the very least, an index/index redundancy, but ensures that the normal node is still fully connected to the network if one of its supernodes fails. Similarly, the goal of full coverage could be relaxed to reduce load. For instance, in many real networks, messages are given a time-to-live so that they do not reach every node. This results both in lower coverage and lower load.

4   Evaluation of Network Topologies

We quantify the strengths and weaknesses of the various topology archetypes in three steps. First, we define metrics that are computable over SIL graphs. Then, we use these metrics to evaluate analytically the strengths and weaknesses of different idealized architectures. Finally, we run simulations to validate our analytical results for less idealized networks. We focus our evaluation on two archetypes: supernode networks, which represent a popular and widely deployed existing architecture, and parallel search clusters, which is a promising new architecture that we discovered from analysis of SIL. Due to space limitations, we will only highlight here some of the results of our evaluation. For a complete discussion of our analytical and simulation results, see [5].

First, we must define metrics to evaluate both the efficiency and the robustness of networks. One measure of efficiency is *load*, which represents the amount of work that is done by each node in the network. In particular, we define load as the number of messages processed by nodes per unit time. There are two types of messages in the network: search messages and index update messages. We treat both types of messages as equally costly to process. A situation where one

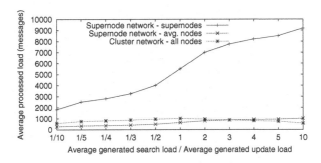

Fig. 4. Load of optimized networks.

type of message is more costly to process can be represented in our framework as a scenario where there is more of one type of message than the other. Another measure of efficiency is *search latency*, or the response time for searches. We calculate this metric by examining the longest path length that queries must take in the network, because the path length is related to the amount of time a user must wait before the query returns all results. Finally, we also examine *fault susceptibility*, which represents the amount that service is degraded after a node fails. We calculate fault susceptibility by finding the node whose failure would cause the largest decrease in coverage, and measuring that decrease.

Next, we can obtain analytical results. Specifically, we examine the load of networks, both because this is most important to ensuring scalability, and also because it is particularly amenable to analytical evaluation. The load on a node X is the result of the search load and update load generated by nodes that send messages to X, and thus the network-wide load depends on the average number of search and update messages generated by nodes in the network. In [5], we define equations for the load on nodes as a function of the rate of search and update messages and the topology of the network. We can use those equations to compare different network archetypes. Imagine a network with 100 nodes, where each node generates 100 messages per unit time, divided between search and index messages. Figure 4 shows the load in cluster and supernode networks as a function of the ratio between the average number of generated search and update messages. As the graph shows, supernode networks have lightly loaded nodes on average but heavily loaded supernodes, especially as the search load in the network increases. This is because supernodes do all of the search processing in the network. In contrast, nodes in a cluster network are much less loaded. In a cluster network, the search processing is shared among all of the nodes, and thus there are no nodes that are overloaded. Moreover, the cluster size can be adjusted based on the load in the network; for example, smaller clusters are better as the search load increases. The result is that a cluster network allows nodes to be lightly loaded, as if they were normal nodes in a supernode network, without needing to have any overloaded supernodes.

Table 1. Simulation parameters

Parameter	Description	Base value
n	Number of nodes	100
NS	Number of supernodes	$1...n$
NC	Number of clusters	$1...n$
SL	Avg. search load generated by a peer	$10...100$
UL	Avg. update load generated by a peer	$10...100$

Our analytical result assumes idealized networks where all clusters are the same size and all supernodes are responsible for the same number of normal nodes. In contrast, real networks are likely to be more "messy" and we wanted to see if the load advantages of cluster networks applied to such messy networks. To do this, we used a simulator to generate several cluster networks, where each network had clusters of varying sizes. Similarly, we generated supernode networks, where the number of normal nodes varied from supernode to supernode. In each network, we chose the number of clusters or supernodes to minimize network-wide load. Table 1 lists the parameters we used to generate networks and calculate load.

The load in our simulated networks matches well with the analysis shown in Figure 4. As in our analytical results, our simulation results (not shown) indicate that the average cluster network node is far less loaded than supernodes, and roughly as heavily loaded as a normal node in a supernode network. The main difference between the simulation and analytical results is that in the simulation, some cluster nodes are up to a factor of two more loaded than the average cluster node. This is because when clusters are different sizes, nodes in large clusters must process more searches than nodes in small clusters. Nonetheless, a supernode is still far more loaded, by up to a factor of seven, than the most heavily loaded node in a cluster network. The problem of overloading is inherent to supernode networks; adding more supernodes does not decrease the search load on existing supernodes, and adding more normal nodes adds more processing capacity but that capacity goes unused. In contrast, a cluster network uses all the processing capacity and is thus inherently more efficient.

In addition to calculating the load in our simulated networks, we also calculated search latency and fault susceptibility. The full results are available in [5]. In summary, cluster networks a far less susceptible to faults than supernode networks, since there are no nodes in a cluster network that take on as much responsibility as supernodes do. The search latency of supernode and cluster networks is roughly comparable.

In summary, cluster networks ensure that no node is overloaded, without significantly increasing load on an average node. This load sharing is vital when there are no nodes in the network that are powerful enough to act as supernodes. Moreover, as a supernode network grows, even powerful supernodes can become overloaded, and thus for pure scalability reasons a cluster network may be preferred. At the same time, if robustness in the face of faults is important, a cluster network may also be preferred, since service in a cluster network will degrade much less after a failure than in a supernode network. Thus, cluster networks, suggested by our SIL model, are a useful alternative to supernode networks for peer-to-peer search.

5   Related Work

Several researchers have examined special algorithms for performing efficient search in peer-to-peer search networks, including parallel random walk searches [8,1], flow control and topology adaptation [9], iterative deepening search [15], routing indices [6] and local indices [15]. Others have suggested that the content can be proactively placed in the network to ensure efficiency [3,9], or that the network be structured with low diameter [10]. Each of these approaches could be used to further optimize the general archetypes described by the SIL model.

A large amount of attention recently has been given to distributed hash tables (DHTs) such as CHORD [14] and CAN [11]. DHTs focus on efficient routing of queries for objects whose names are known, but often rely on a separate mechanism for information discovery [11]. Information discovery is the focus of our work. Moreover, the huge popularity, wide deployment and clear usefulness of Gnutella/Kazaa-style networks mean that optimizing such networks is an important research challenge.

Some investigators have proposed mechanisms for using peer-to-peer networks to answer structured queries. Examples include DHT-based SQL queries [7] and the Local Relational Model [2]. It may be interesting to extend our model for more structured queries. However, there are many research issues in content-based queries, and we have focused on those as a starting point.

Others have performed measurements of Gnutella and Napster [13,12]. However, we know of no studies of deployed supernode networks, which are more widely used than were either Napster or Gnutella at their peak.

6   Conclusion

We have introduced a Search/Index Link model of P2P search networks that allows us to study networks that reduce the load on peers while retaining effective searching and other benefits of P2P architectures. With only four basic link types, our SIL model can represent a wide range of search and indexing structures. This simple yet powerful model also allows us to generate new and interesting variations. In particular, in addition to the supernode and pure search topologies, our SIL model describes topologies such as *parallel search clusters* and *parallel index clusters*. Analytical results, as well as experimental results from our topology simulator, indicate that a parallel search cluster network reduces overloading by allowing peers to fairly share the burden of answering queries, rather than placing the burden entirely on supernodes. This topology makes better use of the aggregate resource of the system, and is useful in situations where placing an extremely high load on any one peer is infeasible. Moreover, our results show that other considerations, such as fault susceptibility, may also point to parallel search clusters as an attractive topology.

References

1. L. Adamic, R. Lukose, A. Puniyani, and B. Huberman. Search in power-law networks. *Phys. Rev. E*, 64:46135–46143, 2001.
2. P.A. Bernstein, F. Giunchiglia, A. Kementsietsidis, J. Mylopoulos, L. Serafini, and I. Zaihrayeu. Data management for peer-to-peer computing: A vision. In *Proc. Workshop on the Web and Databases (WebDB)*, 2002.
3. E. Cohen and S. Shenker. Replication strategies in unstructured peer-to-peer networks. In *Proc. SIGCOMM*, August 2002.
4. B.F. Cooper and H. Garcia-Molina. Ad hoc, self-supervising peer-to-peer search networks. Technical Report, Stanford University Database Group, 2003.
5. B.F. Cooper and H. Garcia-Molina. SIL: Modeling and measuring scalable peer-to-peer search networks (extended version). http://dbpubs.stanford.edu/pub/2003-53, 2003.
6. A. Crespo and H. Garcia-Molina. Routing indices for peer-to-peer systems. In *Proc. Int'l Conf. on Distributed Computing Systems (ICDCS)*, July 2002.
7. M. Harren, J.M. Hellerstein, R. Huebsch, B.T. Loo, S. Shenker, and I. Stoica. Complex queries in DHT-based peer-to-peer networks. In *Proc. 1st Int'l Workshop on Peer-to-Peer Computing (IPTPS)*, 2002.
8. Q. Lv, P. Cao, E. Cohen, K. Li, and S. Shenker. Search and replication in unstructured peer-to-peer networks. In *Proc. of ACM Int'l Conf. on Supercomputing (ICS'02)*, June 2002.
9. Q. Lv, S. Ratnasamy, and S. Shenker. Can heterogeneity make gnutella scalable? In *Proc. of the 1st Int'l Workshop on Peer to Peer Systems (IPTPS)*, March 2002.
10. G. Pandurangan, P. Raghavan, and E. Upfal. Building low-diameter P2P networks. In *Proc. IEEE Symposium on Foundations of Computer Science*, 2001.
11. S. Ratnasamy, P. Francis, M. Handley, R. Karp, and S. Shenker. A scalable content-addressable network. In *Proc. SIGCOMM*, Aug. 2001.
12. M. Ripeanu and I. Foster. Mapping the gnutella network: Macroscopic properties of large-scale peer-to-peer systems. In *Proc. of the 1st Int'l Workshop on Peer to Peer Systems (IPTPS)*, March 2002.
13. S. Saroiu, K. Gummadi, and S. Gribble. A measurement study of peer-to-peer file sharing systems. In *Proc. Multimedia Conferencing and Networking*, Jan. 2002.
14. I. Stoica, R. Morris, D. Karger, M. F. Kaashoek, and H. Balakrishnan. Chord: A scalable peer-to-peer lookup service for internet applications. In *Proc. SIGCOMM*, Aug. 2001.
15. B. Yang and H. Garcia-Molina. Efficient search in peer-to-peer networks. In *Proc. Int'l Conf. on Distributed Computing Systems (ICDCS)*, July 2002.
16. B. Yang and H. Garcia-Molina. Designing a super-peer network. In *Proc. ICDE*, 2003.

Searchable Querical Data Networks

Farnoush Banaei-Kashani and Cyrus Shahabi

Computer Science Department,
University of Southern California,
Los Angeles, California 90089
{banaeika,shahabi}@usc.edu

Abstract. Recently, a new family of massive self-organizing networks has emerged that not only serve as a communication infrastructure, but also mainly as a distributed query processing system. We term these networks *Querical Data Networks (QDNs)*. Peer-to-peer networks are examples of QDN. In this paper, first we identify and characterize QDN as a new family of data networks with common characteristics and applications. Subsequently, as the first step toward realizing the evolved vision of QDN as a large-scale distributed query processing system, we propose an efficiently searchable QDN model based on a recently developed small-world model. We discuss in details how our QDN model enables effective location of the data relevant to a QDN query.

1   Introduction

Recently, a new family of massive self-organizing networks has emerged that not only serve as a communication infrastructure, but also mainly as a distributed query processing system. These networks are significantly different with classical engineered networks (e.g., the Internet) both in the way they are applied and in the characteristics of their components (nodes and links). We term these networks *Querical Data Networks (QDNs)*. Peer-to-peer networks and sensor networks [9,2] are examples of QDN.

This paper is organized in two parts. In the first part, we provide our overview, where we 1) define and characterize QDN as a new family of data networks with common characteristics and applications (Section 2), and 2) review possible database-like architectures for QDNs as querying systems, and discuss design principles and implementation issues in realizing those architectures (Section 3). In the second part (Section 4), as the first step toward realizing the evolved vision of QDNs we focus on a specific problem, namely the problem of effective data location (or search) for efficient query processing in QDNs.

We believe that with QDNs, search optimization is not limited to optimal query routing on the unintelligently generated ad hoc network topology. Considering the flexibility (hence, controllability) of the topology of QDNs (see Section 2), a QDN can self-organize to a *search-efficient topology* that in combination with an intelligent query routing/forwarding mechanism can significantly improve the *searchability* of the QDN. Here, with our searchable QDN model, first

K. Aberer et al. (Eds.): VLDB 2003 Ws DBISP2P, LNCS 2944, pp. 17–32, 2004.

we propose a self-organization mechanism that generates a *small-world* QDN based on a recently developed small-world model [29]. Small-world networks are known to be extremely search-efficient [28]. Although DHTs [20,27,22,31] are also successful in creating efficient topologies, we argue that as a model they are not compatible with characteristics/requirements of QDNs. Particularly, DHTs enforce certain data distribution and replication schemes and impose strict connectivity rules to QDN nodes. On the other hand, the small-world model is the *natural* model for QDNs that completely respects the autonomy of QDN nodes. Second, we complement the generated small-world network topology with query forwarding mechanisms that effectively route the query toward the QDN nodes that store target data relevant to the submitted query.

2   Querical Data Networks (QDNs)

Recently, a family of massive, self-organizing, engineered networks has emerged that bear componental characteristics (e.g., node lifetime) that are significantly different with those of the classical engineered networks such as the Internet, but similar to those of their natural counterparts, so-called *complex systems* such as social networks and biological networks. Besides componental differences, these networks are also *applied* differently as compared with the classical networks. A collection of interrelated data is distributed among the nodes of these networks, where the data are naturally created, collected (e.g., by sensing the physical world), and/or stored. Database-style queries are frequently posed (by nodes themselves, or by an outsider) to retrieve the data or information (i.e., the processed data) from this distributed network of data sources. Hence, the network not only serves as the communication infrastructure, but also mainly and more importantly as a distributed data source and a distributed query processing system. We term these emerging networks *Querical Data Networks (QDNs)*. Here, we enumerate the main componental characteristics and application features of a QDN.

2.1   Componental Characteristics

A network is an interconnection of nodes via links, usually modelled as a graph. Nodes of a QDN are often massive in number and bear the following characteristics:

- *Peer functionality*: All nodes are capable of performing a restricted but similar set of tasks in interaction with their peers and the environment, although they might be heterogeneous in terms of their physical resources. For example, joining the network and forwarding search queries are among the essential peer tasks of every node in a peer-to-peer network.
- *Autonomy*: Aside from the peer tasks mentioned above, QDN nodes are autonomous in their behavior. Nodes are either self-governing, or governed by out-of-control uncertainties. Therefore, to be efficacious and applicable

the QDN engineering should avoid imposing requirements to and making assumptions about the QDN nodes[1]. For example, strict regulation of connectivity (i.e., number of connections and/or target of connections) might be an undesirable feature for a QDN design.

- *Intermittent presence*: Nodes may frequently join and leave the network based on their autonomous decision, due to failures, etc.

On the other hand, links in various QDNs stand for different forms of interaction and communication. Links may be physical or logical, and they are fairly inexpensive to rewire. Therefore, a QDN is "a large-scale federation of a dynamic set of peer autonomous nodes building a transient-form interconnection". Traditional modelling and analysis approaches used for classical networks are either too weak (oversimplifying) or too complicated (overcomplicated) to be effective with large-scale and topology-transient QDNs. The *complex system theory* [5], on the other hand, provides a set of conceptual, experimental, and analytical tools to contemplate, measure, and analyze systems such as QDNs[2].

2.2 Application Features

A QDN is applied as a distributed source of data (a *data network*) with nodes that are specialized for cooperative query processing and data retrieval. The node cooperation can be as trivial as forwarding the queries, or as complicated as in-network data analysis (see Section 3). In order to enable such an application, QDN should support the following features:

- *Data-centric naming, addressing, routing, and storage*: With a QDN, queries are declarative; i.e., query refers to the names of data items and is independent of the location of the data. The data may be replicated and located anywhere in the data network, the data holders are unknown to the querier and are only intermittently present, and the querier is interested in data itself rather than the location of the data. Therefore, naturally QDN nodes should be named and addressed by their data content rather than an identifier in a virtual name space such as the IP address space. Consequently, with data-centric naming and addressing of the QDN nodes [13], routing [16] and storage [19] in QDN are also based on the content. It is interesting to note that non-procedural query languages such as SQL also support declarative queries and are appropriate for querying data-centric QDNs.
- *Self-organization for efficient query processing*: QDNs should be organized for efficient query processing. A QDN can be considered as a database system with the data network as the database itself. QDN nodes cooperate in

---

[1] One can consider peer tasks as *rules of federation*, which govern the QDN but do not violate autonomy of individual nodes.

[2] Further discussion about the complex system theory is beyond the scope of this paper. We refer the interested reader to our work on complex-system-based modelling of the peer-to-peer networks in [4].

processing the queries by retrieving, communicating, and preferably on-the-fly processing of the data distributed across the data network (in Section 3, we explain the benefits of adopting a database system framework to discuss and design query processing in QDNs). To achieve efficiency in query processing with high resource utilization and good performance (e.g., response time, query throughput, etc.), QDN should be *organized* appropriately. In Section 4, we discuss an example organization, where the topology of QDN is structured such that search for data items is performed efficiently. Other examples of organization are: intelligent partitioning of the query to a set of sub-queries to enable parallel processing, or collaborative maintenance of the data catalogue across the QDN nodes. However, the peer tasks of the QDN nodes should be defined such that they *self-organize* to the appropriate organization. In other words, organization must be a collective behavior that emerges from local interactions (defined by peer tasks) among nodes, otherwise the dynamic nature and large scale of QDN renders any centralized micro-management of the QDN unscalable and impractical.

3   Database-System Querying Framework for QDNs

The idea of adopting a DBS querying framework was originally discussed briefly and abstractly in two recent position papers for some specific cases of QDN [10,12]. Here, we define a taxonomy of approaches to generalize this querying framework for the entire family of QDNs.

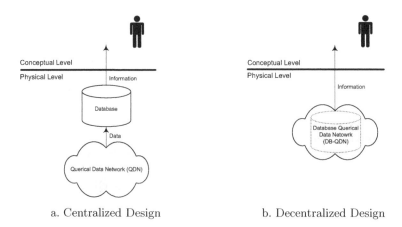

a. Centralized Design   b. Decentralized Design

Fig. 1. Database System Framework for Querying Querical Data Networks (QDNs)

3.1   Taxonomy

Based on the two fundamentally distinct design choices for the physical level of the DBS framework (i.e., centralized and decentralized), we recognize two approaches to implement a DBS-based querying system for QDNs:

1. Database *for* QDN (Figure 1a): This approach corresponds to the querying systems with centralized query processing. These systems are similar to other centralized database applications, where data are collected from some data sources (depending on the host application, the data sources can be text documents, media files, and in this case, QDN data) to be separately and centrally processed.
2. Database-QDN (DB-QDN) (Figure 1b): The systems that are designed based on this approach strive to implement query processing in a decentralized fashion within the QDN; hence, in these systems *"QDN is the database"*.

3.2   Designing a Database-QDN (DB-QDN)

By definition QDNs tend to be large-scale systems and their potential benefits increase as they grow in size. Therefore, between the two types of DBS-based querying systems for QDNs, the database-QDNs (DB-QDNs) are more promising because they are scalable and efficient. Here, we discuss the design issues with these systems.

Design Principles. Among the design principles for distributed query processing at QDNs one can distinguish the following:

1. *In-network query processing*: In-network query processing is the main distinction of DB-QDNs. In-network query processing techniques should be implemented in a distributed fashion, ensuring minimal communication overhead and optimal load-balance.
2. *Transaction processing with relaxed semantics*: Due to the dynamic nature of QDNs, requiring ACID-like semantics for transaction processing in DB-QDNs is too costly to be practical and severely limits scalability of such processing technique. Hence, transaction processing semantics should be relaxed for DB-QDNs.
3. *Adaptive query optimization*: Since QDNs are inherently dynamic structures, optimizing query plans for distributed query execution in DB-QDNs should also be a dynamic/adaptive process. Adaptive query optimization techniques are previously studied in the context of central query processing systems [3].
4. *Progressive query processing*: Distributed query processing tends to be time-consuming. With real-time queries, user may prefer receiving a rough estimation of the query result quickly rather than waiting long for the final result. The rough estimation progressively enhances to the accurate and final result. This approach, termed *progressive* query processing [24], allows users to rapidly obtain a general understanding of the result, to observe the

progress of the query, and to control its execution (e.g., by modifying the selection condition of the query) on the fly.

5. *Approximate query processing*: Approximation techniques such as *wavelet-based* query processing can effectively decrease the cost of the query, while producing highly accurate results [25]. Inherent uncertainty of the QDN data together with the relaxation of the query semantics justify application of approximation techniques to achieve efficiency.

Implementation Issues

Operators. In DB-QDNs, the data is distributed among QDN nodes. An operator is executed by a set of selected QDN nodes, which receive the query (or sub-queries), and perform partial processing and communicate with each other to generate the final result. Therefore, regardless of the type of the operator, the mechanism that defines the implementation of an operator should address the following questions:

1. Which QDN nodes should receive the query (or sub-query)?
2. Which sub-query should each node receive?
3. How should the nodes collaborate to process the query? Or, what is the set of local computation and communication tasks (i.e., peer tasks) that every QDN node should perform such that QDN nodes cooperatively compute the result of the query with optimal cost and performance?

Query Plan Construction and Optimization. With centralized database systems the metrics for query optimization are usually user-centric; e.g., throughput and response time. However, with QDNs physical resources of the system are seriously restricted. Therefore, besides user-centric metrics the query optimizer should consider "resource utilization" as a new optimization metric (probably with higher priority). With these systems, the query optimizer should also optimize the partitioning of the QDN processing power among several parallel operators in a query plan, and in case of multi-user systems, among multiple query plans.

4 QDN Searchability

Toward realizing a Database-QDN (DB-QDN), here we address the first implementation issue mentioned in Section 3.2, *"which QDN nodes should receive the query?"*. This problem arguably reduces to the problem of locating the nodes containing the data relevant to the query. The query declares the required data and the QDN must be *efficiently* searched to locate the corresponding nodes. We term a QDN that self-organizes for efficient search a *searchable* QDN.

To measure searchability, we introduce the following metrics:

1. *Precision and Recall*: Considering *Ret* as the set of QDN nodes that receive the query during the search for data, and *Rel* as the set of nodes that are intended to receive the query (because they store relevant/target data required to process the query), precision (**P**) and recall (**R**) of a search are defined according to the classical definitions of precision and recall:

$$\mathbf{P} = \frac{|Rel \cap Ret|}{|Ret|} \times 100 \qquad \mathbf{R} = \frac{|Rel \cap Ret|}{|Rel|} \times 100$$

   Assuming uniform distribution of the target data among the relevant QDN nodes, **P** and **R** are correlated with the precision and recall of the retrieved data, respectively. The limited amount of data stored at each node of a typical QDN (e.g., sensor network) justifies such a uniform distribution.

2. *Hop-count*: We use hop-count (**H**) as an abstract measure of the search time. Nodes forward the query to their neighbors once at each hop (or time slot). The number of hops a search takes (or is allowed to take, otherwise it will be terminated) to execute is the hop-count of the search.

The combination of these two metrics capture both resource-efficiency and user-centric performance (e.g., response time) of the search. With a fixed hop-count (i.e., limited time for search), higher precision and recall demonstrates better use of the resources; on the other hand, the fewer hops required by a search to achieve a target precision and/or recall, the better is the response time of the search. For example, the flooding-based search is expected to have low precision but high recall in low hop-count. In contrast, a search based on random walk may result in higher precision but lower recall, and requires more hops to achieve high recall.

Here, first we discuss how to organize a QDN for searchability and compare two different approaches to introduce such organization into QDN. Thereafter, we propose a searchable QDN model compatible with one of these approaches.

4.1   Organizing QDNs for Searchability

Without organization, a QDN that is generated by random interconnection of nodes is not efficiently searchable. With such a QDN, since the required data can be located anywhere in the network, nodes lack a sense of direction to forward the query toward the node(s) that potentially hold the required data. All neighbors of a node may equally lead the path to the target data. Therefore, nodes either pick a neighbor randomly and forward the query (i.e., random walk), or forward the query to all neighbors (i.e., flooding). In both cases, search is brute-force.

As we mentioned in Section 2, unlike classical networks, with QDNs the topology is flexible and rewiring the links is fairly inexpensive. Therefore, search optimization is not limited to optimal routing on the available network topology. A QDN can self-organize to a *search-efficient topology*, which in combination with an intelligent and data-centric query routing/forwarding mechanism can significantly improve the searchability of the QDN. To create a search-efficient topology, interconnection between nodes is correlated with "similarity" of the data content of the nodes: the more similar the data content of two nodes, the more likelihood of interconnection. Consequently, with sufficient correlation, nodes with similar data content are clustered to generate highly connected components that correspond to data localities, and the topology is a connected graph of interwoven data localities. Such a topology enhances the searchability in two ways:

1. Directed forwarding: Assuming that a node has (local) knowledge about the data content of the nodes in its neighborhood, the node can selectively forward the query to the neighbor with most similar data to the target data (i.e., data required to process the query). Due to the correlation between data similarity and node connectivity, it is more likely that the selected neighbor lead to the data locality corresponding to the target data. Therefore, the query is effectively routed toward the target data locality and avoids irrelevant paths. Hence, the precision **P** of the search increases.
2. Batch data access: When the query approaches the target data locality, most probably a large collection of the target data can be located all together within a few hops. Hence, the recall **R** of the search is improved too.

Approaches. There are two philosophically different approaches to organize a search-efficient topology: *fabricated* organization, and *natural* organization (i.e., an organization approach that respects natural characteristics of the system components)[3]. Distributed Hash Table (DHT) [20,27,22,31], which is proposed as a model for peer-to-peer networks, is an example of fabricated organization. To generate data locality, with DHT both nodes and data items are randomly assigned unique identifiers from a virtual identifer space. Each data item (or pointer to the data item) is stored at the node with the closest identifier to the identifier of the data item. Finally, nodes are interconnected via a *regular* topology, where nodes that are close in the identifier space are highly interconnected. DHT topology is regulated: all nodes have the same connectivity (same number of neighbors), and selection of the neighbors is strictly dictated by the semantics of the DHT interconnections.

Although DHTs (as the most important realization of the fabricated organization approach) are very successful in creating efficient topologies, we argue that as a model DHT fails to respect natural characteristics/requirements of QDNs. For example, data-to-node assignment via the virtual identifier space violates the natural distribution and replication of the data, where each node autonomously maintains its own and only its own data. Also, regular topology of the DHT imposes strict connectivity rules to autonomous nodes. While similarity of data content itself can be used to generate data localities, using virtual

---

[3] In continuation of our QDN analogy to social networks, one can compare socialistic and capitalistic societies with fabricated and natural QDNs, respectively!

identifier space to introduce virtual similarity is not only unnecessary but also problematic (as mentioned above). Moreover, strict regulation of the topology must be relaxed to allow more flexible connectivity rules that enable trading off efficiency against natural flexibility. In Section 4.2, we provide an example of such a natural organization, which improves searchability of QDNs while respecting their characteristics.

4.2   Our Searchable QDN Model

To develop a *natural* model for searchable QDNs, we adopt and generalize a social network model [29] that is proposed recently to explain the small-world phenomenon in social networks[4]. Here, assuming a relational data model for DB-QDN, we use the following query template to explain the basics of the QDN model:

```
SELECT   *
FROM     r
WHERE    AND_{i∈[1,d]}  (A_i = v_i)
```

where $R(A_1, A_2, ..., A_d)$ is a schema of degree d for the relation r stored at DB-QDN, and v_i is a constant. Later in this section, we generalize this model to other query templates with join clauses and disjunctive predicates.

Basics. We define our QDN model by explaining the following concepts in sequence:

1. Node identity: We define an *identity* for each node based on its data content;
2. Identity-based linking to create the network: We explain how nodes join the QDN by linking to some other QDN nodes, selecting the nodes of "similar" identity with higher probability; and
3. Identity-based routing to forward the queries: We describe how nodes, which know about the identity of their neighbors, route/forward the query to the neighbor that has the most similar identity to the target data content.

Node Identity. The identity of a node is defined such that it represents the data content of the node, just as the cognitive identity of a person which stands for the knowledge-set of the person. For node n, identity I_n is a d-tuple $< a_1, a_2, ..., a_i, ..., a_d >$ defined as follows:

$$I_n = < a_1, a_2, ..., a_i, ..., a_d > = \mathcal{F}(\{t_k | \ tuple \ t_k \in r \ is \ stored \ at \ n\}) \quad (1)$$

[4] In social networks, where individuals are represented as nodes and the acquaintance relationship between them as links, the average length of acquaintance chain between two individuals is logarithmic to the size of the network. The fact that individuals, which only have local knowledge about the network (i.e., they know their close acquaintances), can effectively and cooperatively find these short paths from a source to a target individual is termed the small-world phenomenon [28]. In addition to the small-world model we adopt here, there are other (more aged) models for this phenomenon [6,1,15]; however, we found the model proposed at [29] the most compatible model with the characteristics of QDNs.

where $\mathcal{F}$ is a tuple-aggregation function defined based on a set of d attribute-aggregation functions f_i such that[5]:

$$< a_1, ..., a_i, ..., a_d > \ = \ < f_1(\{t_k[A_1]\}), ..., f_i(\{t_k[A_i]\}), ..., f_d(\{t_k[A_d]\}) >$$

The selection of the aggregation functions f_i is application dependent. However, since QDN nodes often have limited storage that stores few tuples, a simple aggregation function such as AVG is sufficiently accurate in generating an identity that represents the data content of the node. Otherwise, we can avoid aggregation altogether, and represent each node as multiple *virtual* nodes by taking each tuple t_k as a virtual identity. The latter approach increases the size of the QDN, but it is more accurate. Also, with dynamic data content, the identities of the nodes is expected to change. However, since with QDN nodes the data content is often highly autocorrelated, frequent modification of the identity is unnecessary.

In subsequent sections, we explain how we use node identities to 1) organize the network topology to localities of nodes with similar identities (i.e., data content), and 2) route the queries to the node localities that store data content similar to the target data of the query.

Identity-based Linking. We assume the domain D_i of the attribute A_i is a metric space with the similarity measure S_i as the distance function of the space; for example, Hamming distance, Euclidean distance, or even the absolute difference $S(a, b) = |a - b|$ as the similarity measure for numbers, and Edit distance as that of strings. We also assume that node n is potentially able to (or desired to) connect only to nodes from a set of possible nodes Q (e.g., a range of nodes geographically close to n). Node n selects each of its M neighbors as follows: 1) randomly select a dimension i from $[1..d]$, 2) probabilistically select a distance x based on the probability distribution function $p_i(x) = c_i \exp(-\alpha_i x)$, where α_i is a tunable parameter[6] and c_i is the normalization constant, and finally 3) select the node m from Q such that $|x - S_i(I_n[A_i], I_m[A_i])|$ is minimum. The number of neighbors M depends on the local connectivity policy of n and is not enforced by the linking algorithm, although with higher connectivity diameter of the network decreases, and consequently, searchability of the QDN is expected to improve.

Identity-based Routing. According to the searchability metrics, when a query is originated at some node, the QDN nodes should forward/route the query, one hop at a time, such that the query: 1) traverses (as many as possible) the nodes with tuples satisfying the selection condition of the query, and 2) preferably avoids other nodes. With the searchable QDN model, each node is aware of the

---

[5] Notation: $t_k[A_i]$ is the value of the i-th attribute at tuple t_k. $\{t_k[A_i]\}$ is the set of these values for a set of tuples.

[6] The parameter α_i can be considered as the measure of *homophily* at dimension i, i.e., tendency of associating identities that are similar at dimension i to each other.

identity of its neighbors. Assume that the selection condition of the query is represented by the tuple $t < v_1, v_2, ..., v_d >$, where $v_i = NULL$ if the attribute A_i is not conditioned. To forward a query, the node n uses the distance measure U to estimate the *semantic* distance of its neighbor m from the target data content (hence, target node)[7]:

$$U(m, t) = \min_{\{i|v_i <> NULL\}} S_i(I_m[A_i], t[A_i]) \tag{2}$$

Since with homophilic linking, the network distance is correlated with the semantic distance, among all neighbors, the node n selectively chooses to forward the query to the neighbor with minimum semantic distance to the target data content. We term this routing algorithm *selective walk*. There are three conditions that terminate a selective walk:

1. When the node n receives a query for the first time, it creates and maintains a soft state (which expires, if not refreshed) for the query. If the query is received for the second time, this time n forwards the query to the neighbor with the second to minimum semantic distance to the target, and so on. The $(M + 1)$-th time the query is received, it is terminated (i.e., discarded).
2. If the selection condition t of the query (see above) conditions a key of the relation r, the first node that receives the query and locates the target data locally terminates the query, because the target data is expected to be unique.
3. The query carries a TTL (Time-To-Live) value, which is decreased by one each time the query is forwarded. To avoid everlasting looping of the queries, the query is terminated when its TTL equals zero.

Improvements. There are many ways to improve the basic searchable QDN model. Here, we discuss two examples:

Weighted Linking. With normal linking, at step 1 of the neighbor selection procedure (see above) node n selects a dimension *randomly*, to link to a node with similar identity in that dimension. If the distribution of queries conditioned on each dimension/attribute is not uniform across all dimensions, instead of random dimension selection, node n selects the dimension according to the query distribution. This linking approach, termed *weighted linking*, strengthens the correlation between network connectivity and data similarity in those dimensions that are more frequently used at queries, and consequently, improves the searchability of the QDN in those dimensions.

---

[7] The semantic distance measure U is *ultrametric*, i.e., it may violate the triangle inequality.

Wooding. Existence of the data localities in the searchable QDN model encourages a new routing algorithm that we term *wooding*[8]. Wooding starts with selective walk, which leads the query toward the target data locality. The first time a target data item is located signifies the approach to the target locality, where nodes with similar data content are clustered. Therefore, to take advantage of the high recall of the flooding in minimum hop-count (while high precision is ensured at the target data locality), it is reasonable that the routing algorithm is switched from selective walk to flooding. Thus, with wooding the node that receives the first hit during selective walk, marks the query for scope-limited flooding and continues forwarding the query by originating the flooding.

As an alternative (more controlled) wooding algorithm, nodes can fork successively more selective walkers as the semantic distance between the local node and the target data decreases. With this approach, starting with a single selective walker, as the query approaches the target data locality the number of query forwarding branches gradually increase such that close to the target the forwarding algorithm resembles flooding. It is important to note that both wooding algorithms are enabled by the linking policy that generates the data localities in the QDN topology, otherwise wooding in random topologies is ineffective.

Other Queries. We used a selection-query template to explain our searchable QDN model. Leveraging on the main property of the search-efficient topology, i.e., existence of distinct data localities, the model is expandable to support other query templates. The expansion mainly involves customizing the basic routing and applying a different routing method for each particular query template. Also, for application-specific QDNs, the linking method can be customized to optimize the topology for processing the most frequent query templates. Here, we discuss two examples:

Selection. The selection condition in our template query is a simple conjunction of equality literals. More generally, the selection condition is a statement in disjunctive normal form, which consists one or more disjuncts each of which is a conjunction of one or more equality and/or inequality literals. First, to support conjunction of both equality and inequalities literals, the semantic distance function used with selective random walk should be customized as follows:

$$U(m,t) = \min_{\{i|v_i <> NULL\}} \begin{cases} S_i(I_m[A_i], t[A_i]) & (A_i = v_i) \\ (1 - S_i(I_m[A_i], t[A_i])) & (A_i <> v_i) \end{cases}$$

where the distance function S_i is normalized. To process a selection query with disjunctive condition, the source of the query partitions the query to several sub-queries, each as a selection query conditioned by one of the disjuncts, and originates a basic selection query for each sub-query.

---

[8] "Wooding" is an abbreviation for a hybrid routing algorithm of selective **walk** and **flooding**. The verb "to wood" also means "to rage suddenly", which signifies the switching from walking to flooding to rapidly embrace the target data locality when located.

Join. With a multi-relation DB-QDN, each node has multiple virtual identities, one per each relation. Consider the following join query:

```
SELECT   *
FROM     r, s
WHERE    r.A_i = s.B_j
```

To process such a query, we adopt an approach similar to the nested-loop join. The source initially floods the network with the query. At every node n that receives the query (in parallel with others), for each tuple t of r stored locally a selection query is originated with $s.B_j = t[A_i]$ as the selection condition. Subsequently, node n joins the results of the selection queries with the corresponding local tuples, and forwards the final result to the source. To optimize the query processing for resource efficiency, it remains open to study how nodes at the same data locality (i.e., cluster of nodes that store tuples with similar/identical A_i values) can cooperate to share selection queries for the same A_i value. An intelligent cooperation scheme can effectively eliminate the redundant queries. This latter problem is an instance of the third-type implementation issues mentioned in Section 3.2.

4.3   Related Work

In [30] and [18], distributed query processing is discussed in the context of sensor networks, but the effect of the network topology in efficiency of the process is not considered. Also, [1] and [17] propose efficient routing schemes (without any particular linking scheme) for search in peer-to-peer networks assuming an ad hoc organization for the network topology; efficient routing mechanisms in combination with the linking mechanisms that create search-efficient topologies are expected to outperform those search schemes significantly. In [14], [21], and [11] DHTs are adopted as the mechanism to organize the network for efficient data access and retrieval. As we discussed in Section 4.1, DHT is an example of fabricated organization, which is not sufficiently compatible with the characteristics and requirements of QDNs. Similarly, [26] and [9] employ the traditional hierarchy scheme, and [23] uses a hypercube structure to organize the network. Here, we propose an organization scheme based on a small-world model, which as a natural organization model completely respects componental characteristics of the QDN nodes and allows highly efficient query processing as exemplified by the well-known small-world phenomenon. Finally, with "semantic overlays" [8, 7], network nodes are clustered into distinct overlays based on the semantic similarity of their data content in order to create data localities. However, this work does not introduce any routing and intra-linking scheme for semantic overlays.

5   Future Work and Conclusion

In this paper, we identified *Querical Data Networks (QDNs)* as a recently emerging family of networks (such as peer-to-peer networks and sensor networks) that not only serve as a communication infrastructure, but also mainly and more importantly as a distributed query processing system. We discussed the design issues with a Database-QDN (i.e., a QDN that implements distributed query processing in network), and as a first step toward realizing a Database-QDN, we focused on the problem of effective data location for query processing. We proposed a searchable QDN model that self-organizes to a small-world topology and allows effective forwarding of the queries to the nodes containing the target data required for query processing.

We intend to continue studying QDNs extensively. In short terms, we focus on the searchability problem by 1) experimental evaluation of our searchable QDN model and behavioral study of the model across the parameter space (e.g., number of data dimensions, homophilic parameter of the linking scheme, etc.), and 2) developing routing (and/or linking) schemes to support other query templates. In long terms, we turn our attention to other implementation problems discussed in Section 3.2, beginning with the study of cooperative query processing schemes that take advantage of the correlation between data placement and network interconnection in the searchable QDN model to optimize the resource-efficiency of the distributed query processing.

Acknowledgment. This research has been funded in part by NSF grants EEC-9529152 (IMSC ERC), IIS-0082826 (ITR), IIS-0238560 (CAREER) and IIS-0307908, and unrestricted cash gifts from Okawa Foundation and Microsoft. Any opinions, findings, and conclusions or recommendations expressed in this material are those of the author(s) and do not necessarily reflect the views of the National Science Foundation.

References

1. L. Adamic, R.M. Lukose, A.R. Puniyani, and B.A. Huberman. Search in power-law networks. *Physics Review Letters*, 64(46135), 2001.
2. I.F. Akyildiz, W. Su, Y. Sankarasubramaniam, and E. Cayirci. A survey on sensor networks. *IEEE Communications Magazine*, 40(8), August 2002.
3. R. Avnur and J.M. Hellerstein. Eddies: continuously adaptive query processing. In *In Proceedings of ACM International Conference on Management of Data (SIGMOD'00)*, May 2000.
4. F. Banaei-Kashani and Cyrus Shahabi. Criticality-based analysis and design of unstructured peer-to-peer networks as complex systems. In *Third International Workshop on Global and Peer-to-Peer Computing (GP2PC) in conjunction with CCGrid'03*, May 2003.
5. Y. Bar-Yam. *Dynamics of Complex Systems*. Westview Press, 1997.
6. A.L. Barabási and R. Albert. Emergence of scaling in random networks. *Science* 286:509–512, 1999.
7. M. Bawa, G. Manku, and P. Raghavan. SETS: Search enhanced by topic-segmentation. In *Proceedings of the 26th Annual International Conference on Research and Development in Informaion Retrieval (SIGIR'03)*, 2003.
8. A. Crespo and H. Garcia-Molina. Semantic overlay networks. In submission.

9. D. Estrin, R. Govindan, J. Heidemann, and S. Kumar. Next century challenges: Scalable coordination in sensor networks. In *Proceesings of International Conference on Mobile Computing and Networks (MobiCOM'99)*, 1999.

10. R. Govindan, J. Hellerstein, W. Hong, S. Madden, M. Franklin, and S. Shenker. The sensor network as a database. Technical Report 02-771, University of Southern California, 2002.

11. A. Gupta, D. Agrawal, and A. El Abbadi. Approximate range selection queries in peer-to-peer systems. In *Proceedings of the First Biennial Conference on Innovative Data Systems Research*, January 2003.

12. M. Harren, J.M. Hellerstein, R. Huebsch, B.T. Loo, S. Shenker, and I. Stoica. Complex queries in DHT-based peer-to-peer networks. In *Proceedings of the 1st International Workshop on Peer-to-Peer Systems (IPTPS '02)*, 2002.

13. J. Heidemann, F. Silva, C. Intanagonwiwat, R. Govindan, D. Estrin, and D. Ganesan. Building efficient wireless sensor networks with low-level naming. In *Proceedings of the Symposium on Operating Systems Principles*, October 2001.

14. R. Huebsch, N. Lanham, B.T. Loo, J.M. Hellerstein, S. Shenker, and I. Stoica. Querying the inernet with PIER. In *Proceedings of 29th International Conference on Very Large Data Bases (VLDB'03)*, 2003.

15. J. Kleinberg. The small-world phenomenon: an algorithmic perspective. Technical Report 99-1776, Cornell University, 2000.

16. B. Krishnamachari, D. Estrin, and S. Wicker. Modelling data-centric routing in wireless sensor networks. In *Proceedings of INFOCOM'02*, June 2002.

17. Q. Lv, P. Cao, E. Cohen, K. Li, and S. Shenker. Search and replication in unstructured peer-to-peer networks. In *Proceedings of the 16th International Conference on supercomputing (ICS '02)*, June 2002.

18. S.R. Madden, M.J. Franklin, J.M. Hellerstein, and W. Hong. TAG: a Tiny AGgregation service for ad-hoc sensor networks. In *Proceedings of 5th Annual Symposium on Operating Systems Design and Implementation (OSDI)*, December 2002.

19. S. Ratnasamy, D. Estrin, R. Govindan, B. Karp, S. Shenker, L. Yin, and F. Yu. Data-centric storage in sensornets. In *Proceedings of SIGCOMM'02*, 2002.

20. S. Ratnasamy, P. Francis, M. Handley, R. Karp, and S. Shenker. A scalable content-addressable network. In *Proceedings of ACM SIGCOMM '01*, August 2001.

21. S. Ratnasamy, B. Karp, L. Yin, F. Yu, D. Estrin, R. Govindan, and S. Shenker. GHT: A Geographic Hash Table for data-centric storage in sensornets. In *Proceedings of the First Workshop on Sensor Networks and Applications (WSNA)*, 2002.

22. A. Rowstron and P. Druschel. Pastry: Scalable, distributed object location and routing for large-scale peer-to-peer systems. In *IFIP/ACM International Conference on Distributed Systems Platforms (Middleware)*, November 2001.

23. M. Schlosser, M. Sintek, S. Decker, and W. Nejdl. A scalable and ontology-based p2p infrastructure for semantic web services. In *Proceedings of the 2nd International Workshop on Agents and Peer-to-Peer Computing*, 2002.

24. R.R. Schmidt and C. Shahabi. How to evaluate multiple range-sum queries progressively. In *21st ACM SIGACT-SIGMOD-SIGART Symposium on Principles of Database Systems (PODS'02)*, June 2002.

25. R.R. Schmidt and C. Shahabi. Propolyne: A fast wavelet-based algorithm for progressive evaluation of polynomial range-sum queries (extended version). In *VIII. Conference on Extending Database Technology (EDBT'02)*, May 2002.

26. C. Shen, C. Srisathapornphat, and C. Jaikaeo. Sensor information networking architecture and applications. *IEEE Personel Communication Magazine*, 8(4):52–59, August 2001.

27. I. Stoica, R. Morris, D. Karger, M.F. Kaashoek, and H. Balakrishnan. Chord: A scalable peer-to-peer lookup service for internet applications. In *Proceedings of ACM SIGCOMM '01*, August 2001.
28. J. Travers and S. Milgram. An experimental study of the small world problem. *Sociometry*, 32(4):425–443, December 1969.
29. D.J. Watts, P.S. Dodds, and M.E.J. Newman. Identity and search in social networks. *Science*, 296:1302–1305, 2002.
30. Yong Yao and Johannes Gehrke. Query processing in sensor networks. In *Proceedings of the Conference on Innovative Data Systems Research (CIDR)*, January 2003.
31. B.Y. Zhao, J. Kubiatowicz, and A. Joseph. Tapestry: An infrastructure for fault-tolerant wide-area location and routing. Technical Report UCB/CSD-01-1141, UCB, April 2001.

Semantic Overlay Clusters within Super-Peer Networks

Alexander Löser[1], Felix Naumann[2], Wolf Siberski[3], Wolfgang Nejdl[3], and
Uwe Thaden[3]

[1] CIS, Technische Universität Berlin, 10587 Berlin, Germany
aloeser@cs.tu-berlin.de
[2] Computer Sciences, Humboldt University Berlin, 10099 Berlin, Germany
naumann@informatik.hu-berlin.de
[3] Learning Lab Lower Saxony, 30539 Hannover
siberski,nejdl,thaden@learninglab.de

Abstract. When joining information provider peers to a peer-to-peer network, an arbitrary distribution is sub-optimal. In fact, clustering peers by their characteristics, enhances search and integration significantly. Currently super-peer networks, such as the Edutella network, provide no sophisticated means for such a "semantic clustering" of peers. We introduce the concept of semantic overlay clusters (SOC) for super-peer networks enabling a controlled distribution of peers to clusters. In contrast to the recently announced semantic overlay network approach designed for flat, pure peer-to-peer topologies and for limited meta data sets, such as simple filenames, we allow a clustering of complex heterogeneous schemes known from relational databases and use advantages of super-peer networks, such as efficient search and broadcast of messages. Our approach is based on predefined policies defined by human experts. Based on such policies a fully decentralized broadcast- and matching approach distributes the peers automatically to super-peers. Thus we are able to automate the integration of information sources in super-peer networks and reduce flooding of the network with messages.

1 Introduction

Current peer-to-peer (P2P) networks support only limited meta data sets such as simple filenames. Recently a new class of peer-to-peer networks, so called schema based peer-to-peer networks have emerged (see [1,2,3,4,5]), combining approaches from peer-to-peer research as well as from the database and semantic web research areas. Such networks build upon peers that use explicit schemas to describe their content. The meta data describing peers is based on heterogeneous schemata. They allow the aggregation and integration of data from autonomous, distributed data sources. However current schema-based peer-to-peer networks have still the following shortcomings:

- Schema based P2P networks that broadcast all queries to all peers don't scale. Intelligent routing- and network organization strategies are essential in such networks so queries are only routed to a *semantically chosen subset of peers* able to answer parts or whole queries. First approaches to enhance routing efficiency in a clustered network have already been proposed by [6] and [7].

K. Aberer et al. (Eds.): VLDB 2003 Ws DBISP2P, LNCS 2944, pp. 33–47, 2004.

– For most domains usually only a small but well-defined set of meta data standards exists. Peers provide information using such standards. For bridging the heterogeneity between different meta data schemes within the domain, mappings have to be provided. *Clustering peers by their schemes* enables the efficient reuse of such existing mappings within a particular domain.

Both issues, forwarding complex queries to selected peers and integration of small groups of schemas for a particular context benefit either from a search-driven or integration-driven clustering of the network in logically portions. Figure 1 shows peers clustered by their characteristics.

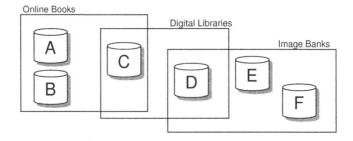

Fig. 1. Semantic Overlay Clusters

There are many challenges building such semantic overlay clusters: What are suitable models describing the nodes and clusters? How can such models matched in a distributed environment? What is a suitable topology? This paper addresses those questions by introducing deeper to semantic overlay clusters (section 3.2), presents a model for information provider peers (section 4), describes clustering policies for describing the demand on peers for an particular cluster (section 5) and shows matching and broadcasting approaches (section 6).

2   Related Work

In previous papers [5][4][8], we have described an RDF-based P2P infrastructure called Edutella (see http://edutella.jxta.org for the source code). It aims at providing access to distributed collections of digital resources through a P2P network. The idea of placing data nodes together, so queries can be efficiently routed and a semantic integration of the nodes is more automat<ed, has been discussed in many research projects. In the field of federated databases the tightly coupled mediator-wrapper architecture [9] was proposed by Wiederhold, enabling a static integration of domain-specific information sources. Matchmaking Infrastructures, such as InfoSleuth [10] or OBSERVER[11], match information provider to information consumers in a centralized way using description logics. In the Artificial Intelligence field the conceptual clustering problem has been widely studied in inductive learning systems, such as in COBWEB[12] and LABYRINTH [13].

Other approaches for routing queries directly to existing clusters are proposed by [6]. However, most systems assume that documents are part of a controlled collection located at a central database and allow only a centralized matching. Recently semantic overlay networks for peer-to-peer systems [7] allow overlays for placing data nodes semantically together. However they allow only the use of limited meta data schemes, such as simple filenames, and are designed for pure peer-to-peer networks, without using advantages of super-peer networks.

3 Clustering in Super-Peer Based Networks

In this section we show the use of super-peer networks for a semantic clustering of information provider. After a short introduction to super-peer networks we present the concept of semantic overlay clusters and an extension to an existing super-peer infrastructure enabling such clusters.

3.1 Super-Peer Networks

Recently a new wave of peer-to-peer systems is advancing an architecture of centralized topology embedded in decentralized systems; such a topology forms a super-peer network. Super-peer networks occupy the middle-ground between centralized and entirely symmetric peer-to-peer networks. They introduce hierarchy into the network in the form of super-peer nodes, peers which have extra capabilities and duties in the network (see [14]). A super-peer is a node that acts as a centralized server to a subset of clients, e.g. information provider and information consumer. Clients submit queries to their super-peer node and receive results from it, as in a hybrid system. However, super-peers are also connected to each other as peers in a pure system are (see also figure 2), routing messages over this overlay network, and submitting and answering queries on behalf of their clients and themselves. Examples of super-peer networks are JXTA[15], Edutella[8] or Morpheus. Because a super-peer network combines elements of both pure and hybrid

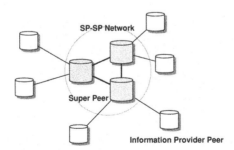

Fig. 2. Super-Peer Network

systems, it has the potential to combine the efficiency of a centralized search with the autonomy, load balancing[16], robustness to attacks and at least semantic interoperability [1] provided by distributed search.

3.2   Semantic Overlay Clustering

In this section we introduce the concept of semantic overlay clusters (SOC). Existing super-peer networks do not provide capabilities for enabling the definition and construction of SOCs yet. However some existing super-peer networks already provide clusters based on the physical network topology, such as JXTA with its group model or Edutella (see [4],[5]). In a super-peer networks a set of clients together with their super-peer forms a cluster. Intra cluster data communication takes place via direct peer to peer links between the clients, inter cluster communication takes place via links between super-peers. So far all the above described methods do not describe the structure of the clusters semantically. For enabling SOC as logical layers above the physical network topology we need a clustering method suitable to match semantically information provider peers to super-peer based clusters. Similar to the definition for semantic overlay networks by [7] we assume existing information provider peers and existing super peers as nodes in a physical network. Both can exchange messages within the network. A semantic overlay cluster (SOC_l) is defined as a link structure within a physical network (N) given a set of links from information provider (p) to a particular super-peer (s): ($SOC_l = p_i, s_j \in N | \exists a link(p_i, s_j, l)$). In addition we assume that each SOC_l supports at least two functions: $Join(p_i, l)$, where links (p_i, s_j, l)) between a super-peer and a information provider peer are created and $Leave(p_i, l)$ where they are dropped.

We focus our work on the realization of the *Join* function. Requests for a join are made by issuing a meta data based model m_i of a particular p_i to the network. We assume that every information provider provides such a model . Furthermore each cluster is related to one super-peer s_j and expresses explicitly its demand for information provider peers by a so called clustering policy c_j. We model a match between a clustering policy c_j and an the model of an information provider m_i as a function $Match(m_i, c_j)$ that returns 1 if there is a match and 0 otherwise (see also figure 3). The total number of matches T for an particular model m is the number of matches over all clustering policies: $T(m, c_j) = \Sigma_j Match(m, c_j)$. Matches can either be exhaustive, partial, fuzzy or ontology-based.

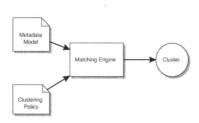

Fig. 3. Metadata Modell-based Clustering Approach

Now we look closer at the components enabling SOCs in a super-peer network:

– **Information provider model.** The models m_i contain a semantic rich description of the underlying peer, including (among others) information about the query and export schema of the peer, quality aspects and classification aspects. Furthermore they should be extensible by application specific annotations. We need to define a schema for these models and also need to ensure that they can be handled at the super-peers.

- **Clustering policies.** Policies c_j describe constraints on information provider peers for each cluster. We use policies to select automatically particular sources from all available information sources, taking into account the underlying model of the information source. Since policies are defined by an human expert, they have to be formalized in some way, so algorithms can match suitable information provider automatically.

- **Matching engines.** Information provider model and clustering policies are matched against each other by a matching function. If a match occurs, a peer joins a super-peer. Matching is detected by a matching engine which implements the matching function $Match_j()$. Matches can either be exhaustive, partial, fuzzy or ontology-based. We do not assume a common matching engine. Rather, each super-peer may select its own matching concepts and local engine implementation, depending on its needs.

- **Model distribution engine.** Since each super-peer owns a separate implementation of a "personal" matching engine and its specific super-peer dependent clustering policy, models of information provider peers willing to join one or more super-peers are distributed to all super-peers in the in super-peer network. This is done by a broadcast.

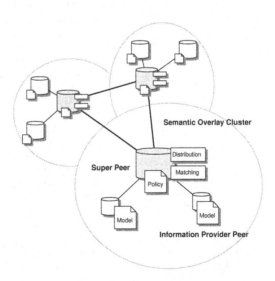

Fig. 4. Super-Peer Network with Clustering Policy and Information Provider Model

Figure 4 illustrates the extension of the "traditional" super-peer architecture. Each super-peer represents a separate semantic overlay cluster. Information provider peers are extended by an information provider model. Super-peers, typically computer with loads of memory and processing power, are extended with the clustering policy, matching and distribution concepts, Furthermore, in this figure not shown, information provider peers may join two or more super-peers.

In the following sections we will describe the elements of our approach in detail. In section 4 we present our information provider model. Section 5 discusses the description of clustering policies and their relation to the information provider model. Section 6 shows how the matching process works for new peers joining the network.

4   The Information Provider Model

The metadata model presented in this section provides an annotation schema designed to support the definition of semantic overlay clusters by local domain experts within the Edutella Network. This model shows a set of attributes for a particular infrastructure. In a semantic overlay cluster environment the model is used for the identification of relevant information provider peers. It consists of 15 attributes, which are either extracted from the information provider peer automatically at runtime (Peer ID, Peer IP, Peer Domain, Completeness, Accuracy, Response Time, Amount of Data) or are manually defined by local domain experts (Peer Schema, Peer Name, Peer Description, Global Classification URI and Taxon Path).The model (see figure 5) consists of five RDF Classes containing several annotations, e.g. annotations for information provider peers such as schema based annotations used in mediator-based information systems, annotations for information quality used in the context of federated information systems, peer-to-peer specific annotations and annotations for classifying peers according to existing taxonomies. The

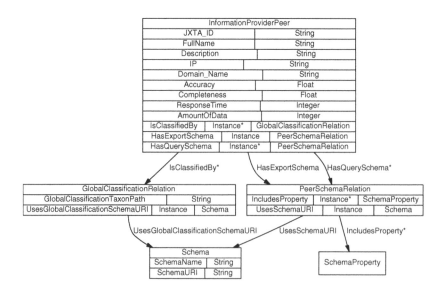

Fig. 5. Edutella Information Provider Peer Metadata Model (extract)

complete model can be taken from *http://nutria.cs.tu-berlin.de/edutella/*. In the following subsections we show the model details.

Since there is no ideal model describing arbitrary information sources, our model should be viewed as a core of relevant attributes; it may be completed by attributes from other models, as with any other RDFS based schema. Other systems do also use peer models to improve the peer-to-peer network characteristics. [14] uses a metric model for improving search in peer-to-peer networks, including annotations such as average aggregate bandwidth, average aggregate processing cost, number of results, satisfaction of the query and time to satisfaction. Semantic characteristics are not taken into account. [17] proposes a model for encoding semantic information as content categorization, security information, visibility of resources at a peer and caching of resources. This model is similar to ours, but it isn't used for clustering and it doesn't contain schema and quality information. The model used in [7] consists of one or several content classifications which are used to form semantic overlay networks, also to avoid searching on nodes that have unrelated content.

4.1 Annotations for a Peer Classification

Classification annotations include mainly information about the peer location, human readable description and its classification within existing taxonomies. We distinguish between the following attributes:

Peer ID. This ID represents a unique identifier of the peer within the network. Since we use the JXTA plattform[15] as underlaying P2P infrastructure we use the JXTA ID URN.

Peer Description. Human readable label, describing the purpose of the peer.

Peer IP. The underlaying IP of the peer.

Peer Domain. The full qualified domain name, e.g. *nutria.cs.tu-berlin.de*

Peer Name. This label contains information human readable information about the peer, e.g. *E-Learn Repository TU Berlin*

Global Classification Scheme URI. Am major problem when classifying a information provider peer is to find a suitable global classification scheme or taxonomy. In the world wide web the classification of web sites has been widely adopted. Examples are Yahoo and DMOZ. This label contains the URL of any recognized "official" taxonomy or any user-defined taxonomy, e.g. *http://www.dmoz.org*

Global Classification Scheme TaxonPath. This label represents an entry in a classification as a path from a more general to more specific entry in a classification, e.g. $Programming/Methodologies/Modeling_Languages/UML/Education/$

4.2 Annotations to Schema Information

Such annotations include schema information such as schemas or attributes used, as well as possibly conventional indexes on attribute values. We build upon the schema-based approaches successfully used in the context of mediator-based information systems [9]. Elements used in a query are matched against the schema information for a particular information provider peer in order to determine if the information provider peer is able to answer the query, see also [18] and [4] for a related approach. A match means that a peer understands and can answer a specific query, but does not guarantee a non-empty answer set. Schema information contain information about query capabilities for a particular peer at different granularities: schema identifiers, schema properties, property value ranges, and individual property values (we already resented concepts in [5] and [4]).

Schema Index. We assume that different peers support different schemas and that these schemas can be uniquely identified. The routing index contains the schema identifier as well as the peers supporting this schema. Queries are forwarded only to peers which support the schemas used in the query. An example are the dc and lom namespaces, they are uniquely identified by an URI.

Property/Sets of Properties Index. Peers might choose to use only parts of (one or more) schemas, i.e. certain properties, to describe their content. While this is unusual in conventional database systems, it is more often used for data stores using semi-structured data, and very common for RDF-based systems. In this kind of index, super-peers use the properties (uniquely identified by namespace/schema ID plus property name) or sets of properties to describe their peers. Examples are dc:subject, dc:language and lom:context. In our model we used the semantics of $http : //www.w3.org/1999/02/22 - rdf - syntax - ns/Property$.

Property Value Range Index. For properties which contain values from a predefined hierarchical vocabulary we can use an index which specifies taxonomies or part of a taxonomy for properties. This is a common case in Edutella, because in the context of the semantic web quite a few applications use standard vocabularies or ontologies. Examples are dc:subject =ccs:networks.

Property Value Index. For some properties it may also be advantageous to create value indexes to reduce network traffic. This case is identical to a classical database index with the exception that index entries do not refer to the resource, but the peer providing it. This index contains only properties that are used very often compared to the rest of the data stored at the peers. Examples are lom:context=undergraduate or dc:language =DE.

4.3   Annotations for Information Quality

In recent times both researchers and practitioners have recognized that reasoning about information quality has become one of the most important tasks when integrating information from autonomous information sources, such as information provider peers [19]. In the following paragraphs, we list information quality criteria that are relevant for the classification of read-only type information sources, like peers. Additionally we provide a short description of how we assess the scores for these criteria.

Completeness. For an information provider peer , completeness is a measure for the "size" of the underlying data source. The size of an information provider peer is measured as the absolute number of available resources. This number is usually provided by the information provider themselves as a form of advertisement. Information provider peers with a higher completeness are of higher quality to users, because the probability to find a suitable resource is higher.

Accuracy is the quotient of the number of correct values in a source and the overall number of values in the source. A value is an instance of an attribute. For our context accuracy is the percentage of data without *data errors*, such as non-unique keys or out of range values. Mohan et al. give a list of possible data errors [20].

Accuracy has been subject of several research projects [21,22]. The impact of data errors on data mining methods and data warehouses gives rise to data cleansing methods. The methods identify and eliminate a variety of data errors. The identification techniques can be used to count errors and thus to assess data quality.

Response Time measures the average delay in milliseconds between submission of a request and reception of the complete response from the information provider peer. The score for this criterion depends on unpredictable factors, such as network traffic, server workload etc. Also, the technical equipment of the information server plays a role as well. Response time can be automatically assessed through *query calibration*; statistics about average response time under different circumstances and times are gathered. They can be updated with each call to the information provider peer and are thus quite accurate.

Amount of Data is the size of the query result, measured in bytes. In contrast to the completeness criterion, amount of data is considered a cost factor; a higher amount of data means more storage and bandwidth needs. Just like response time, amount of data can be assess through the gathering and updating of statistics during actual calls to the information provider peer.

Of course, the list above is only a subjective choice of quality dimensions. Different application domains might need other criteria. For instance, information provider peers based on a fee should include *price* as a cost dimension. For processing-type information provider peers, which are not covered here, different information quality criteria are of importance. Examples of such criteria include *security*, *availability*, and *reliability*.

5 Clustering Policies

Clustering policies express the demand of information provider peers for a particular application domain. They are defined manually by local domain experts. In super-peer networks each super-peer represents a cluster of domain specific information provider peers and is related to exactly one clustering policy. Every cluster policy consists of *rules*, expressing which information provider peers are allowed to join the cluster and which services are denied to enter the cluster. Each rule consists of an event, a constraint, and an action. Table 1 shows five rules we identified so far. An event can be connected to one or many constraints. A typical *constraint* is defined by a property, an operator [1],) and a value, e.g. Peer.Advertisement.Property accuracy > .95. When checking a constraint, the value of the check can be either "TRUE" or "FALSE". In the following example we assume, that a super-peer is only interested in information provider peers providing URLs and metadata of materials related to "UML Education" by using the Dublin Core scheme as export schema, having an accuracy of more then 95 per cent and are classified according the Open Directory (see also Figure 6 as an example for

---
[1] E.g.: =,!=, <,>, INCLUDE, EXCLUDE, SIMILAR-TO, PART-OF-ONTOLOGY,...

Table 1. Possible rules within a clustering policy

No	Event	Constraint	Action	Explanation
1	Enter	True	Approve	a new service is accepted at the cluster
2	Enter	False	Reject	a new service is not accepted and is rejected
3	Leave	-	DeleteEntry	an registered service leaves the cluster
4	Check	True	-	an registered service is re-accepted
5	Check	False	Reject	an registered service is rejected from the cluster

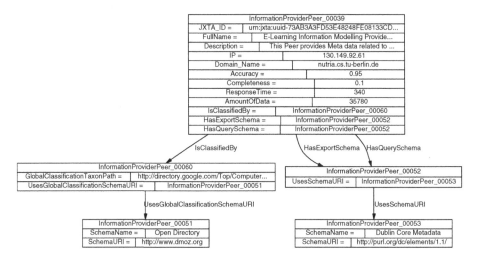

Fig. 6. Edutella Information Provider Peer Example

such an information provider peer). The corresponding policy of the super-peer can be expressed by defining one rule.[2]:

```
ON (Event) Enter

IF (
  (Peer.Advertisement.Property
  HasExportScheme.SchemaURI="http://purl.org/dc/elements/1.1/")
AND (Peer.Advertisement.Property accuracy > .95 )
AND (Peer.Advertisement.Property IsClassifiedBy.URI
  "http://www.dmoz.org")
AND (Peer.Advertisement.Property
  IsClassifiedBy.GlobalClassificationTaxonPath INCLUDES
  "Programming/Methodologies/Modeling_Languages/UML/Education/")
)

DO (Action) Approve(service)
```

---

[2] The above mentioned examples are described by using a pseudo language, similar to Java.

Constraints can be combined conjunctively (AND) and disjunctively (OR). As long as a constraint meets our scheme, we allow the formulation of arbitrary constraints using arbitrary property sets, since most super-peer administrators use their own context specific set. If a super-peer receives a service advertisement containing an unknown property, the property is ignored by the super-peer. If a super-peer misses a property in a service advertisement while checking the value of a constraint, the value of the constraint is "FALSE".

6 Matching and Distributing Metadata Models

In the previous sections we presented concepts extending "classical" super-peer networks. In such a network each super-peer consists of its own clustering policy. Furthermore we allow at each super-peer a local matching engine supporting different kinds of matches. Such local matching engines may implemented by the super-peer administrator according to the domain and context of the super-peer. Since both, clustering policies and matching engines, are distributed over the hole super-peer network the matching process between clustering policies and information provider peers models is two folded:

- Broadcast of the information provider peer model within the whole super-peer network to all super-peers
- Matching of the information provider peer model with each local super-peer specific clustering policy according to the local implemented matching engine

In this section we show approaches for distributing information provider peer models within the super-peer network and show possible matching strategies matching models and clustering policies.

6.1 Distribution

For joining the network an information provider peer chooses an arbitrary super-peer in the network and forwards its model to the super-peer. The super-peer executes two operations, it first matches the model against its clustering policy and allows or denies the join of the peer to its cluster, second it broadcasts the model to all other super-peers in the super-peer network (see figure 7). A broadcast of a model should include a forwarding of the model to all super-peers in the network, every super-peer should only receive the model once. This can be achieved by computing the minimal spanning tree (MST) over the super-peer network from the initiating super-peer. Building a MST is a well-studied problem (see [23]). In the peer-to-peer community this problem has been addressed by many search and broadcast algorithms. Since in super-peer networks the "inner" network is a pure peer-to-peer network, we use an existing algorithm.

There are only a few algorithms which broadcast messages to all peers with a minimum overhead for a very large number of nodes. DHT-based Algorithms, like CAN and CHORD, are developed for simple models of resources, e.g. key value pairs for file sharing, and allow therefore not a broadcast of complex models of information provider peers. Schlosser et.al presented the HyperCuP [24] a highly scalable topology which enables efficient broadcast and search algorithms without any message overhead at all

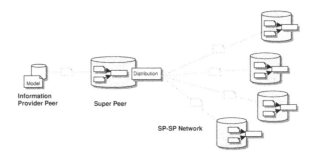

Fig. 7. Matching and distribution of models in the Super-Peer Network

during broadcast, logarithmic network diameter, and resiliency in case of node failures. It is guaranteed that exactly N-1 messages are required to reach all nodes in a topology. Furthermore, the last nodes are reached after $log_b N$ forwarding steps. Any node can be the origin of a broadcast in the network, satisfying a crucial requirement. The algorithm works as follows: A node invoking a broadcast sends the broadcast message to all its neighbors, tagging it with the edge label on which the message was sent. Nodes receiving the message restrict the forwarding of the message to those links tagged with higher edge labels. Other approaches we identified so far are Bayeux, Zhunag et.al.[25], and P-Grid, Aberer [26].

6.2 Matching

Matchmaking concepts between models and clustering policies depend from domain and goal of the super-peer. This includes matching operators at attribute level and matching algorithms behind operators. We can't assume that in the near future a "one size fits all" approach will be available. Therefore each super-peer uses its own matching engine, which matches an information provider peer model against the local super-peer policy. Its interface should include the method $float\ r = match(profile\ p, model\ m)$, with $0 <= r <= 1$. We distinguish so far between four matching approaches:

- **Exact.** In this case an information provider peer only joins a super-peer when its model matches exact with the clustering policy, r can be either 0 or 1.
- **Partial.** The information provider peer may also join the super-peer if only some attributes of the model match with the clustering policy. The result of the match r is calculated as $r = \frac{NumberOfMatchingConstraints}{NumberOfAllConstraints}$. Matching engines for exact and partial matches may be implemented using an RDF-Query language for the RDF-based information provider peer model. Such matchings concepts could be used for the attributes IP, $ResponseTime$, $Accuracy$, $AmountOfData$ and $Completeness$. Matching operators for such matching concepts are for instance $=,!=,<,>,INCLUDE$ and $EXCLUDE$.
- **Similar.** For same attributes of the model, such as $Description$ and $Fullname$, an exact or partial match is sometimes not be successful,e.g. if a description contains the phrase "Database materials" but the policy looks for "data base materials". Both

literals express the same thing, but use different syntax. A match for such attributes occurs if these attributes are syntactically/verbatim similar to the constraints of the policy, expressed by the operator $SIMILAR - TO$. This field has been widely studies in the past. Most search engines such as Google and SMART [27] equate text similarity with content similarity and use keywords and verbatim phrases to identify similar/relevant documents. The result r of the match expresses the similarity, an r near to 0 expresses a low overlapping, an r near 1 a high overlapping between attributes of the model and the clustering policy.

- **Ontology.** This more sophisticated approach includes the collection of attributes which are part of an ontology. Consider the case, a super-peer might be interested in clustering restaurant providers for a specific geographic region. First it has to decide, whether an information provider peer offers materials for this area and uses words as Café, Bar, Tourism and so far, second has to relate the restaurant to an specific geographic area. Existing ontologies such as ChefMoZ could by used to define concepts and relations. An attribute of an information provider peer should consist of a relation to the ontology, at least a $IsPartOf$ relation, e.g. by using the operator $PART - OF - ONTOLOGY$. Calculating the result is difficult, since different relations between different concepts result in different measures of similarity. First approaches for an ontology-based matchmaking have been shown recently by [28].

Since the information provider peer descriptions are based on RDF annotations, and clustering policies could be understood as queries over an RDF graph an straight forward approach of implementing an matching engine would be the use and extension of an existing RDF query language engine, expressing clustering policies by using a RDF query language like RDQL, SeRQL, RQL or an RDF Rule language like TRIPLE. [3] Unfortunately none of the query engines support operators like $SIMILAR - TO$ or $PART - OF - ONTOLOGY$ so far. However existing concepts already shown could be used to extend such engines.

7   Conclusion

This paper makes several novel contributions: We introduced the concept of semantic overlay clusters in super-peer based networks. SOC's are designed for very large, highly distributed networks improving search and semantic interoperability. Especially the super-peer topology, consisting of a super-peer backbone with powerful computers and smaller clients which are linked to these super-peers, is very suitable for this approach. Further on we showed four extensions to an existing super-peer network, allowing a dynamic clustering of information provider peers to super-peer based clusters: RDF-based models for information provider peers formulated by using knowledge from existing approaches of the data base community, clustering policies expressing the demand on information providers based on existing RDF Query languages, distribution

---

[3] We are currently evaluating how clustering rules can be mapped to the RDQL language. In a simple approach all parts of the "IF.. AND.. AND" clauses could be mapped to the AND clauses of the RDQL language. The SELECT part and the WHERE part as well as the USING part could be static, since they do not change.

concepts models for based on the HyperCuP algorithm and finally matching approaches. Implementing the shown concepts within the Edutella network by using existing components is left open to further work.

Acknowledgements. We thank Susanne Busse and Ralf-Detlef Kutsche from CIS, TU-Berlin for reviewing concepts presented and providing the research environment.

References

1. Aberer, K., Cudré-Mauroux, P., Hauswirth, M.:   The chatty web: Emergent semantics through gossiping. In: Proceedings of the Twelfth International World Wide Web Conference (WWW2003), Budapest, Hungary (2003)
2. Halevy, A.Y., Ives, Z.G., Mork, P., Tatarinov, I.: Piazza: Data management infrastructure for semantic web applications. In: Proceedings of the Twelfth International World Wide Web Conference (WWW2003), Budapest, Hungary (2003)
3. Bernstein, P.A., Giunchiglia, F., Kementsietsidis, A., Mylopoulos, J., Serafini, L., Zaihrayeu, I.: Data management for peer-to-peer computing: A vision. In: Proceedings of the Fifth International Workshop on the Web and Databases, Madison, Wisconsin (2002)
4. Nejdl, W., Wolpers, M., Siberski, W., Löser, A., Bruckhorst, I., Schlosser, M., Schmitz, C.: Super-Peer-Based Routing and Clustering Strategies for RDF-Based Peer-To-Peer Networks. In: Proceedings of the Twelfth International World Wide Web Conference (WWW2003), Budapest, Hungary (2003)
5. Löser, A., Nejdl, W., Wolpers, M., Siberski, W.: Information Integration in Schema-Based Peer-To-Peer Networks. In: Proceedings of the 15th International Conference of Advanced Information Systems Engieering (CAiSE 03), Klagenfurt (2003)
6. Ng, C.H., Sia, K.C., King, I.:   Peer clustering and firework query model in the peer-to-peer network. Technical report, Chinese University of Hongkong, Department of Computer Science and Engineering (2003)
7. Crespo, A., Molina, H.G.: Semantic Overlay Networks (2002) Stanford University, Submitted for publication.
8. Nejdl, W., Wolf, B., Qu, C., Decker, S., Sintek, M., Naeve, A., Nilsson, M., Palmér, M., Risch, T.: EDUTELLA: a P2P Networking Infrastructure based on RDF. In: Proceedings of the Eleventh International World Wide Web Conference (WWW2002), Hawaii, USA (2002)
9. Wiederhold, G.: Mediators in the architecture of future information systems. IEEE Computer **25** (1992) 38 – 49
10. Kashyap, V., Sheth, A.:   Information Brokering Across Heterogeneous Digital Data A Metadata-based Approach. Kluwer Academic Publishers, Boston/Dordrecht/London (2000)
11. Mena, E., Kashyap, V., Sheth, A.P., Illarramendi, A.: OBSERVER: An approach for query processing in global information systems based on interoperation across pre-existing ontologies. In: Conference on Cooperative Information Systems. (1996) 14–25
12. Fisher, D.: Knowledge acquisition via incremental conceptual clustering. Machine Learning **2** (1987) 139–172
13. Thompson, K., Langley, P.: Concept formation in structured domains. In: D. Fisher, M. Pazzani, and P. Langley, editors, Concept formation: knowledge and experience in unsupervised learning. Morgan Kaufmann. (1991)
14. Garcia-Molina, H., Yang, B.: Efficient search in peer-to-peer networks. In: Proceedings of ICDCS. (2002)
15. Gong, L.: Project JXTA: A technology overview. Technical report, SUN Microsystems (2001) http://www.jxta.org/project/www/docs/TechOverview.pdf.

16. Yang, B., Garcia-Molina, H.: Designing a super-peer network. In: Proccedings of the ICDE. (March 2003)
17. Jeen Broekstra et.al: A metadata model for semantics-basd peer-to-peer systems. In: In Proceedings of the International Workshop in Conjunction with the WWW03 Budapest. (2003)
18. Aberer, K., Hauswirth, M.: Semantic gossiping. In: Database and Information Systems Research for Semantic Web and Enterprises, Invitational Workshop, University of Georgia, Amicalola Falls and State Park, Georgia (2002)
19. Naumann, F.: Quality-driven Query Answering for Integrated Information Systems. Volume 2261 of Lecture Notes on Computer Science (LNCS). Springer Verlag, Heidelberg (2002)
20. Mohan, S., Willshire, M.J.: DataBryte: A data warehouse cleansing framework. In: Proceedings of the International Conference on Information Quality (IQ), Cambridge, MA (1999) 77–88
21. Hernández, M.A., Stolfo, S.J.: Real-world data is dirty: Data cleansing and the merge/purge problem. Data Mining and Knowledge Discovery **2(1)** (1998) 9–37
22. Galhardas, H., Florescu, D., Shasha, D., Simon, E.: An extensible framework for data cleaning. In: ICDE,, San Diego, CA (2000) 312
23. Gallager, Humblet, Spira: A distributed algorithm for minimum weight spanning trees. In: ACM Transactions on Programming Languages and Systems. Volume 5-1. (1983) 66–77
24. Schlosser, M., Sintek, M., Decker, S., Nejdl, W.: A scalable and ontology-based P2P infrastructure for semantic web services. In: Proceedings of the Second International Conference on Peer-to-Peer Computing, Linköping, Sweden (2002)
25. Zhuang, S.Q., Zhao, B.Y., Joseph, A.D., Katz, R.H., Kubiatowicz, J.D.: Bayeux: An architecture for scalable and fault-tolerant wide-area dissemination. In: Proceedings of ACM/NOSSDAV, Port Jefferson,New York, USA (2001)
26. Aberer, K.: P-grid: A self-organizing access structure for p2p information systems. In: In Proceedings of the Sixth International Conference on Cooperative Information Systems (CoopIS), Trento, Italy (2001)
27. Buckley, C., Singhal, A., Mitra, M., Salton, G.: New retrieval approaches using SMART: TREC 4. In: Proceedings of the Fourth Text REtrieval Conference (TREC-4). (1995) 25–48
28. Tangmunarunkit, H., Decker, S., Kesselman, C.: Ontology-based resource matching - the grid meets the semantic web. In: Proceedings of the First Workshop of Semantics in Peer-to-Peer and Grid Computing in Conjunction witrh the 12. th WWW Conference, Budapest (2003)

Structuring Peer-to-Peer Networks Using Interest-Based Communities

Mujtaba Khambatti, Kyung Dong Ryu, and Partha Dasgupta

Arizona State University, Tempe AZ 85281, USA,
{mujtaba, kdryu, partha}@asu.edu

Abstract. Interest-based communities are a natural arrangement of distributed systems that prune the search space and allow for better dissemination of information to participating peers. In this paper, we introduce the notion of peer communities. Communities are like interest groups, modeled after human communities and can overlap. Our work focuses on providing efficient formation, discovery and management techniques that can be implemented to constantly changing community structures. We provide a mechanism to generate realistic peer-to-peer network topologies that can be used in simulations that evaluate the operation of our algorithms. Our experiments show how searching the peer-to-peer network can take advantage of peer communities to reduce the number of messages and improve the quality of search results.

1 Introduction

The current organization of the Internet allows users to connect to web servers of their interest that are often located using a search engine, such as [1,2,3]. In this paper, we propose an alternative organization built on an overlay network of peers. We provide a model for communication that scales well and efficiently uncovers community structures. We describe how these communities of peers can be used in structuring the peer-to-peer network.

A Peer-to-peer (P2P) system is a distributed system in which peers that have comparable roles and responsibilities, communicate information, share or consume services and resources between them [4]. These systems can harness massive amounts of storage with modest investment and no central authority [5, 6], and are therefore particularly attractive to everyday home computer users, who seem empowered by the ability to share a portion of the authority. The emergence of file-sharing applications, such as Gnutella [5], Freenet [6] and Napster [7], has been the catalyst that drew a lot of attention to P2P systems.

We introduce the notion of peer communities as a generalization of the multiplicity of peer groups (possibly overlapping) involving peers that are actively engaged in the sharing, communication and promotion of common interests. Our concept of peer communities is loosely based on the idea of "interest groups," for example Yahoo Groups [8] or Usenet Newsgroups, except that communities are self-organizing, and are formed implicitly due to the declared interests of human users. We use communities as a more natural arrangement of distributed systems and show how they are helpful in pruning the search space. They also allow

K. Aberer et al. (Eds.): VLDB 2003 Ws DBISP2P, LNCS 2944, pp. 48–63, 2004.

for better dissemination of information to participating peers, thereby reducing unnecessary communication within the P2P network.

Our solution for searching in P2P takes advantage of the self-organization of peers, and their capacity to form communities based on the interests of their human users and the interactions of individual peers. Earlier P2P search techniques, such as flooding, directed flooding, iterative deepening [9], and local indices [9], had the disadvantage that information located farther away from a peer could only be found through a considerable search expense. We believe that the community-based search query propagation provides more efficient searching by targeting one or more communities, irrespective of the current membership of the searching peer. Our technique follows the innate method of searching used by humans in the analogous social network, where queries for unknown items are asked to "those that know." The community-based search technique will allow search operations to be based on content rather than just filenames, as in many existing P2P search techniques [5,6,10,11].

Efficient discovery and management of constantly changing community structures are essential to performing the proposed community-based search query propagation in a populated P2P space. In this paper, we show how these self-configuring communities are formed, discovered and managed, in spite of node failures. Finally, we discuss the mechanics of our community-based search solution and provide some initial evaluations of its performance. To demonstrate the performance of our algorithms, we use simulations to create populated P2P networks.

The paper is arranged as follows. Section 2 provides the motivation; Section 3 introduces some of the terms that we use; Section 4 describes how P2P networks are created; Section 5 illustrates our algorithms for structuring the network; and Section 6 explains the community-based search and provides simulation results. We conclude with Section 7.

2   Motivation

We view P2P networks consisting of an end-to-end overlay network of peers as being analogous to social networks comprising of humans. In fact, many of our proposed solutions for forming, discovering and managing structures in P2P networks, and their use to provide a more efficient search technique were motivated by our observations of similar solutions in social networks. For instance, the inclination of autonomous elements in a social system to form groups and associations leads us to believe that a populated P2P system made up of peers and an end-to-end overlay network, will also form similar community structures. Thus, P2P communities are a natural extension for arranging distributed P2P systems. Like their social network counterpart, these structures also enhance the capabilities of each member.

In this research we focused on understanding these community structures and proposing algorithms that can help manage and utilize P2P communities for better search operations, and consequently create newer P2P applications.

2.1   Forming and Discovering P2P Communities

A P2P community is a non-empty set of peers that share a non-empty set of interests that they have in common. Unlike a group, which is a physical collection of objects, a community is a set of active members, involved in sharing, communicating, and promoting a common interest. Peers in a network can exchange or advertise their interests with their neighbors in order to find peers with whom community relationships can be formed.

We proposed a community formation algorithm [12] that works without any central authority and optimizes the cost of communication. The algorithm is an autonomous procedure that is executed asynchronously by each peer. Through a simple exchange of interests, we demonstrated how communities could be formed. Each peer can then analyze the received interests to discover its community memberships without any additional communication.

2.2   Information Dissemination

P2P communities aid in the better dissemination of useful information amongst peers. For example, suppose node X belongs to a person interested in Amazonian Biological Catapults (ABC). After X declares this interest, it implicitly becomes a member of the community of ABC enthusiasts. Henceforth, all the information that X wants to share can be placed in a public directory that can be read/searched by all members of ABC. This concept can be extended to discover resources, physical devices, and network components. This example is interesting in the context of peer communities with no overlapping interests and is especially applicable in applications that follow the publish-subscribe-notify model [13].

2.3   Pruning the Search Space

Searching for information is one of the key challenges in P2P systems. Centralized searching has a drawback: the indexing and presentation of information are controlled by a central authority. P2P searching allows anyone to put up information in the search index and then cooperatively search the P2P space.

Fig. 1. Example of peer communities linked by a common peer. The vertices represent peers, and edges represent end-to-end connections between peers. The closely connected collection of peers to the left and the similar but smaller collection to the right are assumed to be two separate communities that are linked by a common peer

Consider a digital library built from a collection of peers, in which each peer owns a set of books that it is willing to share with other peers. The subjects of the books that a peer owns form its set of interests. Peers are implicitly grouped into communities based on the common interests they share. Since a peer could own books spanning a variety of subjects, it could be a member of multiple communities.

If the Computer Science (CS) and Medical (M) communities were disjoint, then search operations for medical information performed by a node that belonged to the CS community would not yeild any results. However, if the communities were linked at some point, lets say Q (Q belongs to both communities), then the medical information would be found, but at a great search expense, since, on the average, half of the CS community would be searched before a node from the M community is found.

To mitigate such problems, we need a community based query propagation method. Thus to provide efficient searching, it is better to search for one or more target communities, irrespective of the current membership of the searching node.

3   Terms and Definitions

In this section, we define and explain in detail two of the most commonly used terms in this paper: (i) Interest Attributes, and (ii) Peer Links.

3.1   Interest Attributes

Peer communities are formed based on their common interests. In our model, common interests are represented by attributes, which are used to determine the peer communities in which a particular peer can participate. Attributes can be either explicitly provided by a peer or implicitly discovered from past queries. However, there are privacy and security concerns in using such information, so we divide interests into three classes - *personal*, *claimed*, and *group*.

The full set of attributes for a peer is called *personal attributes*. However, for privacy and/or security reasons, all these attributes may not be used to determine community membership. A user may not want to reveal some of her personal attributes. Hence, a subset of these attributes is explicitly claimed public by a peer. We call these the *claimed attributes*. In addition, we introduce the notion of *group attributes*. Group attributes are location or affiliation-oriented and are needed to form a physical basis for communities. Every node belongs to at least one pre-determined group and has a group attribute that identifies the node as a member of this group. The domain name of an Internet connection may be used as the group identifier.

The group attribute is also considered to be a personal attribute, which may or may not be one of the claimed attributes. It is recommended that a node include the group attribute as part of the claimed attribute set.

The non-empty set of interest attributes that renders a collection of peers to become a community is called the *signature* of that P2P community.

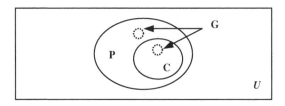

Fig. 2. Venn diagram of interest attribute sets for a peer. U is the universe of all attributes; P is the set of personal attributes; C is the set of claimed attributes; and G indicates the group attribute

3.2   Peer Links

P2P communities are attribute-based; that is, attributes (claimed and group) determine the membership of a node in one or more communities. In addition to attributes we also define an end-to-end overlay network in terms of *links*.

Links are not necessary to form and manage P2P communities. However, they are needed to feasibly run low-cost algorithms for formation and discovery, as it is conceptually and algorithmically simpler to use the notion of a set of *neighbors*[1] when communicating with other peers. To develop a better conceptualization of the nature of peer links, we explain a case where links are essential.

When node 'X' is born, it needs to have one or more logical neighbors. If it has three neighbors, 'A', 'B', and 'C', then we say that it has three links, X→A, X→B, and X→C. Unlike the overlay networks used by Distributed Hash-Table (DHT) based P2P systems, our link based network does not rely on node names, but on user selected neighbors. A peer, 'X' provides the following options that can be implemented to solve the isolation problem:

1. A special bootstrapping node that is present within each domain.
2. A peer that 'X' knows and trusts - a friend.

For a novice/new node, the first option may be the most appropriate. As 'X' ages, it finds other nodes and adds these links to improve the search speed and information access. The linkages are similar to friendships in real life, or to http links in the Web and are directed by humans.

Definition 1. *Link weights are given to each claimed attribute of a peer based on the percentage of links from the peer that can reach, after at most one indirection, other peers claiming the same attribute.*

Link weights are computed after the *escalation* of attributes (described in Section 5.1) and are important in determining the membership of a peer in a community.

---

[1] Neighbors are directly linked peers.

4   Modeling a P2P Network

A P2P network can be thought of as a graph where the nodes represent peers and the edges represent the links between two peers. In this section, we explain two approaches for generating a realistic P2P network topology that could be used to simulate our algorithms.

4.1   The Internet as a P2P Network

The pre-cursor to the Internet (Arpanet) was one of the first P2P networks, which had the ability to connect computers as peers and provide them with equal rights in sending and receiving packets. Therefore, in order to evaluate our proposed algorithms, we initially evaluated them on an Arpanet successor - the Internet - as we know it today. Because it is difficult to make a large number of computers on the Internet run our programs, we wrote a spider program that would crawl a subset of the Internet and create a topological map on which we could simulate our algorithms. The spider program started at a user-specified website, requested its HTML content, and parsed the HTML code to extract all the linked websites. It recorded the websites that lay within a pre-specified domain, such as "asu.edu," and discarded the rest. Thereafter, the spider recursively visited each website from its recorded list, thus repeating the same steps. By programming the spider to travel the Internet domain using an Eulerian path, we could create a map of the web topology, where each node was a website and edges represented a link from one site to another.

Except for a few changes, the web topology graph that we generated closely resembled a P2P network since websites are analogous to peers and http links are manually created and analogous to peer links. One such change required converting the graph from a directed graph to an undirected graph where the edges between the nodes represented bi-directional links between peers. The other reason for this close resemblance was the website content, which was analogous to a peer's interest attributes. Also, the domain specific attribute, such as "cse.asu.edu," is equivalent to the group attribute in a P2P network.

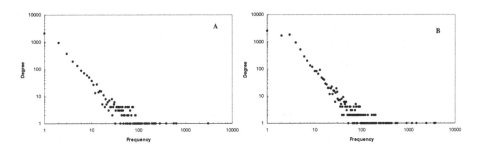

Fig. 3. The graphs show the power-law distribution of the frequency (*X-axis*) vs. degree (*Y-axis*) plot for the web topology graphs of: (*A*) "asu.edu" domain, and (*B*) "umich.edu" domain

Although the web topology graphs demonstrated power-law properties (see Fig. 3), our calculations for small-world behavior identified a problem. In order for a graph or a network to be considered a small-world network, its characteristic path length must be as low as the path length in random graphs and its clustering coefficient (CC) must be as high as the CC in regular graphs. However, both these values were low in our topology graphs. The characteristic path lengths were 2.46 and 2.32 for asu.edu and umich.edu, respectively; and the clustering coefficients were 0.28 and 0.32 in the same order. We attribute this phenomenon to the popular use of increasingly efficient search engines on the Internet. While a few years ago, a website owner placed http links to frequently visited websites on her website so that they could be easily accessible, contemporary search engines efficiently locate websites so that many website owners do not even have to link to the websites of their colleagues and friends any more. The resulting topology graph therefore showed fewer regular links, and calculations for clustering coefficient revealed low values.

4.2   Creating Our Own P2P Network

A P2P network comprising of peers that link to known peers is analogous to social networks, and therefore it should have a high clustering coefficient to represent the interconnected social links amongst circles of friends. We needed to provide a mechanism to ensure that our P2P network topology would exhibit the properties of a small-world network and would also show a power-law distribution for frequency versus degree.

Our next approach involved enforcing certain rules on new peers that wanted to join the P2P system. By virtue of these rules, the P2P system that was formed was a small-world network, which also exhibited a power-law (or scale-free) characteristic for the distribution of the number of neighbors of each peer.

We were inspired by the work of M. Steyvers and J. Tenenbaum [15] on semantic networks and extended the domain of their model to a P2P network that involves peers and links.

The new peer 'X' has to follow the rules below in order to join a P2P system:

1. Peer 'X' selects a single peer, 'A', from a list of known peers (see Section 3.2) that are currently members of the P2P system, such that 'A' is one of the more well-connected peers, i.e., it has, on the average, more links to other peers within the P2P system than the other peers from the list.
2. Peer 'X' creates links to N neighbors of 'A', such that the neighbors of 'A' that have more links to other peers are chosen with a higher probability than the other neighbors.

5   Structuring the P2P Network

We have previously stated two important traits of P2P communities: they are implicitly formed, and their membership depends on the relationships between peers that share common interests. Below, we discuss in detail the techniques that we use to structure peers into communities.

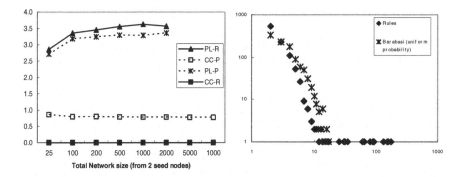

Fig. 4. (*left*) The graph shows the Clustering Coefficient (*CC*) and the characteristic Path Length (*PL*) for various network sizes generated with an initial seed of 2 nodes. The suffixes *P* and *R* indicate P2P and random networks, respectively. (*right*) The graph shows the power-law distribution in a frequency (*X-axis*) Vs degree (*Y-axis*) plot of our rules mechanism compared with the well-known "Barabasi" technique. The network size was 1000 nodes - grown from 2 seed nodes

5.1   Attribute Exchange, Escalation, and Analysis

The exchange of interest attributes is not required in order to form communities. In fact, if all peers only tried to form communities based on their claimed attributes, we could significantly reduce the cost of communication. However, it is possible that a P2P community with signature 'S' might exist. As a result, a peer that has 'S' in its personal attribute set, but does not claim it, will not be able to join this community and avail of the benefits until it claimed 'S'.

Peers, therefore, need to expose (escalate from the personal list to the claimed list) as many attributes as possible in order to join the maximum number communities. This escalation can only be achieved by establishing communication with other peers.

After the escalation of attributes, a peer cannot assume to be a member of a community based on "unescalated claimed attributes". Only after analyzing the received interest attributes will a peer be able to discover the two kinds of communities: (i) the communities that peers are explicitly a part of, by virtue of their common group attribute or other claimed attributes; and (ii) the communities in which peers become members, by virtue of their claimed attribute set after escalations.

5.2   Discovering Community Members

Since interest attributes are constantly changing values, the attribute exchange process needs to occur on a regular basis to keep the P2P system up-to-date and the peers subscribed to the most suitable, existing communities. Then, again, a periodic increase in communication messages might not be suitable for low bandwidth networks, as regular communication will be affected by this increased traffic. Our solution is to opt for *Distributed Discovery* and *P2P Gossiping*. The nature of the Distributed Discovery algorithm enables a peer to become aware of the following information: (1) the approximate size of its communities, (2) the other community members, and (3) various profile information of the member peers, such as peer involvement values, and claimed interest attributes for each peer.

In addition to link weights, peers have *involvement* values associated with every community in which it is a member. Involvement is proportional to the number of peers in the *neighborhood*[2] that claim the signature attributes of a particular community. Therefore peers with a higher value of involvement associated with a community such as 'C', have more peers within their neighborhood that are also members of 'C'. We use the term *seers* when referring to these peers.

In [14] we have shown that information stored on the seers will be available to a large percentage of peers within the community. The Distributed Discovery algorithm described in the same paper was also shown to be a low overhead, simple protocol that was resilient to failures and delays in peers. The protocol used vectors traveling a Hamiltonian path, and it terminated easily. If random peers initiated this protocol within their communities, the end result would be a well-structured P2P network, with peers being aware of the configuration of their communities. Below we describe a variation of the distributed discovery protocol that is bound by a maximum hop-count for discovery in very large communities.

Hop-bound Distributed Discovery. For communities that are extremely large, the Distributed Discovery algorithm will require a long time to conclude. Therefore the initiator will have to remain online for a long time to receive incoming vectors. To overcome this obstacle, we propose an alternative hop-bound Distributed Discovery that works by sending a maximum hop count (h) value along with the vector so that a sub-set of the community can be discovered. At a later stage, a merging algorithm can be executed for the purpose of combining various sub-sets into one community.

The merging algorithm can be executed as a low priority activity, which is not essential to the operation of algorithms, such as community-based search. That being said, the merging algorithm helps structure the P2P network so that the search algorithm will work more efficiently. Fig. 7 below shows the cases that might occur during the hop-bound discovery of a community. Following Fig. 7 is the construct of the merging algorithm:

Case 1: *There exists more than one initiator within h hops.* If the initiators have neighbors within or beyond h hops, then by virtue of the Distributed Discovery algorithm, the vector with the lower identification number survives, and remains as the only initiator in the community until the process is terminated. The ousted initiator knows the identity of the extant initiator. All the results sent to the ousted initiator are forwarded to the extant initiator of the community.

---

[2] The neighborhood of a peer includes neighboring peers and their neighbors.

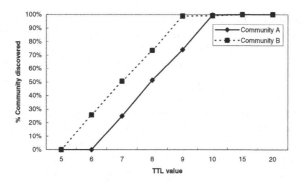

Fig. 5. The above graph shows the increasing percentage of the community discovered as the value of hop count increases. Note that the behavior of the hop-bound distributed discovery is linear. The test was conducted on a network with 4,500 nodes

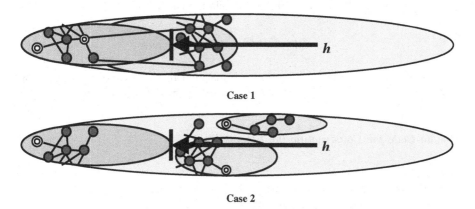

Fig. 6. The figures portray the two cases that might occur during a hop-bound distributed discovery. The large ellipse that encloses everything indicates the actual size of a community ($h = \infty$). The smaller ellipses indicate sub-sets of the community ($h \in \mathbb{N}$), where $\mathbb{N}$ is the set of natural numbers that are discovered. Peers (gray circles) and their links (connecting edges) are shown in the figure. Initiating peers are marked with concentric circles

Case 2: There exists more than one initiator beyond h hops. If the end vectors received by the initiator indicate that the hop count has been reached, then there could be some potential community members beyond h, who might have been involved in their own hop-based discovery. The initiator therefore sends a message to the peers that sent the end vectors requesting them to obtain the identity of the initiator from their neighbors that were not involved in this particular discovery. The initiator with the lowest peer identification value takes over as the new initiator of the merged community. However if no such initiator is found, then this operation of locating an initiator beyond h is repeated periodically so that eventually a merge operation will take place.

Obtaining Bloom Filter Summaries. Bloom filters [16] are compact data structures that probabilistically represent the elements of a set. They support queries of the form, *"Is X an element of the represented set?"* and at the current stage, they have been used in a variety of ways [17,18,19,20].

We extend our proposed Distributed Discovery protocol further by gathering Bloom filter summaries from each participating peer. The initiator creates a Bloom filter from its claimed attributes and sends it along with the vector. Each peer that receives the vector and the filter creates its own Bloom Filter and merges it into the existing filter. After the end vectors and filters are received, the initiator merges all the filters, forming, in this manner, a Bloom Filter that represents a compact summary of the attributes claimed by the peer members of a particular community.

In order to reduce the rate of false positives that result from the probabilistic nature of these data structures, we chose $k = 8$ hash functions and set the Bloom Filter size to $m = 2048$ bits. Based on formula (1) (described in [21], and [22]), we get: $p_{err} \approx 1.\mathsf{E}^{-05}$ for $n = 70$ possible claimed attributes.

$$p_{err} \approx \left(1 - e^{-\frac{kn}{m}}\right)^k \text{ (false positives)} \tag{1}$$

The reasons for this modification are justified in the next section where we employ the Bloom Filter for a Community-Based Search algorithm.

Pseudo-Code for Constructing the Bloom Filter

```
Start-prog
bloomFilter = new bool[m] initialized to false
Foreach attribute in Claimed Attribute List
    Foreach hashFunction hi
        bloomFilter[hi(attribute)] = true
    End-for
End-for
End-prog
```

Pseudo-Code for Merging Bloom Filters

```
Start-prog
mergedFilter = new bool[m] initialized to false
Foreach bFilter in List of Bloom Filters to merge
    Foreach bElement in bFilter
        i = bloomFilter.IndexOf(boolElement)
        mergedFilter[i] = mergedFilter[i] bit-OR bElement
    End-for
End-for
End-prog
```

6   Community-Based Search

Our solution for searching P2P networks takes advantage of the self-organization of peers and their capacity to implicitly form communities. In this section, we briefly describe the mechanics of our search technique and provide some preliminary comparisons with known search algorithms.

6.1   Constructing the Search Query

Any peer that needs to search the P2P network constructs a three-part search query containing: (1) the identity of the peer creating the query, (2) the actual query for an item, and (3) a list of meta-information that describe the item. Meta-information descriptions are analogous to adding the word "television" after "Japanese" while doing an Internet search in order to narrow the search for Japanese televisions.

In an interest-based P2P network, such as the digital library from Section 2.3, a peer might use interest attributes as meta-information to a query. For instance, if the query is for "Vampires," the list of meta-information might include attributes such as, "Twentieth century," "Bram Stoker," and "European authors".

6.2   Processing the Query

To facilitate the search operation, the query is sent to the peer P_S that is most likely to either solve the query or know some peer that can solve it. In our digital library example, a solution to a query could mean that the peer either owns the requested books or can provide information about the peer that owns them. As previously mentioned, this approach is markedly different from the traditional P2P search techniques. The peer P_S is chosen if it is a seer within the appropriate communities. At the end of Section 5, we described how Bloom filter summaries of claimed attributes were obtained for a particular community. At the current stage, the bloom filters are consulted to determine whether a peer claims any attribute from the meta-information list of the query. False positives can occur, thus increasing the overhead of locating P_S.

After the query is constructed, it is sent to the closest peer P_S that is also a seer in a community whose signature contains at least one attribute from the meta-information list. If the querying peer P_Q matches this description, then it is chosen to process the query. Else, P_Q looks for P_S from its immediate neighbors. In the case that P_S is not located, P_Q asks its neighbors to provide the identity of P_S. In the P2P networks generated using the rules described in Section 4.2, we found that the latter case occurs about 32% of the time. In addition, we found that P_S is almost always located after asking the neighbors. The cost involved in locating P_S is amortized over a number of queries because peers remember the identities of the closest peers that are seers of a particular community.

The query is then sent to P_S to be placed on the *blackboards* for the communities in which it is a seer and whose signatures contain at least one attribute from the query's meta-information list. Blackboards are similar to web pages and are independently maintained by a peer. Any peer can view the content on the blackboard of any other peer, provided that it knows the identity of that peer so that the blackboard can be reached. Peers maintain separate blackboards for each community in which they are members.

6.3   Checking Blackboards

Periodically and asynchronously, for each community C that it is a member, a peer visits the blackboard for C, which is maintained by each of its neighbors who are also members of C. If the visiting peer can solve any of the queries on the blackboard, then a message is created and sent to the peer that created the query. The message created could be sent via email to the querying peer.

Regardless of the outcome of the above procedure, the visiting peer copies the queries and places them onto its own blackboard for the community C. Our experiments revealed that even such an asynchronous, background communication amongst peers results in quick and efficient solutions to queries.

6.4   Simulation Results

We simulated the Community-Based Search (CBS) operation over a P2P network created by the rules described in Section 4.2. A set (10% of available peers) of random peers was selected to create queries. The details of the queries were randomly generated from a list of 25 known attributes. On an average, a query had 3 attributes in the meta-information list. The performance of CBS was evaluated against the performance of two well-known search techniques: (1) Gnutella search, a hop-limited breadth-first search of the P2P network beginning from the querying peer; and (2) Hub search, a hop-limited search like Gnutella, except that only one peer, selected for having the maximum number of neighbors, is forwarded the query each time.

In the digital library, the participating peers created two kinds of queries for books: (1) queries containing the title of the book; and (2) queries containing partial book contents or genre descriptions. CBS can operate using either type of query. Our tests were performed using queries that are of type (2). Therefore a solution to a query contained a list of all the peers that matched as many genre descriptions as possible, implying that the peers were likely to be members of the communities $C = \{C_1, \ldots, C_n\}$ whose member/s owned the requested book.

The parameters with which the search techniques were evaluated are: (1) the number of messages required for each search method, and (2) the quality of the solution, which is a measure of the number of peers found that are likely to be members of the maximum communities in C, i.e. the peers found have high link weights for the attributes that matched the genre descriptions.

Fig. 8 shows that CBS consistently requires fewer messages in order to process the queries. Furthermore, CBS scales well when the number of queries increases. On the other hand, the number of messages generated during the Hub-search method (*Hub*) begins to increase rapidly as more queries are created, because each hub forwards queries to all of its neighbors. Although the Gnutella (*Gnu*)

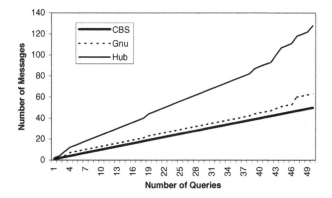

Fig. 7. Evaluation based on number of messages for search operation as the number of querying peers increases (*X-axis*). The results are the average values of 5 separate tests

technique exhibits linear behavior (since hop-limit was set at 5), it still does not out perform CBS in terms of number of messages generated.

Higher link weights (in fig. 8) for attribute 'A' indicate a higher probability that the peer is a member of a community of peers that claim attribute 'A'. For most attribute values, CBS finds a peer with higher link weights than the other two techniques.

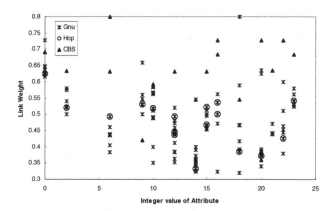

Fig. 8. The graph above displays the link weights of the peers found by the various search techniques. The *X-axis* of the graph corresponds to the attributes converted to an integer value ranging from 0 to 24

7   Conclusion

Peer-to-peer networks are autonomously created, self-organizing, decentralized systems that appeal to everyday home computer users. We have shown that these networks can be organized into interest-based communities using simple formation and discovery algorithms. We explained how a P2P network topology can be generated, and then illustrated our techniques for structuring the P2P network. Finally, we described the community-based search protocol that exploits this arrangement of the P2P network in order to provide better search operations. The results of our simulations showed that community-based search used fewer messages and found peers that were more likely to solve the query than two other well-known search techniques.

References

1. Google. http://www.google.com/
2. Yahoo. http://www.yahoo.com/
3. AltaVista. http://www.altavista.com/
4. Khambatti, M., Ryu, K., Dasgupta, P.: Efficient Discovery of Implicitly Formed Peer-to-Peer Communities. In: Mickle, M.H. (ed.): Int'l. Jour. of Parallel and Distributed Systems and Networks, vol. **5**(4). ACTA Press, Calgary (2002) 155–164
5. Gnutella. http://www.gnutelliums.com/
6. Clarke, I., Sandberg, O., Wiley, B., Hong, T. W.: Freenet: A distributed anonymous information storage and retrieval system. In: Workshop on Design Issues in Anonymity and Unobservability. (Berkeley, CA, USA, 2000) 311–320
7. Napster. http://www.napster.com/
8. Yahoo Groups. http://groups.yahoo.com
9. Yang, B., Garcia-Molina, H.: Efficient Search in Peer-to-peer Networks. In: International Conf. On Distributed Computing Systems. Vienna, Austria, 2002
10. Stoica, I., Morris, R., Karger, D., Kaashoek, F., Balakrishnan, H.: Chord: A Scalable Peer-to-peer Lookup Service for Internet Applications. In: Proc. ACM SIGCOMM, (2001) 149–160
11. Druschel, P., Rowstron, A.: Past: Persistent and anonymous storage in a peer-to-peer networking environment. In: Proc. the 8th IEEE Work. Hot Topics in Operating Systems (HotOS), (Germany, May 2001) 65–70
12. Khambatti, M., Ryu, K., Dasgupta, P.: Peer-to-Peer Communities: Formation and Discovery. In: 14th IASTED Int'l. Conf. Parallel and Distributed Computing Systems (PDCS), (Cambridge, MA, USA, 2002) 497–504
13. Gummadi, R., Hohlt, B.: Efficient Implementation Of A Publish-Subscribe-Notify Model Using Highly-Concurrent B-Trees (unpublished). (2000)
14. Khambatti, M., Ryu, K., Dasgupta, P.: Push-Pull Gossiping for Information Sharing in Peer-to-Peer Communities. In: Int'l Conf. on Parallel and Distributed Processing Techniques and Applications (PDPTA), (Las Vegas, NV, 2003)
15. Steyvers, M., Tenenbaum, J. B.: The large-scale structure of semantic networks: statistical analyses and a model of semantic growth (submitted). To: 25th Annual Meeting of the Cognitive Science Society (CogSci). (Boston, MA, 2003)
16. Bloom, B.: Space/time Trade-offs in Hash Coding with Allowable Errors. In: Communications of the ACM, **13**(7). (1970) 422–426

17. Gribble, S.D., Brewer, E.A., Hellerstein, J.M., Culler, D.: Scalable, Distributed Data Structures for Internet Service Construction. In: Proc. of the Fourth Symposium on Operating Systems Design and Implementation (OSDI 2000), (San Diego, CA, 2000)

18. Gribble, S.D., Welsh, M., Behren, R.v., Brewer, E.A., Culler, D., Borisov, N., Czerwinski, S., Gummadi, R., Hill, J., Joseph, A.D., Katz, R.H., Mao, Z., Ross, S., Zhao, B.: The Ninja Architecture for Robust Internet-Scale Systems and Services. In: Special Issue of Computer Networks on Pervasive Computing, **35**(4). (2001) 473–497

19. Hodes, T.D., Czerwinski, S.E., Zhao, B.Y., Joseph, A.D., Katz, R.H.: An Architecture for Secure Wide-Area Service Discovery. In: ACM Baltzer Wireless Networks: Selected papers from MobiCom 1999. (1999)

20. Kubiatowicz, J., Bindel, D., Chen, Y., Czerwinski, S., Eaton, P., Geels, D., Gummadi, R., Rhea, S., Weatherspoon, H., Weimer, W., Wells, C., Zhao, B.: OceanStore: An Architecture for Global-Scale Persistent Storage. In: Proc. of the Ninth Int'l Conf. on Architectural Support for Prog. Lang. and Operating Systems (ASPLOS 2000), (Cambridge, MA, 2000)

21. Fan, L., Cao, P., Almeida, J., Broder, A.: Summary Cache: A Scalable Wide-Area Web Cache Sharing Protocol. In: Proc. of ACM SIGCOMM '98, (Vancouver, Canada, 1998)

22. Ripeanu, M., Iamnitchi, A.: Bloom Filters – Short Tutorial (unpublished) (2001)

A Robust Logical and Computational Characterization of Peer-to-Peer Database Systems

Enrico Franconi[1], Gabriel Kuper[2], Andrei Lopatenko[1,3], and Luciano Serafini[4]

[1] Free University of Bozen–Bolzano, Faculty of Computer Science, Italy,
{franconi,lopatenko}@inf.unibz.it,
[2] University of Trento, DIT, Italy, kuper@acm.org
[3] University of Manchester, Department of Computer Science, UK
[4] ITC-irst Trento, Italy, serafini@itc.it

Abstract. In this paper we give a robust logical and computational characterisation of peer-to-peer (p2p) database systems. We first define a precise model-theoretic semantics of a p2p system, which allows for local inconsistency handling. We then characterise the general computational properties for the problem of answering queries to such a p2p system. Finally, we devise tight complexity bounds and distributed procedures for the problem of answering queries in few relevant special cases.

1 Introduction

The first question we have to answer when working on a logical characterisation of p2p database systems is the following: what is a p2p database system in the logical sense? In general, it is possible to say that a p2p database system is an integration system, composed by a set of (distributed) databases interconnected by means of some sort of logically interpreted mappings. However, we also want to distinguish p2p systems from standard classical logic-based integration systems, as for example described in [Lenzerini, 2002]. As a matter of fact, a p2p database system should be understood as a collection of independent nodes where the *directed* mappings between nodes have the only role to define how data migrates from a set of source nodes to a target node. This idea has been formulated in [Calvanese *et al.*, 2003], where a framework based on epistemic logic is proposed as a possible solution.

Consider the following example. Suppose we have three distributed databases. The first one (DB_1) is the municipality's internal database, which has a table Citizen-1. The second one (DB_2) is a public database, obtained from the municipality's database, with two tables Male-2 and Female-2. The third database (DB_3) is the Pension Agency database, obtained from a public database, with the table Citizen-3. The three databases are interconnected by means of the following rules:

$$1 : \texttt{Citizen-1}(x) \Rightarrow 2 : (\texttt{Male-2}(x) \lor \texttt{Female-2}(x))$$
(this rule connects DB_1 with DB_2)

K. Aberer et al. (Eds.): VLDB 2003 Ws DBISP2P, LNCS 2944, pp. 64–76, 2004.

$2 : \mathtt{Male\text{-}2}(x) \Rightarrow 3 : \mathtt{Citizen\text{-}3}(x)$
$2 : \mathtt{Female\text{-}2}(x) \Rightarrow 3 : \mathtt{Citizen\text{-}3}(x)$
        (these rules connect DB_2 with DB_3)

In the classical logical model, the $\mathtt{Citizen\text{-}3}$ table in DB_3 should be filled with all of the individuals in the $\mathtt{Citizen\text{-}1}$ table in DB_1, since the following rule is logically implied:

$1 : \mathtt{Citizen\text{-}1}(x) \Rightarrow 3 : \mathtt{Citizen\text{-}3}(x)$

However, in a p2p system this is not a desirable conclusion. In fact, rules should be interpreted only for fetching data, and not for logical computation. In this example, the tables $\mathtt{Female\text{-}2}$ and $\mathtt{Male\text{-}2}$ in DB_2 will be empty, since the data is fetched from DB_1, where the gender of any specific entry in $\mathtt{Citizen\text{-}1}$ is not known. From the perspective of DB_2, the only thing that is known is that each citizen is in the view ($\mathtt{Female\text{-}2} \vee \mathtt{Male\text{-}2}$). Therefore, when DB_3 asks for data from DB_2, the result will be empty.
In other words, the rules

$2 : \mathtt{Male\text{-}2}(x) \Rightarrow 3 : \mathtt{Citizen\text{-}3}(x)$
$2 : \mathtt{Female\text{-}2}(x) \Rightarrow 3 : \mathtt{Citizen\text{-}3}(x)$

will transfer no data from DB_2 to DB_3, since no individual is known in DB_2 to be either definitely a male (in which case the first rule would apply) or definitely a female (in which case the second rule would apply). We only know that any citizen in DB_1 is either male or female in DB_2, and no reasoning about the rules should be allowed.

We shall give a robust logical and computational characterisation of p2p database systems, based on the principle sketched above. We say that our formalisation is *robust* since, unlike other formalisations, it allows for local inconsistencies in some node of the p2p network: if some database is inconsistent it will not result in the entire database being inconsistent. Furthermore, we propose a polynomial-time algorithm for query answering over realistic p2p networks, which does not have to be aware of the network structure, which can therefore change dynamically.

Our work has been influenced by the semantic definitions of [Serafini *et al.*, 2003], which itself is based on the work of [Ghidini and Serafini, 1998]. [Serafini *et al.*, 2003] defined the *Local Relational Model* (LRM) to formalise p2p systems. In LRM all nodes are assumed to be relational databases and the interaction between them is described by coordination rules and translation rules between data items. Coordination rules may have an arbitrary form and allow to express constraints between nodes. The model-theoretic semantics of coordination rules in [Ghidini and Serafini, 1998,Serafini *et al.*, 2003] is non-classical, and it is very close to the *local semantics* introduced in this paper.

Various other problems of data management focusing on p2p systems have been considered in the literature with classical logic-based solutions. We mention here only few of them. In [Halevy *et al.*, 2003b], query answering for relational database- based p2p systems under classical semantics is considered. The case when both GAV and LAV style mappings between peers are allowed is considered. The mapping between data sources is given in the $\mathcal{PPL}$ language allowing for both inclusion and equality of conjunctive queries over data sources and definitional mappings (that is, inclusions of positive queries for a relation), and queries have certain answer semantics. It is proved that in the general case query answering is undecidable and in the acyclic case with only inclusion mappings allowed, the complexity of query answering becomes polynomial (if equality peer mappings are allowed, subject to some restrictions, query answering then becomes co-NP-complete). An algorithm reformulating a query to a given node into queries to nodes containing data is provided. In [Kementsietsidis *et al.*, 2003] mapping tables (similar to translation rules of [Serafini *et al.*, 2003]) are considered. In the article mapping tables under different semantic are considered, as well as constraints on mappings and reasoning over tables and constraints under such conditions. Moreover, see [Gribble *et al.*, 2001] for the data placement problem, [Cooper and Garcia-Molina, 2001] for data trading in data replication, [Halevy *et al.*, 2003a] for the relationship between p2p and Semantic Web, and in general [Lenzerini, 2002] for the best survey of classical logic-based data integration systems.

This paper is organised as follows. At the beginning, the formal framework is introduced; three equivalent ways of defining the semantics of a p2p system will be given, together with a fourth one – the extended local semantics – which is able to handle inconsistency and will be adopted in the rest of the paper. General computational properties will be analysed in Section 3, together with the special case of p2p systems with the minimal model property. Tight data and node complexity bounds for query answering are devised for the Datalog-p2p systems and for the acyclic p2p systems.

2   The Basic Framework

We first define the nodes of our p2p network as general first order logic (FOL) theories sharing a common set of constants. Thus, a node can be seen as represented by the set of models of the FOL theory.

Definition 1 (Local database) *Let I be a nonempty finite set of indexes $\{1, 2, \ldots, n\}$, and C be a set of constants. For each pair of distinct $i, j \in I$, let L_i be a first order function-free language with signature disjoint from L_j but for the shared constants C. A local database DB_i is a theory on the first order language L_i.*

Nodes are interconnected by means of coordination rules. A coordination rule allows a node i to fetch data from its neighbour nodes $j_1, \ldots, j_m$.

Definition 2 (Coordination rule) *A coordination rule is an expression of the form*

$$j_1 : b_1(\mathbf{x}_1, \mathbf{y}_1) \wedge \cdots \wedge j_k : b_k(\mathbf{x}_k, \mathbf{y}_k) \Rightarrow i : h(\mathbf{x})$$

$j_1, \ldots, j_k, i$ are distinct indices, and each $b_l(\mathbf{x}_l, \mathbf{y}_l)$ is a formula of L_{j_l}, and $h(\mathbf{x})$ is a formula of L_i, and $\mathbf{x} = \mathbf{x}_1 \cup \cdots \cup \mathbf{x}_k$.

Please note that we are making the simplifying assumption that the equal constants mentioned in the various nodes are actually referring to equal objects, i.e., they are playing the role of URIs (Uniform Resource Identifiers). Other approaches consider *domain relations* to map objects between different nodes [Serafini *et al.*, 2003]. We will consider this extension in our future work.

A p2p system is just the collection of nodes interconnected by the rules.

Definition 3 (p2p system) *A peer-to-peer (p2p) system is a tuple of the form* $MDB = \langle LDB, CR \rangle$, *where* $LDB = \{DB_1, \cdots, DB_n\}$ *is the set of local databases, and CR is the set of coordination rules.*

A user accesses the information hold by a p2p system by formulating a query to a specific node.

Definition 4 (Query) *A local query is a first order formula in the language of one of the databases* DB_i.

2.1   Global Semantics

In this section we formally introduce the meaning of a p2p system. We say that a global model of a p2p system is a FOL interpretation over the union of the FOL languages satisfying both the FOL theories local to each node and the coordination rules. Here it is crucial the fact that the semantics of the coordination rule is not the expected standard universal material implication, as in the classical information integration approaches. The p2p semantics for the coordination rules states that if the body of a rule is true in any possible model of the source nodes then the head of the rule is true in any possible model of the target node. This different notion from classical first order logic is exactly what we need: in fact, only information which is true in the source node is propagated forward.

Definition 5 (Global semantics) *Let* Δ *be a non empty set of objects including C (see Definition 1), and let* $MDB = \langle LDB, CR \rangle$ *be a p2p system. An interpretation of MDB over* Δ *is a n-tuple* $m \equiv \langle m_1, m_2, \ldots m_n \rangle$ *where each* m_i *is a classical first order logic interpretation of* L_i *on the domain* Δ *that interprets constants as themselves.*
We adopt the convention that, if m is an interpretation, then m_i *denotes the* i^{th} *element of m.*
A (global) model M for MDB – written $M \models_{global} MDB$ *– is a nonempty set of interpretations such that:*

1. *the model locally satisfies the conditions of each database, i.e.,*

$$\forall m \in M. \ (m_i \models DB_i)$$

2. *and the model satisfies the coordination rules as well, i.e., for any coordination rule*

$$j_1 : b_1(\mathbf{x}_1, \mathbf{y}_1) \wedge \cdots \wedge j_k : b_k(\mathbf{x}_k, \mathbf{y}_k) \Rightarrow i : h(\mathbf{x})$$

then for every assignment α – assigning the variables $\mathbf{x}$ to elements in Δ, which is common to all models – the following holds:

$$(\forall m \in M.(m_{j_1} \models \exists \mathbf{y}.b_1(\mathbf{x}_1, \mathbf{y})) \wedge \cdots \wedge (m_{j_k} \models \exists \mathbf{y}.b_k(\mathbf{x}_k, \mathbf{y}))) \rightarrow$$
$$(\forall m \in M.\ (m_i \models h(\mathbf{x})))$$

The answer to a query in a node of the system is nothing else than the tuples of values that, substituted to the variables of the query, make the query true in each global model restricted to the node itself.

Definition 6 (Query answer) *Let $Q_i(\mathbf{x})$ be a local query with free variables $\mathbf{x}$. The answer set of Q_i is the set of substitutions of $\mathbf{x}$ with constants $\mathbf{c}$, such that any model M of MDB satisfies the query, i.e.,*

$$\{\mathbf{c} \in C \times \cdots \times C \mid \forall M.\ (M \models_{\text{global}} MDB) \rightarrow \forall m \in M.\ (m_i \models Q_i(\mathbf{c}))\}$$

This corresponds to the definition of certain answer in the information integration literature.

2.2   Local Semantics

The semantics we have introduced in the previous section is called global since it introduces the notion of a global model which spans over the languages of all the nodes. In this section we introduce the notion of local semantics, where actually models of a p2p system have a node-centric nature which better reflects the required characteristics. We will prove at the end of the Section that the two semantics are equivalent.

Definition 7 *The derived local model $\hat{M}_i$ is the union of the ith components of all the models of MDB:*

$$\hat{M}_i = \bigcup_{\substack{m \in M, \\ M \models_{\text{global}} MDB}} m_i$$

Lemma 1 *The answer set of a local query $Q_i(\mathbf{x})$ coincides with the following:*

$$\{\mathbf{c} \in C \times \cdots \times C \mid \forall m_i \in \hat{M}_i.\ (m_i \models Q_i(\mathbf{c}))\}$$

The above lemma suggests that we could consider somehow $\left\langle \hat{M}_1, \ldots, \hat{M}_n \right\rangle$ as a model for the p2p system. This alternative semantics, which we call local semantics as opposed to the global semantics defined in the previous section, is defined in the following. The notation will sometimes coincide with the one used in the definition of global semantics; its meaning will be clear from the context.

Definition 8 (Local semantics) *A (local) model M for MDB – written $M \models MDB$ – is a sequence $\langle M_1, \ldots, M_n \rangle$ such that:*

1. *each M_i is a non empty set of interpretations of L_i over Δ*
2. *$\forall m_i \in M_i. \ (m_i \models DB_i)$*
3. *for any coordination rule*

$$j_1 : b_1(\mathbf{x}_1, \mathbf{y}_1) \wedge \cdots \wedge j_k : b_k(\mathbf{x}_k, \mathbf{y}_k) \Rightarrow i : h(\mathbf{x})$$

then for each assignment α to the variables $\mathbf{x}$ the following holds:

$$(\forall m_{j_1} \in M_{j_1}.(m_{j_1} \models \exists \mathbf{y}.b_1(\mathbf{x}_1, \mathbf{y}))) \wedge \cdots \wedge$$
$$(\forall m_{j_k} \in M_{j_k}.(m_{j_k} \models \exists \mathbf{y}.b_k(\mathbf{x}_k, \mathbf{y})))) \rightarrow$$
$$(\forall m_i \in M_i. \ (m_i \models h(\mathbf{x}))$$

Definition 9 (Query answer for local semantics) *Let Q_i be a local query. The answer for Q_i is the set of substitutions of $\mathbf{x}$ with constants $\mathbf{c}$ such that any model M of MDB locally satisfies the query, i.e.:*

$$\{\mathbf{c} \in C \times \cdots \times C \mid \forall M. \ (M \models MDB) \rightarrow \forall m_i \in M_i. \ (m_i \models Q_i(\mathbf{c}))\}$$

Theorem 2 *The answer sets of a local query Q_i in the global semantics and in the local semantics coincide.*

A way to understand the difference between global and local semantics would be the following. If

$$M = \{\langle m_1^1, \ldots, m_i^1, \ldots, m_n^1 \rangle, \ldots, \langle m_1^j, \ldots, m_i^j, \ldots, m_n^j \rangle, \ldots\}$$

is a model for a p2p system in the global semantics, then *also*

$$M' = \{\langle m_1^1, \ldots, m_i^j, \ldots, m_n^1 \rangle, \ldots, \langle m_1^j, \ldots, m_i^1, \ldots, m_n^j \rangle, \ldots\}$$

is a model in the global semantics. In other words, there is no formula expressible in the p2p system which distinguishes two models in the global semantics obtained by swapping local models. This is the reason why we can move to the local semantics defined in this section without loss of meaning. In fact, the local semantics itself does not distinguish between the two above cases, and can be therefore considered closer to the intended meaning of the p2p system.

2.3 Autoepistemic Semantics

In this section we briefly introduce a third approach to define the semantics of a p2p system, as suggested in [Calvanese *et al.*, 2003]. This approach can be proved equivalent to the global semantics introduced at the beginning – and therefore equivalent to the local semantics as well.

Let us consider KFOL, i.e., the autoepistemic extension of FOL (see, e.g., [Reiter, 1992]). The previous definition of global semantics can be easily changed to fit in a KFOL framework, so that the p2p system would be expressed in a single KFOL theory Σ. Each D_i would be expressed into KFOL without any change, i.e., without using at all the **K** operator; the coordination rules would be translated into formulas in Σ as

$$\forall \mathbf{x}.\mathbf{K}\exists \mathbf{y}.b(\mathbf{x}, \mathbf{y}) \Rightarrow \mathbf{K}h(\mathbf{x}).$$

It can be easily proved that the answer set as defined above (Definition 6) in the global semantics framework is equivalent to the answer set defined in KFOL as the set of all constants **c** such that

$$\Sigma \models_K \mathbf{K}Q_i(\mathbf{c}) .$$

2.4 Extended Local Semantics to Handle Inconsistency

The semantics defined above does not formalise local inconsistency. In fact as soon as a local database becomes inconsistent, or a coordination rule pushes inconsistency somewhere, both the global and the local semantics say that no model of *MDB* exists. This means that local inconsistency implies global inconsistency, and the p2p system is not robust.

Proposition 3 *For any p2p system such that there is an i such that DB_i is inconsistent, then the answer set of any query $Q_j(\mathbf{x})$ is equal to $C \times \cdots \times C$, for both the global and local semantics.*

In order to have a robust p2p system able to be meaningful even in presence of some inconsistent node, we extend the local semantics by allowing single M_i to be the empty set. This captures the inconsistency of a local database: we say that a local database DB_i is inconsistent if M_i is empty for any model of the p2p system. A database depending on an inconsistent one through some coordination rule will have each dependent view – i.e., the formula in the head of the rules with n free variables – equivalent to Δ^n, and the databases not depending on the inconsistent one will remain consistent. Therefore, in presence of local inconsistency the global p2p system remains consistent.

The following example will clarify the difference between the local semantics and the extended local semantics in handling inconsistency.

Example 1. Consider the p2p system composed of a node DB_1 containing a unary predicate P and an inconsistent axiom $\bot$, and another node DB_2 containing two unary predicates Q and R with no specific axiom on them. Let

$$1 : P(x) \Rightarrow 2 : Q(x)$$

be a coordination rule from DB_1 to DB_2. Even though DB_1 is inconsistent, there is a model $M = \langle M_1, M_2 \rangle$ where M_2 is not the empty set. The answer set of the query $Q(x)$ in 2 is the whole set of constants known to the p2p system. Furthermore, the answer set of the query $R(x)$ in 2 is the empty set. So, in this case the inconsistency does not have an effect through the coordination rule to each predicate of DB_2.

Let us suppose now that M_2 contains in addition the axiom $\exists x \neg Q(x)$. Then, the only model (in the local semantics) is $\langle M_1, M_2 \rangle$ where both M_1 and M_2 are the empty set.

In the case of fully consistent p2p systems, the local semantics and the extended local semantics coincide. In the case of some local inconsistency, the local (or, equivalently, the global) semantics will imply a globally inconsistent system, while the extended local semantics is able to still give meaningful answers.

Theorem 4 *If there is a model for MDB with the local (or global, or autoepistemic) semantics then for each query the answer set with the local (or global, or autoepistemic) semantics coincide with the answer set with extended local semantics.*

3 Computing Answers

In this section, we will consider the global properties of a generic p2p system: we will try to find the conditions under which a computable solution to the query answering problem exists, we will investigate its properties and how to compute it in some logical database language. From now on, we assume the extended local semantics – i.e., the semantics of the p2p system able to cope with inconsistency. We include the sketches of some proofs.

Let us define the inclusion relation between models of a p2p system. A model M is *included* into N ($M \subseteq N$) if for each node i, a set of models of i in M is a subset of a set of models for i in N.

Let CR be a set of coordination rules and M an interpretation of MDB, i.e., a sequence $\langle M_1, \ldots, M_n \rangle$ such that each M_i is a set of interpretations of L_i over Δ. A ground formula A is a *derived fact* for M and CR if either $M \models A$, or $i : \psi \Rightarrow j : A$ is an instantiation of a rule in CR and $M \models \psi$. Please remember that when we write $M \models \psi$ – where M is a model for MDB– we intend the logical implication for the extended local semantics.

Definition 10 (Immediate consequence operator) *Let MDB be a p2p system, CR a set of coordination rules, and M a model of MDB. A model $\hat{M}$ is an immediate consequence for M and CR if it is a maximal model included into M such that each $M_i \in \hat{M}$ contains facts derived by CR from M. The immediate consequence operator for MDB, denoted T_{MDB}, is the mapping from a set of models into a set of models such that for each M, $T_{MDB}(M)$ is an immediate consequence of M.*

Few lemmas about the properties of the consequence operator are in order to prove our main theorem.

Lemma 5 *The operator T_{MDB} is monotonic with respect to model inclusion, i.e., if $M \subseteq N$, then $T_{MBD}(M) \subseteq T_{MDB}(N)$*

Proof. For each rule create a ground instantiation of it. Each ground instance of CR in N is also present in M. This means that for each new formula ψ derivable in N the same formula is derivable in M. So, all models which are refused during the application of the operator in N are also refused in M. Therefore, $T_{MDB}(M) \subseteq T_{MDB}(N)$.

Lemma 6 *The operator T_{MDB} is monotonic with respect to the set of ground instantiations of rules satisfied (the set of ground instances of rules derived at some step of the execution of an operator remains valid for all the subsequent steps).*

Proof. Let's assume that a rule $i : \psi(\mathbf{x}, \mathbf{y}) \Rightarrow j : \phi(\mathbf{x})$ is instantiated for some $\mathbf{x}$, $\mathbf{y}$ at step n for the set of models M_i^n, M_j^n. Clearly, it will remain valid for any step $m > n$, given the semantics of the rules and that $M_i^m \subseteq M_i^n, M_j^m \subseteq M_j^n$.

Lemma 7 *For any initial model M, the operator T_{MDB} reaches a fixpoint which is a model of MDB.*

Proof. Since we begin from a finite set of models, after a finite number of steps we reach a lower bound (possibly the empty set of models): this is a set of models which satisfy *MDB*. In fact, all local FOL theories are satisfied by definition of T_{MDB}, and if some rule in *CR* is not satisfied then an execution of T_{MDB} will lead to a new model, but this would contradict the reaching of the fixpoint. If the empty set of models is reached then *MDB* is trivially satisfied.

The main theorem states that we can use the consequence operator to compute the answer to a query to a p2p system.

Theorem 8 *The certain answer of a query to a p2p system MDB is the certain answer of the query over the model $T_{MDB}^\omega(M_0)$, where M_0 is the model set consisting of the Cartesian product of all the interpretations satisfying the local FOL theories.*

Proof. $\Leftarrow$. If $Q(a)$ is a certain answer, then, since $Q(a)$ is true in any model, it is true in the model resulting by applying the operator to the maximum original set. So, $\{\mathbf{x} \mid MDB \models Q(\mathbf{x})\} \subseteq \{\mathbf{x} \mid T_{MDB}(M_0) \models Q_\mathbf{x}\}$

$\Rightarrow$. Since the original interpretation is the Cartesian product of all local interpretations, then any particular model consisting of a set of local models is a subset of M_0, i.e., $\forall M.M \subseteq M_0$. By monotonicity of the operator, it holds that

$$\forall M.T_{MDB}^\omega(M) \subseteq T_{MDB}^\omega(M_0)$$

Therefore, $\{\mathbf{x} \mid MDB \models Q(\mathbf{x})\} \supseteq \{\mathbf{x} \mid T_{MDB}(M_0) \models Q(\mathbf{x})\}$.

3.1   Computation with Minimal Models

Let us now assume that at each node the minimal model property holds – i.e., in each local database the intersection of all local models is a model itself of the local FOL theory, and it is minimal wrt set inclusion. Let us assume also that the coordination rules are preserving this property – e.g., the body of any rule is a conjunctive query and the head of any rule is a conjunctive query without existential variables. We say that in this case the p2p system enjoys the minimal model property. Then, it is possible to simplify the computation procedure defined by the T_{MDB} operator. In such case the computation is reducible to a "migration of facts". The procedure is crucially simplified if it is impossible to get inconsistency in local nodes (like for Datalog or relational databases).

Definition 11 (Minimal model property) *The consequence operator T_{MDB}^{min} for MDB with the minimal model property is defined in the following way:*

- *at the beginning, the minimal model is given for each node;*
- *at each step, T_{MDB}^{min} computes for each coordination rule a set of derived facts and adds them into the local nodes;*
- *if for a node j an inconsistent theory is derived, then the current model is replaced by the empty set, otherwise the current theory is extended with the derived facts and the minimal model is replaced by the minimal model of the new theory.*

We denote with $T_{MDB}^{min,\omega}$ the fixpoint of T_{MDB}^{min}.

Theorem 9 *If the p2p system has the minimal model property, then for positive queries $Q(\mathbf{x})$*

$$T_{MDB}^{min,\omega}(M_{min}) \models Q(\mathbf{x}) \quad \leftrightarrow \quad MDB \models Q(\mathbf{x})$$

Proof. If M_{min} is the minimal model, then if ψ does not contain negation, $(\forall M$ model of $MDB, M \models \psi) \Leftrightarrow M_{min} \models \psi$. Let us assume that we execute $T_{MDB}(M_0)$, where M_0 is the set of all the models of each node. Assume that at step i of the execution of $T_{MDB}^{min}(M_{min})$ we get the minimal model of the outcome of step i of the execution of $T_{MDB}(M_0)$ (which is evidently true for step 0). The set of derived facts for each node at step $i+1$ for T_{MDB} will be the same as for T_{MDB}^{min}, so that at step $i+1$ the theories for the execution of T_{MDB} and T_{MDB}^{min} will be the same. By definition of T_{MDB}^{min}, this will give a minimal model at the $i+1$ step. If at step n T_{MDB} reaches a fixpoint, then T_{MDB}^{min} reaches a fixpoint as well with the minimal model corresponding to the models devised by T_{MDB}. Since Q is a positive query, the thesis is proved.

This theorem means that a p2p system with nodes and coordination rules with the minimal model property collapses to a traditional p2p and data integration system like [Halevy *et al.*, 2003b,Lenzerini, 2002] based on classical logic. A special case is when each node is either a pure relational database or a Datalog-based deductive database (in either case the node enjoys the minimal model property), and each rule has the body in the form of a conjunctive query and the head in the form of a conjunctive query without existential variables. We call such a system a Datalog-p2p system. In such case, it is possible to introduce a simple "global program" to answer queries to the p2p system. The global program is a single Datalog program obtained by taking the union of all local Datalog programs and of the coordination rules expressed in Datalog, plus the data at the nodes seen as EDB.

We are able to precisely characterise the data and node complexity of query answering in a Datalog-p2p system. The data complexity is the complexity of evaluating a fixed query in a p2p system with a fixed number of nodes and coordination rules over databases of variable size – as input we consider here the total size of all the databases. The node complexity, which we believe is a relevant complexity measure for a p2p system, is the complexity of evaluating a fixed query over a databases of a fixed size with respect to a variable number of nodes in a p2p system with a fixed number of coordination rules between each pair of nodes. It turns out that the worst case node complexity is rather high.

Theorem 10 (Complexity of Datalog-p2p) *The data complexity of query answering for positive queries in a Datalog-p2p system is in PTIME, while the node complexity of query answering a Datalog-p2p system is EXPTIME-complete.*

Proof. The proof is obtained by reducing the problem to a global Datalog program and considering complexity results for Datalog

It can be shown that the node complexity becomes polynomial under the realistic assumption that the number of coordination rules is logarithmic with respect to the number of nodes.

3.2   A Distributed Algorithm for Datalog-p2p Systems

Clearly, the global Datalog program devised in the previous Section is not the way how query answering should be implemented in a p2p system. In fact, the global program requires the presence of a *central* node in the network, which knows all the coordination rules and imports all the databases, so that the global program can be executed. A p2p system should implement a *distributed* algorithm, so that each node executes locally a part of it in complete autonomy and it may delegate to neighbour nodes the execution of subtasks, so that there is no need for a centralised authority controlling the process.

In [Serafini and Ghidini, 2000] a distributed algorithm for query answering has been introduced, which is sound and complete for an extension of Datalog-p2p systems. In that work, a Datalog-p2p system is called a *definite deductive multiple database*, where domain relations translating query results from the different domains of the various nodes are also allowed. So, we can fully adopt this procedure in our context by assuming identity domain relations. In this paper we do not give the details of the distributed algorithm, which can be found in [Serafini and Ghidini, 2000,Casotto, 1998].

3.3   Acyclic p2p Systems

A p2p system is acyclic if the dependency graph induced by the coordination rules is acyclic. The acyclic case is worth considering since the node complexity of query answering is greatly reduced – it becomes quadratic – and more expressive rules are allowed.

Theorem 11 (Complexity of acyclic p2p) *Answering a conjunctive query in an acyclic p2p system with coordination rules having unrestricted conjunctive queries both at the head and at the body is in PTIME. If a positive query is*

allowed at the head of a coordination rule then query answering becomes coNP-complete. In both cases the node complexity of query answering is quadratic, and it becomes linear in the case of the network being a tree.

Proof. The proof follows by reducing to the problem of query answering using views (see, e.g., [Lenzerini, 2002]).

This result extends Theorem 3.1 part 2 of [Halevy *et al.*, 2003b].

A distributed algorithm for an acyclic p2p system would work as follows. A node answers to a query first by populating the views defined by the heads of the coordination rules of which the node itself is target with the answer to the queries in the body of such rules, and then by answering the query using such views. Of course, answering to the queries in the body of the rules involve recursively the neighbour nodes.

It is possible to exploit the low node complexity of acyclic systems (which have a tree-like topological structure) to build more complex network topologies still with a quadratic node complexity for query answering. The idea is to introduce in an acyclic network the notion of fixed size autonomous subnetworks where cyclic rules are allowed, and a *super-peer* node is in charge to communicate with the rest of the network. This architecture matches exactly the notion of super-peer in real p2p systems like Gnutella.

4   Conclusions

In this paper, we propose a new model for the semantics of a p2p database system. In contrast to previous approaches our semantics is not based on the standard first-order semantics.

In our opinion, this approach captures more precisely the intended semantics of p2p systems. It models a framework in which a node can request data from another node, which can involve evaluating a query locally and/or requesting, in turn, data from a third node, but *can not* involve evaluating complex queries over the entire network, as would be the case if the network was an integrated system as in standard work on data integration.

One interesting consequence is in the way we handle inconsistency. In a p2p system, with many independent nodes, there is a possibility that some nodes will contain inconsistent data. In standard approaches, this would result in the whole database being inconsistent, an undesirable situation. In our framework, the inconsistency will not propagate, and the whole database will remain consistent.

The results we have presented show that the original, global, semantics and an alternative, local, semantics are in fact equivalent, and we then extended it in order to handle inconsistency. We also give an algorithm for query evaluation, and some results on special cases where queries can be evaluated more efficiently.

Directions for future work include studying more thoroughly the complexity of query evaluation, as well as special cases, for example ones with appropriate network topologies, for which query evaluation is more tractable. Another issue is that of *domain relations*. These were introduced in [Serafini *et al.*, 2003] to capture the fact that different nodes in a p2p system may not use the same underlying domains, and show how to map one domain to another. Such relations are not studied in the current paper, and their integration in our framework is another area for future research.

References

[Calvanese *et al.*, 2003] Diego Calvanese, Elio Damaggio, Giuseppe De Giacomo, Maurizio Lenzerini, and Riccardo Rosati. Semantic data integration in P2P systems. In *Proc. of the International Workshop On Databases, Information Systems and Peer-to-Peer Computing*, September 2003.

[Casotto, 1998] Camilla Casotto. Un algoritmo distribuito per l'interrogazione di basi di dati federate. Master thesis, ITC-irst, 1998.

[Cooper and Garcia-Molina, 2001] Brian Cooper and Hector Garcia-Molina. Peer to peer data trading to preserve information. Technical report, Stanford University, 2001.

[Ghidini and Serafini, 1998] Chiara Ghidini and Luciano Serafini. Distributed first order logics. In Franz Baader and Klaus Ulrich Schulz, editors, *Frontiers of Combining Systems 2*, Berlin, 1998. Research Studies Press.

[Gribble *et al.*, 2001] Steven Gribble, Alon Halevy, Zachary Ives, Maya Rodrig, and Dan Suciu. What can databases do for peer-to-peer? In *WebDB Workshop on Databases and the Web*, 2001.

[Halevy *et al.*, 2003a] Alon Halevy, Zachary Ives, Peter Mork, and Igor Tatarinov. Peer data management systems: Infrastructure for the semantic web. In *WWW Conference*, 2003.

[Halevy *et al.*, 2003b] Alon Y. Halevy, Zachary G. Ives, Dan Suciu, and Igor Tatarinov. Schema mediation in peer data management systems. In *ICDE*, 2003.

[Kementsietsidis *et al.*, 2003] Anastasios Kementsietsidis, Marcelo Arenas, and Renee J. Miller. Mapping data in peer-to-peer systems: Semantics and algorithmic issues. In *Proceedings of the SIGMOD International Conference on Management of Data (SIGMOD'03)*, 2003.

[Lenzerini, 2002] Maurizio Lenzerini. Data integration: a theoretical perspective. In *Proceedings of the twenty-first ACM SIGMOD-SIGACT-SIGART symposium on Principles of database systems*, pages 233–246. ACM Press, 2002.

[Reiter, 1992] Raymond Reiter. What should a database know? *Journal of Logic Programming*, 14(2,3), 1992.

[Serafini and Ghidini, 2000] Luciano Serafini and Chiara Ghidini. Using wrapper agents to answer queries in distributed information systems. In *Proceedings of the First Biennial Int. Conf. on Advances in Information Systems (ADVIS-2000)*, 2000.

[Serafini *et al.*, 2003] Luciano Serafini, Fausto Giunchiglia, John Mylopoulos, and Philip A. Bernstein. Local relational model: A logical formalization of database coordination. In *CONTEXT 2003*, pages 286–299, 2003.

Semantic Data Integration in P2P Systems

Diego Calvanese, Elio Damaggio, Giuseppe De Giacomo,
Maurizio Lenzerini, and Riccardo Rosati

Dipartimento di Informatica e Sistemistica
Università di Roma "La Sapienza"
Via Salaria 113, I-00198 Roma, Italy
{Calvanese,Damaggio,Giacomo,Lenzerini,Rosati}@dis.uniroma1.it

Abstract. In this paper, we study the problem of data integration in
P2P systems. Differently from the traditional setting, data integration
in these systems is not based on the existence of a global view. Instead,
each peer exports data in terms of its own schema, and information integration is achieved by establishing mappings among the various peer
schemas. We present a framework that captures this general architecture, and then we discuss the problem of characterizing the semantics
of such framework. We show that the usual approach of resorting to a
first-order logic intepretation of P2P mappings, leads both to a poor
modeling of the whole system, and to undecidability of query answering,
even for mappings of a restricted form. This motivates the need of a new
semantics for P2P system. We then present a novel proposal, based on
epistemic logic, and show that not only it adequately models the interactions among peers, but it also supports decidable query answering. In
particular, for the restricted form of mapping mentioned above, query
answering is polynomial with respect to the size of data stored in the
peers.

1 Introduction

Most of the formal approaches to data integration refer to an architecture based
on a global schema and a set of sources. The sources contain the real data, while
the global schema provides a reconciled, integrated, and virtual view of the
underlying sources. One of the challenging issues in these systems is to answer
queries posed to the global schema. Due to the architecture of the system, query
processing requires a reformulation step: the query over the global schema must
be re-expressed in terms of a set of queries over the sources [12,13,17,15].

In this paper, we study the problem of data integration in peer-to-peer systems. In these systems every node (peer) acts as both client and server, and provides part of the overall information available from a distributed environment,
without relying on a single global view. A suitable infrastructure is adopted for
managing the information in the various nodes. Napster[1], which made the P2P
idea popular, employs a centralized database with references to the information

---

[1] http://www.napster.com/

K. Aberer et al. (Eds.): VLDB 2003 Ws DBISP2P, LNCS 2944, pp. 77–90, 2004.

items (files) on the peers. Gnutella, another well-known P2P system, has no central database, and is based on a communication-intensive search mechanism. More recently, a Gnutella-compatible P2P system, called Gridella [1], has been proposed, which follows the so-called Peer-Grid (P-Grid) approach. A P-Grid is a virtual binary tree that distributes replication over community of peers and supports efficient search. P-Grid's search structure is completely decentralized, supports local interactions between peers, uses randomized algorithms for access and search, and ensures robustness of search against node failures.

As pointed out in [10], current P2P systems focus strictly on handling semantic-free, large-granularity requests for objects by identifier, which both limits their utility and restricts the techniques that might be employed to distribute the data. These current sharing systems are largely limited to applications in which objects are described by their name, and exhibit strong limitations in establishing complex links between peers. To overcome these limitations, data-oriented approaches to P2P have been proposed recently [11,2,10]. For example, in the Piazza system [10], data origins serve original content, peer nodes co-operate to store materialized views and answer queries, nodes are connected by bandwidth-constrained links and advertise their materialized views to share resources with other peers.

Differently from the traditional setting, integration in data-oriented P2P systems is not based on a global schema. Instead, each peer represents an autonomous information system, and information integration is achieved by establishing P2P mappings, i.e., mappings among the various peers. Queries are posed to one peer, and the role of query processing is to exploit both the data that are internal to the peer, and the mappings with other peers in the system. To stress the data-oriented nature of the framework, we refer to "semantic data integration", in the sense that we assume that the various peers export data in terms of a suitable schema, and mappings are established among such peer schemas. A peer schema is therefore intended to export the semantics of information as viewed from the peer.

In this paper, we present a framework that captures this general architecture (Section 2), and then discuss the problem of characterizing the semantics of such framework (Section 3). We argue that, although correct from a formal point of view, the usual approach of resorting to a first-order logic interpretation of P2P mappings (followed for example by [6,11,2]), has several drawbacks, both from the modeling and from the computational perspective. In particular, query answering under the first-order semantics is undecidable, even for restricted forms of P2P systems, called *simple* P2P systems, i.e., for the case where the various peers are empty first-order theories. Motivated by these observations, several authors proposed suitable limitations to the form of P2P mappings, such as acyclicity.

Based on the above mentioned drawbacks, we propose a new semantics for P2P systems, with the following aims: *(i)* we want to take into account that peers are autonomous modules, and the modular structure of the P2P system should be explicitly reflected in the definition of its semantics; *(ii)* we do not want to limit a-priori the topology of the mapping assertions between the peers in the system; *(iii)* we seek for a semantic characterization that leads to a setting where query answering is decidable, and possibly, polynomially tractable.

We base our proposal of a new semantics for P2P systems on epistemic logic, and we show that not only it adequately models the interactions among peers, but it also supports decidable query answering. In particular, for simple P2P systems, we devise a query answering algorithm which runs in polynomial time with respect to the size of data stored in the peers (Section 4).

2   Framework

In this section, we set up the general framework for peer-to-peer (P2P) systems. We refer to a fixed, infinite, denumerable, set Γ of constants. Such constants are shared by all peers, and are the constants that can appear in the P2P system. Moreover, given a (relational) alphabet A, we denote with $\mathcal{L}_A$ the set of function-free first-order logic (FOL) formulas whose relation symbols are in A and whose constants are in Γ. A *FOL query* of arity n over an alphabet A is written in the form

$$\{\mathbf{x} \mid body(\mathbf{x})\}$$

where $body(\mathbf{x})$ is an open formula of $\mathcal{L}_A$ with free variables $\mathbf{x} = x_1, \ldots, x_n$. A *conjunctive query* (CQ) of arity n over an alphabet A is written in the form

$$\{\mathbf{x} \mid \exists \mathbf{y}\ cbody(\mathbf{x}, \mathbf{y})\}$$

where $cbody(\mathbf{x}, \mathbf{y})$ is an conjunction of atoms of $\mathcal{L}_A$ involving the free variables (also called the distinguished variables of the query) $\mathbf{x} = x_1, \ldots, x_n$, the existentially quantified variables (also called the non-distinguished variables of the query) $\mathbf{y} = y_1, \ldots, y_m$, and constants from Γ.

A P2P system is constituted by a set of peers, and a set of mappings among peers. We first concentrate on describing the structure of a single peer. Following the basic ideas presented in [11], we define a peer P as a triple $P = (G, S, L)$, where:

- G is the *schema* of P, which is defined, starting from an alphabet A_G, as a set of formulas of $\mathcal{L}_{A_G}$. We call A_G the *alphabet* of P.
- S is the *(local) source schema* of P, that is simply a finite relational alphabet, which is called the *local alphabet* of P.
- L is a set of *(local) mapping assertions* between G and S. Each local mapping assertion has the form

$$cq_S \rightsquigarrow cq_G$$

where cq_S and cq_G are two conjunctive queries of the same arity, over the source schema S and over the peer schema G, respectively.

Intuitively, the source schema describes the structure of the data sources of the peer (possibly obtained by wrapping physical sources), where the real data managed by the peer are stored, while the peer schema provides a virtual view of the information managed by, and exported by the peer. The mapping assertions establish the connection between the elements of the source schema and those of the peer schema. In particular, an assertion of the form $cq_S \rightsquigarrow cq_G$ specifies that all the data satisfying the query cq_S over the sources also satisfy the concept in the peer schema represented by the query cq_G. This form of mapping is the most expressive one among those studied in the data integration literature. Indeed, in terms of the terminology used in data integration, a peer in our setting corresponds to a GLAV *data integration system* [9] managing a set of sound data sources S defined in terms of a (virtual) global schema G.

A P2P system is constituted by a set of peers and a set of mappings that specify the semantic relationships between the data exported by the peers. Formally, a *P2P system* is a pair $\mathcal{S} = (\mathcal{P}, \mathcal{M})$, where $\mathcal{P}$ is a finite set of peers, and $\mathcal{M}$ is a finite set of P2P-mapping assertions. Each *P2P mapping assertion* has the form

$$q_1 \rightsquigarrow q_2$$

where

- q_1, called the *tail* of the assertion, is a FOL query over the union of the alphabets of the peers in $\mathcal{P}$,
- q_2, called the *head* of the assertion, is a FOL query over the alphabet of a single peer, and
- q_1 and q_2 are of the same arity.

Intuitively, a P2P mapping assertion $q_1 \rightsquigarrow q_2$, where q_2 is a query over the schema of a peer P, expresses the fact that P can use, besides the data in its local sources, also the data retrieved by q_1 from the peers over which q_1 is expressed. Such data are mapped to the schema of P according to what is specified by the query q_2. Observe that P2P mapping assertions may be cyclic, in the sense that no limitation is imposed on the graph representing such assertions. This graph contains one node for every relation symbol in the peer schemas, and one arc from the node corresponding to R_1 to the node corresponding to R_2 if there is a P2P mapping assertion whose tail mentions R_1 and whose head mentions R_2.

Finally, we assume that queries are posed to a single peer of the system. More precisely, a *query* over a P2P system $\mathcal{S} = (\mathcal{P}, \mathcal{M})$ is a first-order query over the peer schema of a single peer in $\mathcal{P}$.

3   Semantics

In this section, we first define the semantics of one peer (subsection 3.1), and then we discuss two mechanisms for specifying the semantics of the whole P2P system. The first mechanism (subsection 3.2), adopted in most formal approaches to P2P data integration, is based of FOL. Motivated by several drawbacks of this approach, we propose a new semantics, based on epistemic logic (subsection 3.3).

In what follows, a database (DB) for a schema $\mathcal{T}$ is simply a set of collection of relations, one for each symbol in the alphabet of $\mathcal{T}$. Also, if q is a query of arity n and $\mathcal{DB}$ is a database, we denote with $ans(q, \mathcal{DB})$ the set of tuples (of arity n) in $\mathcal{DB}$ that satisfy q.

3.1   Semantics of One Peer

In order to assign formal meaning to a peer $P = (G, S, L)$, we conceive P as a FOL theory T_P, called "peer theory", defined as follows:

- The alphabet of T_P is obtained as union of the alphabet $\mathcal{A}_G$ of G and the alphabet of the local sources S of P,
- The axioms of T_P are the formulas specified as follows:
  - there is one formula of the form

  $$\forall \mathbf{x} \ (cq_S(\mathbf{x}) \rightarrow cq_G(\mathbf{x}))$$

  for each local mapping assertion $cq_S \rightsquigarrow cq_G$ in L
  - T_P includes all the formulas expressing the schema G.

We make a simplifying assumption on the domain of the various databases. In particular, we assume that the databases involved in our framework (both the databases conforming to the local schemas, and those conforming to the peer schemas) share the same infinite domain Δ, fixed once and for all. We also assume that the constants in Γ (see the previous section) have the same, fixed, interpretation in all databases, i.e., to each constant $c \in \Gamma$ is associated, once and for all, a certain domain element $d \in \Delta$. Moreover, we assume that Γ contains a constant for each element in Δ, and that different constants are interpreted as different domain elements. It follows that Γ is actually isomorphic to Δ, so that we can use (with a little abuse of notation) constants in Γ whenever we want to denote domain elements.[2]

Now, the semantics of P directly follows from its characterization in FOL, and the assumption above on the interpretation domain. However, in order to point out the role of local sources in P, we specialize the notion of FOL semantics by starting with a *local source database* for P, i.e., a finite database $\mathcal{D}$ for the source schema S. Based on $\mathcal{D}$, we now specify which is the information content of the peer schema G at the extensional level. We call *peer database* for P any database for G. A peer database $\mathcal{B}$ for P is said to be a *model of P with respect to $\mathcal{D}$* if:

- $\mathcal{B}$ satisfies all the formulas expressing the meaning of G,
- $\mathcal{B}$ satisfies every mapping assertion in L, where $\mathcal{B}$ satisfies the mapping assertion $cq_S \rightsquigarrow cq_G$ if every tuple that satisfies cq_S in $\mathcal{D}$ satisfies also cq_G in $\mathcal{B}$.

Finally, we specify the semantics of queries posed to a peer. As we said before, such queries are expressed in terms of the alphabet $\mathcal{A}_G$, i.e., in terms of the symbols in the peer schema G of P. Given a local source database $\mathcal{D}$ for P, the answer $ans(q, P, \mathcal{D})$ to a query q in P with respect to $\mathcal{D}$, is the set of tuples $\mathbf{t}$ of constants in Γ such that $\mathbf{t} \in ans(q, \mathcal{B})$ for *every* peer database $\mathcal{B}$ that is a model of P with respect to $\mathcal{D}$. The set $ans(q, P, \mathcal{D})$ is called the set of *certain answers* to q in P with respect to $\mathcal{D}$.

In the next two subsections, we turn our attention to the problem of specifying the semantics of the whole P2P system.

---

[2] In other words the constants in Γ act as *standard names* [16].

3.2   FOL Semantics for P2P Systems

The first approach we discuss for assigning semantics to a P2P system, is the FOL approach, followed by [6,14,11]. In this approach, one associates to a P2P system $\mathcal{S} = (\mathcal{P}, \mathcal{M})$ a *single* FOL theory, obtained as the union of the various peer theories, plus suitable FOL formulas corresponding to the P2P mapping assertions. In particular, we have one mapping formula

$$\forall \mathbf{x}\ \ (q_1(\mathbf{x}) \to q_2(\mathbf{x}))$$

for each P2P mapping assertion $q_1 \rightsquigarrow q_2$.

In this formalization, the models of the whole P2P system $\mathcal{S}$ are simply the FOL models of the corresponding FOL theory. Although correct from a formal point of view, we argue that this formalization has two main drawbacks:

- Since this approach considers the whole P2P system as a single flat FOL theory, in the formalization the structure of the system in terms of peers is actually lost. In other words, the formulas of the various peers, and the mapping between peers become formulas of the theory, without any formal distinction of their roles.
- One of the implications of the above observation is that, even if we restrict the general framework in such a way that the various peers are *decidable* FOL theories (in particular, empty theories), query answering in the whole P2P system is actually undecidable, as illustrated in the next section. This is why, in [11,14], the authors propose syntactic restrictions on the mapping assertions (e.g., acyclicity).

The above drawbacks suggest that it is worth exploring other kinds of semantics for P2P systems.

3.3   A New Semantics for P2P Systems Based on Epistemic Logic

Based on the above mentioned drawbacks, we propose a new semantics for P2P systems, with the following aims:

- We want to take into account that peers in our context are to be considered autonomous sites, that exchange information. In other words, peers are modules, and the modular structure of the system should be explicitly reflected in the definition of its semantics.
- We do not want to limit a-priori the topology of the mapping assertions among the peers in the system. In particular, we do not want to impose acyclicity of assertions.
- We seek for a semantic characterization that leads to a setting where query answering is decidable, and possibly, polynomially tractable.

We base our proposal of a new semantics for P2P systems on epistemic logic[3]. Due to space limitations, we cannot delve into the details of epistemic logic here.

---

[3] Technically we resort to epistemic FOL with standard names, and therefore with a fixed domain, and rigid interpretation of constants [16].

We simply describe its basic notions. In epistemic logic, the language is the one of FOL, except that, besides the usual atoms, one can use another form of atoms, namely:

$$\mathbf{K}\alpha$$

where α is again a formula. Intuitively, the formula $\mathbf{K}\alpha$ is interpreted as the objects that are *known* to satisfy α, i.e., that satisfy α in all possible FOL models (of the kind seen so far, in our case).

An *epistemic logic theory* is simply a set of axioms that are formulas in the language of epistemic logic. The semantics of an epistemic logic theory is based on the notion of epistemic interpretation. We remind the reader that we are referring to a unique interpretation domain Γ. An *epistemic interpretation* $\mathcal{E}$ is a pair $(\mathcal{I}, \mathcal{W})$, where $\mathcal{I}$ is a FOL interpretation, $\mathcal{W}$ is a set of FOL interpretations, and $\mathcal{I} \in \mathcal{W}$. The notion of satisfaction of a formula in an epistemic interpretation $\mathcal{E} = (\mathcal{I}, \mathcal{W})$ is analogous to the one in FOL, with the provision that the interpretation for the atoms is as follows:

- a FOL formula constituted by an atom $f(\mathbf{x})$ (where $\mathbf{x}$ are the free variables in F) is satisfied in $(\mathcal{I}, \mathcal{W})$ by the tuples of constants $\mathbf{t}$ such that $f(\mathbf{t})$ is true in $\mathcal{I}$,
- an atom of the form $\mathbf{K}\alpha(\mathbf{x})$ is satisfied in $(\mathcal{I}, \mathcal{W})$ by the tuples of constants $\mathbf{t}$ such that $\alpha(\mathbf{t})$ is satisfied in all the pairs $(\mathcal{J}, \mathcal{W})$ such that $\mathcal{J} \in \mathcal{W}$.

Note that our definition of epistemic interpretation is a simplified view of a Kripke structure of an S5 modal system, in which every epistemic interpretation is constituted by a set of worlds, each one connected to all the others by means of the accessibility relation. Indeed, in our setting each world corresponds to a FOL interpretation, and the accessibility relation is left implicit by viewing the whole structure as a set.

An *epistemic model* of an epistemic logic theory is an epistemic interpretation that satisfies every axiom of the theory. In turn, an axiom constituted by the formula α is satisfied by an epistemic interpretation $(\mathcal{I}, \mathcal{W})$ if, for every $\mathcal{J} \in \mathcal{W}$, the epistemic interpretation $(\mathcal{J}, \mathcal{W})$ satisfies α. Observe that in order for an epistemic interpretation $(\mathcal{I}, \mathcal{W})$ to be a model of a theory, the axioms of the theory are required to be satisfied in every $\mathcal{J} \in \mathcal{W}$. Hence, with regard to the satisfaction of axioms, only $\mathcal{W}$ counts.

Observe that in epistemic logic the formula $\mathbf{K}(\alpha \vee \beta)$ has an entirely different meaning with respect to the formula $\mathbf{K}\alpha \vee \mathbf{K}\beta$. Indeed, the former is satisfied in an interpretation $(\mathcal{J}, \mathcal{W})$ if for every $\mathcal{I} \in \mathcal{W}$, there is at least one among $\{\alpha, \beta\}$, α or β is satisfied in $\mathcal{I}$. Conversely, the latter requires that there is one formula among α and β that is satisfied in all $\mathcal{I} \in \mathcal{W}$. Observe also that, if α is a FOL formula, there is a striking difference between $\mathbf{K}\exists x.\alpha(x)$ and $\exists x.\mathbf{K}\alpha(x)$. In particular, for $\exists x.\mathbf{K}\alpha(x)$ to be satisfied in $(\mathcal{I}, \mathcal{W})$ there must be a constant $c \in \Gamma$ such that $\alpha(c)$ is satisfied in every $\mathcal{J} \in \mathcal{W}$.

We formalize a P2P system $\mathcal{S} = (\mathcal{P}, \mathcal{M})$ in terms of the epistemic logic theory $E_{\mathcal{S}}$, called P2P theory, constructed as follows:

- the alphabet is the disjoint union of the alphabets of the various peer theories, one corresponding to one peer in $\mathcal{P}$[4]
- all the formulas of the various theories T_P belong to $E_{\mathcal{S}}$,
- there is one formula in $E_{\mathcal{S}}$ of the form

$$\forall \mathbf{x} \ ((\mathbf{K} \ q_1(\mathbf{x})) \rightarrow q_2(\mathbf{x}))$$

for each P2P mapping assertion $q_1 \rightsquigarrow q_2$ in $\mathcal{M}$.

Note that the formalization of the P2P mapping assertions in terms of the formulas specified above intuitively reflects the idea that only what is *known* by the peers mentioned in the tail of the assertion is transferred to the peer mentioned in the head.

Now, the semantics of the P2P system $\mathcal{S}$ directly follows from the above characterization in epistemic logic. However, as we did for the case of one peer, in order to point out the role of local sources in the various peers, we specialize the notion of epistemic semantics by starting with a collection of source databases, one for each peer in $\mathcal{P}$

Let $\mathcal{D}_1, \ldots, \mathcal{D}_n$ be n local source databases for the peers $P_1, \ldots, P_n$ in $\mathcal{P}$. We call *source database* $\mathcal{D}$ *for* $\mathcal{S}$ based on $\mathcal{D}_1, \ldots, \mathcal{D}_n$ the disjoint union of $\mathcal{D}_1, \ldots, \mathcal{D}_n$. Moreover, let $\mathcal{B}_1, \ldots, \mathcal{B}_n$ be n models of $P_1, \ldots, P_n$ with respect to $\mathcal{D}_1, \ldots, \mathcal{D}_n$, respectively. The disjoint union of $\mathcal{B}_1, \ldots, \mathcal{B}_n$ is called a *FOL model* for $\mathcal{S}$ based on $\mathcal{D}$.

We can now introduce the notion of epistemic interpretation for $\mathcal{S}$: an *epistemic interpretation* for $\mathcal{S}$ based on $\mathcal{D}$ is a pair $(\mathcal{I}, \mathcal{W})$ such that $\mathcal{I}$ is a FOL model for $\mathcal{S}$ based on $\mathcal{D}$, $\mathcal{W}$ is a set of FOL models for $\mathcal{S}$ based on $\mathcal{D}$, and $\mathcal{I} \in \mathcal{W}$. Taking into account the semantics of epistemic logic described above, it is easy to see that an *epistemic model* for $\mathcal{S}$ based on $\mathcal{D}$ is any epistemic interpretation for $\mathcal{S}$ based on $\mathcal{D}$ that satisfies all the axioms corresponding to the P2P mapping assertions in $\mathcal{M}$. In particular, an epistemic interpretation $(\mathcal{I}, \mathcal{W})$ for $\mathcal{S}$ based on $\mathcal{D}$ satisfies the P2P mapping assertion $q_1 \rightsquigarrow q_2$ if, for every tuple $\mathbf{t}$ of objects in Γ, the fact that $q_1(\mathbf{t})$ is satisfied in every FOL models in $\mathcal{W}$ implies that $q_2(\mathbf{t})$ is satisfied in $\mathcal{J}$, for each $\mathcal{J} \in \mathcal{W}$.

Let q be a query over one peer of $\mathcal{S}$. The *certain answer* $ans_k(q, \mathcal{S}, \mathcal{D})$ to q in $\mathcal{S}$ based on $\mathcal{D}$ is the set of tuples $\mathbf{t}$ of objects in Γ such that $q(\mathbf{t})$ is satisfied in every epistemic model $(\mathcal{I}, \mathcal{W})$ of $\mathcal{S}$ based on $\mathcal{D}$, i.e., the set of tuples $\mathbf{t}$ of objects in Γ such that, for every every epistemic model $(\mathcal{I}, \mathcal{W})$ of $\mathcal{S}$ based on $\mathcal{D}$, $q(\mathbf{t})$ is satisfied in $\mathcal{I}$.

4   Query Answering

In this section we address query answering in P2P systems. We start by noticing that query answering in the general framework is obviously undecidable. Indeed, since peer schemas are arbitrary FOL theories, it is undecidable even to answer

---

[4] In order to get the disjoint union, we may simply rename the predicates of the schemas of the various peers by prefixing the peer identifier.

boolean queries posed to a P2P system constituted by a single peer. So, it makes sense to introduce some restriction to make query answering more manageable.

Here we focus on a specific restricted setting. In particular, we call a P2P system $\mathcal{S} = (\mathcal{P}, \mathcal{M})$ *simple* if it satisfies the following restrictions:

1. peer theories are empty, i.e., each peer schema of $\mathcal{S}$ simply consists of a relational alphabet;
2. P2P mapping assertions in $\mathcal{M}$ are expressed using conjunctive queries, i.e., a P2P mapping assertion is an expression of the form $q_1 \rightsquigarrow q_2$, where q_1 and q_2 are conjunctive queries of the same arity, q_1 is expressed over the union of the alphabets of the peers, and q_2 is expressed over the alphabet of a single peer.
3. the language for querying the P2P system is *union of conjunctive queries (UCQ)*, i.e., a query over a P2P system is a UCQ over the alphabet of a single peer.

Such a restricted framework allows us to isolate the complexity coming from the P2P mappings. Indeed, since we have dropped constraints (axioms) in the various peer schemas, we are avoiding the introduction of complexity coming from the structure of such schemas. Also, having restricted the queries used in the P2P mapping and the queries posed to the P2P system to conjunctive (union of conjunctive) queries, which are well investigated in data integration, allows us to understand the complexity coming out of the core structure of the P2P system itself.

Interestingly, if we adopt the FOL semantics for simple P2P systems, query answering remains undecidable. This is mainly due to the presence of cycles in the P2P mapping assertions [7].

One of the contributions of our work is that, if we instead adopt the epistemic semantics, we get decidability for query answering. We show this by providing a sound and complete algorithm for query answering in simple P2P systems.

In particular, we show that, given an UCQ q posed to a simple P2P system S, and given a source database $\mathcal{D}$ for $\mathcal{S}$, one can construct a finite (relational) database RDB on the alphabet $\mathcal{A}_\mathcal{S}$ that is the union of the alphabet of the peer schemas in $\mathcal{S}$, such that for each tuple $\mathbf{t}$ of constants in Γ, $\mathbf{t} \in ans_\mathbf{k}(q, \mathcal{S}, \mathcal{D})$ if and only if $\mathbf{t} \in ans(q, RDB)$. Intuitively, such a finite database RDB constitutes a "representative" of all the epistemic models for $\mathcal{S}$ based on $\mathcal{D}$ with respect to the query q.

The database RDB contains, as objects, constants in Γ and new constants, called below *fresh values*, coming from an infinite, denumerable set of constants Φ, disjoint from Γ. To construct RDB, we make use of the following algorithm:

Algorithm build-rdb$(\mathcal{S}, \mathcal{D})$
Input: simple P2P system $\mathcal{S} = (\mathcal{P}, \mathcal{M})$, with $\mathcal{P} = \{P_1, \ldots, P_n\}$,
         source database $\mathcal{D}$ for $\mathcal{S}$
Output: database RDB on $\mathcal{A}_\mathcal{S}$
$RDB \leftarrow \emptyset$;
(a) **for** $i = 1, \ldots, n$ **do** $RDB \leftarrow$ retrieve-local-mapping$(\mathcal{S}, P_i, D, RDB)$;
(b) **repeat**

$RDB' \leftarrow RDB$;
$RDB \leftarrow$ retrieve-P2P-mapping$(\mathcal{M}, RDB)$
until $RDB' = RDB$;
return RDB

Informally, the algorithm proceeds as follows: first, through the local mapping assertions, it retrieves data from the local sources of the peers, and stores such data in the database RDB; then, through the P2P mapping assertions, it adds new data to RDB, until no new data can be added.

To compute the database RDB, the algorithm resorts to two subroutines, retrieve-local-mapping and retrieve-P2P-mapping. The first one retrieves data from the local sources of the peers according to the local mapping assertions, while the second one derives new data according to the P2P mapping assertions. In order to define such operations, we introduce the following notation. Given a conjunctive query $q = \{\mathbf{x} \mid \exists \mathbf{y}.cbody(\mathbf{x}, \mathbf{y})\}$, a tuple $\mathbf{t}$ of the same arity of $\mathbf{x}$, and a database $\mathcal{DB}$ whose objects are in $\Gamma \cup \Phi$, we denote with $fresh(q, \mathbf{t}, \mathcal{DB})$ the set of atoms obtained by instantiating the distinguished variables in q by $\mathbf{t}$ and the existentially quantified variables in q by some fresh values not already occurring in $\mathcal{DB}$. In other words, $fresh(q, \mathbf{t}, \mathcal{DB})$ is the set of atoms that form the conjuncts of $cbody(\mathbf{t}, \mathbf{v})$ where each v in $\mathbf{v}$ is a fresh value not occurring in $\mathcal{DB}$.

Below we define the algorithm retrieve-local-mapping that, given a simple P2P system $\mathcal{S} = (\mathcal{P}, \mathcal{M})$, a peer $P = (G, S, L)$ in $\mathcal{P}$, a source database $\mathcal{D}$ for $\mathcal{S}$ and a database RDB on $\mathcal{A}_{\mathcal{S}}$, adds to RDB all the facts that are consequence of the local mapping assertions in L evaluated over $\mathcal{D}$.

Algorithm retrieve-local-mapping$(\mathcal{S}, P, \mathcal{D}, RDB)$
Input: simple P2P system $\mathcal{S} = (\mathcal{P}, \mathcal{M})$,
         peer $P = (G, S, L)$ in $\mathcal{P}$,
         source database $\mathcal{D}$ for $\mathcal{S}$,
         database RDB on $\mathcal{A}_{\mathcal{S}}$
Output: database RDB' on $\mathcal{A}_{\mathcal{S}}$
$RDB' \leftarrow RDB$;
for each $q_s \rightsquigarrow q_g \in L$ **do**
   for each $\mathbf{t} \in ans(q_s, \mathcal{D})$ **do**
     if $\mathbf{t} \notin ans(q_g, RDB')$
     then $RDB' \leftarrow RDB' \cup fresh(q_g, \mathbf{t}, RDB')$
return RDB'

Then, we define the algorithm retrieve-P2P-mapping that, given a set of P2P mapping assertions $\mathcal{M}$ and a database RDB on $\mathcal{A}_{\mathcal{S}}$, adds to RDB all the facts that are consequences of the assertions $\mathcal{M}$ evaluated over RDB.

Algorithm retrieve-P2P-mapping$(\mathcal{M}, RDB)$
Input: P2P mapping assertions $\mathcal{M}$,
         database RDB on $\mathcal{A}_{\mathcal{S}}$
Output: database RDB' on $\mathcal{A}_{\mathcal{S}}$
$RDB' \leftarrow RDB$;

for each $q \rightsquigarrow q_i \in \mathcal{M}$ **do**
   for each tuple $\mathbf{t}$ of constants in Γ such that $\mathbf{t} \in ans(q, RDB')$ **do**
      if $\mathbf{t} \notin ans(q_i, RDB')$
      then $RDB' \leftarrow RDB' \cup fresh(q_i, \mathbf{t}, RDB')$
return RDB'

The next theorem proves termination of the algorithm build-rdb.

Theorem 1. *Let* $\mathcal{S} = (\mathcal{P}, \mathcal{M})$ *be a simple P2P system,* $\mathcal{D}$ *a source database for* $\mathcal{S}$, *and* q *a UCQ of arity* n *over the alphabet of a single peer in* $\mathcal{P}$. *Then, the algorithm* build-rdb$(\mathcal{S}, \mathcal{D}, q)$ *terminates, and returns a finite database RDB on* $\mathcal{A}_{\mathcal{S}}$ *whose objects are constants in* Γ *and fresh values in* Φ.

The next theorem gives us soundness and completeness of the technique presented here, with respect to the epistemic semantics, for simple P2P systems.

Theorem 2. *Let* $\mathcal{S} = (\mathcal{P}, \mathcal{M})$ *be a simple P2P system,* $\mathcal{D}$ *a source database for* $\mathcal{S}$, q *a UCQ of arity* n *over the alphabet of a single peer in* $\mathcal{P}$, *and RDB the database returned by* build-rdb$(\mathcal{S}, \mathcal{D}, q)$. *Then, for each tuple* $\mathbf{t}$ *of constants in* Γ, $\mathbf{t} \in ans(q, RDB)$ *if and only if* $\mathbf{t} \in ans_{\mathbf{k}}(q, \mathcal{S}, \mathcal{D})$.

Informally, the proof of the above theorem is based on the fact that the finite database RDB computed by the algorithm build-rdb constitutes a "representative" of all the (generally infinite) models for $\mathcal{S}$ and $\mathcal{D}$. Based on such a property, the evaluation of the query q with respect to $\mathcal{S}$ and $\mathcal{D}$ is equivalent to the evaluation of q over the database RDB.

Finally, we analyze the complexity of the algorithm with respect to the size of data stored in the peers of $\mathcal{S}$, i.e., the size of the source database $\mathcal{D}$ for $\mathcal{S}$ (data complexity). The next theorem gives us a polynomial time bound in data complexity.

Theorem 3. *Let* $\mathcal{S} = (\mathcal{P}, \mathcal{M})$ *be a simple P2P system,* $\mathcal{D}$ *be a source database for* $\mathcal{S}$, q *a UCQ of arity* n *over the alphabet of a single peer in* $\mathcal{P}$, *and* $\mathbf{t}$ *a tuple of arity* n *of constants in* Γ. *The problem of establishing whether* $\mathbf{t} \in ans_{\mathbf{k}}(q, \mathcal{S}, \mathcal{D})$ *is in PTIME in data complexity.*

The result follows from the following observations:

1. As it is immediate to verify, the algorithm retrieve-local-mapping runs in polynomial time in data complexity, and therefore the data complexity of step (a) of the algorithm build-rdb is polynomial as well.
2. In the algorithm retrieve-P2P-mapping, for each assertion $q \rightsquigarrow q_i \in \mathcal{M}$, only the answers to the query q that are tuples of constants in Γ are considered, which implies that the number of instances of the P2P mapping assertion $q \rightsquigarrow q_i$ that cause the addition of new tuples in RDB' is bound by c^h, where c is the number of constants occurring in the P2P source database $\mathcal{D}$ and h is the arity of the query q. Consequently, the maximum number of iterations that can be executed by step (b) of the algorithm build-rdb is bound by $a \cdot c^k$, where a is the number of assertions in $\mathcal{M}$ and k is the

maximum arity of the conjunctive queries occurring in $\mathcal{M}$. Hence, step (b) of the algorithm build-rdb runs in polynomial time data complexity, and the size of the database RDB computed by the algorithm is also polynomial with respect to the size of the source database $\mathcal{D}$ for $\mathcal{S}$.

3. Checking whether $\mathbf{t} \in ans(q, RDB)$ is polynomial (actually LOGSPACE) in data complexity, being q an UCQ.

5   Conclusions

In this paper we have presented a general framework for data-oriented P2P systems, and we have discussed possible methods for specifying the semantics of such systems. Motivated by several drawbacks in the usual FOL formalization of data-oriented P2P systems, we have proposed a novel semantics for data integration in these systems, and we have shown that, at least for simple P2P systems, query answering under the new semantics is not only decidable, but can be done in polynomial time with respect to the size of data stored in the peers. The main objective of our work was to study the fundamental aspects of P2P data integration, and, therefore, we made several assumptions that may be too restrictive in real applications. One direction to continue our research work is to relax some of these assumptions. In particular:

- The purpose of the algorithm presented in Section 4 was to show relevant formal properties of the proposed semantics, in particular that it supports polynomial time data complexity in computing the answers to queries posed to simple P2P systems. However, the algorithm is based on a bottom-up computation that does not exploit in any way the structure of the query. While such an approach is appropriate in a data-exchange context [7,8], where one aims at materializing the integrated data independently of a particular query, by exploiting the structure of the query one could substantially improve efficiency of query answering. Indeed, we are working on a top-down algorithm for query answering under the epistemic semantics, that is driven by the query and the structure of mappings and avoids computing integrated data that are not relevant for the query.
- Although we have assumed here that P2P mappings mention only one peer in their heads, our results can be extended to the case of more expressive forms of mappings, in particular allowing conjunctive queries over more than one peer in the head.
- Peer schemas in simple P2P systems are specified just in terms of an alphabet. Obviously, more expressive forms of schema may be needed in real settings. Interestingly, by exploiting the results presented in [3,4,5], it is possible to show that both the technique described in Section 4, and the query-driven algorithm mentioned above, can be generalized to a setting where peer schemas contain important classes of constraints, such as key and foreign key constraints.
- In our formal framework we assumed the existence of a single, common set of constants for denoting the interpretation domain of all the peers. In real applications, this is a too strong assumption, as the various peers are

obviously autonomous in choosing the mechanisms for denoting the domain elements. The issue of different vocabularies of constants in different peers is addressed, for example, in [2], and we believe that our approach can be extended in order to incorporate such kinds of techniques to deal with this problem.

– Finally, in our current formalization, if the information that one peer provides to another peer is inconsistent with the information known by the latter, the whole P2P system is logically inconsistent. Again, this is a strong limitation when one wants to use the framework in real applications. Data reconciliation and cleaning techniques may mitigate such a problem in some cases. More generally, to deal with this problem, we are investigating suitable extensions of the epistemic semantics presented here, in the line of [5].

References

1. K. Aberer, M. Punceva, M. Hauswirth, and R. Schmidt. Improving data access in P2P systems. *IEEE Internet Computing*, 2002.
2. P. A. Bernstein, F. Giunchiglia, A. Kementsietsidis, J. Mylopoulos, L. Serafini, and I. Zaihrayeu. Data management for peer-to-peer computing: A vision. In *Proc. of the 5th Int. Workshop on the Web and Databases (WebDB 2002)*, 2002.
3. A. Calì, D. Calvanese, G. De Giacomo, and M. Lenzerini. Data integration under integrity constraints. *Information Systems*, 2003. To appear.
4. A. Calì, D. Lembo, and R. Rosati. On the decidability and complexity of query answering over inconsistent and incomplete databases. In *Proc. of the 22nd ACM SIGACT SIGMOD SIGART Symp. on Principles of Database Systems (PODS 2003)*, pages 260–271, 2003.
5. A. Calì, D. Lembo, and R. Rosati. Query rewriting and answering under constraints in data integration systems. In *Proc. of the 18th Int. Joint Conf. on Artificial Intelligence (IJCAI 2003)*, 2003. To appear.
6. T. Catarci and M. Lenzerini. Representing and using interschema knowledge in cooperative information systems. *J. of Intelligent and Cooperative Information Systems*, 2(4):375–398, 1993.
7. R. Fagin, P. G. Kolaitis, R. J. Miller, and L. Popa. Data exchange: Semantics and query answering. In *Proc. of the 9th Int. Conf. on Database Theory (ICDT 2003)*, pages 207–224, 2003.
8. R. Fagin, P. G. Kolaitis, and L. Popa. Data exchange: Getting to the core. In *Proc. of the 22nd ACM SIGACT SIGMOD SIGART Symp. on Principles of Database Systems (PODS 2003)*, pages 90–101, 2003.
9. M. Friedman, A. Levy, and T. Millstein. Navigational plans for data integration. In *Proc. of the 16th Nat. Conf. on Artificial Intelligence (AAAI'99)*, pages 67–73. AAAI Press/The MIT Press, 1999.
10. S. Gribble, A. Halevy, Z. Ives, M. Rodrig, and D. Suciu. What can databases do for peer-to-peer? In *Proc. of the 4th Int. Workshop on the Web and Databases (WebDB 2001)*, 2001.
11. A. Halevy, Z. Ives, D. Suciu, and I. Tatarinov. Schema mediation in peer data management systems. In *Proc. of the 19th IEEE Int. Conf. on Data Engineering (ICDE 2003)*, 2003.
12. A. Y. Halevy. Answering queries using views: A survey. *Very Large Database J.*, 10(4):270–294, 2001.

13. R. Hull. Managing semantic heterogeneity in databases: A theoretical perspective. In *Proc. of the 16th ACM SIGACT SIGMOD SIGART Symp. on Principles of Database Systems (PODS'97)*, pages 51–61, 1997.
14. C. Koch. Query rewriting with symmetric constraints. In *Proc. of the 2nd Int. Symp. on Foundations of Information and Knowledge Systems (FoIKS 2002)*, volume 2284 of *Lecture Notes in Computer Science*, pages 130–147. Springer, 2002.
15. M. Lenzerini. Data integration: A theoretical perspective. In *Proc. of the 21st ACM SIGACT SIGMOD SIGART Symp. on Principles of Database Systems (PODS 2002)*, pages 233–246, 2002.
16. H. J. Levesque and G. Lakemeyer. *The Logic of Knowledge Bases.* The MIT Press, 2001.
17. J. D. Ullman. Information integration using logical views. In *Proc. of the 6th Int. Conf. on Database Theory (ICDT'97)*, volume 1186 of *Lecture Notes in Computer Science*, pages 19–40. Springer, 1997.

Defining Peer-to-Peer Data Integration Using Both as View Rules

Peter McBrien[1] and Alexandra Poulovassilis[2]

[1] Dept. of Computing, Imperial College London, pjm@doc.ic.ac.uk
[2] School of Computer Science and Information Systems, Birkbeck College,
Univ. of London, ap@dcs.bbk.ac.uk

Abstract. The loose and dynamic association between peers in a peer-to-peer integration has meant that, to date, implementations of peer-to-peer systems have been based on the exchange of files identified with a very limited set of attributes, and no schema is used to describe the data within those files. This paper extends an existing approach to data integration, called both-as-view, to be an efficient mechanism for defining peer-to-peer integration at the schema level, and demonstrates how the data integration can be used for the exchange of messages and queries between peers.

1 Introduction

The Internet has made available to almost all computer users the basic physical capability to exchange data. The challenge today is how to effectively harness this physical connectivity in order to effectively share data between users in a manner where their participation in data integration is not subject to centralised control, but instead is conducted in a **peer-to-peer (P2P)** fashion.

In [MP03] we described the **both-as-view (BAV)** approach to data integration, and compared it with the alternative approaches **global-as-view (GAV)** and **local-as-view (LAV)** [Len02]. In BAV, schemas are mapped to each other using a sequence of bidirectional schema transformations which we term a transformation **pathway**. From these pathways it is possible to extract a definition of the global schema as a view over the local schemas (*i.e.* GAV) and it is also possible to extract definitions of the local schemas as views over the global schema (*i.e.* LAV). The BAV approach has been implemented as part of the AutoMed data integration system being developed at Birkbeck and Imperial Colleges (see http://www.doc.ic.ac.uk/automed).

As we discussed in [MP02,MP03], one advantage of BAV over GAV and LAV is that it readily supports the evolution of *both* global and local schemas, including the addition or removal of local schemas. Such evolutions can be expressed as extensions to the existing pathways. New view definitions can then be regenerated from the new pathways as needed for query processing. This feature makes BAV very well suited to the needs of P2P data integration, where peers may join or leave the network at any time, or may change their set of local schemas, published schemas, or pathways between schemas. This paper describes how BAV can be used in this setting.

K. Aberer et al. (Eds.): VLDB 2003 Ws DBISP2P, LNCS 2944, pp. 91–107, 2004.

Previous work on data integration in P2P environments has used combinations of LAV and GAV rules between schemas and a combination of GAV and LAV query processing techniques [HIST03,HIMT03]. In our approach described here, we specify a BAV pathway between any pair of schemas. Due to the implicit presence of a GAV specification within such BAV pathways, and assuming no cycles in the inter-connection network between schemas, query answering in our approach is normally a simple matter of query unfolding using the GAV parts of the BAV pathways. However, it would also be possible to extract the LAV parts of the BAV pathways and use LAV query rewriting techniques.

A similar approach to ours is taken by [CDD+03] in this proceedings, where the GLAV rules [FLM99] are used to specify the constructs of each schema in terms of the constructs of some set of other peer schemas, and hence it is possible to write rules that specify the mapping in both directions between schemas.

Other complementary work to ours has been carried out within the Edutella project [Nej03,LNWS03] which uses a superpeer based network topology to provide better scalability than pure peer-to-peer networks. RDF Schema is used as the common data model for heterogeneous information sources. Routing indexes at superpeers store information about the metadata available at the peers directly connected to them, and aid in the forwarding of query requests only to relevant peers. Correspondence assertions between global and local schema constructs are stored at the superpeers, and these correspondence assertions could be generated using the BAV techniques we describe here.

The need for a superpeer is avoided in the **local relational model (LRM)** [BGK+02], where peers are directly related by a combination of a **domain relation** that specifies how the data types of the peers are related, together with **coordination formulae** that specify that if one predicate is true in one peer, then another predicate is true in another peer. The BAV approach has previously been shown to provide such a direct mapping between data sources [MP99a], and between different data modelling languages [MP99b].

The approach we present in this paper combines the advantages of Piazza and LRM, by having common virtual **superpeer schemas** — allowing peers to reuse the existing integration of other peers with the superpeer schema — but having no physical superpeer nodes that may act as a bottleneck in the system — in particular, we show how any peer can combine the different integrations of other peers with a superpeer schema in order to form direct pathways between peers for query and update processing.

We begin the paper with an overview of the BAV data integration approach. In Section 3 we describe how BAV can be extended to apply in a P2P setting, having originally been developed for a federated or mediated architecture. Then in Section 4 we describe one approach to P2P data integration using BAV, showing how update and query requests can be exchanged between peers via superpeer schemas. In Section 5 gives a more detailed comparison of our approach with closely related work. Finally we give a summary and our conclusions.

2   An Overview of BAV Data Integration

The basis of the BAV approach to data integration is a low-level **hypergraph-based data model (HDM)** and a set of primitive schema transformations for schemas expressed in this HDM [PM98,MP99a]. Facilities are provided for defining higher-level modelling languages and primitive schema transformations for them in terms of this lower-level HDM. For example, previous work has shown how relational, ER, UML, XML, RDF and semi-structured data models can be defined in terms of the HDM [MP99b,MP01,WP03,Kit03]. For each type of modelling construct of each modelling language (*e.g.* Relation, Attribute, Primary Key and Foreign Key in a relational model; Element, Attribute and Parent-Child relationship in XML) there will be a set of primitive schema transformations for adding such a construct to a schema, removing such a construct from a schema and, in the case of constructs with textual names, renaming such a construct.

Schemas are incrementally transformed by applying to them a sequence of such primitive schema transformations $t_1, \ldots, t_r$. Each primitive transformation t_i makes a 'delta' change to the schema by adding, deleting or renaming just one schema construct.

The general form of a primitive transformation that adds a construct c of type T to a schema s in order to generate new schema s' is $\mathsf{add}T(c, q_s)$, where q_s is a query over s specifying the extent of c in terms of the existing constructs of s. The logical semantics of this kind of transformation are

$$\forall \boldsymbol{x} \, . \, c(\boldsymbol{x}) \leftrightarrow q_s(\boldsymbol{x})$$

and for this reason we term add an **exact transformation**. In the AutoMed system, q_s is expressed in a functional **intermediate query language (IQL)** [JPZ03], and we shall use IQL for example queries in this paper.

When it is not possible to specify the exact extent of the new construct c being added in terms of the existing schema constructs, the primitive transformation $\mathsf{extend}T(c, q_s)$ must be used instead of add. The logical semantics of this kind of transformation are

$$\forall \boldsymbol{x} \, . \, c(\boldsymbol{x}) \leftarrow q_s(\boldsymbol{x})$$

and so we term extend a **sound transformation**. The query q_s may just be the constant Void, indicating that the extent of the new construct cannot be specified even partially. In this case the query can be omitted from the transformation, and a value of Void is implied.

In a similar manner, the exact transformation $\mathsf{delete}T(c, q_s)$ when applied to schema s' generates a new schema s with construct c of type T removed. The extent of c may be recovered using the query q_s on s, and

$$\forall \boldsymbol{x} \, . \, c(\boldsymbol{x}) \leftrightarrow q_s(\boldsymbol{x})$$

Note that this implies that from a primitive transformation $\mathsf{delete}T(c,q_s)$ used to transform $s' \to s$ we can automatically derive that $\mathsf{add}T(c,q_s)$ transforms $s \to s'$, and *vice versa*.

When it is not possible to specify the exact extent of the construct c being deleted from s' in terms of the remaining schema constructs, the sound transformation contract$T(c, q_s)$ must be used instead of delete, where

$$\forall \boldsymbol{x} . c(\boldsymbol{x}) \leftarrow q_s(\boldsymbol{x})$$

Again, it is possible that q_s may just be Void, indicating that the extent of c cannot be specified even partially, in which case it can be omitted from the transformation. Note that from a primitive transformation contract$T(c, q_s)$ used to transform $s' \to s$ we can automatically derive that extend$T(c, q_s)$ transforms $s \to s'$, and *vice versa*.

Finally, the transformation rename$T(c, c')$ causes a construct c of type T in a schema s to be renamed to c' in a new schema s', where in logical terms

$$\forall \boldsymbol{x} . c(\boldsymbol{x}) \leftrightarrow c'(\boldsymbol{x})$$

Note that this implies that from rename$T(c, c')$ used to transform $s \to s'$ we can automatically derive that rename$T(c', c)$ transforms $s' \to s$, and *vice versa*.

GAV defines a global schema as a set of views v over the local schemas, and LAV defines a local schema as a set of views v over a global schema. We relate v to a set of BAV schema constructs by a rule of the form $v(\boldsymbol{x}) = c_0(\boldsymbol{x_0}), \ldots, c_n(\boldsymbol{x_n})$ where $c_0(\boldsymbol{x_0}), \ldots, c_n(\boldsymbol{x_n})$ is a lossless decomposition of $v(\boldsymbol{x})$. For example, assuming the specification of the relational data model in terms of the HDM we gave in [MP03], if v is a relation $r(\boldsymbol{k}, a_1, \ldots, a_n)$ where $\boldsymbol{k}$ are its key attributes and $a_1, \ldots, a_n$ its non-key attributes, then c_0 would be a **Relation** construct $r(\boldsymbol{k})$ and $c_1, \ldots, c_n$ would be **Attribute** constructs $r\_a_1(\boldsymbol{k}, a_1), \ldots, r\_a_n(\boldsymbol{k}, a_n)$.

In [JTMP03] we discuss how LAV, GAV and GLAV views can be extracted from a BAV pathway $s_{local} \to s_{global}$. For a GAV view v defining a construct of s_{global} in terms of constructs of s_{local}, the algorithm uses the add and extend transformations that create $c_1, \ldots, c_n$. If all these transformations are exact then, in the terminology of [Len02], v is an **exact** view definition. If any one of $c_1, \ldots, c_n$ is defined using a sound transformation, then v is a **sound** view definition. For a LAV view v defining a construct of s_{local} in terms of constructs of s_{global}, the same algorithm is applied to the reverse pathway $s_{global} \to s_{local}$ (which, in BAV, is automatically derivable from $s_{local} \to s_{global}$). The only difference is that what in the GAV case were sound view definitions will in the LAV case be **complete** view definitions with respect to the global schema. Extraction of GLAV view definitions uses LAV view extraction and in addition also uses the bodies of add and extend transformations to generate GLAV rules (see [JTMP03]).

3   Developing BAV for P2P Data Integration

When building an integrated database, one must consider both the **logical integration** of the schemas and their logical extents, and the **operational integration** of the actual data, defining where data is to be materialised (*i.e.* permanently stored) and where data will be virtual (*i.e.* may be queried, but not permanently stored). We make the assumption that the logical extent of the local schemas equates to the materialised data within such schemas. In past work on data integration, there have been three basic approaches to the operational integration of data:

- **Virtual global schema**: in the **federated database** [SL90] and **mediator** [Wie92] approaches, data is only materialised in local schemas. Any queries on the global schema are answered by rewriting the queries to execute on one or more local schemas, and the logical extent of the global schema equates to results of those queries. Hence the operational extent of the global schema is virtual, and equates to its logical extent.
- **Materialised global schema**: in the **data warehouse** approach [JLVV02], data is materialised in both local and global schemas, and queries on each are answered directly from the data held within each schema. Hence the operational extent of the global schema is fully materialised. However the logical extent of the global schema is defined in the same way as for the federated database approach.
- **Partial virtual global schema**: in the **workflow** approach [vdAvH02], the global schema is implied by some message format standard, and the logical extent of the global schema is the union of all the valid messages that all the local schemas may generate in the format. The operational extent of the global schema is simply those messages that are in transit at any one time.

In P2P networks, local schemas will be autonomous and membership of the network is likely to be highly dynamic. Thus, maintaining a materialised global schema is likely to be unachievable in practise, and even answering queries on the global schema is difficult due to the varying nature of the local schemas. Hence we regard the workflow model as the most promising for development as a basis for P2P integration, but we use **superpeer schemas** (see Section 4 below) to make explicit the notion of a global schema that is only implied in the workflow approach. We do not assume physical superpeer nodes; rather, we rely on peers publishing via a directory service such as UDDI [Bel02] their integration with standard superpeer schemas that might be owned by any peer.

3.1   BAV Sound Queries and Complete Queries

To use BAV for P2P data integration, it is now necessary that we are able write transformation rules that capture the looser relationship between local and global schemas. BAV sound transformation rules allow local schemas to provide a lower bound on what data is available in the global schema, but up to now BAV did not have a method of specifying that the logical extent of the global schema is an upper bound on the logical extent of the local schema. For the purposes of applying BAV to P2P data integration, we now extend it to support this facility. In particular, we extend the extend and contract transformations discussed above to take a second query as an argument:

The transformation $\mathsf{extend}T(c, q_l, q_u)$ adds a new construct c of type T to a schema s to form a schema s', where q_l determines from s what is the minimum extent of c in s' (and may be Void if no lower bound on the extent can be specified) and q_u determines from s what is the maximal extent of c in s' (and may be Any if no upper bound on the extent can be specified). We write the extent of c, $Ext(c)$, specified by such a transformation as an interval $[q_l, q_u]$. In logical terms it means that

$$\forall \boldsymbol{x} \,.\, c(\boldsymbol{x}) \leftarrow q_l(\boldsymbol{x}) \ \wedge \ \forall \boldsymbol{x} \,.\, c(\boldsymbol{x}) \rightarrow q_u(\boldsymbol{x})$$

Note that the semantics of add are such that $\mathsf{add}T(c, q_s) \equiv \mathsf{extend}T(c, q_s, q_s)$.

Similarly, the transformation $\mathsf{contract}T(c, q_l, q_u)$ removes a construct c of type T from a schema s' to form a new schema s, where q_l determines from s what is the minimum extent of c in s', and q_u determines from s what is the maximal extent of c in s'. As before, q_1 may be Void and q_u may be Any. In logical terms it means that

$$\forall \boldsymbol{x} \,.\, c(\boldsymbol{x}) \leftarrow q_l(\boldsymbol{x}) \ \wedge \ \forall \boldsymbol{x} \,.\, c(\boldsymbol{x}) \rightarrow q_u(\boldsymbol{x})$$

Note that the semantics of delete are such that $\mathsf{delete}T(c, q_s) \equiv \mathsf{contract}T(c, q_s, q_s)$.

We refer to the first query in an extend or contract transformation as defining the **sound** extent of the construct, and the second query as defining the **complete** extent; and the transformation as a whole is a **sound-complete** transformation. In the terminology of [Len02], when used to generate GAV views the first query generates sound views and the second query generates complete views. When used to generate LAV views the first query generates complete views and the second query sound views.

In general, a construct c in a global schema will be derived from a number of local schemas $l_1, \ldots, l_n$ with an extent $[q_{l_i}, q_{u_i}]$ derived from each local schema. Hence, there will be a number of lower bound queries over the local schemas, $q_{l_1}, \ldots, q_{l_n}$, and a number of upper bound queries, $q_{u_1}, \ldots, q_{u_n}$. The extent of c will have a lower bound which is the union of all the lower bounds, and an upper bound which is the intersection of all the upper bounds. Hence, writing the extent of c as an interval, we have $Ext(c) = [q_{l_1} \cup \ldots \cup q_{l_n}, q_{u_1} \cap \ldots \cap q_{u_n}]$.

4   P2P Data Integration via Superpeer Schemas

With the extentions proposed in the previous section, BAV could in principle be used to map directly between peer schemas. However, defining pairwise mappings between peer schemas does not scale as the number of schemas grows. Thus, we explore in this section a method of undertaking P2P BAV data integration via superpeer schemas. We also give a method for message exchange and query processing in this P2P integration framework.

We assume that in a P2P network peers are able to create schemas and make them available to the other peers (*i.e.* to publish them) — we term such publicly available schemas **superpeer** schemas. We will see below how BAV transformations with sound queries and complete queries within them give a natural method for defining superpeer schemas.

In addition to such public schemas, peers may also manage one or more local schemas, which may be either materialised or virtual. Each peer is able to create transformation pathways between its own local schemas and superpeer schemas made public by itself or other peers. Such pathways can be stored at the peer, but we assume that peers are able to publish the fact that they support a pathway to a superpeer schema (without necessarily publishing the actual pathway). A superpeer schema has a logical extent that is the union of all the peer schemas from which there exists a pathway to the superpeer schema.

Suppose now a peer P wishes to send a query or update request formulated with respect to one of its local schemas, l, to other peers that have access to data semantically related to l. P can find out to which superpeer schemas, s, there exists in its own metadata repository a pathway $l \rightarrow s$. P can also find out which other peers support pathways to s. Suppose P' is such a peer; then P can request from P' its set of pathways to s. Suppose $l' \rightarrow s$ is one of this set of pathways. P can then combine the reverse pathway $s \rightarrow l'$ with its own pathway $l \rightarrow s$ to obtain a pathway from l to l' (consisting of $l \rightarrow s$ followed by $s \rightarrow l'$). P can then use this pathway to translate a query or update request expressed on its own schema l to an equivalent query or update expressed on l' which can then be sent to P' for processing.

4.1   Method for Generating Pathways

To integrate a peer schema ps_i with a superpeer schema sps, the following steps can be followed in order to generate a pathway $ps_i \rightarrow sps$:

1. Decide which constructs of sps have no relationship with ps_i and use extend transformations with a [Void,Any] extent to add these constructs.
2. For each remaining construct c in sps, use extend transformations on ps_i in order to derive c with a sound query that specifies how constructs in ps_i can be used to derive global instances of c.
3. Decide which constructs of ps_i have no relationship with sps, and use contract transformations with a [Void,Any] extent to remove these constructs.
4. For each remaining construct c in ps_i, use contract transformations on ps_i in order to derive c with a complete query that specifies how constructs in sps can be used to derive local instances of c.

4.2   An Example

The schemas in Figure 1 are adapted from the example given in [BGK+02]. Peer schema PS$_1$ is the schema for a hospital's patient database. Each patient is assigned a unique hospital identifier (hid) and a record is kept of their national insurance number (ni), name, sex, age, and the name of their gp (General Practitioner, or family doctor). Patients receive treatments. Each treatment has a unique identifier (tid), and a record is kept of the patient (via their hid), date, description and the Consultant who authorised the treatment.

Peer PS_2 is the schema for the database maintained by General Practitioner Dr Davies. He identifies his patients by their ni number and records their first name (fName), last name (lName), sex and address. His database also records in the event table all treatments and consultations for each of his patients as plain text descriptions within the field desc.

PS_1 hpatient(<u>hid</u>,ni,name,sex,age,gp)
    treatment(<u>tid</u>,*hid*,date,desc,consultant)

PS_2 patient(<u>ni</u>,fName,lName,sex,address)
    event(<u>ni,date</u>,desc)

SPS_1 allPatients(<u>ni</u>,name,sex,gp)
    allTreatments(<u>ni,date</u>,desc)

Fig. 1. Peer schemas

In Figure 1, a possible superpeer schema SPS_1 is given. Let us suppose that the hospital owning PS_1 wishes to exchange the information in its hpatient table, which we denote PS_1.hpatient, with other peers. Any patient record in PS_1 might be sent to another peer conforming to SPS_1. Conversely, a patient record from another peer conforming to SPS_1 might be imported into PS_1. The BAV pathway from PS_1 to SPS_1 is as follows:

$PS_1 \rightarrow SPS_1$

① contractTable($\langle\!\langle$treatment, tid, hid, date, desc, consultant$\rangle\!\rangle$, Void, Any)
② extendTable($\langle\!\langle$allTreatments, ni, date, desc$\rangle\!\rangle$, Void, Any)
③ contractAtt($\langle\!\langle$hpatient, age$\rangle\!\rangle$, Void, Any)
④ contractAtt($\langle\!\langle$hpatient, hid$\rangle\!\rangle$, Void, Any)
⑤ extendTable($\langle\!\langle$allPatients, ni, name, sex, gp$\rangle\!\rangle$, $\langle\!\langle$hpatient, ni, name, sex, gp$\rangle\!\rangle$, Any)
⑥ contractTable($\langle\!\langle$hpatient, ni, name, sex, gp$\rangle\!\rangle$, Void, $\langle\!\langle$allPatients, ni, name, sex, gp$\rangle\!\rangle$)

The first two transformations above mean that no association is drawn between the PS_1.treatment and SPS_1.allTreatments tables. The next two transformations remove information about patients' ages and hospital identifier from the schema. Transformation ⑤ indicates that SPS_1.allPatients is a superset of PS_1.hpatient, while the final transformation ⑥ indicates that PS_1.hpatient is a subset of SPS_1.allPatients.

Also note that the contractTable and extendTable transformations are a shorthand for a sequence transformations on the Rel construct and its associated Att constructs. For example, contractTable is defined as follows, where k denotes the sequence of primary key attributes of relation r:

$$\text{contractTable}(\langle\!\langle r, a_1, \ldots, a_n \rangle\!\rangle, q_1, q_2) = \text{contractRel}(\langle\!\langle r \rangle\!\rangle, \pi_{\boldsymbol{k}} q_1, \pi_{\boldsymbol{k}} q_2)$$
$$\text{contractAtt}(\langle\!\langle r, a_1 \rangle\!\rangle, \pi_{\boldsymbol{k},a_1} q_1, \pi_{\boldsymbol{k},a_1} q_2)$$
$$\ldots$$
$$\text{contractAtt}(\langle\!\langle r, a_n \rangle\!\rangle, \pi_{\boldsymbol{k},a_n} q_1, \pi_{\boldsymbol{k},a_n} q_2)$$

The composite transformations extendTable, addTable and deleteTable are similarly defined in terms of a sequence of extend, add and delete primitive transformations on the Rel construct and its associated Att constructs.

As we saw in Section 3.1 above, each BAV primitive transformation has an automatically derivable reverse transformation, in that each add/extend transformation is reversed by a delete/contract transformation with the same arguments, while each rename transformation is reversed by another rename transformation with the two arguments swapped. Hence the BAV pathway $SPS_1 \rightarrow PS_1$ is automatically derivable as the reverse of the above pathway $PS_1 \rightarrow SPS_1$:

$SPS_1 \rightarrow PS_1$

⑥ extendTable($\langle\!\langle$hpatient, ni, name, sex, gp$\rangle\!\rangle$, Void, $\langle\!\langle$allPatients, ni, name, sex, gp$\rangle\!\rangle$)

⑤ contractTable($\langle\!\langle$allPatients, ni, name, sex, gp$\rangle\!\rangle$, $\langle\!\langle$hpatient, ni, name, sex, gp$\rangle\!\rangle$, Any)

④ extendAtt($\langle\!\langle$hpatient, hid$\rangle\!\rangle$, Void, Any)

③ extendAtt($\langle\!\langle$hpatient, age$\rangle\!\rangle$, Void, Any)

② contractTable($\langle\!\langle$allTreatments, ni, date, desc$\rangle\!\rangle$, Void, Any)

① extendTable($\langle\!\langle$treatment, tid, hid, date, desc, consultant$\rangle\!\rangle$, Void, Any)

Similarly, let us suppose that Dr Davies maintaining PS_2 wishes to exchange the information contained in his patient table with other peers. Any patient record in PS_2 might be sent to another peer conforming to SPS_1. Conversely, a patient record from another peer conforming to SPS_1 might be imported into PS_2. The BAV pathway from PS_2 to SPS_1 is as follows:

$PS_2 \rightarrow SPS_1$

⑦ contractTable($\langle\!\langle$event, ni, date, desc$\rangle\!\rangle$, Void, Any)

⑧ extendTable($\langle\!\langle$allTreatments, ni, date, desc$\rangle\!\rangle$, Void, Any)

⑨ addAtt($\langle\!\langle$patient, gp$\rangle\!\rangle$, [(x, 'Davies') | x $\leftarrow$ $\langle\!\langle$patient$\rangle\!\rangle$])

⑩ addAtt($\langle\!\langle$patient, name$\rangle\!\rangle$, [(x, concat(y_1, ' ', y_2)) |
   $\quad$ (x, y_1) $\leftarrow$ $\langle\!\langle$patient, fName$\rangle\!\rangle$; (x, y_2) $\leftarrow$ $\langle\!\langle$patient, lName$\rangle\!\rangle$])

⑪ deleteAtt($\langle\!\langle$patient, fName$\rangle\!\rangle$, [(x, substring(z, 0, pos(z, ' '))) |
   $\quad$ (x, z) $\leftarrow$ $\langle\!\langle$patient, name$\rangle\!\rangle$]

⑫ deleteAtt($\langle\!\langle$patient, lName$\rangle\!\rangle$, [(x, substring(z, pos(z, ' ') + 1)) |
   $\quad$ (x, z) $\leftarrow$ $\langle\!\langle$patient, name$\rangle\!\rangle$]

⑬ contractAtt($\langle\!\langle$patient, address$\rangle\!\rangle$)

⑭ extendTable($\langle\!\langle$allPatients, ni, name, sex, gp$\rangle\!\rangle$, $\langle\!\langle$patient, ni, name, sex, gp$\rangle\!\rangle$, Any)

⑮ contractTable($\langle\!\langle$patient, ni, name, sex, gp$\rangle\!\rangle$, Void, $\langle\!\langle$allPatients, ni, name, sex, gp$\rangle\!\rangle$)

Again the pathway $SPS_1 \rightarrow PS_2$ is automatically derivable as the reverse of this. The pathway $PS_1 \rightarrow PS_2$ is just the composition of $PS_1 \rightarrow SPS_1$ and $SPS_1 \rightarrow PS_2$. Similarly, the pathway $PS_2 \rightarrow PS_1$ is the composition $PS_2 \rightarrow SPS_1$; $SPS_1 \rightarrow PS_1$ or, equivalently, the reverse of $PS_1 \rightarrow PS_2$

Such BAV pathways between peers, going via common superpeer schemas, can be used for translating messages between peers. Starting with a message expressed with respect to a schema of one peer, say PS_1, the transformations in the pathway to a schema of another peer, say PS_2, can be used to translate the message so that it is expressed in terms of PS_2. Messages may contain update requests or query requests, both of which can be translated using the techniques we described in [MP99a] in the context of federated database architectures but which apply also in this context. The translation uses the queries present within each transformation to incrementally rewrite the message, and we discuss it in more detail now.

4.3   Sending Update Requests over BAV Pathways

We assume that update requests to be sent from a data source S_1 to another data source S_2 will be of the form insert m, delete m, or update m for some expression m. The message translation process has two aspects, the first performing a **logical translation** of the message so that it *may* be applied to S_2, and the second performing an **operational interpretation** of the message to decide if it *should* be applied to S_2.

For the logical translation, we regard the data as having a lower bound d_l which is minimum set of values that should be inserted, deleted or updated, and an upper bound d_u which is the maximal set of values that should be inserted, deleted or updated. We write this range as the interval $[d_l, d_u]$. When some data d is to be sent from S_1 to S_2, we begin with $[d, d]$ appearing within the message expression m. The translation then proceeds as follows for each successive transformation t in the transformation pathway $S_1 \rightarrow S_2$:

1. if $t = rename(c, c')$, rename all occurrences of c in m by c';
2. if $t = add(c, q)$ and q is not Void, add c to m with range $[q,q]$.
3. if $t = extend(c, q_l, q_u)$ and q_u is not Void, add c to m with range $[q_l, q_u]$. The value of its associated extent will be within $[q_l, q_u]$ but this is decided by the operational aspect of the process.
4. if $t = contract(c, q_l, q_u)$ or $t = delete(c, q)$ and c appears in m then remove c from the m.

The operational aspect of the process determines how the values associated with constructs that appear in *extend* transformations are handled: if the logical value for a construct derived from a pathway is $[q_l, q_u]$, the **maximal** interpretation will give the construct the value q_u and the **minimal** interpretation will give the construct the value q_l.

For sending data from a peer schema ps_i to a peer schema ps_j via a superpeer schema sps, we define the **superpeer minmax interpretation** as taking the minimal interpretation for deriving the extent of constructs in sps from ps_i, and then the maximal interpretation for deriving the extent of constructs in ps_j from sps. Intuitively, the superpeer minmax interpretation ensures that only definite information from ps_i is transmitted to ps_j, and that all such information is transmitted. Example 1 illustrates this process applied to a message to convert an insert request expressed on PS_1 to an insert request expressed on PS_2, using the superpeer maxmin interpretation.

Example 1 Using pathways to update requests Suppose the update request insert hpatient(10000,'ZS341234P','Joe Bloggs','M',56,'Davies') is to be sent from PS_1 to PS_2. Transformations ③ and ④ convert the record to
$$\text{hpatient('ZS341234P','Joe Bloggs','M','Davies')}$$
making it union compatible with allPatients in schema SPS_1. Transformation ⑤ then states that this hpatient data is a lower bound of what should be inserted into allPatients in the superpeer schema SPS_1, and using the superpeer minmax interpretation, giving the range of values of the message in SPS_1 as:

[allPatients('ZS341234P','Joe Bloggs','M','Davies'),

allPatients('ZS341234P','Joe Bloggs','M','Davies')]

Transformation ⓯ then states upper bound of the the patient record in PS_2 is that of allPatients in SPS_1. Transformation ⓭ then inserts a Void value for the patient's address while transformations ⓬, ⓫ and ⓾ break up and replace the name attribute to make the record

patient('ZS341234P','Joe','Bloggs','M','Davies',Void)

Finally, transformation ⑨ removes the gp attribute; note that the query associated with this transformation allows one to reject records which do not have Void or 'Davies' as the gp attribute. This finally gives

insert patient('ZS341234P','Joe','Bloggs','M',Void)

as the message that will be sent to PS_2. If the address is nullable, then this insertion can be applied at PS_2 without further processing. However if address cannot be Null, the insertion will be rejected. A user must then be prompted to find the value of the address attribute before the insertion can be performed. □

4.4   Sending Query Requests over BAV Pathways

We assume that query requests to be sent from a data source S_1 to another data source S_2 will be of the form query e where e is some IQL expression expressed on the constructs of S_1. The message translation process again has two aspects, the first performing a **logical translation** of the message so that is *may* be applied to S_2, and the second performing an **operational interpretation** of the message.

The logical translation of e proceeds as follows for each successive transformation t in the pathway $S_1 \to S_2$:

1. if $t = rename(c, c')$, rename all occurrences of c in e by c';
2. if $t = add(c, q)$ or $t = extend(c, q_l, q_u)$ ignore t as c cannot appear within the current query expression e;
3. if $t = del(c, q)$ replace all occurrences of c in e by the interval $[q, q]$;
4. if $t = contract(c, q_l, q_u)$ replace all occurrences of c in e by the interval $[q_l, q_u]$;

The operational aspect of the process determines how the interval queries associated with constructs that appear in *contract* transformations are handled: if an interval query is $[q_l, q_u]$, the **maximal** interpretation will select q_u and the **minimal** interpretation will select q_l.

For sending query requests from a peer schema ps_i to a peer schema ps_j via a superpeer schema sps, we define the **superpeer maxmin interpretation** as taking first the maximal interpretation for selecting queries over the intermediate schema sps, and then the minimal interpretation for selecting queries over the target schema ps_j. Intuitively, the superpeer maxmin interpretation ensures that only definite information from ps_j will be used to answer the query request and that all such information will be used.

Example 2 Using pathways to translate queries Suppose the following query is to be sent from PS_1 to PS_2:

$[(x, n) \mid x \leftarrow \langle\!\langle hpatient\rangle\!\rangle; (x, s) \leftarrow \langle\!\langle hpatient, sex\rangle\!\rangle; s = 'F'; (x, n) \leftarrow \langle\!\langle hpatient, ni\rangle\!\rangle]$

Transformation ⑥ results in this query on the superpeer SPS_1, where the notation $q_1 .. q_2$ denotes a pair of set-valued queries respectively returning a lower and upper bound:

$[(x, n) \mid x \leftarrow Void..\langle\!\langle allPatients\rangle\!\rangle; (x, s) \leftarrow Void..\langle\!\langle allPatients, sex\rangle\!\rangle; s = 'F';$
$(x, n) \leftarrow Void..\langle\!\langle allPatients, ni\rangle\!\rangle]$

Retaining only the upper bound queries, by the superpeer maxmin interpretation, gives:

$[(x, n) \mid x \leftarrow \langle\!\langle allPatients\rangle\!\rangle; (x, s) \leftarrow \langle\!\langle allPatients, sex\rangle\!\rangle; s = 'F';$
$(x, n) \leftarrow \langle\!\langle allPatients, ni\rangle\!\rangle]$

Transformation ⓮ now results in this query on schema PS_2:

$[(x, n) \mid x \leftarrow \langle\!\langle patient\rangle\!\rangle..Any; (x, s) \leftarrow \langle\!\langle patient, sex\rangle\!\rangle..Any; s = 'F';$
$(x, n) \leftarrow \langle\!\langle patient, ni\rangle\!\rangle..Any]$

Retaining only the lower bound queries, by the superpeer maxmin interpretation, gives this final query on PS_2:

$[(x, n) \mid x \leftarrow \langle\!\langle patient\rangle\!\rangle; (x, s) \leftarrow \langle\!\langle patient, sex\rangle\!\rangle; s = 'F'; (x, n) \leftarrow \langle\!\langle patient, ni\rangle\!\rangle]$

After this is evaluated at PS_2, the resulting set of records can be translated back to PS_1 using the translation scheme for update requests in Section 4.3. □

Example 3 Queries which cannot be answered As an example of P2P query processing involving unavailable information suppose the following query is to be sent from PS_1 to PS_2:

$[(x, n) \mid x \leftarrow \langle\!\langle hpatient\rangle\!\rangle; (x, a) \leftarrow \langle\!\langle hpatient, age\rangle\!\rangle; a > 65; (x, n) \leftarrow \langle\!\langle hpatient, ni\rangle\!\rangle]$

Transformations ③ and ⑥ result in this query on the intermediate schema SPS_1:

$[(x, n) \mid x \leftarrow Void..\langle\!\langle allPatients\rangle\!\rangle; (x, a) \leftarrow Void..Any; a > 65;$
$(x, n) \leftarrow Void..\langle\!\langle allPatients, ni\rangle\!\rangle]$

Applying the maxmin interpretation, this becomes:

$[(x, n) \mid x \leftarrow \langle\!\langle allPatients\rangle\!\rangle; (x, a) \leftarrow Any; a > 65; (x, n) \leftarrow \langle\!\langle allPatients, ni\rangle\!\rangle]$

Transformation ⓮ results in this query on schema PS_2:

$[(x, n) \mid x \leftarrow \langle\!\langle patient\rangle\!\rangle..Any; (x, a) \leftarrow Any; a = 'F'; (x, n) \leftarrow \langle\!\langle patient, ni\rangle\!\rangle..Any]$

Applying the maxmin interpretation, this finally simplifies to:

$[(x, n) \mid x \leftarrow \langle\!\langle patient\rangle\!\rangle; (x, a) \leftarrow Any; a = 'F'; (x, n) \leftarrow \langle\!\langle patient, ni\rangle\!\rangle]$

The presence of Any in the above query implies an absence of information and the query will evaluate to the empty set: as we would expect, no information can be extracted from PS_2 for the original query since it involves people's ages, about which there is no information in SPS_1.   □

In general, a peer may wish to assemble results to a query from more than one peer that can provide such results, or from all such peers. This is easily supported in our framework:

Suppose a peer P wishes to send a query request formulated with respect to one of its local schemas, l, to other peers that have access to data semantically related to l. P can find out to which superpeer schemas, s, there exists in its own metadata repository a pathway $l \rightarrow s$. P can also find out which other peers support pathways to s and request from them the pathways from their local schemas to s. P can then construct a set of pathways from its local schema l going via a superpeer schema s to other peers' local schemas. A query request can be sent individually to each of these local schemas and the data returned merged at P in order to answer the original query expressed on l.

We note that multiple levels of superpeer schemas are possible with our approach, c.f. [BRM02], and the inter-connection network between schemas in our P2P network may be a tree of arbitrary depth as opposed to having just one level. At present we assume no cycles in this inter-connection network, and it is an area of further work to explore what their impact would be on query processing, c.f. [HIST03]. For translating update requests and data sent from one peer schema l to another l', we can use 'minmax' semantics with respect to the lowest common ancestor superpeer schema, sps, of l and l' while for translating queries from l to l' we can use 'maxmin' semantics with respect to sps.

We finally note that the BAV approach can also handle OO models. Once a BAV pathway has been specified between two schemas, any query that uses inheritance needs to be rewritten to make that inheritance explicit, before being translated using the techniques described above, and then making the inheritance implicit again. For example, suppose we had a subclass of hpatient called inpatient in PS_1 which inherits the attributes of hpatient. The query $\langle\langle\text{inpatient}, \text{name}\rangle\rangle$ on PS_1 would first be translated to $[(x, y) \mid (x) \leftarrow \langle\langle\text{inpatient}\rangle\rangle; (x, y) \leftarrow \langle\langle\text{hpatient}, \text{name}\rangle\rangle]$ before being translated using the techniques already described.

4.5   Changes to an Integration Network and Schema Evolution

The highly dynamic nature of P2P integration means that we must handle two types of changes in an efficient manner. First, a peer might wish to change what parts of one of its local schemas are taking part in an integration network. Second, the local schemas or superpeer schemas may evolve, and thus we need to reuse the old integration network to form a new one.

To handle alterations to what constructs of a local schema take part in an integration network we simply need to keep a record of what actions were taken when performing steps (1)–(4) in Section 4.1, and see if those actions need to be reviewed. In particular, if it is decided that a superpeer construct is now to be related to the peer schema, then the transformation for the construct covered by step (1) would be replaced by one or more covered by step (2). If a construct in the peer schema is then in part derivable from the superpeer schema, then the transformation for the construct covered by step (3) would be replaced by one or more covered by step (4).

In our running example, it might be decided to relate treatment information held in PS_1 with that in SPS_1. This will cause an update to pathway $PS_1 \rightarrow SPS_1$ to be made, replacing the subpathway where the treatment table was contracted (transformations ① and ②) by a new subpathway that transforms PS_1.treatment into SPS_1.allTreatments as follows:

⑯ addAtt($\langle\!\langle$treatment, ni$\rangle\!\rangle$, $[(x, z) \mid (x, y) \leftarrow \langle\!\langle$treatment, hid$\rangle\!\rangle$;
        $(y, z) \leftarrow \langle\!\langle$hpatient, ni$\rangle\!\rangle]$)
⑰ deleteAtt($\langle\!\langle$treatment, hid$\rangle\!\rangle$, $[(x, z) \mid (x, y) \leftarrow \langle\!\langle$treatment, ni$\rangle\!\rangle$;
        $(z, y) \leftarrow \langle\!\langle$hpatient, ni$\rangle\!\rangle]$)
⑱ contractAtt($\langle\!\langle$treatment, consultant$\rangle\!\rangle$, Void, Any)
⑲ contractAtt($\langle\!\langle$treatment, tid$\rangle\!\rangle$, Void, Any)
⑳ extendTable($\langle\!\langle$allTreatments, ni, date, desc$\rangle\!\rangle$, $\langle\!\langle$treatment, ni, date, desc$\rangle\!\rangle$, Any)
㉑ contractTable($\langle\!\langle$treatment, ni, date, desc$\rangle\!\rangle$, Void, $\langle\!\langle$allTreatments, ni, date, desc$\rangle\!\rangle$)

Evolution of peer or superpeer schemas can be handled using our existing techniques for schema evolution in BAV [MP02]. The approach is that any evolution of a schema should be described as a BAV pathway from the original schema. It is then possible to reason about the composite pathway between other schemas, the old schema and the new schema. For example, let us suppose that a peer decides to publish a new version of $\mathsf{SPS_1}$ called $\mathsf{SPS_1'}$ such that allPatients now includes an attribute age. This may be expressed by the single-transformation pathway $\mathsf{SPS_1} \to \mathsf{SPS_1'}$:

㉒ extendAtt($\langle\!\langle$allPatients, age$\rangle\!\rangle$, Void, Any)

Now if a peer schema $\mathsf{PS_3}$ integrates with $\mathsf{SPS_1'}$ via pathway $\mathsf{PS_3} \to \mathsf{SPS_1'}$ it is possible to exchange messages and data between $\mathsf{PS_1}$ and $\mathsf{PS_2}$ and the new schema $\mathsf{PS_3}$ using the techniques already described.

4.6   Optimising Pathways

Once schema evolution has taken place over a period of time, it is likely that some degree of redundancy may exist in pathways. Also, given the use of the pathway for certain types of query processing, some elements of the pathway may be removed to optimise the processing of the pathway during query and message reformulation between schemas.

Using the techniques of [Ton03], the pathways may be analysed to determine if the integration of the peer schemas with superpeer schemas might be refined after schema evolution. For example, considering the pathway $\mathsf{PS_1} \to \mathsf{SPS_1'}$ which now consists of ⑯ –㉑ , ③ –⑥ , ㉒ , it can be shown that ㉒ may be reordered to appear just before ⑤ if we change ⑤ to include the age attribute, and change ㉒ to operate on the hpatient table instead of the allPatients table. A suggestion can then be made to the peer managing PS_1 that the age attribute of hpatient might be included in the data integration since there is an apparently redundant contract and extend of the $\langle\!\langle$hpatient, age$\rangle\!\rangle$ construct.

Once a particular operational interpretation has been decided upon for a long term exchange of messages between a set of peers, it also is possible to adapt techniques in [Ton03] to simplify pathways to give a direct pathway between the peer schemas. For example, if we have a large number of updates to send form $\mathsf{PS_1}$ to $\mathsf{PS_2}$ under minmax semantics, we may reorder transformations from the $\mathsf{PS_1} \to \mathsf{PS_2}$ so that we have the subpathway:

⑤ extendTable($\langle\!\langle$allPatients, ni, name, sex, gp$\rangle\!\rangle$, $\langle\!\langle$hpatient, ni, name, sex, gp$\rangle\!\rangle$, Any)
❶❺ extendTable($\langle\!\langle$patient, ni, name, sex, gp$\rangle\!\rangle$, Void, $\langle\!\langle$allPatients, ni, name, sex, gp$\rangle\!\rangle$)

Then taking the minimum extent of ⑤ (since it is originally before SPS_1) and the maximum extent of ⑮ (since it was originally after SPS_1) gives the simplified transformation:

㉓ extendTable($\langle\langle$patient, ni, name, sex, gp$\rangle\rangle$, Void, $\langle\langle$hpatient, ni, name, sex, gp$\rangle\rangle$)

Note that this simplified pathway is *only* suitable for message exchange between the peers using minmax semantics; since it does not form a semantically correct relationship between the peers. This is because it is incorrectly stating the $PS_2 : \langle\langle$patient$\rangle\rangle$ is a subset of $PS_1 : \langle\langle$hpatient$\rangle\rangle$.

5   Comparison with Related Approaches

In the context of data integration, GLAV is regarded as subsuming the expressive capabilities of LAV and GAV. Thus we focus our comparison here on examining how BAV compares with GLAV. In the original GLAV work [FLM99], rules were permitted to have a conjunction of source schema relations in their head. In [MH03] this was extended to allow any query expressed in the source schema query language to appear in the head of a GLAV rule. In [CDD+03], the distinction between source and global schemas is removed, and any number of GLAV rules may be specified between schemas, hence in part moving towards the BAV approach of specifying rules for each schema being integrated. However, [CDD+03] does not differentiate between sound, complete and exact rules, as GLAV rules are always sound.

In [CDD+03], integrating schemas PS_1, PS_2, ... PS_n, there might be GLAV rules $PS_1 \leftarrow PS_2, PS_3, \ldots, PS_n$, $PS_2 \leftarrow PS_1, PS_3, \ldots, PS_n$, *etc.* By contrast, BAV can define a single network of transformations that integrates the peer schemas. This may be done by direct association between peers or, as described in this paper, via one or more superpeer schemas. One advantage of the BAV approach is that it separates the logical specification of a mapping between schemas from the procedural aspects of performing query or update processing over the mapping. Another advantage of BAV is that it allows common concepts shared between schemas to be explicitly stated. For example, if hospitals insisted that all patients register with a GP (*i.e.* hospital_patient $\subseteq$ gp_patient), then in BAV we could integrate hospital peer schemas to specify a superpeer schema containing $\langle\langle$hospital_patient$\rangle\rangle$, and integrate GP peer schemas to specify a superpeer schema containing $\langle\langle$gp_patient$\rangle\rangle$, and then relate the two superpeer schemas by:

extendTable($\langle\langle$gp_patient, . . .$\rangle\rangle$, $\langle\langle$hospital_patient, . . .$\rangle\rangle$, Any)

contactTable($\langle\langle$hospital_patient, . . .$\rangle\rangle$, Void, $\langle\langle$gp_patient$\rangle\rangle$)

By contrast in GLAV, each hospital would need to state a rule saying that its patients were a subset of gp_patient, in effect repeating the definition of gp_patient at every peer, and omitting the concept of hospital_patient.

6   Summary and Conclusions

We have defined in this paper an extension to the BAV data integration approach to allow it to specify both sound queries and complete queries in transformations, and have demonstrated how this extension may be used for P2P data integration.

The sound queries are used where a minimum answer is required, and serve as the basis for moving data from peer schemas to superpeer schemas, and for answering queries on a superpeer schema from a peer schema. The complete queries are used where a maximal answer is required, and serve as the basis for moving data from superpeer schemas to peer schemas, and for answering queries on a peer schema from a superpeer schema. Hence we use 'minmax' semantics in moving data from a peer schema via a superpeer schema to another peer schema, and 'maxmin' semantics in moving queries over a similar path.

We have shown how the pathways are easy to update to reflect changes in the P2P data integration, and our previous work [MP02] has demonstrated how we handle schema evolution. Redundancy in the pathways between schemas may be removed using the techniques described in [Ton03].

The BAV approach has been adopted within the AutoMed data integration system (`http://www.doc.ic.ac.uk/automed`). All source schemas, intermediate schemas and global schemas, and the pathways between them are stored in AutoMed's metadata repository [BMT02], and a suite of tools have been developed for creating and editing a schema integration network, processing queries (using GAV query processing) [JPZ03], and analysing the contents of schemas to suggest integration rules. Future work will extend this suite of tools to support the new P2P extensions reported in this paper. We also plan to apply this technology in the SeLeNe project (`http://www.dcs.bbk.ac.uk/selene`) which is investigating techniques for semantic integration of RDF/S descriptions of learning objects stored in P2P networks.

References

[Bel02]   T. Bellwood *et al.* UDDI version 3.0. Technical report, UDDI.ORG, July 2002.

[BGK+02]   P.A. Bernstein, F. Giunchiglia, A. Kementsietsidis, J. Mylopoulos, L. Serafini, and I. Zaihrayeu. Data management for peer-to-peer computing: a vision. In *Proceedings of WebDB02*, pages 89–94, 2002.

[BMT02]   M. Boyd, P.J. McBrien, and N. Tong. The automed schema integration repository. In *Proceedings of BNCOD02*, volume 2405 of *LNCS*, pages 42–45. Springer-Verlag, 2002.

[BRM02]   Z. Bellahsene, M. Roantree, and L. Mignet. A functional architecture for large scale integration. Technical report, Univ. of Montpellier, 2002.

[CDD+03]   D. Calvanese, E. Damagio, G. De Giacomo, M. Lenzerini, and R. Rosati. Semantic data integration in P2P systems. In *Proceedings of DBISP2P*, Berlin, Germany, 2003.

[FLM99]   M. Friedman, A. Levy, and T. Millstein. Navigational plans for data integration. In *Proc. of the 16th National Conference on Artificial Intelligence*, pages 67–73. AAAI, 1999.

[HIMT03]   A. Y. Halevy, Z. G. Ives, P. Mork, and I. Tatarinov. Piazza: Data management infrastructure for semantic web applications. In *WWW 2003*, 2003.

[HIST03]   A. Y. Halevy, Z. G. Ives, D. Suciu, and I. Tatarinov. Schema mediation in peer data management systems. In *Proceedings of ICDE03*. IEEE, 2003.

[JLVV02]   M. Jarke, M. Lenzerini, Y. Vassiliou, and P. Vassiliadis. *Fundamentals of Data Warehouses*. Springer-Verlag, 2nd edition edition, 2002.

[JPZ03]   E. Jasper, A. Poulovassilis, and L. Zamboulis. Processing IQL Queries and Migrating Data in the AutoMed toolkit. Technical report, AutoMed TR Number 20, 2003. Available from `http://www.doc.ic.ac.uk/automed/`.

[JTMP03]   E. Jasper, N. Tong, P.J. McBrien, and A. Poulovassilis. View generation and optimisation in the automed data integration framework. Technical report, AutoMed TR Number 16, Version 3, 2003. Available from `http://www.doc.ic.ac.uk/automed/`.

[Kit03]   S. Kittivoravitkul. Transformation-based approach for integrating semi-structured data. Technical report, AutoMed Project, http://www.doc.ic.ac.uk/automed/, 2003.

[Len02]   M. Lenzerini. Data integration: A theoretical perspective. In *Proceedings of PODS 2002*, pages 233–246. ACM, 2002.

[LNWS03]   A. Loser, W. Nejdl, M. Wolpers, and W. Siberski. Information integration in schema-based peer-to-peer networks. In *Proceedings of CAiSE 2003*, LNCS. Springer-Verlag, 2003.

[MH03]   J. Madhavan and A.Y. Halevy. Composing mappings among data sources. In *Proceedings of 29th Conference on VLDB*, pages 572–583, 2003.

[MP99a]   P.J. McBrien and A. Poulovassilis. Automatic migration and wrapping of database applications — a schema transformation approach. In *Proceedings of ER99*, volume 1728 of *LNCS*, pages 96–113. Springer-Verlag, 1999.

[MP99b]   P.J. McBrien and A. Poulovassilis. A uniform approach to inter-model transformations. In *Advanced Information Systems Engineering, 11th International Conference CAiSE'99*, volume 1626 of *LNCS*, pages 333–348. Springer-Verlag, 1999.

[MP01]   P.J. McBrien and A. Poulovassilis. A semantic approach to integrating XML and structured data sources. In *Proceedings of 13th CAiSE*, volume 2068 of *LNCS*, pages 330–345. Springer-Verlag, 2001.

[MP02]   P.J. McBrien and A. Poulovassilis. Schema evolution in heterogeneous database architectures, a schema transformation approach. In *Advanced Information Systems Engineering, 14th International Conference CAiSE2002*, volume 2348 of *LNCS*, pages 484–499. Springer-Verlag, 2002.

[MP03]   P.J. McBrien and A. Poulovassilis. Data integration by bi-directional schema transformation rules. In *Proceedings of ICDE03*. IEEE, 2003.

[Nej03]   W. Nejdl *et al.* Super-peer-based routing and clustering strategies for RDF-based peer-to-peer networks. In *WWW 2003*, 2003.

[PM98]   A. Poulovassilis and P.J. McBrien. A general formal framework for schema transformation. *Data and Knowledge Engineering*, 28(1):47–71, 1998.

[SL90]   A. Sheth and J. Larson. Federated database systems. *ACM Computing Surveys*, 22(3):183–236, 1990.

[Ton03]   N. Tong. Database schema transformation optimisation techniques for the automed system. In *Proceedings of BNCOD*, volume 2712 of *LNCS*, pages 157–171. Springer-Verlag, 2003.

[vdAvH02]   W. van der Aalst and K. van Hee. *Workflow Management: Models, Methods, and Systems*. MIT Press, 2002.

[Wie92]   G. Wiederhold. Mediators in the architecture of future information systems. *IEEE Computer*, 25(3):38–49, March 1992.

[WP03]   D. Williams and A. Poulovassilis. Representing RDF and RDF Schema in the HDM. Technical report, AutoMed Project, http://www.doc.ic.ac.uk/automed/, 2003.

Coordinating Peer Databases Using ECA Rules

Vasiliki Kantere[1], Iluju Kiringa[2], John Mylopoulos[1],
Anastasios Kementsietsidis[1], and Marcelo Arenas[1]

[1] Dept. of Computer Science, University of Toronto
[2] School of Inf. Technology and Engineering, University of Ottawa

Abstract. Peer databases are stand-alone, independently developed databases that are linked to each other through acquaintances. They each contain local data, a set of mapping tables and expressions, and a set of ECA rules that are used to exchange data among them. The set of acquaintances and peers constitutes a dynamic peer-to-peer network in which acquaintances are continuously established and abolished. We present techniques for specifying data exchange policies on-the-fly based on constraints imposed on the way in which peers exchange and share data. We realize the on-the-fly specification of data exchange policies by building coordination ECA rules at acquaintance time. Finally, we describe mechanisms related to establishing and abolishing acquaintances by means of examples. Specifically, we consider syntactical constructs and executional semantics of establishing and abolishing acquaintances.

1 Introduction

Peer-to-Peer (P2P) networking is establishing itself as an architecture of choice for a certain number of popular applications such as file sharing, distributed processing, and instant messaging. A P2P architecture involves nodes, called *peers*, which act as both clients and servers, and participate in a common network by autonomously controlling and evolving its topology. Using appropriate protocols, new peers may join or leave the network at will.

Building on the P2P model of computing, data management techniques are now being developed for query, update, and transaction processing in a P2P network involving peers that are databases [3,5]. The architecture of such a P2P network consists of a collection of *peer databases* that are located at nodes of the P2P network. Each peer database is managed by a peer data management system (PDBMS). Typically, a PDBMS has a P2P layer that interoperates the peer database with other peers. In order for such an interoperation to take place, an acquaintance must be established between the peer databases. A peer database establishes at least one *acquaintance* with other peers that are already part of the P2P network. Doing so, it joins the P2P network. The acquainted peers are called *acquaintees*. Acquaintees share and coordinate data over their acquaintance. Acquaintances are transient since they may evolve over time as peers join and leave the network. An acquaintance is established between peers that belong to the same *interest group*. The later is a community of peers centred around a common business (e.g. airline, genomic, hospital, and university databases) [4].

K. Aberer et al. (Eds.): VLDB 2003 Ws DBISP2P, LNCS 2944, pp. 108–122, 2004.

We assume that the peer databases do not share any global database schema and administrative authority. Moreover, the availability of their data is strictly local.

Syntactically, the peer language includes the usual constructs for querying and updating data. It also includes constructs that allow the user to establish or abolish acquaintances between peers. Semantically, an acquaintance outgoing from a peer is qualified by a subset of the mapping tables and expressions, as well as by a set of coordination rules. The former constrain the data exchange over the acquaintance, and the latter coordinate that exchange.

In this paper, we describe algorithms used by PDBMSs for establishing and abolishing acquaintances. We give several examples of coordination rules expressed in an extension of the standard SQL3 triggers. We also consider syntactical constructs used to establish or abolish acquaintances between peers. Finally, we give execution semantics for these constructs. Specifically, we make the following contributions:

- Using the concept of mapping tables introduced in [7], we present new techniques for specifying data exchange policies on-the-fly based on constraints on the way in which peers exchange and share data. Unlike many approaches used in data integration systems [9], we do not consider design-time, uniform access to a collection of heterogeneous data. Rather we consider a setting in which data coordination plays a key role. Here, each PDBMS defines and manages its own view of the shared data, and defines its own sharing and co-ordination policies based on Event-Condition-Action (ECA) rules provided by interest groups.
- We realize the on-the-fly specification of data exchange policies by selecting coordination ECA rules at acquaintance time from domain-specific rule libraries, rather than having them designed for particular peers by database designers. This way of selecting active rules contributes to a vision of a P2P database technology that can be used by end-users to establish acquaintances between peers in a flexible and cost-effective way.
- We focus on setting up and abolishing acquaintances between PDBMSs. We describe mechanisms to that end and illustrate them by means of examples. These mechanisms create logical meta-data and ECA rules on-the-fly to guide the exchange of data.

This work is part of the Hyperion project conducted at the Universities of Toronto and Ottawa [1].

This paper is organized as follows. Section 2 motivates the use of ECA rules for coordinating peer databases; it also reviews the notions of mapping tables and expressions. Section 3 summarizes the architecture of Hyperion. Mechanisms used by peer databases for joining and leaving a peer network are described in Section 4. Here, we show how ECA rules are generated on-the-fly and from a library of generic rules for setting up coordination between peers. Section 5 treats related work. Finally, Section 6 concludes the paper and indicates how the framework presented here is being extended in various ways.

OA_Passenger OA_Ticket

pid	name
1	Lachance
2	Smith
3	Moore

pid	fno	meal
1	OA229	Veal
2	OA378	Trout

QA_Passenger QA_Fleet

pid	name
1	Michel
2	Lachance

aid	type	capacity
B-1	Bombard. 27	140
B-2	Embraer L12	130
B-3	Boeing 737	117

OA_Flight

fno	date	dest	sold	cap
OA229	01/05	Mont.	120	256
OA341	01/15	Tor.	160	160
OA378	01/21	S.F.	90	124

QA_Flight

fno	date	to	sold	aid
QA2132	01/07	Dorv.	67	B-3
QA1187	01/15	LBP	118	B-2
QA1109	01/15	MDC	164	B-1

QA_Reserve

pid	fno
1	QA2132
2	QA1187
2	QA1109

(a) Ontario-Air Database Instance   (b) Quebec-Air Database Instance

Fig. 1. Instances for the two airline databases

2   ECA Rules for Coordinating Peer Databases

2.1   Motivating Example: Mapping Tables and Expressions

We consider two airline-ticket reservation peer databases $Ontario-Air\_DB$ and $Quebec-Air\_DB$ belonging to two fictitious airlines Ontario Air and Quebec Air, respectively. Assume that these databases manage reservations for flights originating in Ottawa. Their schemas are as follows:

OA_Passenger (pid, name)
OA_Flight   (fno, date, dest, sold, cap)
OA_Ticket   (pid, fno, meal)

(a) Schema for the Ontario-Air database

QA_Fleet   (aid, type, capacity)
QA_Passenger (pid, name)
QA_Flight   (fno, date, to, sold, aid)
QA_Reserve   (pid, fno)

(b) Schema for the Quebec-Air database

Ontario-Air stores identifications and names for each passenger. It stores flight numbers, dates, destinations, number of tickets sold, and capacities of flights. Finally, it stores identifiers, flight numbers, and meal requests of passengers. Quebec-Air stores passenger identifiers and names, and the number, date, destination airport code, number of tickets sold and the airplane identifier for each flight. Quebec-Air also stores a table containing the passenger identifiers and the corresponding flight numbers. Finally, Quebec-Air stores information about its fleet, i.e., the identifier of each plane together with the corresponding type and capacity. Figure 1 shows instances of the two peer database schemas.

Ontario-Air and Quebec-Air can aim at coordinating their activities by establishing an acquaintance. The goal of such an acquaintance can be to favour an exchange of flight information and to coordinate their flights to various locations. Since the schemas of both peer databases are heterogeneous, no data exchange can take place before a form of homogenization is undertaken. In the more traditional context of data integration (see e.g. [9]), views are used to facilitate some form of data exchange across heterogeneous schemas. Usually, to adopt our terminology, these views constraint the *content* of source peer databases in order to determine the content of target peer databases. However, two major assumptions of the PDBMS setting precludes the use of the data integration approach: peer databases are supposed to be autonomous with respect to their contents, and the very large number of involved peers makes any static approach to the reconciliation process of peer contents inadequate. Rather we focus on techniques for coordinating data exchange between peers by looking for ways of constraining, not the contents of the peers, but the data exchange itself. We propose using mapping tables [7] and expressions [1],and an appropriate extension of SQL3 triggers as a way of constraining data exchange across heterogeneous boundaries. Figure 2(a) shows an example of the former construct, and Figure 2(b)-(c) shows examples of the latter.

Intuitively, mapping tables are binary tables that provide a correspondence between data values of acquaintees. Implicitly, they also provide a rudimentary schema-level correspondence. As an example, the mapping table 2(b) associates city names mentioned in the Ontario-Air database to airport codes mentioned by the Quebec-Air database, and the table 2(c) gives correspondences between flight numbers mentioned by the two peer databases.

Intuitively, a mapping expression relates two different schemas. It realizes a schema level correspondence of two different peers. Syntactically, it is expressed in some first order, Datalog-like language. The mapping expression of Figure 2(a) says that, in the context of data exchange, any flight of Quebec-Air is considered a flight of Ontario-Air, and not necessarily vice-versa. Here, we assume that the mapping expression is created at the Ontario-Air database.

$$\text{OA\_Flight(fno,date,dest,sold,cap)} \supseteq \text{QA\_Flight(fno,date,dest,sold,cap)}$$

Mapping expression 2(a)

dest	to
Tor.	LBP
Tor.	ILD
Mont.	Dorv.
Mont.	Mira.
Ottawa	MDC

OA.fno	QA.fno
OA229	QA2132
OA341	QA1187
OA341	QA1108

Mapping table 2(b) Mapping table 2(c)

Fig. 2. Mapping tables and expressions

Once the two databases are acquainted, and mapping tables or expressions are in place, the peers can use each other's contents during query answering and data coordination. In [1], the use of mapping tables in query answering is outlined and illustrated.

2.2   ECA Rules for PDBMSs

The Language: Apart from querying, peers are also able to coordinate their data with those of their acquaintances. For some applications, run-time reconciliation will not be sufficient and we will want to reconcile the data as it is updated. In this example, suppose the two partner airlines wish to reconcile their data to conform to the mapping expression of Figure 2(a). Using this mapping expression, we can derive a rule to ensure the two databases stay consistent as new passengers are entered into the Quebec-Air peer. To enforce this rule, and other similar business rules, we propose a mechanism which uses event-condition-action (ECA) rules with the distinctive characteristic that events, conditions and actions in rules refer to multiple peers. An example of such an ECA rule is given below.

```
create trigger passengerInsertion
after     insert on QA_Passenger
          referencing new as NewPass
for each row
begin
          insert into OA_Passenger values NewPass
          in Ontario-Air_DB;
end
```

According to this rule, an event that is detected in the Quebec-Air database causes an action to be executed in the Ontario-Air database. Specifically, each passenger insertion in the QA_Passenger relation generates an event which triggers the rule above. The rule has no condition while its action causes the insertion of an identical passenger tuple in the OA_Passenger relation.

The rule above is expressed in a language extending SQL3 triggers [8]. An SQL3 trigger is an ECA rule that bears an explicit name. Each trigger is associated with a specific table, and only insertions, deletions, and updates on this table can activate the associated trigger. SQL3 events are simple. Conditions are SQL queries, and actions are SQL statements that will be executed on the database. There are two sorts of triggers, namely the AFTER and BEFORE triggers. The former are activated before the occurrence of their activating event, and the later are activated after their activating event has occurred.

A rule of our language extends a typical SQL3 trigger by explicitly mentioning the database in which the event, condition, and action occurs. It also contains a richer event language to permit the expression of complex active behavior encountered in peer coordination. The rule above is a example of a typical rule for enforcing the consistency of peers that coordinate their work. In this paper, we illustrate the rule language and its use in coordinating data exchange between different peers. We also outline its execution semantics below. We leave its formal definition out of the scope of this paper.

Interaction with Mapping Tables: The mappings in the mapping tables are intimately related to values that are stored in the Ontario-Air and Quebec-Air databases. Therefore, it is natural to keep in the mapping tables only the associations between values that exist in the actual instances of the relation schemas of those databases. This means that insertions and deletions of values into the instances of Ontario-Air and Quebec-Air databases may result in an update of mapping tables to avoid discrepancies between the databases of both peers and the mapping tables relating them.

Using our running example, the following discussion further illustrates the updating of mapping tables. Whenever there is a deletion of a tuple in OA_Flight, there is an ECA rule that removes the appropriate tuple in the mapping table of Figure 2(c). Of course such a rule may not be needed for many cases of mapping tables. For example, as far as Figure 2(b) is concerned, even if there is a deletion of all flights of Ontario-Air to New-York, we wouldn't like to delete the respective information from Figure 2(b), because we will probably need it in the future. However, in the case of Figure 2(c), if a cancelled Ontario-Air flight becomes active, again it may not correspond to the same flight of Quebec-Air database. Thus, deleting the corresponding tuples from Figure 2(c) when a flight is cancelled is a reasonable action. The following rule illustrates how deletion in the mapping table of Figure 2(c) might be dealt with:

create trigger flightDeletion
after   **delete on** *OA_Flight*
            referencing old as *OldFlight*
for each row
begin
            delete from *MT2c* **where** *MT2c.fnoOA = OldFlight.fno*
end   ▪

Here, *MT2c* is the relation name of the mapping table of Figure 2(c).

3   System Architecture

This section also summarizes the architecture of Hyperion [1]. Figure 3 represents a generic architecture for the envisioned data management framework. The architecture consists of a collection of PDBMSs located at nodes $N_1, \cdots, N_m$ of a P2P network. The various acquaintances that exist in the network induce the existence of communities of peers that coordinate their data. Such groups are called *interest groups* [4]. On the left hand side of Figure 3, two such groups, delimited by thin dashed lines, are depicted. Each PDBMS coordinates many of its typical database activities such as queries, updates, and transactions with its acquaintees in a transparent way. Our proposal assumes concepts such as absence of any global database schema, transient PDBMSs, distributed (or no)

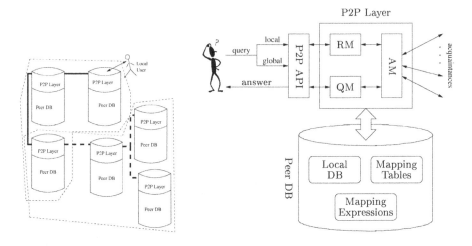

Fig. 3. Architecture for a PDBMS

administrative authority, locally available data, strict local access to a single database, etc.

Figure 3, right hand side (taken from [1]), depicts the architecture of a PDBMS with its main functionalities. A PDBMS consists of three main components: an interface (P2P API), a P2P layer, and a DBMS. For simplicity, we do not show the local management system layer that manages a peer database. This contains local data along with mapping tables and expressions that are used in data exchange with other peers. The P2P API is the interface for posing queries and specifying whether these are to be executed only locally or remotely. Through an acquaintance manager, the P2P layer allows a PDBMS to establish or abolish an acquaintance (semi-)automatically at runtime, thereby inducing a *logical* peer-to-peer network. More specifically, the acquaintance manager uses mapping tables as constraint on the data exchange between peer databases to automatically check the consistency of a set of mapping constraints and infer new ones. In [7], these capabilities are shown to be of practical importance in establishing new acquaintances. We will return to this issue below.

4   Setting Up and Abolishing Acquaintances

In this section, we describe the algorithms used by peer databases for joining and leaving a peer network. Syntactically, the peer language includes constructs that allow the user to establish or abolish acquaintances between peers. Semantically, an acquaintance is a kind of bookkeeping instance that interface two peers. Figure 4 depicts the constraints of an acquaintance.

4.1   Setting Up Acquaintances

To join a network, a peer N_i, must establish an acquaintance with a known peer, say N_j, which is already part of the network. We assume, for simplicity, that acquaintances are explicitly established by a user, most probably a database administrator. To that end, the peer language includes the following construct in its syntax:

```
set acquaintance to <peer database>
    [using mapping tables <list of mapping table names>]
    [using mapping expressions <list of mapping expression
names>]
    [belonging to <Interest Group>]
```

Using this construct, a peer database administrator establishes explicit acquaintances between her database and other existing ones. When an acquaintance is established, it is coupled with several constraints. The most important of these constraints are mapping tables and expressions which – as stated earlier – constrain the exchange of data between peers, and coordination rules (written in the ECA language outlined above) which are guidelines for such an exchange.

Now we give details on the algorithm used by a peer to establish an acquaintance. Assume that peer N_i issues the following command for establishing an acquaintance:

```
set acquaintance to Nj
```

Then the following algorithm is used for completing this request:

Phase 1. Semi-automatically generate mappings as follows:

1. Use a matching algorithm to get an initial match between schemas of the peers N_i and N_j. Such a matching will most probably not be correct or complete, and may have to be revised manually by the administrator.
2. Create mapping expressions and views.
3. Use the match obtained in step 1 to create and populate an initial set of mapping tables.
4. Send a copy of the mapping table instances to N_j.

Phase 2. Generate consistency-enforcing rules from mapping expressions obtained in Phase 1, and generate rules for maintenance of mapping tables.

Phase 3. Add N_j to the list of N_i's acquaintees.

The algorithm above does not use initial mapping tables. To process a request with an initial list $M_1, \cdots, M_n$ of mapping tables, it suffices to replace step 3 of phase 1 in the algorithm above by the mere use of the given mappings tables. The algorithm above also does not use initial coordination rules. We could assume that an initial list of coordination rules is used in setting up an acquaintance. However, though this is not precluded in principle, we prefer to think of such a list of initial rules being brought in on-the-fly from an interest group, rather than being designed for particular peers by database designers. The main reason for doing this is that we want to create a technology that is end-user oriented.

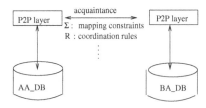

Fig. 4. A constrained acquaintance

4.2   Generic Rules for Interest Groups

The simple acquaintance algorithm given above assumes that all peers belong to a single universal group of peers. However, it seems appropriate to classify peers into interest groups. We assume that an interest group has standard schemas known to all members of the group. For the airline domain, for example, we have schema S_A for airline peer databases, schema S_{TA} for travel agencies, schema S_{RA} for regional airlines. Rules are written for common patterns of data exchange and coordination among S_A, S_{TA}, and S_{RA}. When a particular set of peers, say airline a_1, travel agency ta_1 and regional airline ra_1 decide to coordinate with a given rule R_1, they need to bind/match their respective schemas to the schema with respect to which R_1 was defined in order to find appropriate mappings. With these bindings in place, all that is left is agreement among a_1, ta_1, and ra_1 that they indeed want to coordinate with rule R_1. This detail is left out.

When peers join the network, they need to register as belonging to certain interest groups. By default, the interest group will be a distinguished catch all interest group to which all peers belong. It also means that some domain experts use the rule language outlined in Section 2.1 to define possible coordinations among members of different interest groups. We assume that *generic rules* are created with respect to the standard schema of an interest group, and then adapted for specific databases that belong to the interest group. In fact, a generic rule may involve the standard schemas of more than one interest group. For simplicity, we also assume that the standard schema and generic rules are stored at every member of the interest group.

By means of an example, we now illustrate step by step a mechanism for setting up acquaintances in the presence of interest groups. In the example below, we will use the following terminology. A schema mapping is a correspondence between schema elements of two peers. We call a mapping "strict" if it represents an identity function that maps each value of an attribute A of the first peer to itself in the second peer. For example, the values of the attribute "date" in the Ontario-Air database are mapped to itself in the Quebec-Air database. We call a mapping "loose" if it represents any function that possibly maps different values of the same attribute. Finally, a view is conceived in its traditional meaning.

Assume the schemas of Ontario-Air and Quebec-Air given in Section 2.1 and that both peers belongs to the interest group *Airlines*.

Step 1. Suppose that the interest group *Airlines* has the following standard schema, called S_A:

    Ticket(pid, name, fno, meal)
    Flight(fno, date, destination)
    FlightInfo(fno, sold, cap, aid, type)

Then, the schema mappings for Ontario-Air and Quebec-Air databases would be as follows:
For Ontario-Air, we have the following mappings $M_{S_A \rightarrow OA}$:

    M_{OA_1}: OA_Passenger(pid, name) ← Ticket(pid, name, fno, meal)
    M_{OA_2}: OA_Ticket(pid, fno, meal) ← Ticket(pid, name, fno, meal)
    M_{OA_3}: OA_Flight(fno, date, dest, sold, cap) ← Flight(fno, date, dest),
                FlightInfo(fno, sold, cap, aid, type)

From the three mappings above, Ontario-Air marks M_{OA_2} as a loose one (because the database administrator thinks that the mapping of fnos may not be very accurate, because she knows that usually airlines use different flight numbers). Also, M_{OA_3} is marked as a loose one (because the administrator suspects that different airlines consider different things as destinations). Finally, M_{OA_1} is marked as a strict mapping.
For Quebec-Air, we have the following mappings $M_{S_A \rightarrow QA}$:

    M_{QA_1}: QA_Passenger(pid, name) ← Ticket(pid, name, fno, meal)
    M_{QA_2}: QA_Reserve(pid, fno) ← Ticket(pid, name, fno, meal)
    M_{QA_3}: QA_Flight(fno, date, to, sold, aid) ← Flight(fno, date, to),
                FlightInfo(fno, sold, cap, aid, type)
    M_{QA_4}: QA_Fleet(aid, type, capacity) ← FlightInfo(fno, sold, capacity, aid, type)

M_{QA_2} and M_{QA_3} are marked as loose mappings and M_{QA_1} and M_{QA_4} as strict ones.
Step 2.
A. We try to define **views** between the schemas of Ontario-Air and Quebec-Air. We observe from $M_{S_A \rightarrow OA}$ and $M_{S_A \rightarrow QA}$ that the mappings M_{OA_1} and M_{QA_1} are defined over the same set of attributes. Therefore we create the trivial view:

    V1: OA_Passenger(pid, name) ⟵ QA_Passenger(pid, name)

Also, we observe that the sets of attributes of the mappings M_{OA_2} and M_{QA_2} overlap. Thus we map the one with the more attributes to the one with less attributes using the following view:

    V2: QA_Reserve(pid, fno) ⟵ OA_Ticket(pid, fno, meal).

Finally, from the mappings M_{OA_3}, M_{QA_3}, and M_{OA_4}, we derive the view:

    V3: OA_Flight(fno, date, dest, sold, cap) ⟵
                QA_Flight(fno, date, dest, sold,aid), QA_Fleet(aid, type, cap)

where 'to' is renamed as 'dest' and 'capacity' as 'cap'.

B.We now try to define **mapping tables** between the schemas of Ontario-Air and Quebec-Air using views V1–V3. View V1 comes from schema mappings that were strict. Thus, it can stand by itself and we can use it as it is. However, V2 comes from two loose schema mappings. Thus, we understand that we need additional information to use this view: we need a mapping of values in order to fix the 'looseness' of the mappings of attributes 'fno'. Thus, we create a mapping table MT_1(OA.fno, QA.fno). Now we search to find if we can derive more mapping tables. Also, V3 comes from loose schema mappings, both because 'looseness' on the attribute 'fno' and the attribute 'dest'. For 'fno' we have already created a mapping table. For 'dest' and 'to' we create the mapping table MT_2(OA.dest, QA.to).

Step 3. We now ask the user/administrator if she wants to create mapping expressions either on the already created views or any new ones from scratch The user creates a mapping expression from view V1. Let the corresponding mapping expression be

$$\text{ME: OA\_Passenger(pid, name)} \supseteq \text{QA\_Passenger(pid,name)}$$

As seen in Section 2.1, the mapping expression ME has an executional meaning and does not refer to the structure of the relations.

Step 4. The user populates the mapping tables MT1 and MT2 as shown in Figure 2.

Step 5.

A. Using the mapping expression ME, we create the following rule to ensure consistency over the acquaintance link between Ontario-Air and Quebec-Air databases:

```
create trigger enforceME
after      insert on QA_Passenger
           referencing new as New in Quebec-Air_DB
for each row
begin
           insert into OA_Passenger values (New.pid, New.name)
           in Ontario-Air_DB
end
```

B. For the maintenance of mapping tables MT_1 and MT_2, we create maintenance rules. Generally the administrator has to decide which kind of rules are needed for the maintenance of a mapping table according to the nature of information that it keeps. Whenever there is a deletion of a tuple in OA_Flight, there is a rule that removes the corresponding tuple in MT_2. The rule flightDeletion given in Section 2.2 captures this interaction with mapping tables.

Step 6. Now suppose the following active behavior that involves two airline peers: DB_A and DB_B agree that whenever a DB_A flight is oversold, a new flight should be created by DB_B to accommodate new passengers. The following is a generic rule that captures this behavior:

create trigger AFullFlight
before   update of *sold* **on** *FlightInfo*
           referencing new as *New*
           referencing old as *Old* **in** *DB_A*
when   *New.sold = New.cap*
for each row
begin
        insert into *Flight* **values** *(New.fno, date, New.destination);*
        insert into *FlightInfo* **values** *(New.fno, 0, New.cap, New.aid, New.type)*
        in *DB_B*
end

When this rule is customized for Ontario-Air and Quebec-Air peer databases, we get the following rule:

create trigger OAAFullFlight
before   update of *sold* **on** *OA_Flight*
           referencing new as *New*
                    old as *Old*
           in *Ontario-Air_DB*
when   *New.sold = New.cap*
for each row
begin
        insert into *QA_Flight* **values**
        (map(New.fno), date, map(New.dest), 0, null)
        in *Quebec-Air_DB*
end

This rule means that, whenever a reservation is *about* (thus the use of "before") to fail due to a full Alpha Air flight, a new flight is going to be created by Quebec-Air to accommodate all passengers that Ontario-Air could not accommodate.

Notice that the action part of the rule above contains an insertion of a new tuple which is a transformation of the updated Ontario-Air flight tuple. This transformation is accomplished using the mapping tables.

Ontario-Air database, into the table *QA_Reserve* of the Quebec-Air database. The rule engine must use the mapping tables at run-time to solve the discrepancies that may arise between the values of the two databases.

Step 7. Quebec-Air is added to the list of acquaintees of Ontario-Air and vice-versa.

Now we give details on the algorithm for establishing an acquaintance in presence of interest groups. Assume that peer N_i issues the following command:

```
set acquaintance to N_j
       belonging to SIG
```

Then the following algorithm is used for completing this request:

If N_j does not belongs to SIG, then follow the simple algorithm of Section 4.1. Otherwise, do the following:

1. For both N_i and N_j, if there are no mappings between the standard schema S_{SIG} of SIG and the actual schemas of S_{N_i} of N_i and S_{N_j} of N_j, then create such mappings.
2. Given the mappings $M_{i \to SIG}$ from S_{N_i} to S_{SIG}, and $M_{SIG \to j}$ from S_{SIG} to S_{N_j}, infer (using algorithms of [7]) a mapping $M_{i \to j}$ from S_{N_i} to S_{N_j}. Use $M_{i \to j}$ to create mapping tables and views between N_i and N_j.
3. Create mapping expressions.
4. Populate the mapping tables, and send a copy of the mapping table instances to N_j.
5. Generate consistency-enforcing rules from mapping expressions obtained in step 2,and generate rules for maintenance of mapping tables.
6. Customize the generic rules of SIG according to the final views and mapping tables obtained in step 2 and activate the customized rules.
7. Add N_j to the list of N_i's acquaintees.

4.3   Abolishing Acquaintances

A peer N_i, may abolish one or more acquaintances with known peers, say $N_{j_1}, \cdots, N_{j_l}$. Again, for simplicity, we assume that acquaintances are explicitly abolished by a user. For this task, the peer language includes the following construct:

    abolish acquaintance to <peer database>

When an acquaintance is abolished, the various constraints that were attached to it are dropped. Dropping a constraint can be as simple as locally disabling it. However, abolishing an acquaintance can lead to the peer leaving the network if the abolished acquaintance was the only one that the peer had. Therefore dropping a constraint can also be as hard as filling the gap left behind by the vanishing peer. To abolish all the acquaintances of a peer all together, the language contains the construct `leave`.

The following gives details on the algorithm used by a peer to abolish an acquaintance. Assume that peer N_i issues the following command for abolishing an acquaintance:

    abolish acquaintance to N_j

This is executed as follows:

If N_j is not the only N_i's acquaintee, then do the following:

1. Send a message to N_j to disable any copies of the mapping tables that originated in N_i that it may have.
2. Disable any mapping tables, mapping expressions, and coordination rules that is coupled to the acquaintance $\langle N_i, N_j \rangle$.

Otherwise, do the following:

1. Send a marker to N_j.
2. Steps 2 and 3 as above.

The `leave` command is executed by abolishing all the acquaintances using the algorithm above.

Notice that the "marker" mentioned in the algorithm above is a proxy that the very last peer that was acquainted with a vanishing peer will keep as an indication that the vanishing peer was at some point in the network and has left. We will not elaborate on this marker here. It suffice to mention that this marker can be used to decide on what to do when a query is being answered or an event is being detected while some peers have left the network.

5   Related Work

Our architecture adds details to the *local relational model* presented in [3] and extended in [1]. We view peer databases as local relational databases which establish or abolish acquaintances between them to build a P2P network. In [3], each acquaintance is characterized both by a mapping between the peer involved and by a first-order theory that gives the semantic dependencies between the peers. There, it was also indicated that the first-order theory that characterizes the semantic dependencies between the peers can be implemented as ECA rules. In the present paper, we start spelling out the details of this implementation.

That ECA rules constitute an important mechanism for supporting data coordination has been recognized mainly in the context of multidatabase systems, e.g. in [10,2,6]. Here, distributed rules involving several databases of the kind "If event E_1 occurs in DB_1, E_2 occurs in DB_2, and E_1 precedes E_2 then carry out transaction T in DB_3" is recognized. Executing such distributed rules requires coordination among peer databases DB_1, DB_2 and DB_3. Therefore, it would naturally be useful to add active functionality to P2P MDBSs. The work in [6] presents a first attempt to study implementation issues for distributed ECA rules as a mechanism of P2P interoperability. However, much work remains to be done on this topic in terms of dealing with the management of seamless addition and removal of peers in the network. Like ours, the proposal for a peer database architecture given in [4], is inspired by the theoretical foundations laid down in [3]. It also mentions the importance of ECA rule for coordinating data exchange between peers. Unlike ours, [4] does not focus on details of how ECA rules can be used for such an endeavour. Finally, in the context of information integration within a common domain, usual solutions (e.g., *global-as-view* and *local-as-view* [9]) that address heterogeneity involve constructing views that reconcile heterogeneous sources in the logical structures. Instead, we consider that metadata is required for data sharing across highly heterogeneous worlds which are often hard to reconcile.

6   Conclusions

We have described techniques for specifying data exchange policies on-the-fly based on constraints (expressed as mapping tables and as generic ECA rules) on the way in which peers exchange and share data. We considered a setting in which a PDBMS defines and manages its own view of the shared data, and defines its own sharing and coordination policies based on ECA rules provided by interest groups. The on-the-fly specification of data exchange policies is realized by building coordination ECA rules at acquaintance time, as opposed to having them being created at design-time for particular peers by experts. This on-the-fly generation of active rules contributes to our vision of a P2P database technology that is end-user oriented and where establishing acquaintances between peers is done in a flexible, and cost-effective way.

The coordination framework presented here is being extended in various ways. First, we are investigating a complete extension of SQL3 triggers for the peer database setting. For this extension, we are studying a suitable execution model that combines the execution model for SQL3 triggers [8] and the one proposed for the multidatabase context in [6]. Second, the notion of acquaintance type, denoting the level of privileges attached to the acquaintance, is useful in practice. For example, Ontario-Air may have established an acquaintance with Quebec-Air that is of a higher degree of privileges than an existing acquaintance it has with Alberta-Air. We are studying types as a further constraint that characterizes acquaintances. Finally, we started investigating appropriate notions of query processing and transaction management.

References

1. M. Arenas, V. Kantere, T. Kementsietsidis, I. Kiringa, R.J. Miller, and J. Mylopoulos. The hyperion project: from data integration to data coordination. *SIGMOD RECORD*, September 2003.
2. R. Arizio, B. Bomitali, M. Demarie, A. Limongiello, and P.L Mussa. Managing inter-database dependencies with rules + quasi-transactions. In *Third International Workshop on Research Issues in Data Engineering: Interoperability in Multidatabase Systems*, p. 34–41, Vienna, April 1993.
3. P. Bernstein, F. Giunchiglia, A. Kementsietsidis, J. Mylopoulos, L. Serafini, and I. Zaihrayeu. Data Management for Peer-to-Peer Computing: A Vision. In *Proc. of the Int'l Workshop on the WEB and Databases*, 2002.
4. F. Giunchiglia and I. Zaihrayeu. Making peer databases interact - a vision for an architecture supporting data coordination. In *Proceedings of the Conference on Information Agents*, Madrid, September 2002.
5. S. Gribble, A. Halevy, Z. Ives, M. Rodrig, and D. Suciu. What can databases do for peer-to-peer? In *Proc. of the Int'l Workshop on the WEB and Databases*, 2001.
6. V. Kantere. A rule mechanism for p2p data management. Technical report, University of Toronto, 2003. CSRG-469.
7. A. Kementsietsidis, M. Arenas, and R. J. Miller. Data mapping in peer-to-peer systems: Semantics and algorithmic issues. In *ACM SIGMOD*, 2003.
8. K. Kulkarni, N. Mattos, and R. Cochrane. Active database features in SQL3. In N. Paton, editor, *Active Rules in Database Systems*, p. 197–219. Springer, 1999.
9. M. Lenzerini. Data Integration: A Theoretical Perspective. In *Proc. of the ACM Symp. on Principles of Database Systems*, p. 233–246, 2002.
10. C. Turker and S. Conrad. Towards maintaining integrity in federated databases. In *3rd Basque International Workshop on Information Technology*, Biarritz, France, July 1997.

An Adaptive and Scalable Middleware for Distributed Indexing of Data Streams

Ahmet Bulut[1], Roman Vitenberg[1], Fatih Emekçi[1], and Ambuj K. Singh[1]

Computer Science Department, UCSB, Santa Barbara, CA 93106, USA
{bulut,romanv,fatih,ambuj}@cs.ucsb.edu,
http://www.cs.ucsb.edu/{~bulut,~romanv,~fatih,~ambuj}

Abstract. We are witnessing a dramatic increase in the use of data-centric distributed systems such as global grid infrastructures, sensor networks, network monitoring, and various publish-subscribe systems. The visions of massive demand-driven data dissemination, intensive processing, and intelligent fusion in order to build dynamic knowledge bases that seemed infeasible just a few years ago are about to come true. However, the realization of this potential demands adequate support from middleware that could be used to deploy and support such systems.

We propose a peer-to-peer based distributed indexing architecture that supports scalable handling of intense dynamic information flows. The suggested indexing scheme is geared towards providing timely responses to queries of different types with varying precision requirements while minimizing the use of network and computational resources. Our solution bestows the capabilities provided by peer-to-peer architectures, such as scalability and load balancing of communication as well as adaptivity in presence of dynamic changes. The paper elaborates on database and peer-to-peer methodologies used in the integrated solution as well as non-trivial interaction between them, thereby providing a valuable feedback to the designers of these techniques.

1 Introduction

Data streams are becoming an increasingly important class of datasets. They find applications in sensor networks, stock tickers, news organizations, telecommunications networks, and data networks. Network service providers channelize logs of network usage in great detail from routers into data processing centers to use them in trend-related analysis. The amount of data generated in such applications can become too large to maintain in memory. This prompts a need in techniques and architectures for scalable stream processing.

A significant amount of research has been devoted to this problem in databases, with the objective to maintain a summary of statistical information that can be used to answer client queries quickly while meeting certain precision requirements (see [8] for a discussion). While mostly focusing on query semantics, these works introduce algorithms for mining data streams in centralized settings wherein all streams and queries arrive at a single location. In practice,

K. Aberer et al. (Eds.): VLDB 2003 Ws DBISP2P, LNCS 2944, pp. 123–137, 2004.

however, data stream systems such as sensornets, network monitoring systems, and security sensors in military applications consist of a multitude of streams at different locations. The core of such system architectures is formed by *data centers* (also called *sensor proxies* or *base stations* to which sensors send information for processing), which coordinate their data handling for providing collaborative data mining and fusion, and for responding to various types of user queries. Typically, data centers can be dispersed over significant distances and communication between them is expensive.

Emerging peer-to-peer based technologies such as CAN [32], Chord [35], Pastry [34], and Tapestry [38] that are introduced as general solutions for Internet-based peer-to-peer applications, bear the potential to lay ground for the underlying communication stratum in distributed data stream systems as they provide the means to uniformly distribute the load of processing stream data and queries as well as the burden of communication due to data propagation across all nodes and links in the system. Furthermore, these technologies aim at adaptive accommodation of dynamic changes, which facilitates a seamless addition of new data streams and data centers to the system as well as handling of various possible failures, e.g., data center crashes. Additionally, some content-based routing schemes, such as GHT [33], have been introduced specifically for sensornets and similar specialized environments. However, most works in this area focus on network-level communication and various aspects of message routing while not being concerned with the typical issues of database applications such as the semantics and precision requirements of queries.

We propose an adaptive and scalable middleware for data stream processing in a distributed environment. Our integrated middleware solution harnesses the potential of the peer-to-peer paradigm with the purpose of fast and efficient stream data mining and timely response to queries while minimizing the amount of network and computational resources consumed by data centers and network links. Specifically, our work exploits the scalability and load balancing of communication as well as adaptivity in presence of dynamic changes provided by peer-to-peer schemes. The proposed architecture is geared towards efficient handling of similarity queries and adequate support for inner product queries, which are among the most popular types of queries in complex data stream applications.

The paper elaborates on both database and peer-to-peer methodologies used in the integrated solution as well as non-trivial interaction between them, thereby providing a valuable feedback to the designers of these techniques. Furthermore, the proposed middleware relies on the standard distributed hashing table interface provided by content-based routing schemes rather than on a particular implementation. This makes our architecture more general and portable because it can be used on top of any existing content-based routing implementation tailored to a specific data stream environment.

2   Data Stream Computation Model and Query Models

A data stream consists of an ordered sequence of data points $\langle \ldots, x_i, \ldots \rangle$. The value of each data point lies in a bounded range, $[R_{min}, R_{max}]$. We consider a system where there are M streams, and where we are interested in only the N most recent values of each stream. A stream processing engine processes data streams and computes synopses to provide approximate answers to user queries.

We categorize queries posed on data streams into two general categories: inner-product queries and similarity queries. For each of these query categories, we give some examples and define the queries formally.

2.1   Inner Product Queries

Inner product queries are important for statistics computation and condition specification. Examples include

- What is the average closing price of Intel for the last month ? (stock data processing)
- What is the average duration of a TCP session for the day ? (network data processing)
- Notify when the weighted average of last 20 body temperature measurements of a patient exceed a threshold value! (medical sensor data processing)

Formally, an inner product query is a quadruple (S_{id}, I, W, δ), where S_{id} denotes the stream identifier, I denotes the index vector (the data items of interest), W denotes the weight vector (the individual weights corresponding to each data item), and a precision δ within which the result $I \cdot W$, the inner product of I and W, needs to be computed. Simple point and range queries can be expressed as inner product queries [8].

2.2   Similarity Queries

Similarity queries enable detection of primary trends and discovery of patterns in dynamic data streams. Examples include

- Identify time periods during which a set of companies had a similar profit pattern as Intel had last month!
- Find all pairs of companies whose closing prices over the last month correlate within a certain threshold value ϵ!
- Which temperature sensors currently report on a temperature in some range, or exhibit some temperature behavior pattern?
- Which links or routers in a network monitoring system have been experiencing significant fluctuations in the packet handling rate over the last 5 minutes?
- How many computers in a large scale network have recorded some pattern of remote accesses, which may be an indication of an intruder trying to gain control over the system?

A similarity query is formally defined as follows: given a sequence database, D, a query sequence, Q, and a similarity threshold ϵ, find all the subsequences in D that are ϵ-similar to the query sequence Q. The distance measure we use is the L_2 norm of the *normalized* sequences which is preserved under orthonormal transforms. We note that normalization of sequences is a linear operation in this context. Therefore, streaming algorithms can be devised to normalize sequences on the fly due to the linearity of the transformations used.

3   Centralized Querying and Summarization

3.1   Related Work

Theoretical methods have been developed for comparing data streams under various L_p distances [10], for clustering and computing the k-median [30], and for computing aggregates over data streams [12,16]. Various histogramming algorithms, provably optimal [24] and near optimal approaches [19], have been proposed for maintaining the distribution of a single-attribute stream. The idea of random sketches for computing frequency moments of a data stream is introduced in [3]. In the literature, the sketches have been used extensively for computing approximate answers over data streams [14,17].

Design and implementation issues for building Data Stream Management Systems (DSMS) [4] for sensor networks [13,28], Internet databases [9] and telecommunications networks [11] have been explored in the database community. Query processing over data streams is an active research area mainly focused on characterization of memory requirements [1,26].

In our earlier work, SWAT [8], we examined how to summarize a single data stream in an online manner. The technique uses $O(\log N)$ space for a stream of size N. The update cost for each incoming data point is constant (this follows from an amortized analysis). For an inner product query, the technique computes an approximate answer in polylogarithmic time.

The most pioneering work on similarity search in sequence databases is using Fourier transform for feature extraction from time-sequences [2]. This idea is further extended to subsequence matching [15] and to efficient handling of variable length similarity queries [25]. Piecewise constant approximation and its variations for dimensionality reduction are addressed in [27]. We refer the interested reader to [37] for a discussion of similarity search using Fourier transforms and wavelet transforms.

3.2   Proposed Central Solution

Naive approaches to answer especially similarity queries are infeasible. First, the number of streams in the system can be arbitrarily large. Second, a stream can be arbitrarily long. Third, the online arrival of new values require fast processing. This prompts a need to design scalable index structures. A multi-dimensional index structure [6,7] can be built on a subset of data stream features on the

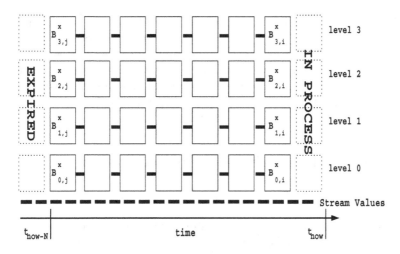

Fig. 1. Composite index structure

fly using an orthonormal transformation such as Discrete Fourier Transform (DFT), Discrete Cosine Transform (DCT), Discrete Wavelet Transform (DWT), and Karhunen-Loeve Transform (SVD). Later, this index structure can be used for efficient similarity search.

Figure 1 shows a prototype of our index structure, which can be used to answer inner product queries and similarity queries. We use DWT (or DFT) to extract features from the subsequences of a stream at multiple resolutions. With each arrival of a new stream value, we apply the transformation starting from the lowest resolution up to some pre-specified resolution level, J ($J = 3$ in Figure 1). At each resolution level, we combine every c of the feature vectors obtained in the previous step into a box, or a Minimum Bounding Rectangle (MBR) that is the tightest hyper-rectangle that bounds a given set of feature vectors in a high dimensional space. Later, this box is inserted into a level-specific index. The index at a given level combines information from all the streams. However, each elementary box inserted into the index is specific to a single stream. In other words, the index at a given level is an agglomeration of stream specific MBRs. The feature vectors at a specific resolution are obtained by considering a sliding window of a fixed length. The window size doubles as we go up a level. This adaptivity is useful for answering queries of variable lengths [25]. The MBRs belonging to a specific stream are also threaded together in order to provide a sequential access to the summary information about the stream. In general, when sufficiently many stream values have arrived, we will need to compute a transform at each level at each data arrival. For example, the level-4 index structure considered in Figure 1 needs to compute 4 forward transforms (corresponding to window sizes $4, 8, 16, 32$) at each data arrival. We reduce this per-item processing time by computing transformation coefficients incrementally using the linearity of the transformation as noted in [8]. A faster per item-processing time is further achieved by employing a batch-computation technique similar to the one proposed in [39].

The inherent assumption in all of the solutions considered so far is that all streams arrive at a single location where they are processed and stored. On the contrary, in most of the real world applications such as sensornets and Internet databases, the streams arrive at possibly diverse locations. This requires that systems should be enabled with efficient distributed query processing over widely dispersed data sources in order to better utilize limited system resources. We describe our distributed system design next.

4   Distributed Querying and Summarization

4.1   Motivation

Consider a naive system solution that stores information about each stream at the data center closest to the stream. Inner product queries over a specific stream can be handled at the querying site if the site has the summary information for the stream. Otherwise, the query has to be propagated to the data center where the stream information is explicitly captured. The location of this data center is found out by using a location service.

While storing all data at the nearest data center is adequate for inner product queries that are interested in individual values of a specific stream, it does not provide a viable solution for general similarity queries. If a system stores information about each stream at the data center closest to this stream, answering such queries requires communication with every data center in the system with the purpose of collecting information, which is highly inefficient. However, if such preprocessing is done by a single data center which is responsible for answering all queries, this data center will immediately become a bottleneck in the system: In addition to being overloaded with the burden of queries and data processing thereby limiting the system scalability, a failure of this single node will render the whole system completely non-functional for the duration of the recovery operation. We refer the interested reader to [20] for a detailed discussion of fault-tolerance issues in various schemes.

An architecture for sensornet data processing is proposed in [18]. This architecture is based on a bidirectional multi-hierarchical distributed index structure for streams that exhibit spatio-temporal dependencies. However, this work restricts its consideration to point and range queries, and does not address similarity queries. Furthermore, it is not clear how efficient the described index structure is: Each generated stream value has to be disseminated through one of the hierarchies in their scheme, which may be prohibitively expensive for systems with multiple data streams generating large volumes of data. Additionally, a query interested in a wide range of values (possibly with spatial constraints) needs to undergo a complex decomposition into multiple sub-queries, each sub-query being sent to a different node in the system. The overall message complexity for such queries may be high.

The main challenge of the distributed indexing scheme is to provide fast and efficient stream data mining and timely response to queries while minimizing the amount of network and computational resources consumed by data centers and network links. We seek to uniformly distribute the load of processing stream data and queries as well as the burden of communication due to data propagation across all nodes and links in the systems.

4.2   Exploiting the Content-Based Routing Paradigm

The underlying communication stratum of our solution is based on the content-based routing paradigm. Various content-based routing approaches have been designed for different types of networks: GHT [33] was introduced specifically for sensornets while CAN [32], Chord [35], Pastry [34] and Tapestry [38] were introduced as general solutions for Internet-based peer-to-peer applications. However, the common idea behind most schemes is to map both summaries and data centers to the same universe of integer *keys*. Each key is *covered* by some data center (e.g., the one which maps to the closest key value.) A message containing a summary is sent not to a specific data center but rather to the key to which the summary maps. The system automatically routes the message to the data center which covers the key in the message. Such key-based routing allows the system to quickly adapt to dynamic changes, such as a failure or addition of individual data centers to the system: such small changes in the configuration only affect a small fraction of the node-to-key mapping, which is local to the region where the change occurs.

Furthermore, virtually all content-based routing schemes provide the same interface for the applications, which consists of the following basic primitives: a) **send** operation to send a message to a destination determined by the given key, b) **join** and **leave** operations for a node to join or leave the system, and c) **deliver** operation that invokes an application upcall upon message delivery. The solution we propose relies on this interface without assuming any particular implementation. The **join** and **leave** operations are used in the straightforward manner by data centers to change the system configuration dynamically. Below, we provide an overview of how the proposed architecture uses **send** and **deliver** primitives in order to exchange information between data centers.

4.3   Middleware Prototype

The middleware we propose for the distributed stream model provides the following primitives for data stream application (see Figure 2, the application view layer): one primitive to post a new stream data value, and several primitives for client queries of different types. We assume that the infrastructure of data centers provides the necessary geographical coverage. Every stream value and client query arrives at the closest data center for this stream or client by using the means that are external to the proposed middleware while the middleware is responsible for the information exchange between data centers with the purpose of efficient and scalable data handling.

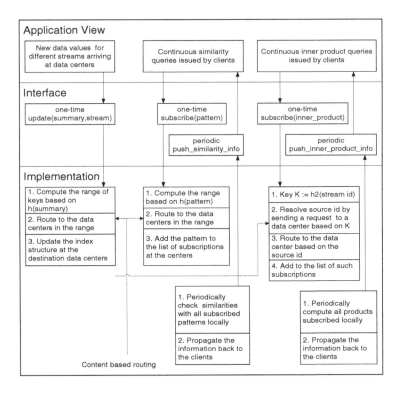

Fig. 2. Process overview in response to data arrival and queries of different types

4.4   Handling Inner Product Queries

Inner product queries over a specific stream can be handled at the querying
site if the site has the summary information for the stream. Otherwise, the
query has to be propagated to the data center where the stream information
is explicitly captured. The location of this data center is found out by using a
location service which is provided as part of a content-based routing scheme. A
significant amount of work on the peer-to-peer paradigm is devoted to making
location services more efficient and scalable by using caching, replication, and
other similar techniques.

4.5   Handling Similarity Queries

After a new summary (feature vector) is computed as described in Section 3, this
summary is sent to the data center that is selected based on the summary value.
Figure 3 gives a simplistic overview of the system in operation. We use a single
value as the summary value for simplicity. The idea is that similar summaries
and patterns are routed to the same or neighbor data centers. A query that is
interested in a certain pattern is routed to the data center that is determined
by this pattern. When a data center receives a query, it only has to check if

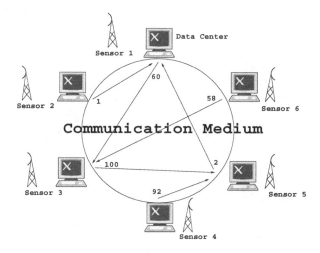

Fig. 3. Content based routing and look-up of stream summaries

the query pattern matches any summary this data center or its neighbors know about.

In order for this scheme to operate efficiently, the mapping between summary values and data centers should satisfy two properties:

- **Locality Preservation**: Similar summaries should be mapped to data centers that are close to each other. This ensures that similarity detection involves only communication between neighbor nodes.
- **Uniformity**: Non-correlated summaries and query patterns should be distributed uniformly over the set of data centers. This property guarantees an even distribution of the burden of data and query processing across all nodes and links.

As described in Section 4.2, a message is routed by a content-based routing scheme based on a key that is given by the application that uses the scheme. One challenge of designing a middleware for efficient distributed stream summarization is to provide a mapping between data summaries and keys that preserves locality and exhibits uniformity. One possibility is to use a DFT-based mapping such as the technique used in [39] for detecting correlations between thousands of streams in a non-distributed environment. In this work, each stream is mapped to a pair of DFT coefficients, and streams with close pairs of coefficients are compared with each other. A possible alternative technique would be to use a wavelet-based mapping for spatio-temporal decomposition [29]. For efficiency of the scheme, the mapping used has to provide a uniform distribution of the load for uncorrelated streams among the participating nodes.

We compare different types of mappings for uniformity on a variety of datasets. We present some preliminary results that we obtained on Standard and Poor 500 index (S&P500) historical stock data [21]. S&P500 Stock Exchange Historical Data consists of data for 500 different stocks. Each stock, x,

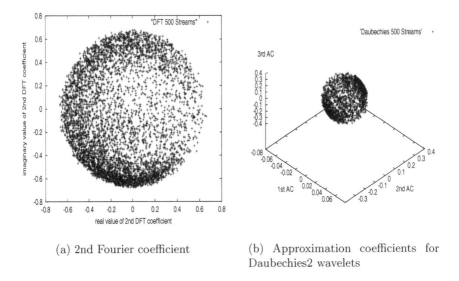

(a) 2nd Fourier coefficient

(b) Approximation coefficients for Daubechies2 wavelets

Fig. 4. Distribution of summaries on Stock Dataset of S&P500

is normalized to have mean, μ_x, 0 and standard deviation, σ_x, 1. Normalization can be done on the fly as new values stream in due to the linearity of transformations used. Figure 4 shows the distribution of summaries computed using (a) 2nd Fourier coefficient (1st Fourier coefficient, μ_x, equals to 0 for all streams) and (b) three Daubechies2 approximation coefficients. As we can see, the mapping exhibits uniformity to some extent, which is an indication of a good balance of resource consumption across data centers and network links.

4.6   Adaptive Methods for Reducing Message Complexity

In our proposed approach, stream summaries are sent to a data center that may be located far away from the stream itself. If every new value generated by the stream caused updated summary information to be sent to a remote data center, this would incur high bandwidth consumption and potentially long lags in query responses. To address this problem, we propose to store ranges of values (i.e., MBRs) instead of precise summaries, similar to the techniques we devised for centralized stream summarization as described in Section 3: a summary computed on a stream of data can be viewed as a point $p \in \Re^k$ in a high dimensional space with dimension k. Grouping every c of these feature vectors into an MBR is a data-independent space reduction technique called *fixed boxing scheme* that has been successfully used in spatial access methods. Since subsequent summary values for the same stream exhibit strong locality, the fixed boxing scheme significantly reduces the amount of communication induced by propagation of data

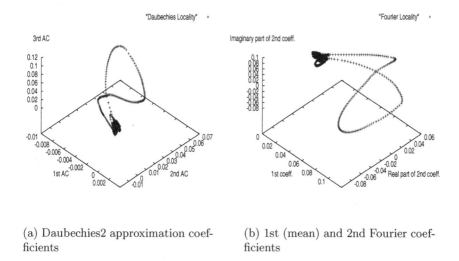

(a) Daubechies2 approximation coefficients

(b) 1st (mean) and 2nd Fourier coefficients

Fig. 5. Locality of summaries computed on Host Load trace data

summaries. We justify this claim on the summaries computed for a Host Load trace [22] as shown in Figure 5.

We consider more intelligent space reduction techniques called *adaptive boxing schemes* that are data-dependent. The approach we propose is to group a set of feature vectors $x_1, x_2, x_3, \ldots, x_i$ into an MBR such that for all j ($2 \leq j \leq i$):

$$x_1[k] - \epsilon \leq x_j[k] \leq x_1[k] + \epsilon \text{ for } 1 \leq k \leq f . \qquad (1)$$

holds for given a sufficiently small ϵ, *adaptivity parameter*. In order to gain better insight about the impact of using various boxing schemes in our distributed architecture, we have conducted experiments with these schemes in the centralized settings. Figure 6 shows the tradeoff between accuracy and space. We observe that accuracy of the indexing improves significantly for smaller values of adaptivity parameter while the space consumption deteriorates as there will be more MBRs produced at fine grain. With this insight, we envision that the size of the MBR affects our decentralized system performance in the following ways:

1. An inner product query may be interested in a precision higher than the one limited by the current MBR dimensions. Such queries need to be propagated to the original data stream source in order to be answered with desired precision, which is an expensive operation. The percentage of such queries increases with the volume of the MBR.
2. The probability of intersection of an MBR with a similarity query sphere increases with the volume of the MBR. This, in turn, increases the false positives rate and results in more messages being communicated.

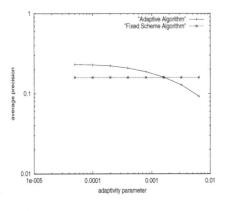
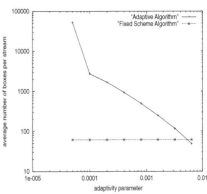

(a) Effect of adaptivity parameter on accuracy

(b) Effect of adaptivity parameter on space usage

Fig. 6. Performance comparison of adaptive boxing scheme with fixed boxing scheme on 100 Synthetic data streams

Additionally, we will adapt the adaptive precision setting technique for caching ranges in the client-server model [31] in order to adjust the low and high boundaries of an MBR along each dimension.

4.7   Variable Selectivity Queries

Similarity queries with varying selectivity may pose a problem in our design. Answers to such queries may contain many streams whose summaries are mapped to and stored at a significant number of data centers that are not even direct neighbors of each other. In order to provide an efficient similarity detection for queries with varying selectivity, we propose the following feature space partitioning scheme:

– Data centers are organized into a hierarchy of clusters, similar to the one used in [5] for application layer multicast. At the bottom level, all data centers are divided into small constant size clusters of neighbor data centers. For each cluster, a leader is chosen to represent the nodes in this cluster. Then, all leaders of the bottom level clusters are divided into the next level clusters by their proximity to each other. This process is repeated until a single leader is chosen for all nodes at the topmost level.

– When a new summary arrives at some data center that belongs to the bottom level cluster C, this data center (in addition to storing the summary locally) forwards it to the leader of C. The leader of C, in its turn, forwards the summary to the leader of the next level cluster, etc. As a result of this technique, the higher we go up the hierarchy of cluster leaders, the larger is the feature space covered at the corresponding data center.

- When a data center receives a similarity query with an interest volume larger than what the center covers, it forwards the query to its bottom level cluster leader. If the feature space covered by the leader is still not large enough, the next level leader is contacted. This process recursively proceeds until we reach the root of the hierarchy.

This scheme induces a hierarchical feature space partitioning where each update to a summary has to be propagated up through the hierarchy of cluster leaders until it reaches the root of the hierarchy. This inefficiency can be eliminated due to the observation that lower cluster centers can act as an information source for higher level clusters and can provide varying levels of consistency as in the case of "summary-to-data center" mapping. A data center that sends a summary to the leader of its cluster in the hierarchy can increase the size of the approximation MBR. This scheme ensures that nodes at the upper levels of the hierarchy need to be updated less frequently at the expense of having less precise information.

4.8   Other Aspects of the Proposed Approach

Additional issues that we currently investigate include adaptively adjusting the mapping function to eliminate hot spots and employing replication of summaries with the purpose of achieving better fault-tolerance and load-balancing:

- **Adaptive adjusting of the mapping function**: While the uniformity of a mapping function is one of our objectives, it ensures an even distribution of summaries across all data centers only if streams are not correlated. However, if many streams are correlated, their summaries will be clustered in the same region resulting in a high load at a small group of data centers. In order to address this issue, we will adjust the mapping function dynamically.
- **Replication for fault-tolerance and load-balancing**: Even if all summaries are distributed uniformly across the data centers, a high load can arise as a result of many queries being interested in some particular data pattern. In this case, we can replicate the summary of high interest on neighbor data centers. We are currently devising a scheme that is based on the existing techniques that provide adaptive caching by considering the current query-to-update ratio [23,36].

5   Concluding Remarks

We are currently developing a middleware prototype that provides support for distributed data stream management as described in Section 4. The objective of the benchmark prototype is to test the performance of our approach by simulating a system with hundreds to tens of thousands of data centers and streams. To achieve this goal, we will use peer-to-peer simulators such as that of Chord [35]. In simulations, we are going to measure the *stress* and *stretch* characteristics: The stretch of a message (a query or summary) is the number of hops it has to traverse from the source to the destination. This characteristic is important for evaluating the response time of a service. The stress of a node or a link is the number of messages that pass through this node or link. This is a load indicator for individual system components.

We will study the communication complexity and response time of the system through an extensive set of experiments on various underlying network types for various workloads (i.e., query types) and datasets in the presence of dynamic changes to the system (i.e, data center joins and failures). We will analyze how each aspect of the system design considered in Section 4, namely adaptive computation of MBR boundaries, construction of a hierarchy of clusters, adaptive adjustment of the mapping function, and replication for load balancing, affects the system performance according to the quality metrics stated earlier.

References

1. A.Arasu, B. Babcock, S. Babu, J. McAlister, and Jennifer Widom. Characterizing memory requirements for queries over continuous data streams. In *PODS*, pages 221–232, 2002.
2. R. Agrawal, C. Faloutsos, and A. Swami. Efficient similarity search in sequence databases. In *FODO*, pages 69–84, 1993.
3. N. Alon, Y. Matias, and M. Szegedy. The space complexity of approximating the frequency moments. In *STOC*, pages 20–29, 1996.
4. B. Babcock, S. Babu, M. Datar, R. Motwani, and J. Widom. Models and issues in data stream systems. In *PODS*, pages 1–16, 2002.
5. Suman Banerjee, Bobby Bhattacharjee, and Christopher Kommareddy. Scalable Application Layer Multicast. In *SIGCOMM*, August 2002.
6. N. Beckmann, H. P. Kriegel, R. Schneider, and B. Seeger. The R*-tree: An efficient and robust access method for points and rectangles. In *SIGMOD*, pages 322–331, 1990.
7. S. Berchtold, D. A. Keim, and H-P. Kriegel. The X-tree: An index structure for high-dimensional data. In *VLDB*, pages 28–39, 1996.
8. A. Bulut and A. K. Singh. SWAT: Hierarchical stream summarization in large networks. In *ICDE*, pages 303–314, 2003.
9. J. Chen, D. J. DeWitt, F. Tian, and Y. Wang. NiagaraCQ: a scalable continuous query system for Internet databases. In *SIGMOD*, pages 379–390, 2000.
10. G. Cormode, M. Datar, P. Indyk, and S. Muthukrishnan. Comparing data streams using hamming norms (how to zero in). In *VLDB*, pages 335–345, 2002.
11. C. Cortes, K. Fisher, D. Pregibon, and A. Rogers. Hancock: A language for extracting signatures from data streams. In *KDD*, pages 9–17, 2000.
12. M. Datar, A. Gionis, P. Indyk, and R. Motwani. Maintaining stream statistics over sliding windows. In *ACM SODA*, pages 635–644, 2002.
13. A. Deshpande, S. Nath, P. B. Gibbons, and S. Seshan. Cache-and-query for wide area sensor databases. In *SIGMOD*, pages 503–514, 2003.
14. A. Dobra, M. Garofalakis, J. Gehrke, and R. Rastogi. Processing complex aggregate queries over data streams. In *ACM-SIGMOD*, pages 61–72, 2002.
15. C. Faloutsos, M. Ranganathan, and Y. Manolopoulos. Fast subsequence matching in time-series databases. In *ACM-SIGMOD*, pages 419–429, 1994.
16. J. Gehrke, F. Korn, and D. Srivastava. On computing correlated aggregates over continual data streams. In *ACM-SIGMOD*, pages 13–24, 2001.

17. A. C. Gilbert, Y. Kotidis, S. Muthukrishnan, and M. Strauss. Surfing wavelets on streams: One-pass summaries for approximate aggregate queries. In *The VLDB Journal*, pages 79–88, 2001.
18. B. Greenstein, D. Estrin, R. Govindan, S. Ratnasamy, and S. Shenker. DIFS: A Distributed Index for Features in Sensor Networks. In *IEEE SNPA*, May 2003.
19. S. Guha and N. Koudas. Approximating a data stream for querying and estimation: Algorithms and performance evaluation. In *ICDE*, pages 567–576, 2002.
20. I. Gupta, R. van Renesse, and K. P. Birman. Scalable Fault-tolerant Aggregation in Large Process Groups. In *ICDSN*, July 2001.
21. http://kumo.swcp.com/stocks/. S&P500 historical stock exchange data.
22. http://www.cs.nwu.edu/~pdinda/LoadTraces/. CMU host load data.
23. Y. Huang, R. H. Sloan, and O. Wolfson. Divergence caching in client server architectures. In *PDIS*, pages 131–139, 1994.
24. H. V. Jagadish, N. Koudas, S. Muthukrishnan, V. Poosala, K. C. Sevcik, and T. Suel. Optimal histograms with quality guarantees. In *VLDB*, pages 275–286, 1998.
25. T. Kahveci and A. K. Singh. Variable length queries for time series data. In *ICDE*, pages 273–282, 2001.
26. J. Kang, J. F. Naughton, and S. D. Viglas. Evaluating window joins over unbounded streams. In *ICDE*, pages 341–352, 2003.
27. E. Keogh, K. Chakrabarti, S. Mehrotra, and M. Pazzani. Locally adaptive dimensionality reduction for indexing large time series databases. In *ACM SIGMOD*, pages 151 – 162, 2001.
28. S. Madden and M. J. Franklin. Fjording the stream: An architecture for queries over streaming sensor data. In *ICDE*, pages 555–566, 2002.
29. S. Mallat. *A Wavelet Tour of Signal Processing*. Academic Press, 2 edition, 1999.
30. L. O'Callaghan, N. Mishra, A. Meyerson, S. Guha, and R. Motwani. High-performance clustering of streams and large data sets. In *ICDE*, pages 685–694, 2002.
31. C. Olston, J. Widom, and B. T. Loo. Adaptive precision setting for cached approximate values. In *ACM-SIGMOD*, pages 355–366, 2001.
32. S. Ratnasamy, P. Francis, M. Handley, and R. Karp. A Scalable Content-Addressable Network. In *SIGCOMM*, August 2001.
33. S. Ratnasamy, B. Karp, L. Yin, F. Yu, D. Estrin, R. Govindan, and S. Shenker. GHT: A Geographic Hash Table for Data-Centric Storage in SensorNets. In *ACM WSNA*, September 2002.
34. A. Rowstron and P. Druschel. Pastry: Scalable, Distributed Object Location and Routing for Large-Scale Peer-to-Peer Systems. In *IFIP/ACM Middleware*, November 2001.
35. I. Stoica, R. Morris, D. Karger, M. Kaashoek, and H. Balakrishnan. Chord: A Scalable Peer-to-Peer Lookup Service for Internet Applications. In *ACM SIGCOMM*, August 2001.
36. O. Wolfson, S. Jajodia, and Y. Huang. An adaptive data replication algorithm. *ACM Transactions on Database Systems*, 22(2):255–314, 1997.
37. Y. Wu, D. Agrawal, and A. E. Abbadi. A comparison of DFT and DWT based similarity search in time-series databases. In *CIKM*, pages 488–495, 2000.
38. B. Zhao, J. Kubiatowicz, and A. Joseph. Tapestry: An Infrastructure for Fault-Resilient Wide-Area Location and Routing. Technical Report UCB/CSD-01-1141, U. C. Berkeley, 2001.
39. Y. Zhu and D. Shasha. Statstream: Statistical monitoring of thousands of data streams in real time. In *VLDB*, pages 358–369, 2002.

Building Content-Based Publish/Subscribe Systems with Distributed Hash Tables

David Tam, Reza Azimi, and Hans-Arno Jacobsen

Department of Electrical and Computer Engineering,
University of Toronto, Toronto ON M5S 3G4, Canada
{tamda, azimi, jacobsen}@eecg.toronto.edu

Abstract. Building distributed content–based publish/subscribe systems has remained a challenge. Existing solutions typically use a relatively small set of trusted computers as brokers, which may lead to scalability concerns for large Internet–scale workloads. Moreover, since each broker maintains state for a large number of users, it may be difficult to tolerate faults at each broker. In this paper we propose an approach to building content–based publish/subscribe systems on top of distributed hash table (DHT) systems. DHT systems have been effectively used for scalable and fault–tolerant resource lookup in large peer–to–peer networks. Our approach provides predicate–based query semantics and supports constrained range queries. Experimental evaluation shows that our approach is scalable to thousands of brokers, although proper tuning is required.

1 Introduction

Publish/subscribe systems are becoming increasingly popular in building large distributed information systems. In such systems, subscribers specify their interests to the system using a set of subscriptions. Publishers submit new information into the system using a set of publications. Upon receiving a publication, the system searches for matching subscriptions and notifies the interested subscribers. Unlike the client/server model, the publish/subscribe model decouples time, space, and flow between publishers and subscribers, which may lead to benefits such as reduced program complexity and resource consumption.

There are at least two major classes of publish/subscribe systems: (i) topic–based and (ii) content–based. In topic–based systems, subscribers join a group containing a topic of interest. Publications that belong to the topic are broadcasted to all members of the group. Therefore, publishers and subscribers must explicitly specify the group they wish to join. Topic–based systems are similar to the earlier group communication and event–notification systems (e.g. in newsgroups).

In content–based publish/subscribe systems, the matching of subscriptions and publications is based on content and no prior knowledge is needed (e.g. the set of available topics). Therefore, these systems are more flexible and useful since subscribers can specify their interests more accurately using a set of predicates.

K. Aberer et al. (Eds.): VLDB 2003 Ws DBISP2P, LNCS 2944, pp. 138–152, 2004.

The main challenge in building such systems is to develop an efficient matching algorithm that scales to millions of publications and subscriptions.

Publish/subscribe systems can be implemented centrally or in a distributed manner. Centralized systems have the advantage of retaining a global image of the system at all times, enabling intelligent optimizations during the matching process. Examples of intelligent matching algorithms can be found in [1], [2], [3], [4], and [5]. Major disadvantages of centralized systems are the lack of scalability and fault–tolerance. Distributed publish/subscribe systems have been introduced to address these problems [6] [7]. However, the main difficulty in building distributed content–based systems is the design of an efficient distributed matching algorithm. Existing distributed content–based systems such as [6] typically rely on a small number of trusted brokers that are inter–connected using a high–bandwidth network. In some scenarios, such configurations may not offer adequate scalability. As well, they do not provide a satisfactory level of fault–tolerance since crashing a single broker may result in a large number of state transfer operations during recovery.

Recently, distributed hash tables (DHTs) [8] [9] [10] [11] have emerged as an infrastructure for efficient, scalable resource lookup in large peer–to–peer distributed networks. Such systems are decentralized, scalable, and self–organizing (i.e. often as well, they automatically adapt to the arrival, departure and failure of nodes in the network). Such characteristics make DHTs attractive for building distributed applications. In fact, DHTs have successfully been used in several application domains, such as distributed file systems [12] [13] [14] [15]. It has also been shown that topic–based publish/subscribe systems can be built on top of DHTs [16]. Although there have been several attempts in building content–based publish/subscribe systems on top of peer–to–peer systems [17] [18], there remains much to be explored. Compared to our system, the systems described in [17] and [18] exploit the underlying DHT infrastructure to different degrees.

In this paper, we present a simple approach to building a distributed content–based publish/subscribe system on top of a DHT. More specifically, we use a topic–based system (Scribe) [16] that is implemented using a DHT (Pastry) [10]. In our approach, topics are automatically detected from the content of subscriptions and publications through the use of a *schema*, which is a set of guidelines for selecting topics. The schema is application–specific and can be provided by the application designer after some statistical analysis. Schemas are similar to database schemas used in RDBMS. With this approach we can significantly increase the expressiveness of subscriptions compared to purely topic–based systems. However, our scheme does not fully provide the query semantics of a traditional content–based system. Queries are not completely free–form but must adhere to a predefined template. Moreover, issues of fault–tolerance in subscription storage have yet to be explored in our system, although fault–tolerance in DHT routing and multicast routing can be transparently handled by Pastry and Scribe, respectively. We implement our scheme on top of the existing DHT simulator included in Pastry.[1] Our evaluation shows that with a carefully designed schema, it is possible to achieve accurate, efficient and scalable matching.

The remainder of the paper is organized as follows. In Section 2, we review related work, including a brief overview of DHT systems. In Sections 3 and 4, we describe the key features of our design. In Section 5, the experimental platform and our results are presented and discussed. In Section 6, we conclude and suggest directions for future work.

2   Related Work

In a typical DHT system, each node has a unique identifier (*nodeId*). Also, each message can be associated with a *key* of the same type as the nodeIds. Keys and nodeIds are typically uniformly distributed. Given a message and its corresponding key, a DHT system routes the message to the node whose nodeId is numerically closest to the message key (*home node*). Given a uniform distribution of the nodeIds and keys, the routing task is evenly distributed among the nodes of the network. The message routing algorithm works based on the key and nodeId digits (in any base). Therefore, routing usually requires $O(logN)$ hops, where N is the total number of nodes in the network. In order to tolerate node failures or network disconnections, several methods are used to replicate messages to a set of neighboring nodes of the home node. Also, in order to increase locality, a proximity metric may be defined to reflect the latency and bandwidth of the connection between any pair of nodes. Such a proximity metric along with keys are used in finding the optimal route between nodes.

Scribe [16] is a topic–based publish/subscribe system (a.k.a. a multicast infrastructure) that is built on top of Pastry [10], a DHT system developed at Rice University. Subscribers join topics of interest, where each topic is identified with a Pastry–level key. Therefore, for each topic there is a Pastry node whose nodeId is numerically closest to the topic key (topic root). Publications are submitted to the corresponding topics. Each publication is then multicasted to all subscribers of the topic. Scribe is a simple, well–structured topic–based system. However, it does not support content–based subscriptions and publications.

SIENA [6] is a distributed content–based event notification system which can be used to implement a publish/subscribe system. Routing is performed in the overlay network based on the content of messages. However, SIENA is not based on a DHT networking substrate. Therefore, it cannot take advantage of the inherent scalability and fault–tolerance of such an infrastructure.

In content–based publish/subscribe systems, the handling of range queries is an important capability to possess. It allows for higher expressiveness and a more elegant interface to the system. A number of projects, as described below, have attempted to address this issue in peer–to–peer systems.

Extensions to CAN [9] have been proposed and evaluated in [19] to enable range queries. The DHT hash function is modified to use a Hilbert space filling

---

[1] We used FreePastry, which is an open–source implementation of Pastry.

curve to map an attribute value to a location in the CAN key space. This curve enables proximity in the attribute value space to correspond to proximity in the key space. With such a configuration, routing and searching in the key space corresponds to routing and searching in the attribute value space. While the work addresses range queries of a single attribute, extending the technique to handle range queries of multiple attributes has yet to be addressed. It is not clear whether handling multiple attributes can be accomplished by simply applying the technique multiple times. As explained by Andrzejak et al., the extension of this technique to handle multiple attributes in a single enhanced DHT system is an interesting problem and remains to be completed.

SkipNet [20] offers an alternative and complimentary technology to DHTs. Using a distributed form of the skip lists data structure, SkipNet is able to control both routing and data placement in an overlay network. Harvey et al. briefly suggest that the use of skip lists enables SkipNet to inherit the ability to perform range queries in an efficient and flexible manner. The implementation and evaluation of range queries in SkipNet has yet to be reported. P–Grid [21] is yet another alternative to DHTs, which uses a distributed binary tree rather than a hash table.

Finally, in [22] Gupta et al. develop a peer–to–peer data sharing architecture for providing approximate answers to range queries by finding similar ranges. They use a locality–sensitive hashing scheme to co–locate similar ranges. Although the contribution of the work is important in providing DBMS–like query processing in peer–to–peer systems, for practical content–based publish/subscribe the hash function error rate of this approach may become too high. In [23], Sahin et al. extend CAN to approximately process basic range queries as well.

3   Design

Our approach bridges the gap between topic–based and content–based systems by automatically organizing the content into several topics. For each publication and subscription we build a set of topics for submission to a topic–based system. Automatically building such topics requires that the content provided by the user application follows certain rules and constraints. We call such rules and constraints the *schema*. Each application domain may have a different schema, and the system is capable of handling multiple domain schemas simultaneously.

3.1   Domain Schema

For each application domain, we define a schema to describe the general format of subscriptions and publications that belong to the domain. The idea of a domain schema is similar to a DBMS–style schema. The purpose of using a domain schema is to limit the number of possible combinations of messages that must be generated and sent out in the DHT system. This technique enables us to feasibly transform a topic–based publish/subscribe system into a content–based

Table 1. An example of a schema table for "COMPUTERS" with three indices. The first index is useful to subscribers concerned mainly with price and visible quality. The second index is useful to subscribers concerned mainly with processing power. The third index is useful to subscribers concerned mainly with storage capacity combined with processing power

Order	Type/Unit	Name	Values	Index 1	Index 2	Index 3
1	USD	Price	1000 .. 5000	√		
2	String	CPU	PII, PIII, P4, Celeron		√	√
3	MHz	Clock	200 .. 3000		√	
4	Mbyte	RAM	64 .. 1024		√	
5	Gbyte	HDD	10.. 200			√
6	Inch	Monitor	14 .. 20	√		
7	String	CD	CDROM, CDRW, DVD			√
8	String	Quality	New, Used, Demo	√		

system. The schema must be broadcasted to all nodes that are running relevant applications prior to the operation of such applications. Each domain is identified with a unique ID (name) so that the system can handle multiple application domains simultaneously. For instance, the publish/subscribe system may be used by a stock market and an auction network simultaneously.

Each schema consists of several tables, each with a standard name. For each table, we maintain information about a set of attributes, including their type, name, and constraints on possible values. We assume the table attributes are ordered. Also for each table, there is a set of *indices* that are used for the actual lookup in the network. Each index is an ordered collection of strategically selected attributes. Selecting the optimal set of attributes for indices is essential to achieving acceptable performance. Similar to indices in database systems, it is imperative to choose attributes that are more of a user's concern, and hence, more likely to be used by the users for lookup. Table 1 shows a simple example of a schema table. It contains three indices corresponding to users with various interests. Currently, we require application designers to intelligently specify domain schemas manually. Designers could be assisted by profiles from a centralized content–based system to identify important attributes and their values.

3.2 Basic System Operation

When a request (publication or subscription) is submitted to the system, it is inspected to extract several *index digests*. Each index digest is a string of characters that is formed by concatenating the attribute type, name, and value of each attribute in the index. For the example schema in Table 1, some possible topic digests would be [*USD: Price: 1000: Inch: Monitor: 19: String: Quality: Used*] and [*String: CPU: PIII: MHz: Clock: 650: Mbyte: RAM: 512*]. In the simple case, we assume that subscribers provide exact values for each attribute. Handling range queries is discussed in Section 3.5. The use of schemas is a key technique in significantly reducing the number of topic digests and corresponding messages. Without a schema, the above technique would require a digest for every possible combination of predicates in every subscription. The maximum number of such digests would be 2^N, where N is the number of predicates in the subscription. Such requirements would generate an extremely large number of messages and render the system infeasible.

A given subscription can be submitted to the system only if it specifies all attribute values for at least one of the indices in the corresponding schema table. In such a case, the composed index digest is translated to a DHT *hash key*. The subscription is then sent to the key's home node by the DHT system.[2] When a publication with attribute values that match the subscription is submitted to the system, the same hash key is generated and therefore the publication is delivered to the same node in the network. Such a matching is partial since only a subset of the subscription predicates are matched in this way. The key's home node is responsible for completing the matching process by comparing the publication with all submitted subscriptions to the node. A standard centralized matching algorithm can be used in the home node for this purpose. Nodes with subscriptions that completely match the publication are notified by the hash key home node.

3.3   Event Notification Multicast Tree

A problem with the basic scheme is that home nodes may become overloaded with the task of processing publications and subscriptions. An improvement to the scheme is to build a multicast tree structure to enable better distribution of these tasks. A multicast tree can be constructed for all nodes that have subscribed to a certain hash key. The *root* of the tree is the hash key's home node, and its branches are formed along the routes from the subscriber nodes to the root. Similar to the root node, the internal nodes in the tree may or may not have subscribed to the index key.

The Scribe multicast tree infrastructure is exploited by our system to achieve scalable performance. To implement efficient multicasting, Scribe builds a multicast tree rooted at each topic root node as follows. When a subscription finds its route to the topic root, all intermediate nodes along the route are added to the multicast notification tree unless they already belong to it. Under this particular scenario, routing stops upon encountering the edge of the corresponding multicast tree. This optimization enables the subscription operation to be efficient and completely distributed. The multicast tree structure significantly reduces the total number of messages generated by subscribers by allowing subscriptions to be submitted to lower levels of the tree, obviating the need to traverse the entire route to the root node. Moreover, the lower level nodes absorb most of the work targeted at the root node and therefore prevent the root node from being a bottleneck in the matching process.

---

[2] The home node itself may or may not have subscribed to this hash key.

For multicasting, the publication is first sent to the topic root, from which the publication is sent all the way down the multicast tree. Such an infrastructure can significantly reduce (i) the number of messages generated by publishers and (ii) notification latency. Event notification is accomplished in $O(logN)$ time, where N is the number of nodes. Further details about the Scribe multicast infrastructure can be found in [16]. In Section 3.4 and Section 3.5 we describe how the Scribe multicast tree is exploited to improve the basic matching scheme.

3.4   Handling False Positives

Since the predicates of a subscription may be used in several indices, some of the publications that are sent to an index home node may not match all predicates of a subscription. In fact, they match only the subset of subscription predicates that were specified in the index. We use the term *miss* to refer to a received publication that partially matches a submitted subscription but does not fully match it. We use the term *hit* to refer to a received publication that fully matches a submitted subscription. To filter out the misses, exact matching is performed at the receiver node by using conventional matching algorithms. Since subscriptions and publications are uniformly distributed in the network, such a matching process occurs in a distributed manner and therefore scales well with the number of publications. Moreover, the use of multicast trees for event notification allows for further distribution of the matching process among the nodes of the multicast tree rather than concentrating it solely on the root node. For index values that are frequently used, the multicast tree grows proportionately to the number of users that use the index value, and therefore the matching load is automatically balanced. The impact of false positives is examined in our experiments and is illustrated by a variety of *hit rate* curves (see Fig. 1 and Fig. 2).

3.5   Range Queries and Disjunctive Forms

A potential complexity in content–based subscriptions is that the constraint on some attributes may be specified as a range rather than an exact value. A naive approach in handling such queries is to build hash keys only for indices that do not include range predicates. The disadvantage of this approach is two–fold. First, for some subscriptions, range predicates may be present in all possible indices so that no indices can be used for submission. This solution suggests dropping such subscriptions and hence, results in a less practical system. Second, this solution limits the index selection policy, and therefore might result in less accurate partial matching.

   Another method of handling range predicates is to build a separate index hash key for every attribute value in the specified range. This solution is only adequate for attributes whose value domains are not large. For instance, in Table 1 there may be a handful of possible values for the *Monitor* attribute. However, for other attributes such as *Price*, a value range might include thousands of possible values.

Our solution for these types of attributes is to divide the range of values into intervals and use interval indicators as values for building hash keys. For instance, for the *RAM* attribute, one may suggest that there are four possible intervals: *less than 128*, *128–256*, *256–512*, and *greater than 512*. Therefore, the predicate $RAM > 384\,Mbyte$ would belong to two keys: $RAM = 256\text{--}512$ and $RAM = greater\ than\ 512$. Of course, the matching that occurs with this scheme is partial, and the actual complete matching must be performed at one of the nodes in the multicast tree. Given a probability distribution function for an attribute, it is possible to improve the division of value intervals by choosing interval boundaries so that the collective probability of each interval is equal. This means that for value subranges that are queried frequently, the intervals are finer–grained. For instance in Table 1, the density of values for the *Clock* attribute may be higher near main–stream processors frequencies (2.0 GHz – 2.5 GHz) than those of older processors (less than 1.0 GHz) or high performance processors (greater than 2.5 GHz).

By having a handful of values for each attribute, we may be able to confine the total number of hash keys for a subscription to the order of tens. As we will show in Section 5.4, it is possible to maintain acceptable performance with this solution since the cost of a subscription in a multicast tree–based system is relatively low.

Similar to range queries, disjunctive form subscriptions may be treated as a set of separate conjunctive subscriptions, where hash keys are generated for each separate subscription.

3.6   Duplicate Notifications

Another problem with the basic scheme is that it is possible that a publication is sent several times to a single subscriber if the subscriber has used several indices. One solution to this problem is for the subscriber to maintain a list of publications it has seen (given that each publication has a unique identifier), and discard duplicate publication messages. Such a list may be relatively small, since the average propagation time for a publication is small. Therefore, it is expected that publication duplicates are received by the subscriber within a relatively short interval. Thus, the subscriber may be able to set a short deadline for each publication and purge its copy from the list after the deadline.

A better solution is to prevent a subscriber from submitting more than one index digest, rather than to allow it to submit an index digest for every applicable index. In this case, the subscriber must submit the index digest corresponding to the index that is the most important. This solution would only work if publications specify values for all attributes, which we believe will be the common case since publishers are information sources. If a publication does not specify a value for an attribute in an index, the publication would be missed by subscribers that used only that index. In our experiments, publishers specify values for all attributes.

4 Implementation

We have implemented our approach on top of Scribe/Pastry. Our choice of plat-form was not fundamental to our design and we could have built our system on top of any DHT system. We found it advantageous to exploit the multicast tree infrastructure of Scribe, although it could have been manually implemented if it did not exist. The Scribe/Pastry platform is implemented in Java. It simulates a network of nodes with arbitrary size. Networks are associated with a prox-imity metric to improve locality. However, such optimizations are transparent to our system. The platform allows us to bind a Java object to each node as the *application*. The object must implement an interface that provides at least two functions: *receiveHandler()* and *forwardHandler()*. The former is called by the Pastry system when a message is delivered to a node, whereas the latter is called when a node is located along a route and is forwarding a message to some other node. With this programmability, we have been able to embed the func-tionality of a content–based publish/subscribe system in the application object. Moreover, we instrumented the calls to these methods to collect statistics and understand the behavior of the system.

5 Evaluation

As a preliminary DHT content–based publish/subscribe system, the main per-formance goal is scalability. We want to ensure that as the size of the system grows, performance remains relatively reasonable. In this section, we evaluate the feasibility of the system.

The metric we used was the number of messages exchanged in the system. This metric is a reasonable, first–order measurement of the system. Since dis-tributed systems deal with communication and computation of physically sepa-rate nodes, measuring traffic characteristics is important. Detailed metrics con-cerning communication characteristics, such as latency and bandwidth consump-tion have yet to be gathered. This area is a subject of future work.

Measuring the number of messages offers a first–order evaluation of the sys-tem performance. Therefore, we examine the impact of changes in various system parameters on the number of messages. Such parameters include the number of publications and subscriptions, the number of nodes in the system, and the number of range predicates in a subscription.

5.1 Experimental Setup

Pastry/Scribe includes a network simulator, enabling us to simulate 1000s of nodes within one physical computer. We used the ToPSS [2] workload generator to generate synthetic workloads.

The workload followed the schema table described in Table 2. This schema table defines possible values of the attributes. For instance, *Price* can have a value of {*1, 2, 3, 4, 5*}. Although some of the value ranges seem inappropriate,

Table 2. Workload schema table

Order	Type	Name	Values	Index 1	Index 2	Index 3	Index 4
1	Integer	Price	1 to 5	√	√	√	√
2	Integer	Volume	1 to 5	√	√	√	√
3	Integer	Color	1 to 5	√	√	√	√
4	Integer	Size	1 to 5	√	√	√	
5	Integer	Temperature	1 to 2	√	√		
6	Integer	Circumference	1 to 2	√			

we used them for simplicity. In reality, the DHT is not concerned with whether the possible values of *Color* are {*red, green, blue, cyan, magenta*} or whether the possible values are {*1, 2, 3, 4, 5*}. These values are used as input into a hash function that generates a fixed–size key. For any particular attribute, integer values are randomly generated by the workload generator with a uniform distribution within the specified range. For this particular workload, there are $5 \times 5 \times 5 \times 5 \times 2 \times 2 = 2500$ unique hash key values.

We recognize that this workload does not necessarily represent a real–world application. However, it provides a simple example of what a fairly typical subscription or publication may look like. Results produced by this workload can be easily understood and analyzed. Moreover, it is difficult to find a real–world content–based publish/subscribe system from which we could obtain workload traces.

Although the chosen schema size in Table 2 is small, an examination of Table 1 may help predict the impact of schema growth. For example, if the number of attributes in Table 1 were to increase dramatically, we would expect only a moderate increase in the number of indices in the application domain. This pattern appears plausible due to the inherent nature of indices. Since an index is formed for a set of commonly used attributes, the number of indices is largely independent of the number of attributes available. Therefore, schema size should have limited impact on performance.

As for the size of value ranges (the number of intervals for a given attribute), this parameter may also have a limited impact on performance. A more important characteristic is the distribution of range queries across the intervals. For example, in a particular application domain, range queries on a particular attribute may often intersect only two intervals, regardless of the number of available intervals. In this case, only two corresponding hash keys are submitted. Our experiments can be viewed as examining the performance impact of up to five intervals of intersection.

5.2   Event Scalability

Figure 1 shows the scalability of the system in terms of the number of events. That is, the impact of the number of subscriptions and publications on the number of messages exchanged. The number of nodes was fixed at 1000 nodes. On the x–axis of the graph, 10000 subscriptions and publications refers to 10000 random subscriptions followed by 10000 random publications.[3] We used an equal number of subscriptions and publications for simplicity. We also show how various hit rates affected the number of messages generated. Hit rate is the proportion of delivered publications that fully match the subscriptions maintained by a node.

To enforce a 100 % hit rate, the schema index consisted of all attributes in Table 2 (Index 1). To enforce other hit rates, we exploit the fact that the workload generator randomly chooses attribute values in a uniformly distributed manner. To attain the 50 % hit rate, the schema index consisted of the first 5 attributes (Index 2). To attain the 25 % hit rate, the schema index consisted of the first 4 attributes (Index 3). Finally, to attain the 5 % hit rate, the schema index consisted of the first 3 attributes (Index 4).

The first observation from Fig. 1 is that message traffic for any particular hit rate grows approximately quadratically with the number of subscriptions and publications. This growth is reasonable since both subscriptions and publications are increased simultaneously.

The second observation is on the incremental impact of the various hit rates shown by the separate curves in the graph. One might expect that a 50 % hit rate means that a node receives twice as many publication messages than were really destined for the node. Similarly, at a 25 % hit rate four times as many publication messages would have been generated compared to the 100 % hit rate configuration. Interestingly, the results showed lower than expected increases.

Our experiments indicated that 72 % of the total messages shown in the y-axis of Fig. 1 were publication messages. This composition is for 40000 subscriptions and publications, with a 100 % hit rate. Therefore, at a hit rate of 50 %, we expected a 72 % increase in total messages but observed only a 46 % increase. At a 25 % hit rate, we expected an increase of $(72 + 72 + 72) = 216\%$ in total messages but observed only a 123 % increase.

These lower than expected increases were due to the use of multicast notification trees. When publication notifications are triggered, only a few additional messages are needed to reach an additional subscribing node. This phenomenon leads to the smaller observed increase in message traffic between the various hit rate curves.

A low hit rate, such as the 5 % curve, shows relatively steep traffic increase compared to higher hit rates, such as 25 %, 50 %, or 100 %. These results suggest that it is important to have a well–designed schema such that the indices used incur hit rates greater than 25 %. Other complementary techniques, such as subscription summaries [7], may be applicable in reducing message size.

In our current implementation, exact matching of publications to subscriptions is done at the leaves of the multicast notification trees. The results in Fig. 1 could be further improved by implementing exact matching higher up in the multicast tree. However, such reductions in message traffic must be carefully balanced against increased processor load on the nodes performing the exact

---

[3] There is no correlation between subscriptions and publications. That is, there is no guarantee that every subscription will be matched by at least one publication.

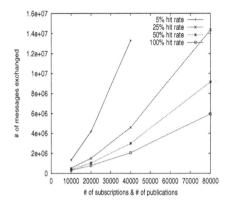

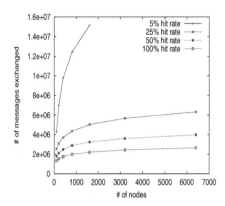

Fig. 1. Scalability in the number of events. 1000 nodes

Fig. 2. Scalability in the number of nodes. 40000 subscriptions, 40000 publications

matching. In summary, there is a trade–off between message traffic and node processor workload.

5.3   Node Scalability

Figure 2 shows the scalability of the system in terms of the number of nodes. The system used a fixed number of events consisting of 40000 random subscriptions followed by 40000 random publications. The value 40000 was arbitrarily chosen since it represented a middle point in the range of values used in Fig. 1. The results show that the system scales well for most hit rates (except for perhaps the 5 % hit rate). Again, these results further suggest that is it important to have a well–designed schema such that the indices used incur hit rates greater than 25 %.

5.4   Impact of Range Queries

Figure 3 shows the impact of range queries. In order to isolate this impact, we use Index 1 (Table 2). The "0 range" curve represents a workload without any range queries. For the "1 range" curve, the first attribute (*Price*) is allowed to specify a range. It may have specifications such as $Price = x$, or $Price < y$, or $Price > z$. The choice among $\{<,=,>\}$ is chosen randomly using a uniform distribution. All other attributes specify exact values. Similarly, for the "2 range" curve, the first and second attributes (*Price* and *Volume*) are allowed to specify ranges.

These results suggest that range queries have a moderate and acceptable impact on the system. In the "1 range" curve, the *Price* attribute has 5 possible values. For each range query, an average of 3 index digests are submitted, given a uniformly random distribution. The selection of the *operator* $\{<,=,>\}$ is also

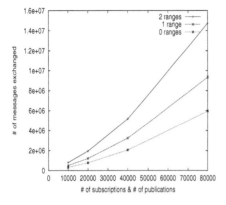
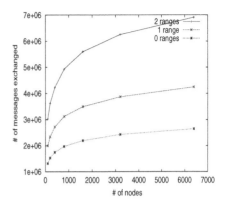

Fig. 3. Impact of range queries. 1000 nodes

Fig. 4. Scalability in the number of nodes with range queries. 40000 subscriptions, 40000 publications

uniformly distributed. Given that $P(o)$ is the probability of a particular operator o, and $E(o)$ is the expected number of index digest submissions for that operator, then the expected number of index digest submissions per subscription is

$$
\begin{aligned}
E(s) &= P(<)E(<) + P(=)E(=) + P(>)E(>) \\
E(s) &= \tfrac{1}{3} \times 3 \quad + \quad \tfrac{1}{3} \times 1 \quad + \quad \tfrac{1}{3} \times 3 \\
E(s) &= \quad 2.33 \ .
\end{aligned}
\tag{1}
$$

Similarly, we expected publications to require 2.33 times as many messages since there are roughly 2.33 times as many interested subscribers. Due to these expected increases in both the subscription and publication components, we therefore expected 2.33 times as many total messages as the "0 range" curve. In contrast, the results show only 1.6 times as many messages (at 40000 subscriptions and publications). Similarly for the "2 range" curve, we expected 5.43 times as many messages as the "0 range" curve. In contrast, the results show only 2.5 times as many messages. These beneficial results are due to the use of multicast notification trees. Subscriptions are registered efficiently and additional publication notifications incur low incremental costs.

Figure 4 shows the impact of range queries on node scalability. Similar to Section 5.3, the system used a fixed number of events consisting of 40000 random subscriptions followed by 40000 random publications. The results show that the system scales well while supporting range queries.

6   Conclusion and Future Work

We have developed a technique to implement a content–based distributed peer–to–peer DHT–based publish/subscribe system on top of an existing topic–based system. We found that the use of a multicast tree infrastructure was critical to achieving good performance. Our design offers an interesting and unexplored point in the design space of publish/subscribe systems. Our design point exists somewhere between a fully centralized content–based system and a fully distributed topic–based system. As a compromise, our system is a fully distributed, content–based system with some restrictions on the expression of content. The content must follow and fit within a well–defined schema for that particular application domain.

Since this content–based publish/subscribe system is an early prototype, there is plenty of future work to be done. Our next step is to perform a more detailed examination of the benefits of the multicast tree infrastructure. Other tasks include (i) adding more features to enable execution of real–world workloads, (ii) performing detailed modeling of the peer–to–peer network, and (iii) examining fault–tolerance. This paper represents on–going research conducted under the p2p–ToPSS project (peer–to–peer–based Toronto Publish/Subscribe System).

We recognize that an endless number of experiments can be run, with many possible combinations of workload parameters. In particular, using locality–sensitive distributions in the workload generator, rather than a uniform distribution, should produce an interesting set of comparative results. However, to achieve some level of workload validity, guidelines on how these parameters vary in relation to each other need to be researched. We are currently not aware of any well–accepted, standard set of workloads for content–based publish/subscribe systems.

Guidelines for good schema design for an application domain remain an important open research question. Determining the optimal set of indices for a particular application domain may require intimate knowledge of the application domain, such as the typical query behavior of users. Achieving an optimal index may require selecting attributes that are commonly specified but can uniquely identify a subscription.

References

1. Fabret, F., Jacobsen, H.A., Llirbat, F., Pereira, J., Ross, K.A., Shasha, D.: Filtering algorithms and implementation for very fast publish/subscribe systems. ACM SIGMOD Record **30** (2001) 115–126
2. Ashayer, G., Leung, H.K.Y., Jacobsen, H.A.: Predicate matching and subscription matching in publish/subscribe systems. In: Proc. of Workshop on Distributed Event-Based Systems (DEBS), Vienna, Austria (2002) 539–546
3. Petrovic, M., Burcea, I., Jacobsen, H.A.: S-ToPSS: Semantic Toronto publish/subscribe system. In: Proc. of Conf. on Very Large Data Bases, Berlin, Germany (2003) 1101–1104
4. Liu, H., Jacobsen, H.A.: Modeling uncertainties in publish/subscribe. In: Conf. on Data Engineering (to appear). (2004)
5. Burcea, I., Muthusamy, V., Petrovic, M., Jacobsen, H.A., de Lara, E.: Disconnected operations in publish/subscribe. In: IEEE Mobile Data Management (to appear). (2004)

6. Carzaniga, A., Rosenblum, D.S., Wolf, A.L.: Achieving scalability and expressiveness in an Internet-scale event notification service. In: Proc. of ACM Symp. on Principles of Distributed Computing (PODC), Portland, OR (2000) 219–227
7. Triantafillou, P., Economides, A.: Subscription summaries for scalability and efficiency in publish/subscribe. In: Proc. of Workshop on Distributed Event-Based Systems, Vienna, Austria (2002) 619–624
8. Kaashoek, F.: Distributed hash tables: Building large-scale, robust distributed applications. Presentation: ACM Symp. on PODC (2002)
9. Ratnasamy, S., Francis, P., Handley, M., Karp, R., Shenker, S.: A scalable content–addressable network. In: Proc. of ACM SIGCOMM, San Diego, CA (2001) 161–172
10. Rowstron, A., Druschel, P.: Pastry: Scalable, decentralized object location and routing for large-scale peer-to-peer systems. In: Proc. of IFIP/ACM Conf. on Distributed Systems Platforms, Heidelberg, Germany (2001) 329–350
11. Stoica, I., Morris, R., Karger, D., Kaashoek, F., Balakrishnan, H.: Chord: A scalable peer-to-peer lookup service for Internet applications. In: Proc. of ACM SIGCOMM, San Diego, CA (2001) 149–160
12. Adya, A., Bolosky, W.J., Castro, M., Cermak, G., Chaiken, R., Douceur, J.R., Howell, J., Lorch, J.R., Theimer, M., Wattenhofer, R.P.: FARSITE: Federated, available, and reliable storage for an incompletely trusted environment. In: Proc. of USENIX Symp. on Operating Systems Design and Implementation (OSDI), Boston, MA (2002) 1–14
13. Dabek, F., Kaashoek, M.F., Karger, D., Morris, R., Stoica, I.: Wide-area cooperative storage with CFS. In: Proc. of ACM Symp. on Operating Systems Principles (SOSP), Banff, Canada (2001) 202–215
14. Muthitacharoen, A., Morris, R., Gil, T.M., Chen, B.: Ivy: A read/write peer-to-peer file system. In: Proc. of USENIX Symp. on OSDI, Boston, MA (2002) 31–44
15. Rowstron, A., Druschel, P.: Storage management and caching in PAST, a large-scale, persistent peer-to-peer storage utility. In: Proc. of ACM SOSP, Banff, Canada (2001) 188–201
16. Castro, M., Druschel, P., Kermarrec, A.M., Rowstron, A.: SCRIBE: A large-scale and decentralized application-level multicast infrastructure. In: IEEE Journal on Selected Areas in Communication. Volume 20. (2002) 1489–1499
17. Pietzuch, P.R., Bacon, J.: Peer-to-peer overlay broker networks in an event-based middleware. In: Proc. of Workshop on DEBS, San Diego, CA (2003)
18. Terpstra, W.W., Behnel, S., Fiege, L., Zeidler, A., Buchmann, A.P.: A peer-to-peer approach to content-based publish/subscribe. In: Proc. of Workshop on DEBS, San Diego, CA (2003)
19. Andrzejak, A., Xu, Z.: Scalable, efficient range queries for grid information services. In: Proc. of IEEE Conf. on Peer-to-Peer Computing, Linköping, Sweden (2002) 33–40
20. Harvey, N.J.A., Jones, M.B., Saroiu, S., Theimer, M., Wolman, A.: SkipNet: A scalable overlay network with practical locality properties. In: Proc. of USENIX Symp. on Internet Technologies and Systems, Seattle, WA (2003)
21. Aberer, K., Hauswirth, M., Punceva, M., Schmidt, R.: Improving data access in P2P systems. IEEE Internet Computing 6 (2002) 58–67
22. Gupta, A., Agrawal, D., El Abbadi, A.: Approximate range selection queries in peer-to-peer systems. In: Proc. of Conf. on Innovative Data Systems Research, Asilomar, CA (2003)
23. Sahin, O.D., Gupta, A., Agrawal, D., El Abbadi, A.: Query processing over peer–to–peer data sharing systems. Technical Report UCSB/CSD-2002-28, University of California at Santa Barbara, Department of Computer Science (2002)

AmbientDB: Relational Query Processing in a P2P Network

Peter Boncz and Caspar Treijtel

CWI, Kruislaan 413, 1098 SJ Amsterdam, The Netherlands
{P.Boncz,C.Treijtel}@cwi.nl

Abstract. A new generation of applications running on a network of nodes, that share data on an ad-hoc basis, will benefit from data management services including powerful querying facilities. In this paper, we introduce the goals, assumptions and architecture of AmbientDB, a new peer-to-peer (P2P) DBMS prototype developed at CWI. Our focus is on the query processing facilities of AmbientDB, that are based on a three-level translation of a global query algebra into multi-wave stream processing plans, distributed over an ad-hoc P2P network. We illustrate the usefulness of our system by outlining how it eases construction of a music player that generates intelligent playlists with collaborative filtering over distributed music logs. Finally, we show how the use of Distributed Hash Tables (DHT) at the basis of AmbientDB allows applications like the P2P music player to scale to large amounts of nodes.

1 Introduction

Ambient Intelligence (AmI) refers to digital environments in which multimedia services are sensitive to people's needs, personalized to their requirements, anticipatory of their behavior and responsive to their presence. The AmI vision is being promoted by the MIT Oxygen initiative [14] and is becoming the focal point of much academic and commercial research. The AmbientDB project at CWI is performed in association with Philips, where the target is to address data management needs of ambient intelligent consumer electronics. In prototyping AmbientDB, CWI builds on its experience with DBMS kernel construction obtained in PRISMA [25] and Monet [4].

We believe there is a common set of data management needs of AmI applications, and in the AmbientDB project we investigate new directions in DBMS architecture to address these. Figure 1 illustrates an example scenario, where a hypothetical ambient-intelligence enriched "amP2P" audio player automatically generates good playlists, fitting the tastes, probable interests and moods of the listeners present to the available music content. The amP2P player uses a local AmbientDB P2P DBMS to manage its music collection as well as the associated meta-information (among others how and when the music was played and appreciated).

In the case of the amP2P player in Figure 1, the main idea is to exploit the wealth of knowledge about music preferences contained in the playlist logs

K. Aberer et al. (Eds.): VLDB 2003 Ws DBISP2P, LNCS 2944, pp. 153–168, 2004.

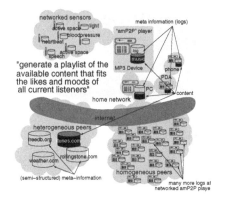

Fig. 1. Music Playlist Scenario

```
create distributed table AMP2P.USER (
    USERID varchar, PROFILE text)
primary key (USERID);

create distributed table AMP2P.SONG (
    SONGID varchar, NAME varchar,
    ARTIST varchar, ALBUM varchar,
    LENGTH integer, FILENAME varchar)
primary key (SONGID);

create partitioned table AMP2P.LOG (
    LOGID integer, SONGID varchar,
    USERID varchar, START daytime,
    DURATION integer)
primary key (LOGID);
```

Fig. 2. Example Music Schema

of the thousands of online amP2P users, united in a global P2P network of AmbientDB instances. The amP2P player could also use AmbientDB to regularly query home sensors, such as active spaces that tell who is listening (in order to select music based on recorded preferences of these persons), and even use speech, gesticulation or mood detectors, to obtain feedback on the appreciation of the currently playing music. Additionally, it could use AmbientDB to query outside information sources on the internet to display additional artist information and links while music is playing, or even to incorporate tracks that can be acquired and streamed in from commercial music sites.

We define the goal for AmbientDB to provide full relational database functionality for standalone operation in autonomous devices, that may be mobile and disconnected for long periods of time. However, we want to enable such devices to cooperate in an ad-hoc way with (many) other AmbientDB devices when these are reachable. This justifies our choice for P2P, as opposed to designs that suppose a central server. We restate our motivation that by providing a coherent toolbox of data management functionalities (e.g. a declarative query language powered by an optimizer and indexing support) we hope to make it easier to create adaptive data-intensive distributed applications, such as envisioned in ambient intelligence.

1.1   Assumptions

Upscaling: We assume the amount of cooperating devices to be potentially large (e.g. in agricultural sensor networks, or our example of on-line amP2P music players). Flexibility is our goal here, as we also want to use AmbientDB in home environments and even as a stand-alone data management solution. Also, we want to be able to cope with ad-hoc P2P connections, where AmbientDB nodes that never met before can still cooperate.

Downscaling: AmbientDB needs to take into account that (mobile) devices often have few resources in terms of CPU, memory, network and battery (devices range from the PC down to smart cards [3] or temperature sensors).

Schema integration: While we recognize that different devices manage different semantics which implies a need for heterogeneous schema re-mapping
support (a.k.a. " model management" [7,18]), in this paper we assume a
situation where all devices operate under a common global schema. As the
functionality of the AmbientDB schema integration component evolves, the
schema operated on by the query processor will increasingly become a virtual
schema that may differ widely from the local schema stored at each node.

Data placement: We assume the user to be in final control of data placement
and replication. This assumption is made because in small mobile devices,
users often prefer to have the final word on how scarce (storage) resources
are used. This is a main distinction with other work on distributed data
structures such as DHTs [22,8] and SDDSs [16], where data placement is
determined solely by the system.

Network failure: P2P networks can be quite dynamic in structure, and any
serious internet-scale P2P system must be highly resilient to node failures.
AmbientDB inherits the resilience characteristics of Chord [8] for keeping
the network connected over long periods of time. When executing a query,
it uses the Chord *finger* table to construct on-the-fly a *routing tree* for query
execution purposes. Such a routing tree only contains those nodes that participate in one user query and thus tends to be limited in size and lifetime.
Our assumption is that while a query runs, the routing tree stays intact (a
node failure thus leads to query failure, but the system stays intact and the
query could be retried).

Since our work touches upon many sub-fields of database research[15,11], we
highlight the main differences. *Distributed database* technology works under the
assumption that the collection of participating sites and communication topology is known a priori. This is not the case in AmbientDB. *Federated database*
technology is the current approach to heterogeneous schema integration, but is
geared towards wrapping and integrating statically configured combinations of
databases. In *mobile database* technology, one generally assumes that the mobile
node is the (weaker) client, that at times synchronizes with some heavy centralized database server over a narrow channel. Again, this assumption does not
hold here. Finally, P2P *file sharing* systems [19,23] do support non-centralized
and ad-hoc topologies. However, the provided functionality does not go beyond
simple keyword text search (as opposed to structured DB queries).

1.2   Example: Collaborative Filtering in a P2P Database

Let us now go back to the problem of intelligently managing and navigating
music, using P2P database technology. We assume that our "amP2P" player has
access to a local content repository that consists of the digital music collection
of the family. This collection – typically in the order of a few thousands of
songs – is distributed among a handful of electronic devices owned by family
members (PC, PDAs, mobile phones, mp3 players). These devices may have
(mobile) access to the internet. The amP2P application would be based on an

instance of AmbientDB running in each of these devices. The devices running AmbientDB form a self-organizing P2P network connecting the nodes for sharing all music content in the "home zone", and a possibly huge P2P network consisting of all amP2P devices reachable via the internet, among which only the meta-information is shared.

Figure 2 shows the schema created by the amP2P application consisting of three tables (USER, SONG, and LOG), that all appear in the global schema "AMP2P" in AmbientDB. Using these structures, the amP2P application registers which users are active on each device, and what music they play. These are *distributed* tables, which means that seen on the global level (over all devices connected in an AmbientDB network) they are formed by the union of all (overlapping) horizontal fragments of these tables stored on each device.

As people choose songs to listen to, they generate entries in their LOG table. The amP2P player exploits the patterns in these logs using collaborative filtering techniques. Our approach can be compared to a memory-based implicit voting scheme [6]. The vote $v_{i,j}$ corresponds to the vote of user i on item j. The predicted vote for the active user for item j is defined as $p_{a,j} = \overline{v}_a + \kappa \sum_{i=1}^{n} w(a,i)(v_{i,j} - \overline{v}_i)$, where $w(a,i)$ is a "weight" function, $\overline{v}_i$ is the average vote for user i and κ is a normalizing factor. We consider fully playing a song as a "vote". For approximating the weight function between the active user and another user, the active user chooses an *example song* as an input for the query. We define our weight function $weight(user_a, user_i)$ to be the times the example song has been *fully* played by user i. Figure 3 shows how this is expressed in a database query: first we compute the listen count for the example song for all users, then we again join this result with the log to compute the weighted vote for all songs, and take the highest 100 songs.

1.3   Overview

In Section 2, we describe the general architecture of AmbientDB. In Section 2.2 we focus on query execution in AmbientDB, outlining its three-level query execution process, where global abstract queries are instantiated as global concrete queries (and rewritten) before being executed as (multi-) "wave" dataflow operator plans over a P2P routing tree. In Section 3 we describe how Distributed Hash Tables (DHTs) fit in AmbientDB as database indices on global tables, and

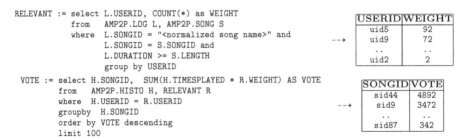

Fig. 3. Collaborative Filtering Query in SQL

show how these can optimize the queries needed by the amP2P music player. After outlining some of the many open challenges and discussing related work, we conclude in Section 4.

2   AmbientDB Architecture

In the following, we describe the major architectural components of AmbientDB. The *Distributed Query Processor* gives applications the ability to execute queries on (a subset of) all ad-hoc connected devices as if it was a query to a central database on the union of all tables held on all selected devices. This is the focus of our paper.

The *P2P Protocol* of AmbientDB uses Chord [8] to connect all nodes in a resilient way, and as the basis for implementing global table indices as Distributed Hash Tables (DHTs). Chord was selected as it provides an elegant, simple yet powerful DHT, with an open-source implementation as well as simulator available. At its core, Chord is a scalable lookup and

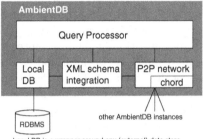

Local DB is a wrapper around any (external) data store.

routing scheme for possibly huge and P2P IP overlay networks made out of unreliable connections. On top of that, the AmbientDB P2P protocol adds functionality for creating temporary (logical) routing trees These routing trees, that are used for routing query streams, are subgraphs of the Chord network. When processing a query, we consider the node that issues the query as root.

The *Local DB* component of AmbientDB node may store its own local tables, either internally in an embedded database, or in some external data source (e.g. RDBMS). In that case, the local DB component acts as a "wrapper" component, commonly used in distributed database systems [15]. The Local DB may or may not implement update and transaction support and its implemented query interface may be as simple as just a sequential scan. However, if more query algebra primitives are supported, this provides query optimization opportunities.

The *Schema Integration Engine* allows AmbientDB nodes to cooperate under a shared global schema even if they store data in different schemas, by using view-based schema mappings [7]. An often forgotten dimension here is providing support for schema evolution within one schema, such that e.g. old devices can be made to work with newer ones. Note that AmbientDB itself does not attack the problem of constructing mappings automatically, but aims at providing the basic functionality for applying, stacking, sharing, evolving and propagating such mappings [18].

2.1   Data Model

AmbientDB provides a standard relational data model and a standard relational algebra as query language (thus it will be easily possible to e.g. create an SQL front-end). The queries that a user poses are formulated against *global* tables. The data in such tables may be stored in many nodes connected in the AmbientDB P2P network. A query may be answered only on the local node, or using data from a limited set of nodes or even against all reachable nodes.

Figure 4 shows that, a global table can be either an Local Table (LT), Distributed Table (DT) or Partitioned Table (PT). Each node has a private schema, in which *Local Tables* (LT) can be defined. Besides that, AmbientDB supports global schemata that contain global tables T, of which all participating nodes N_i in the P2P network carry a table instance T_i. Each local instance T_i may also be accessed as a LT in the query node. A *Distributed Table* (DT) is defined over a set of nodes Q that participate in some global query, as the union of local table instances at all nodes $T_Q = \cup T_i \forall i \in Q$. As we support ad-hoc cooperation of AmbientDB devices that never met before, tuples may be replicated at various nodes without the system knowing this beforehand. The *Partitioned Table* (PT) is a specialization of the distributed table, where all *participating tuples* in each T_i are disjunct between all nodes. One can consider a PT a consistent snapshot view of the abstract table. A Partitioned Table has the advantage over a DT that exact query answers can often be computed in an efficient distributed fashion, by broadcasting a query and letting each node compute a local result without need for communication. Whether a tuple participates in a partitioned table, is efficiently implemented by attaching a bitmap index (i.e. a boolean column) $T_i.Q$ to each local table T_i (see Figure 4). This requires little storage overhead, since adding one extra 64-bit integer column to each tuple suffices to support 64 partitioning schemes. Such partitioning schemes are typically only kept for the duration of a query, such that typically no more than a handful will coexist.

In AmbientDB, data placement is explicit, and we think that users sometimes need to be aware in which node tuples – stored in a DT/PT – are located. Thus, each tuple has a "virtual" column called #NODEID which resolves to the node-identifier (a special built-in AmbientDB type) where the tuple is located. This allows users to introduce location-specific query restrictions (return tuples only from the same node where some other tuples where found), or query tuples only from an explicit set of nodes.

2.2   Query Execution in AmbientDB

Query execution in AmbientDB is performed by a three level translation, that goes from the abstract to the concrete and then the execution level. A user query is posed in the "abstract global algebra," which is shown in Table 1. This is a standard relational algebra, providing the operators for selection, join, aggregation and sort. These operators manipulate standard relational tables, and take parameters that may be (lists of) functional expressions. Lists are denoted List<Type>, list instances <a,b,c>.

Any Table mentioned in the leaves of an abstract query graph, resolves to either a LT, DT, or PT (Figure 4). Thus, when we instantiate the parameters of an abstract relational operators, we get a *concrete* operator invocation. Table 2 shows the concrete operators supported in AmbientDB, where for reasons

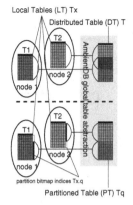

Local Tables (LT) Tx
Distributed Table (DT) T

Partitioned Table (PT) Tq

Fig. 4. LT, DT & PT

Table 1. The Abstract Global Algebra

abstract global algebra
`Select(Table t; Expr cond; List<Expr> result)→Table`
`Aggr(Table t; List<Expr> groupby, result)→Table`
`Join(Table left,right;Expr cond;List<Expr> result)→Table`
`Order(Table t; List<Expr> orderby, result)→Table`
`TopN(Table t; List<Expr> orderby, result; int limit)→Table`

data model
`Column(String name; int type)`
`Key(bool unique; List<Column> columns; Table table)`
`Table(String nme;List<Column> cols;List<Key> prim,forgn)`

expressions
`Expr(int type)`
`Expr::ConstExpr(String printedValue)`
`Expr::ColumnExpr(String columnName)`
`Expr::OperatorExpr(String opName, List<Expr>)`

of presentation, each operator signature is simplified to consist only of the `Table` parameters and a return type. The signatures are shown for all concrete instantiations of the previously defined abstract operators plus two extra operators (partition and union), which are not present on the abstract level.

Starting at the leaves, an abstract query plan is made concrete by instantiating the abstract table types to concrete types. The concrete operators then obtained have concrete result types, and so the process continues to the root of the query graph, which is (usually) required to yield a local result table, hence a LT. Not all combinations of parameter instantiations in abstract operators are directly supported as concrete operators by AmbientDB, thus the AmbientDB query processor must use rewrite-rules to transform an abstract plan into a valid concrete query plan. AmbientDB does support the purely *local* concrete variant of all abstract operators, where all `Tables` instantiate to LTs. In combination with the concrete `union`, which collects all tuples in a DT or PT in the query node into a LT, we see that any abstract plan can trivially be translated into a supported query plan: substitute each DT or PT by a $\texttt{union}_{merge}\texttt{(DT)}$, that creates an LT that contains all tuples in the DT. However, in many cases more efficient alternative query plans will exist. Such plan rewriting should be part of the rewriting done by a query optimizer that looks for an efficient plan.

Each concrete signature roughly corresponds with a particular query execution strategy. Apart from the purely local execution variants, the unary operators `select`, `aggr` and `order` support distributed execution (*dist*), where the operation is executed in all nodes on their local partition (LT) of a PT or DT, producing again a distributed result (PT or DT). On the execution level, this means that the distributed strategy broadcasts the query through the routing tree, after which each node in the tree executes the LT version of the operator on its fragment of the DT. Thus, in distributed execution, the result is again dispersed over all nodes as a PT or DT.

The $\texttt{aggr}_{merge}$ variant is equivalent to $\texttt{aggr}_{local}\texttt{(union}_{merge}\texttt{(DT))}$:LT, but is provided separately, because aggregating sub-results in the nodes ("in network

Table 2. The Concrete Global Algebra

Concrete Global Algebra (T_1, $T_2 \in \{DT, PT\}$)
Union(T_1 t; List<Expr> key, result)→LT # merge DT/PT into a LT
Partition(DT t; List<Expr> key)→PT # identifies duplicates

select$_{local}$(LT)→LT	join$_{local}$(LT,LT)→LT	aggr$_{local}$(LT)→LT
select$_{dist}$(T_1)→T_1	join$_{broadcast}$(LT,T_1)→T_1	aggr$_{merge}$(T_1)→LT
select$_{chord}$(DHT)→LT	join$_{split}$(LT$_1$,T_1)→T_1	aggr$_{dist}$(T_1)→DT
order$_{local}$(LT)→LT	join$_{foreignkey}$(T_1,DT)→T_1	union$_{merge}$(T_1)→LT
order$_{dist}$(T_1)→T_1	topn$_{local}$(LT)→LT	union$_{elim}$(T_1)→LT

Table 3. The Dataflow Algebra

	Local Dataflow Algebra
n	scan(Buffer b)→Dataflow
s	select(Dataflow d; Expr cond; List<Expr> result)→Dataflow
a	aggr(Dataflow d; List<Expr> groupBy,aggr)→Dataflow
o	order(Dataflow d; List<Expr> orderby,result)→Buffer
n	topn(Dataflow d; List<Expr> orderby,result, int n)→Buffer
j	join(Dataflow d_l, d_r; List<Expr> key$_l$,key$_r$,result) # merge-join on dataflows ordered on key
m	merge(Dataflow d_l,d_r; List<Expr> key)→Dataflow # merges key-ordered dataflows, returning tuples in order # adds column $t.\#cnt$: number of consecutive tuples with equal key # and $t.\#nr$: which ascends 0,1, etc.. in each such equal-key chunk
t	split(Dataflow d; List<Buffer><$b_1..b_n$>; List<Expr><$f_1..f_n$>)→Dataflow # returns equal stream and $\forall t \in$d: insert t in $b_i, \forall i : f_i(t) = true$

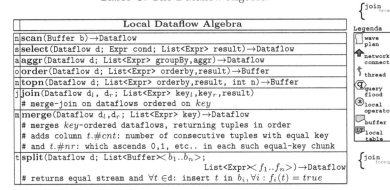

Fig. 5. Mappings

processing") reduces the fragments to be collected in the query node and can save considerable bandwidth [17].

Apart from the purely *local* join, there are three `join` variants. The first is the *broadcast* join, where a LT at the query node is joined against a DT/PT, by broadcasting the LT, and joining it in each node with its local table. Secondly, the *foreignkey* join exploits referential integrity to minimize communication. In AmbientDB, each node is in principle autonomous, which implies that viewed locally, its database should be consistent (have referential integrity). Therefore, join of a local table into a PT or DT over a foreign key, will be able to find all matching tuples locally. Thus, the operator can just broadcast the query and execute such joins locally (much like the *dist* strategy). The third variant is the *split* join (between an LT and DT), which can be used if the join predicate contains a restriction on `#NODEID` (thus specifying which node a tuple should be located). In this case, the LT relation is not broadcasted through the spanning tree, rather it is split when forwarded at each node in a local part (for those tuples where the `#NODEID` resolves to the local node) and in a part for each child in the routing tree. This reduces bandwidth consumption from $O(T * N)$ to $O(T * log(N))$, where T is the amount of tuples in the DT and N is the number of nodes.

The `partition` is a special operator that performs double elimination: it creates a PT from a DT by creating a tuple *participation bitmap* at all nodes. Such an index records whether that tuple in a DT participates in the newly defined PT, at the cost of 1 bit per tuple. In order to be able to use the *dist* operators, we should convert a DT to a PT. Implementation details for partition can be found in [5].

2.3   Dataflow Execution

AmbientDB uses dataflow execution [25] as its query processing paradigm, where a *routing tree* that connects all nodes through TCP/IP connections is used to pass bi-directional tuple streams. Each node receives tuples from its parent, processes them with regards to local data, and propagate (broadcast) data to its children. Also, the other way around, it receives data from its children, merges it (using query operators) with each other as well as with local data and passes the resulting tuples back to the parent. When a query runs, it may cause multiple simultaneous such *waves*, both upward and downward.

The third translation phase for query execution in AmbientDB consists of translating the concrete query plan into *wave-plans*, where each individual concrete operator maps onto one or more waves. Each wave, in turn consists of a graph of *local dataflow algebra operators* (this dataflow algebra is shown in Table 3). In the plans we denote each dataflow operator by a single letter, and we use an arrow going out of a buffer to denote an implicit `scan` operator. Dataflow operators may read multiple tuple streams but always produce one output stream, such that each wave-plan can be executed by one separate thread, that invokes the root a graph of nested *iterators*, where each iterator corresponds with a dataflow algebra operator (i.e. the Volcano iterator model [10]). The leaves of the dataflow query graphs either scan a LT, or read tuples from a neighbor node in the routing tree via a communication *buffer* (we consider a LT also a buffer). Queries that consist of multiple waves pass data from one to the other using buffers that are shared between waves (holding DT/PT fragments produced by a concrete operator that serve as input for the next).

In Figure 5, we show the mapping on wave plans for some concrete algebra operators. These operators typically broadcast their own query request first (depicted by a hexagon). The *dist* plans for `select`, `aggr`, `order` (top), and the foreign-key `join` (bottom) execute a buffer-to-buffer local operator in each node, without further communication. The broadcast `join`, however, propagates a tuple wave through the network, which is shown in the middle of Figure 5. It uses the `split` operator with `true` arguments to pass all tuples to the communication buffers of all children, while the tuple stream (which is already ordered on key) is piped into the merge-join with an LT that has been ordered as a first step. The result is put in a local result buffer in each node, effectively forming a DT/PT. The dataflow algebra operators shown in Table 3 use as algorithms resp. scan-select, quick-sort, merge-join, heap-based top-N and ordered aggregation, which are all stream-based and require little memory (at least no more than the memory used to hold the LTs present). These algorithms were chosen to allow queries to run even on devices with little computational resources.

2.4   Executing the Collaborative Filtering Query

Now we show an example of query execution in AmbientDB using the collaborative filtering query from Figure 3. Its translation into two concrete algebra queries is shown in Figure 6.

The RELEVANT query, that computes the relevance of each user, starts with a distributed select on the example song in the LOG DT. As also illustrated in Figure 8 the query is broadcast, and then in each node that stored the LOG DT, a selection is executed. This local result is streamed into a foreign-key join to the local SONG DT partition, in order to filter out those log records where the song was not played fully. Those result table fragments are then materialized in the $order_{dist}$ on USERID, which is required by the subsequent aggregation. The aggregated values then start to stream back to the query node, passing through a $aggr_{merge}$ in each node that sums all partial results.

```
LT RELEVANT :=
   aggr_merge(DT T4 :=
      aggr_dist(DT T3 :=
         order_dist(DT T2 :=
            join_foreignkey(DT T1 :=
               select_dist(DT L :=
                  AMP2P.LOG,
                  <L.USERID, L.SONGID, L.DURATION>,
                  <L.SONGID == "normalized song name">),
                  DT S := AMP2P.SONG,
                  <T1.DURATION >= S.LENGTH AND
                     T1.SONGID == S.SONGID>, <T1.USERID>),
               <T2.USERID>, <T2.USERID>),
            <T3.USERID>,
            <T3.USERID, TIMESPLAYED := count()>),
         <T4.USERID>,
         <T4.USERID, WEIGHT := sum(T4.TIMESPLAYED)>)

LT VOTE :=
   topn_local(LT T6 :=
      aggr_merge(DT T5 :=
         aggr_dist(DT T4 :=
            join_foreignkey(
               DT S := AMP2P.SONG, DT T3 :=
               order_dist(DT T2 :=
                  join_broadcast(
                     LT R := RELEVANT R, DT T1 :=
                     order_dist(
                        DT L := AMP2P.LOG,
                        <L.USERID>, <L.USERID,L.SONGID>),
                        <R.USERID == T1.USERID>,
                        <T1.SONGID,T1.DURATION, R.WEIGHT>),
                     <T2.SONGID>,
                     <T2.SONGID, T2.DURATION, T2.WEIGHT>),
                  <T3.SONGID == S.SONGID AND
                     T3.DURATION >= S.LENGTH>,
                  <T4.SONGID>,
                  <T4.SONGID, VOTE := sum(T3.WEIGHT)>),
               <T5.SONGID>,
               <T5.SONGID, VOTE := sum(T4.VOTE)>),
            <T6.VOTE>, <T6.SONGID, T5.VOTE>, 100)
```

Fig. 6. Concrete Algebra Example Query

The VOTE query then computes a relevance prediction for each song, by counting the times each user has (fully) listened to it and multiplying this by the just computed user's weight. We broadcast-join RELEVANT with the LOG on all nodes, in order to attach the user's weight to each log-record. As RELEVANT is ordered on USERID, we need to distributively sort LOG before merge-joining it. The resulting DT fragments are again distributively re-ordered on SONGID to allow quick foreign-key join into SONG (to exclude songs that were not played fully). All weights are then summed in an ordered aggregation that exploits the ordered-ness on SONGID, again in a distributed and merged aggregate. We take the top-100 of the resulting LT.

While this may seem already a complex query, we call this the "naive" strategy, as it will have scalability problems both with the number of users/nodes and number of songs. The first query will produce a large list of all users that have ever listened to the example song (not just those who particularly like the song), which will hog resources from all nodes in the network. The second query even takes more effort, as it

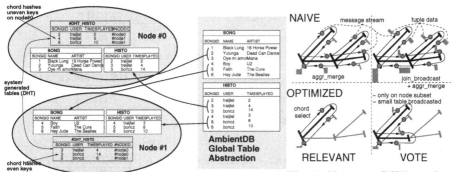

Fig. 7. DT and DHT in AmbientDB

Fig. 8. Naive vs. DHT acceler-
ated Network Bandwidth Usage

will send basically all log records to the query node for aggregation! In the next
section, we will describe how a slightly modified version of this query might be
supported much more efficiently in an AmbientDB enriched with DHTs.

3   DHTs in AmbientDB

Distributed Hash Tables (DHTs) are useful lookup structures for large-scale P2P
applications that want to query data spread out over many nodes, as a DHT
allows to quickly reduce the amount of nodes involved in answering a query with
high recall. In AmbientDB, an entire DT (or a subset of its columns) may be
replicated in a *clustered index*. Our goal here is to enable the query optimizer to
automatically accelerate queries using such DHTs.

We use Chord [8] to implement such clustered indices as DHTs, where each
AmbientDB node contains the index table partition that corresponds to it (i.e.
the key-values of all tuples in the index partition hash to a *finger* that Chord
maps on that node). Invisible to users, DHT indices can be exploited by a query
optimizer to accelerate lookup queries. Getting the benefit of such advanced
P2P structures via AmbientDB and its query language is an example of the
simplification of distributed application engineering we are after (programmers
are currently forced to hardcode such accelerators in their application).

We defined an additional concrete operator select$_{chord}$(DT):LT that uses the
DHT index on a DT to accelerate equi-selection on the index keys (see also Table 2). It is implemented in the dataflow level, by routing a message to the Chord
finger on which the selection key-value hashes, and retrieving all corresponding
tuples as an LT via a TCP/IP transfer.

As AmbientDB is intended to work even in fully ad-hoc encounters between
nodes, the indices defined on distributed tables might be only partially filled at
any point of time. Also, due to local resource constraints, the DHT may discard
some of its inserts when it would exceed its maximum capacity at that node, so
it may never be fully complete. Using a non-complete index for selecting in a
table reduces the number of tuples found. At this moment, we decided that the

```
RELEVANT :=
    select USERID, SUM(TIMESPLAYED) as WEIGHT
    from   AMP2P.HISTO
    where  SONGID = ''<normalized song name>''      --+
    group by USERID
    order by WEIGHT descending
    limit 10

RELEVANTNODES :=
    select R.USERID, R.WEIGHT, H.#NODEID as LOCATION
    from   AMP2P.HISTO H, RELEVANT R                 --+
    where  H.SONGID = ''<normalized song name>'' and
           H.USERID = R.USERID

VOTE :=
    select H.SONGID, SUM(H.TIMESPLAYED * RN.WEIGHT) AS VOTE
    from   AMP2P.HISTO H, RELEVANTNODES RN
    where  H.USERID = RN.USERID                      --+
    groupby  H.SONGID
    order by VOTE descending
    limit 100
```

USERID	WEIGHT
uid5	92
uid9	72
..	..
uid2	2

USERID	WEIGHT	LOCATION
uid5	92	node1
uid5	92	node2
uid9	72	node4
..	..	..
uid2	2	node1
uid2	2	node2

SONGID	VOTE
sid44	4892
sid9	3472
..	..
sid87	342

Fig. 9. Optimized collaborative filtering query in SQL

AmbientDB end-user should decide explicitly whether an index may be used, where a default behavior can be based on a *minimum coverage* threshold[1].

3.1   Example: Optimized Collaborative Filtering

We now describe how the indexing feature of AmbientDB can be used to optimize the queries needed by our example amP2P music player to generate playlists.

```
create distributed table
AMP2P.HISTO(SONGID varchar, USERID varchar,
            TIMESPLAYED integer)
primary key (SONGID,USERID,#NODEID);

create distributed index
AMP2P.HISTO(SONGID,USERID,TIMESPLAYED) on (SONGID);
```

```
delete AMP2P.HISTO;
insert into AMP2P.HISTO
select L.SONGID, L.USERID, count(*) as  TIMESPLAYED
from AMP2P.LOG L, AMP2P.SONG S
where L.SONGID = SG.SONGID and
      L.DURATION >= SG.LENGTH
group by L.SONGID, USERID
order by L.USERID, SONGID;
```

Fig. 10. Extensions To The Music Schema

We introduce an extra HISTO table as a pre-computed histogram of fully-listened-to songs per device. Working with somewhat stale log data should not be a problem for the playlist generation problem, as long as the re-computation refresh rate is faster than the pace of change in human music taste. Thus, using HISTO instead of LOG directly reduces the histogram computation cost of our queries. Additionally, in the schema declaration of Figure 10, we created a *distributed index* on HISTO. As depicted in Figure 7, this leads to the creation of a DHT. The system-maintained indexed table is called #DHT_HISTO and carries an explicit #NODEID column for each tuple. Since the tuples indexed in the DHT partition stem from other nodes, the #NODEID column is stored explicitly in a DHT rather than implicitly as in a LT, DT or PT.

Using this (indexed) HISTO table, we reformulate our query in Figure 9. First, we determine those 10 users that have listened most to the example song and

---

[1] An AmbientDB node can use the percentage of its own local tuples having been inserted up-to-date in the index as an estimate of index coverage in the DT.

retain their weight using a top-N query. The DHT makes this selection highly efficient: it involves just one remote node, and taking only the top-N listeners severely reduces the size of the result. We assume here that the influence extorted by listeners with a low weight can be discarded, and that a small sample of representative users is good enough for our playlist. Second, we ask for the explicit #NODEID locations of the selected relevant HISTO tuples. The reason for doing so is that we want to convey to AmbientDB that the last query involves a limited set of nodes such as to reduce the communication and query processing overhead in all other nodes. Note that this optimization also modifies the original query, as the user might have LOG entries on other nodes than those where he listened to the example song (though this is improbable). Third, we compute the weighted top-N of all songs on only those nodes as our final result.

Figure ?? shows the detailed concrete algebra plans for the optimized query plans. We use $select_{chord}$(HISTO) to directly identify the node with HISTO tuples of the SONGID of the example song, and retrieve RELEVANT (this is contrasted by a full network query and larger result in the naive strategy; as illustrated in Figure 8). Locally in the query node, we then compute the RELEVANT_USERS and RELEVANT_NODES tables as the top-10 listeners to that query resp. all nodes where those top listeners have listened to that song. Further queries only concern this node subset, as we use the $join_{split}$ to route tuples only selectively to the HISTO DT, in order to compute the weighted scores for all (user,song) combinations in that subset, which are aggregated in two phases (distributed and merge) to arrive at the predicted vote.

Though at this stage we lack experimental confirmation, it should be clear that performance is improved in the optimized strategy that only accesses 11 nodes w.r.t. the naive strategy that flooded the entire network twice with the entire contents LOG table (as also illustrated in Figure 8).

3.2 Future Work

At the time of this writing, AmbientDB is under full construction, with the first priorities being in the distributed query processor (including basic optimizer) and the networking protocol. The (Java) prototype being built is designed such that the codebase can be used both in the real DBMS as well as inside a network simulator (we are currently using NS2 [21]). In the near future, we hope to obtain our first performance results on the query strategies described here.

While we now use the $join_{split}$ to selectively route tuples from root to leaves, we intend to experiment with *on-the-fly* subset construction of routing trees. In our optimized example, all nodes of interest become available as a list of node-ids in RELEVANT_NODES.LOCATION. One can envision a trivial divide & conquer algorithm that selects some neighbours from this list (e.g. based on pinging a small random sample and taking the fastest ones), makes them your neighbours in the new IP overlay, divides the remaining node-list among them, and repeats the process there. Having a dedicated subnet may reduce the experienced latency by a factor log(N/M) (where N is tot total amount of nodes and M is the size of the subset), and even more importantly, reduces network bandwidth usage by a factor N/M. This creates a routing tree that is somewhat optimized to the latencies between peers, whereas a purely Chord-based network is randomly formed in that respect. Continuing on the issue of creating a physical-network aware P2P logical networking structure, we may experiment with other DHT algorithms such as Pastry [24] that take network proximity into account.

The dataflow algorithms presented should be considered starting points and can be optimized in many ways. In [5] we show an optimized join technique that uses a semijoin-like reduction strategy [1,2], to optimize the projection phase in a join such that only those attribute values actually in the join result are fetched exactly once. Since AmbientDB often sends streams of ordered key values over the network, it might also be worthwhile to investigate (lightweight) compression protocols to compress these streams in order to reduce the network bandwidth consumption. A finally possible scalability improvement is to distinguish between powerful and weak nodes, putting only the powerful *backbone* nodes in the Chord ring. The weak *slave* nodes (e.g. mobile phone) would look for a suitable backbone and transfer all their data to it, removing themselves as a bottleneck from the query routing tree.

3.3   Related Work

Recently, database research has ventured into the area of *in-network query processing* with TinyDB [17]. The major challenge there is to conserve battery power while computing continuous (approximate) aggregate queries over an ad-hoc physical P2P radio network between a number of very simple sensors ("motes"). It turns out that executing the queries in the network (i.e. in the motes) is more efficient than sending individual messages to a base station from each mote, where many interesting optimization opportunities are opened by the interaction between the networking protocol and query processing algorithms. AmbientDB directly builds on this work, extending the ideas in TinyDB from aggregate queries only to full-fledged relational query algebra. A second strain of recent related research are P2P data sharing protocols that go beyond Gnutella in scalability. Chord, CAN and Pastry [8,22,24] use distributed hash-tables (DHT) or other distributed hashing schemes to efficiently map data items into one node from a potentially very large universe of nodes. Thus, data stored in such networks is relocated upon entrance to the node where the hashing function demands it should be. While these algorithms are highly efficient, they are not directly applicable in AmbientDB, where data placement on a device is determined explicitly by the user. As described, AmbientDB can use DHTs for system-maintained index structures, that are not managed explicitly by the end-user. Another effort of designing complex querying facilities in P2P systems is presented in [13]. In this paper an algorithm for join over a DHT is presented. This approach inserts all tuples to be joined on-the-fly in a CAN DHT [22], using a symmetric pipelined hash-join like [25].

In the database research community, there has been significant interest in Scalable Distributed Data Structures (SDDSs), such as LH* [16], with a focus on automatic scaling and load balancing in query loads with both high read-

and update-rates. An important difference with DHTs is that SDDSs make a distinction between clients and servers and are thus not "pure" P2P structures. Also, DHTs are designed for a network of unreliable connections, whereas SDDSs lack the resilience features that are necessary to stay connected in such harsh circumstances.

Some recent research has addressed the problem of heterogeneous schema integration in P2P systems. Bernstein et al. propose a formal framework called the *Local Relational Model* as a model for denoting manipulating schemas and mappings between them in P2P nodes [9]. In the case of the Piazza system, known techniques for (inverse) schema mappings in the relational domain are extended to XML data models [12]. In future work on AmbientDB, we hope to build on this work for creating our XML schema integration component.

As for P2P database architecture work, we should mention PeerDB [20], which shares similar goals to AmbientDB, but with a focus on handling heteronegenous ad-hoc schemata. The system uses agent technology to implement extensible query execution. It matches schemas in an ad-hoc, Information Retrieval like approach, based on keywords attached to table and column names.

4   Conclusion

The major contribution of our research is a full query processing architecture for executing queries in a declarative, optimizable language, over an ad-hoc P2P network of many, possibly small devices. We adopt dataflow execution on ordered streams and arrive at execution patterns that propagate in parallel multiple ordered tuple waves through the subset of all participating nodes. We have shown how Distributed Hash Tables (DHTs) can be incorporated seamlessly in the architecture to support efficient global indices that can transparently accelerate queries. In principle, data sharing and querying in the network is on a purely ad-hoc basis, where data can be replicated on the fine-grained tuple level. As for future work, we see ample opportunities to further refine our query processing strategies, both in the area of query execution (join, partition, or distributed top-N), as well as in optimizing the networking protocol. In the next few months we will conduct first experiments and obtain performance results.

References

1. P. Apers, A. Hevner, and S. Yao. Optimization algorithms for distributed queries. *IEEE Transactions on Software Engineering*, 9(1):57–68, 1983.
2. P. Bernstein and D. Chiu. Using semi-joins to solve relational queries. *Journal of the ACM (JACM)*, 28(1):25–40, 1981.
3. C. Bobineau, L. Bouganim, P. Pucheral, and P. Valduriez. Picodbms: Scaling down database techniques for the smartcard. In *Proc. VLDB Conf.*, 2000.
4. P. Boncz. *Monet: A Next-Generation DBMS Kernel For Query-Intensive Applications*. PhD thesis, Universiteit van Amsterdam, May 2002.
5. P. Boncz and C. Treijtel. AmbientDB: Relational query processing in a p2p network. Technical Report INS-R0305, CWI, June 2003.

6. J. Breese, D. Heckerman, and C. Kadie. Empirical Analysis of Predictive Algorithms for Collaborative Filtering. In *Proc. Conf. on Uncertainty in Artificial Intelligence*, July 1998.

7. A. Doan et al. Reconciling schemas of disparate data sources: a machine-learning approach. In *Proc. SIGMOD Conf.*, pages 509–520, 2001.

8. I. Stoica et al. Chord: A scalable Peer-To-Peer lookup service for internet applications. In *Proc. SIGCOMM Conf.*, pages 149–160, 2001.

9. P. Bernstein et al. Data management for peer-to-peer computing: A vision. In *Proc. WebDB Workshop*, 2002.

10. G. Graefe. Encapsulation of parallelism in the volcano query processing system. In *Proc. SIGMOD Conf.*, pages 102–111, 1990.

11. G. Graefe. Volcano – an extensible and parallel query evaluation system. *IEEE TKDE*, 6(1):120–135, 1994.

12. S. Gribble, A. Halevy, Z. Ives, M. Rodig, and D. Suciu. What can peer-to-peer do for databases, and vice versa? In *Proc. WebDB Workshop*, 2001.

13. M. Harren, J. Hellerstein, R. Huebsch, B. Loo, S. Shenker, and I. Stoica. Complex queries in dht-based peer-to-peer networks. In *Proc. IPTPS Workshop*, 2002.

14. S. Hedberg. Beyond desktop computing: Mit's oxygen project. *Distributed Systems Online*, 1, 2000.

15. D. Kossmann. The state of the art in distributed query processing. *ACM Computing Surveys (CSUR)*, 32(4):422–469, 2000.

16. W. Litwin, M.-A. Neimat, and D. Schneider. LH* – Linear Hashing for Distributed Files. In *Proc. SIGMOD Conf.*, 1993.

17. S. Madden, M. Franklin, J. Hellerstein, and W. Hong. Tag: a tiny aggregation service for ad-hoc sensor networks. In *Proc. OSDI'02 Symposium*, 2002.

18. S. Melnik, E. Rahm, and P. Bernstein. Rondo: A programming platform for generic model management. In *Proc. SIGMOD Conf.*, 2003.

19. Napster, http://opennap.sourceforge.net/, 2003.

20. W. Ng, B. Ooi, K.-L. Tan, and A. Zhou. PeerDB: A P2P-based System for Distributed Data Sharing. In *Proc. ICDE Conf.*, 2003.

21. The network simulator – ns-2, http://www.isi.edu/nsnam/ns/, April 2003.

22. S. Ratnasamy, P. Francis, M. Handley, R. Karp, and S. Schenker. A scalable content-addressable network. In *Proc. SIGCOMM Conf.*, pages 161–172, 2001.

23. Matei Ripeanu, Adriana Iamnitchi, and Ian Foster. Mapping the gnutella network. *IEEE Internet Computing*, 6(1):50–57, 2002.

24. A. Rowstron and P. Druschel. Pastry: Scalable, distributed object location and routing for large-scale p2p systems. In *Proc. IFIP/ACM Middleware*, 2001.

25. A. Wilschut and P. Apers. Dataflow query execution in a parallel main-memory environment. *Distributed and Parallel Databases*, 1(1):103–128, 1993.

Towards a Unifying Framework for Complex Query Processing over Structured Peer-to-Peer Data Networks

Peter Triantafillou and Theoni Pitoura

Computer Technology Institute and
Department of Computer Engineering and Informatics,
University of Patras, Greece
{peter, tpit}@ceid.upatras.gr

Abstract. In this work we study how to process complex queries in DHT-based Peer-to-Peer (P2P) data networks. Queries are made over tuples and relations and are expressed in a query language, such as SQL. We describe existing research approaches for query processing in P2P systems, we suggest improvements and enhancements, and propose a unifying framework that consists of a modified DHT architecture, data placement and search algorithms, and provides efficient support for processing a variety of query types, including queries with one or more attributes, queries with selection operators (involving equality and range queries), and queries with join operators. To our knowledge, this is the first work that puts forth a framework providing support for all these query types.

1   Introduction

Recently, P2P architectures that are based on Distributed Hash Tables (DHTs) have been proposed and have since become very popular, influencing research in Peer-to-Peer (P2P) systems significantly. DHT-based systems provide efficient processing of the routing/location operations that, given a query for a document id, they locate (route the query to) the peer node that stores this document. Thus, they provide support for exact-match queries. To do so, they rely, in general, on lookups of a distributed hash table, which creates a structure in the system emerging by the way that peers define their neighbors. For this reason, they are referred to as structured P2P systems, as opposed to systems like Gnutella[1], MojoNation[2], etc, where there is no such structure and, instead, neighbors of peers are defined in rather ad hoc ways.

There are several P2P DHTs architectures (Chord[3], CAN[4], Pastry[5], Tapestry[6], etc.). From these, CAN and Chord are the most commonly used as a substrate upon which to develop higher layers supporting more elaborate queries.

CAN ([4]) uses a d-dimensional virtual address space for data location and routing. Each peer in the system owns a zone of the virtual space and stores the data objects that are mapped into its zone. Each peer stores routing information about O(d) other peers, which is independent of the number of peers, N, in the system. Each data object is mapped to a point in the d-dimensional space. When a request for a data object is submitted, it is routed towards the point that the object is mapped in the

K. Aberer et al. (Eds.): VLDB 2003 Ws DBISP2P, LNCS 2944, pp. 169–183, 2004.

virtual space. Each peer on the path passes the request to one of its neighbors which is closer to the destination in the virtual space. The average routing path for exact match lookup is $O(dN^{1/d})$ hops.

Chord ([3]) hashes both the key of a data object into an m-bit identifier, and a peer's IP address into an m-bit identifier, for a value of m that is large enough to make the probability of two peers or keys hashing to the same identifier negligible. Identifiers are ordered in an identifier circle modulo 2^m, called the Chord ring. The keys' identifiers map to peers' identifiers using consistent hashing (i.e. a function succ(k), for k being the identifier for the data object's key). The peers maintain routing information about other peers at logarithmically increasing distance in the Chord ring (i.e. in tables stored in each peer, called finger tables). Therefore, when an exact match query for a data object is submitted in a Chord P2P architecture, the querying peer hashes the attribute's value, locates the peer that stores the object, and uses the routing information stored in the finger tables to forward the query to this peer. As a result, Chord requires $O(logN)$ routing hops for location/routing operations.

There are also other than DHTs structured P2P systems, which build distributed, scalable indexing structures to route search requests, such as P-Grid. P-Grid ([7]) is a scalable access structure based on a virtual distributed search tree. It uses randomized techniques to create and maintain the structure in order to provide complete decentralization.

Although P2P networks provide only exact-match query capability, researchers in data management have recently began to investigate how they could enhance P2P networks to reply to more complex queries. This led to research addressing specific query types, such as range queries, join, aggregation, etc. However, a proposal of a framework upon which all complex query types could be efficiently supported in a P2P architecture is very much lacking.

With this work we attempt to present a unifying framework for efficiently supporting complex querying in P2P networks. Given the prominence of DHT-based architectures, we will assume a DHT architecture as our substrate, hoping that in this way our work can leverage existing research results to develop a comprehensive query processing system for P2P networks.

2   Related Work

Gribble et al. ([8]) investigate how P2P systems can gain the strengths of data management systems in semantics, data transformation and data relationships, which could enable them to provide complex queries capabilities. Towards that direction, they define the dynamic data placement problem in P2P systems and propose a decentralized, globally distributed P2P query processor, which would give answers to aggregations, range, and more complex queries in P2P systems. However, in this work they do not provide specific solutions to query processing since their query processor is still in an initial phase.

In the following sections, we briefly present existing work in addressing specific query types, such as range queries, queries involving join, and/or aggregation operators, etc.

2.1   Supporting Range Queries

Gupta et. al [9] propose an architecture for relational data shared in a P2P system based on Chord, and a hashing-based method to provide *approximate* answers to range queries. Specifically, given a range, this approach considers the set of values that the range consists of, computes an integer for each one of the values by applying a min-wise independent permutation hash function ([10]) on each value, and finally takes the minimum of the resulting integers, as the identifier for that range. The min-wise independent permutations have the property to hash similar ranges to the same identifier with high probability (locality sensitive hashing). Since they use Chord ([3]) to map ranges to peers, range lookup is performed in O(logN) hops, where N is the number of peers.

Sahin, et al. ([11]) extend the CAN ([4]) DHT system for d=2. The virtual hash space for a single attribute is a 2-dimensional square bounded by the lower and higher values of the attribute's domain. The space is further partitioned into zones, and each zone is assigned to a peer. That peer stores the results of the range queries whose ranges hashes into the zone it owns, as well as routing information about its neighbors - owners of its adjacent zones. When a range query is submitted, it is routed towards the range's zone through the virtual space. Once the query reaches that zone, the results stored at this zone are checked. If the results are found locally, they are returned. Otherwise, the query is forwarded to the left and top neighbors that may contain a potential result (recursively). The basic idea of this forwarding is that smaller sets of tuples that are answers to the original range query may be cached at peers that contain supersets of the given range.

Andrzejak and Xu ([12]) also propose a CAN-based extension for range querying, in grid information infrastructures. A subset of the grid servers is responsible for subintervals of the attribute's domain, the *interval keepers* (IK). Each server reports its current attribute value to the appropriate IK. Additionally, each IK owns a zone in the logical d-dimensional space. For efficient range queries, the Space Filling Curves, and especially the Hilbert curve ([13]) for R^2 mapping and its generalization for R^d are used to map the intervals to the zones (the Hilbert curve has the property of proximity preservation). When a range query is issued, the problem is how to route the query to the IK whose interval intersects the query range. There are many techniques to perform efficient routing for range queries, the best of which is propagating the query in two waves: the first one to the neighbors that intersect the query and have higher interval than the current node, and the second wave to those that have lower interval.

2.2   Supporting Multi-attribute Queries

To our knowledge, there is no efficient solution to address specifically this problem. Researchers either leave this issue to address it in the future, or address it by using separate instances of DHTs for each one of the attributes. However, such a solution is not efficient since it requires many replicas of same data objects in different peers, one for each of the index attributes.

An interesting work is presented in Felber et. al ([14]), although they do not aim at answering complex database-like queries, but rather at providing practical techniques for searching data using more advanced tools than keyword lookups. They create multiple indexes, organized hierarchically, which permit users to access data in many different ways (query-to-query mapping). Given a broad query, the system recursively queries itself until it finds the desired data items, which are stored on only one or few of the nodes. The good property of this system is that it does not replicate data at multiple locations, but it provides a key-to-key service, by storing at each node only the indexes to other nodes, which store the answers to more specific queries.

2.3   Supporting Join Queries – Aggregation

Harren et. al ([15]) propose a three-tier architecture: data storage, (any) DHT overlay network, and a Query Processor on top. Specifically, they partition the DHT identifier space into *namespaces* (relations). They also build a hierarchical identifier space on top of the flat identifier space, by partitioning the identifiers in multiple fields, in order to manage multiple data structures. *Joining* relations R and S is implemented by using multicast to distribute the query to all peers in the DHT network. The algorithm locally scans tables R and S, and republishes the resulted tuples in a temporary namespace using the join attributes as its identifier (i.e. it re-hashes the tuples in the DHT). Mini-joins are performed locally as new tuples arrive (i.e. they perform pipelined hash join), and the results are forwarded to the requestor. The same work addresses also projection, join, group by, and aggregation operations in a similar way. In a more recent publication of this work in Huebsch et. al ([16]), their distributed query engine, called PIER, is designed, implemented and tested over a DHT overlay network.

3   The Proposed Framework

3.1   The Problem

We assume a P2P network, with nodes/peers publishing, storing, and sharing data. In our framework, data is organized in relations and each data object is described by a tuple with a number of attributes. For example, in a file sharing P2P system, files are described by their metadata, such as name, type, date, author, etc. forming tuples.

Our study starts from simpler queries, which we call *rudimentary* queries, and proceeds to more complex queries. To facilitate this we have defined a number of *query types*, for both the categories, according to the involvement of different parameters in the expression of the query, such as:

   a.   One or more attributes, forming single or multi-attribute queries, coined *SA or MA,* respectively
   b.   One or more conditions (single or multi-condition queries, respectively), using conditional operators (i.e. union (OR), intersection (AND))
   c.   Different operators applied on the attributes, such as equality and range operators
   d.   Special functions applied on the data, such as aggregations (i.e. count, sum, average, maximum/minimum, etc), grouping, ordering, etc.
   e.   Single or multi-relation queries coined, *SR, or MR,* respectively.

3.2   The Approach

We will classify expected queries into *"rudimentary"* and *"non-rudimentary"* queries, and define *query types* for each of the above categories. We will analyze how to support each query type, starting from rudimentary queries. The non-rudimentary query types that are combining features from these rudimentary types will be supported using the corresponding mechanisms for each involved rudimentary query type.

Based on the above we have classified the expected queries into the following query types:

Rudimentary Queries

[SR, SA, =]:	referring to a query over a single-relation, single-attribute, single-condition with an equality operator.
[SR, SA, < >]:	referring to a query as above, but with a range operator.
[MR, MA, join]:	referring to a query over multiple joined relations

Non-rudimentary Queries

[SR, MA, =]:	referring to a query over multiple attributes with equality operators.
[SR, MA, <>]:	referring to a query over multiple attributes with range operators.
[MR, MA, =]:	referring to a query over multiple relations, over multiple attributes with equality operators.
[MR, MA, <>]:	referring to a query over multiple relations over multiple attributes with range operators.
[MR, MA, =, sf]:	referring to a query over multiple relations over multiple attributes, with *special functions, such* aggregate functions (sum, count, avg, min, max, etc), grouping, ordering, etc.

We currently address only integers as the attribute's domain, and leave other data types, such as strings, dates, Boolean for future work (an approach for strict substring searches using n-grams is presented in [15]).

In the following sections we examine each of the above query types separately aiming to find a single, efficient solution for all query types. As far as we know, there is no single approach that offers a 'global' solution, supporting all query types above. Our goal is to provide this and set a framework for further improvements and extensions for higher-level query languages (i.e. semantically enriched query languages, such as XML).

In the proposed framework we will use Chord, because of its simplicity, its popularity within the P2P community (which has led to it being used in a number of P2P systems), but also because of its good performance (logarithmic in terms of routing hops and routing state) and robustness.

4   The Proposed Architecture

4.1   The Infrastructure

First, we assume that data stored in the P2P network is structured in only one relation R $(DA_1, DA_2, .. DA_k)$, where k is the number of attributes, DA_i the attribute domains, and A_i the name of the attributes, for each $i \in \{1, 2, .. k\}$. For simplicity, we assume that all k attributes are used to index data (i.e. we ignore attributes that are not used for indexing, since they do not affect the proposed architecture; we assume that these can be stored in the tuples and recalled each time we access the tuples).

Each tuple $(a_1, a_2, .. a_k)$ in R, with $a_i \in DA_i$, for each $i \in \{1, 2, .. k\}$, holds a primary key, or simply *key*, which is a distinct identifier. This key can be either one of the attributes of the tuple, or can be calculated separately based on one or more of the attributes.

Based on Chord, our protocol associates with each peer P an m-bit identifier, n, from the set $\{0, 1, .. 2^m\text{-}1\}$, using a base hash function, such as SHA-1([17]), on the peer's IP address. Similarly, it associates with each tuple $(a_1, a_2, .. a_k)$ in R with key t, an m-bit identifier from the same set $\{0, 1, .. 2^m\text{-}1\}$, using a similar hash function on t. The identifiers, which are elements of the set $\{0, 1, .. 2^m\text{-}1\}$, are ordered in an identifier circle modulo 2^m, i.e. the Chord ring[1], which is also referred to as the DHT identifier space.

Furthermore, we use consistent hashing to map tuples to peers, and specifically, we use the function $succ()$: $\{0, 1, .. 2^m\text{-}1\} \rightarrow \{0, 1, .. 2^m\text{-}1\}$, similarly to Chord. Each tuple $(a_1, a_2, .. a_k)$ with key t is routed and stored on the first peer whose identifier is equal to or follows t in the identifier space. This peer is called the successor peer of identifier t and is denoted by succ(t). Each peer n maintains routing information in the following structures:

a) *finger table*, where each entry l is the first peer that succeeds n by at least $2^{l\text{-}1}$ on the ring (mod 2^m), for $1 \leq l \leq m$, and ,

b) link to its *predecessor* peer.

Given this setup, the system is able to reply to queries of type [SR, SA, =], when the queried attribute is the key of a tuple.

4.2   The Enhancements to the Infrastructure

In this section, we describe how to enhance the Chord architecture to enable it to support the other rudimentary query types for *any attribute*. To do this, we proceed as follows: for each tuple and for one of its, say, k (index) attributes, we hash the attribute value of the tuple and insert it to a peer in the DHT identifier space, using the Chord data insertion protocol and a special hash function (which we will define below).

---

[1]   From this point forward, when we refer to a peer n, we consider that n is its identifier, and for a key t of a tuple that t is its key identifier (otherwise, it is mentioned specifically).

In order to support range queries for a single-attribute, we should somehow be able to keep ordering information for the values of that attribute. A simple solution to this is to use *order-preserving (i.e. monotonic) hash* functions to hash the attribute values to the identifier space. Then, tuples at the Chord ring are stored in an ordered form (say, ascending) by the values of this attribute.

For every $i \in \{1, 2, .. k\}$ we define an *order-preserving hash function* $h_i: DA_i \rightarrow \{0, 1, .. 2^m-1\}$, such that:

$$value_1 < value_2 \Rightarrow h_i(value_1) \leq h_i(value_2), \text{ for any } value_1, value_2 \in DA_i. \quad (1)$$

There are many order-preserving hash functions we could use, however, it is quite improbable that they also provide *randomness* and *uniformity*.

Here, we use k order-preserving hash functions, one for each (index) attribute, as follows. Let us say that $DA_i = <low_i, high_i>$ for an attribute A_i and we assume that $2^m > |DA_i|$. Then, we partition the identifier space into $2^m / s_i$ ranges, each of size s_i, such that:

$$s_i = 2^m / \left(high_i - low_i + 1\right). \quad (2)$$

Then, for every value $a_i \in DA_i$, we define,

$$h_i : DA_i \rightarrow \{0, 1, ... 2^m - 1\}, \quad h_i(a_i) = \left\lceil \left(a_i - low_i\right) \times s_i \right\rceil. \quad (3)$$

Now we turn to presenting the basic algorithm for data (tuple) insertion. A node join/leave algorithm is accommodated by executing the join/leave protocol of Chord.

Data Insertion

A tuple $(a_1, a_2, .. a_k)$ with key t is inserted in the network, using Chord's consistent hashing function. We store the tuple in the peer succ(t).

In addition, we apply order-preserving hashing over each one of its k (index) attribute values, $a_1, a_2, .. a_k$, and find the m-bit identifiers $h_1(a_1)$, $h_2(a_2)$, .. $h_k(a_k)$. We apply succ() to each one of the k hashed values and store the tuple in the peers with identifiers succ($h_i(a_i)$), for each $i \in \{1, 2, .. k\}$.

Therefore, for each tuple inserted in the network, we store (k+1) maximum replicas of this tuple: one copy of the tuple with consistent hashing over its key, and k replicas distributed in the peers in an order-preserving form based on its k attributes.

To maintain k more replicas of each tuple may be inefficient, as far as storage requirements are concerned and requires more processing time for data updates to keep replicas mutually consistent, as well as more overhead when nodes join/leave the network. On the other hand, it is indisputable that replicas of data in a DHT network are required given the frequent topology changes, if data availability is to remain at reasonable levels. Furthermore, this approach keeps routing hops for lookups significantly low, since range and join queries can be processed efficiently – as we will describe below.

A way to overcome the increased replica-related overhead is to allow only one copy of a tuple to be stored; specifically, the one stored using consistent hashing on the tuple's key, t, i.e. the tuple stored at the succ(t) peer. The other k peers, whose id is produced by order-preserving hashing for each one of the k attributes, could only store the value of the attribute hashed (needed to compare during lookup) and a link to the succ(t) peer. In this way however, we would increase the peers' state, by adding to the finger table and the predecessor more pointers to peers, indexed by the values of their k attributes. This alternative architecture would also increase lookup and join processing, as we describe below.

5   Processing Queries

5.1   Rudimentary Query Types

As described above, there are three rudimentary types, and their processing is described below.

Query Type [SR, SA, =]

Processing of this query type is based on the Chord lookup algorithm, utilizing the finger table entries of peers, which are maintained as the Chord protocol prescribes. In the pseudocode below n is the requestor.

```
INPUT: aᵢ ∈ DAᵢ, for i ∈ {1, 2, .. k}
OUTPUT: a list of tuples, with value aᵢ of attribute Aᵢ
BEGIN
calculate hᵢ(aᵢ),using the order-preserving hash
          function hᵢ
n_target = Chord_lookup hᵢ(aᵢ)  on peer n
request-and-receive from n_target  the desired tuples
END
```

The data store at peer n_target is locally searched for those tuples of relation R for which $A_i = a_i$.

Since processing of this query type is based solely on the Chord lookup algorithm, it follows that the query type is resolved in O(logN) routing hops. (A proof of this is fairly straightforward and is left out of this paper).

Query Type [SR, SA, <>]

Similarly, given a range query with a range (*low*, *high*) of an attribute, we hash using the order-preserving hash function used for that attribute over *low* and *high*, and find peers succ(h_i(low)) and succ(h_i (high)). Because of the order-preserving hashing, the requested tuples are stored in the peers from succ(h_i (low)) to succ(h_i (high)), and are retrieved by following the successor links within the Chord ring. Specifically, at first the query is forwarded from *n* to succ(h_i(low)), which forwards the query to its successor, and this is repeated, till the query reaches the peer with identifier succ(h_i (high)).

```
INPUT: (low, high) ⊆ DAᵢ, for i ∈ {1, 2, .. k}
OUTPUT: a list of tuples, with values of attribute Aᵢ
        falling within the range (low, high)
BEGIN
calculcate hᵢ(low) and hᵢ(high),using the order-
        preserving hash function hᵢ
n_start = Chord_lookup hᵢ(low) on peer n
n_end = Chord_lookup hᵢ(high) on peer n
forward (query, n, n_end) to n_start
receive tuples
END

Forward (query, n, n_end) executed on node nⱼ
INPUT (low, high) ⊆ DAᵢ, for i ∈ {1, 2, .. k}
OUTPUT: a list of tuples, with values of attribute Aᵢ
        falling within the range (low, high)
BEGIN
local_find(R, Aᵢ, aᵢ), with aᵢ ∈ (low, high)
send matching tuples to node n
if nⱼ != n_end
        forward (query, n, n_end) to its successor
END
```

The above algorithm calls the Chord lookup algorithm to find the peer storing the value *low* of the queried attribute, therefore it needs O(logN) routing hops for this task. Subsequently, the query will be forwarded to all nodes falling between succ(h_i(high)) and succ(h_i(low)), successively, following each time the successor link of the current node (it is a direct link and, therefore it needs O(1) hop each time). Therefore, forwarding needs as many routing hops as the number of nodes lying between succ(h_i(high)) and succ(h_i(low)), which may be from O(1) to O(N)! Therefore, the above algorithm needs O(N) routing hops in the worst case and O(logN) hops in the best. This worst case performance is of course undesirable and resembles performance of lookup algorithms in unstructured P2P networks.

For this reason we enhance our architecture using a number of special peers, called *range guards*.

Enhancing the Architecture Using Range Guards

We select a number of peers, called range guards, *RG*, to keep replicas of all tuples whose values of a specific attribute fall in a specific range. Each RG also maintains routing information for their neighbor RG, i.e for the RGs responsible for the succeeding range.   Additionally, there are direct links in each peer to its corresponding RG.

Specifically, we partition the domain DA of an attribute A into *l* partitions (buckets). To achieve load balancing distribution among the RGs, the partitions should be such that each RG keeps an equal number of tuples. Since this is application-dependent and hard to accomplish, we partition DA into *l* continuous and disjoint ranges of *size* $s = |DA| / l$ (|DA| is the size of domain DA). This means that we divide the attribute domain into l equal-sized subranges - equal to the number of partitions desired, and therefore, l RGs are defined.

We repeat partitioning for each one of the attributes over which we expect range queries to be common.

Range Queries Using Range Guards

A range query is now forwarded into the Range Guards, the ones whose union of their ranges is the *minimum* range (L, H) such that: (low, high) $\subseteq$ (L, H).

As above, given a range (low, high) of an attribute, we hash using an order-preserving hash function over *low* to find the peer succ(h_i(low)). We then forward the query to its corresponding RG, which locally looks up for the requested tuples and sends the matched ones back to the requestor. Then, we compare high≤H. If it is true, the algorithm ends, since all the requested tuples are lying in the RGs that have been already accessed. Otherwise, the RG forwards the query to its successor RG, which repeats the same process.

Therefore, this algorithm requires O(logN) routing hops to access succ(h_i(low), and O(l) routing hops to forward the query from one RG to the next until the query results have been completely gathered. Since l << N, it is obvious that the algorithm is significantly more efficient that the one presented before. Specifically, if we set l=logN, we have log(N) RGs in the network, and a range query would need O(logN) + O(logN) = O(logN) routing hops. Alternatively, we can set $l = \sqrt{N}$ and then the load on each RG will be significantly smaller, while still obtain much better performance and specifically O($\sqrt{N}$).

On the other hand, this enhancement requires more storage for routing information in a peer, since every peer should also keep a link to its corresponding RG. Additionally, we require the existence of l range guard peers with enhanced processing and storage capacity, able to store and process requests for a significant proportion of our data. However, in peer-to-peer data management settings, peers will be able to store complete database systems which implies a willingness and ability to store large amounts of data. Furthermore, this is not unrealistic, since many peers in the network have been proven to be altruistic and/or more powerful, willing and capable to offer their resources and thus play the role of RGs. In fact, a hot trend within the networking and distributed systems P2P research community is to exploit the heterogeneity with respect to the capabilities of peers (bandwidth, processing power, storage) in order to improve routing efficiency ([18]). With the notion and exploitation of range guards we can harness this power heterogeneity of peers in order to facilitate the efficient processing of range queries.

Additionally, with this extended architecture, there are more replicas of the tuples stored in the network. To avoid this degree of data redundancy, we could follow the alternative discussed earlier, and keep only a link to the succ(t), as well as a link to its corresponding RG. This alternative still only costs O(l) routing hops.

Query Type [MR, MA, join]

Using our enhanced architecture with range guards, we are able to reply to equality and range queries for a single attribute - and single relation- efficiently. In this section we examine join queries, both without and with range guards.

Let us assume that we have 2 relations, $R\ (DA_1,\ DA_2\ ,\ ..\ DA_k)\ and\ S\ (DB_1,\ DB_2\ ,\ ..\ DB_l)$, where DA_i and DB_j, for $i \in \{1, 2, .. k\}$ and $j \in \{1, 2, .. l\}$ are the attribute domains of the relations. Both R and S will be represented in the proposed architecture with the approach presented before.

The join query type can be expressed in SQL as:

```
SELECT *
FROM R, S
WHERE R.a = S.b
```

where R.a and S.b are attributes of relations R and S respectively [2].

Note that our architecture ensures that nearby values of attributes are hashed into the same (or near-by) peers, if the domains of the attributes are the same. Specifically, from the definition of the order-preserving hash function h, the following holds, if the domains of R.a and S.b are the same set:

$$R.a = S.b \Rightarrow h(R.a) = h(S.b) \Rightarrow succ(h(R.a)) = succ(h(S.b)) \qquad (4)$$

This means that we do not have to transfer tuples from any of the two relations between different peers to compare them, since those tuples from R that may join with tuples from S are stored at the same peer. Therefore, the join is performed at each peer locally, and results are transferred to the requestor. This is an implementation of a *hash join method* ([19]). However, we should ask all peers in the network in order to find all solutions, which implies a cost of O(N) routing hops resulting in very high network bandwidth requirements and peer node processing loads.

Thus, this approach is not efficient, but significant improvements could be achieved by employing the following optimization techniques (they reduce latency but not the number of hops):

- At each peer, locally scan only those tuples of a relation that their join attributes hash at that peer. (Remember that each peer stores many tuples after hashing each one of the k attributes of the relation). This would reduce time by k, since there are k +1 replicas of all tuples in the whole network, and we scan only one copy of each.).
- Use pipelining to pass partial results to the requestor (users are impatient and we do not have to wait for all results).

However, join processing is still inefficient, since we still have to multicast the query to almost all peers in the network. Therefore, we need to improve join performance. To this end, we employ range guards, as presented earlier.

---

[2] We examine only equijoins, although nonequijoins would be similarly implemented, since the hashing functions we use maintain the correct ordering of the tuples.

Join Queries Using Range Guards
For the values of each join attribute and for all relations, which most possibly will participate in a join operation, we create range guards, as defined earlier. Therefore, a RG stores all tuples whose join attribute values fall in the corresponding range.

The join method in this case is based on *hash-partitioned join* ([19]). According to this method, a hash function - also referred as *split* - is used to partition the tuples in each relation into a fixed number of disjoint sets. The sets are such that a tuple hashes into a given set if the hashed value of its join attributes falls in the range of values for that set. Then, the tuples in the first set of one relation can match only with the tuples in the first set of the second relation. Thus, the processing of different pairs of corresponding partitions from the two sets are independent of other sets.

We split the domain of the join attributes into l partitions and assign each partition to one of the l RGs. Therefore, the query is sent to only those l RGs (not to all peers in the network, as before). This means that, in case l=O(log(N), or $l = O(\sqrt{N})$ *we* would have similar performance improvements for the processing of joins to those discussed for the processing of range queries. Tuples in partition pairs from both relations may be joined by a *simple hash join*, or any other join method.

Alternative Architecture for Multi-Attribute Query Processing
There is often the case when a few specific attributes are used together in queries. In this case, we could alternatively, use hashing on a combination of these (two or more) attributes.

For example, given a query such as :

```
SELECT attributes
FROM R
WHERE A = Avalue AND B = Bvalue AND C = Cvalue
```

We proceed as follows: We place tuples on the Chord ring as before, except now we hash once only using the tuple's attribute values on A, B, and C, instead of placing the tuple each time at a different Chord node, using a hash on A, then on B, and finally on C.

This would enable faster query processing, since with a single Chord lookup we would reach the peer storing only tuples of interest. However, extensions are required for this approach to enable efficient answers to range queries (such as to define an order on the attribute's vectors, and then an order-preserving hash function over more than one attribute). A special case would be hashing over all k attributes of a tuple (when looking for specific items).

5.2   Non-rudimentary Query Types

Query Type [SR, MA, =]
This query type is handled similar with the query type [SR, SA, =], except that the lookup algorithm runs more than once, one for each of the equality-conditions, to find the peers where the requested tuples can be found. For each selected tuple satisfying a query constraint, the tuple ids are used to possibly discard those tuples that do not satisfy the whole query constraint.

Specifically, hashing is performed for all given values of all attributes to find the corresponding number of peers, where the requested tuples are stored. All matched tuples, are sent back to the requestor, where final processing takes place to ensure that the whole query constraint (over all named attributes) is satisfied.

A number of optimizations can be performed in this algorithm, borrowed from the traditional methods in distributed query processing ([20]), in addition to preprocessing of the conditions (i.e. AND, OR, etc) which may significantly improve efficiency.

Query Type [SR, MA, <>]
Similarly with above, we run the rudimentary query type [SR, SA, <>] more than once, one for each of the range-conditions, to find the peers where the requested tuples can be found. Similar techniques to handle the conditions are applied here.

Query Type [MR, MA, =]
We have described above how our enhanced architecture is able to handle more than one relation. This query type is handled similarly with [SR, MA, =], and runs more than once, one for each of the relations. A special case of this query type may be join (i.e. when equality involves attributes of different relations).

Query Type [MR, MA, <>]
As above, the query type [SR, MA, <>] runs more than once.

Query Type [MR, MA, =, sf]
Special cases of this query type, such as the ones involving grouping and ordering, can be handled easily, by using the query types [SR, SA, =] and [SR, SA, <>] and calculating special functions over selected tuples.

Moreover, since tuples are stored in the network in an ordered form, the calculation of a number of functions, such as min, max, average, etc. can be done using similar techniques from ordered lists in combination with the function succ(n). However, with respect to the sum operation, we need to access all peers. Therefore, in that case we can employ range guards to reduce routing hops.

6   Comparison with Related Work

The work presented here is a straightforward approach to develop a unifying framework to enable structured (Chord-based) P2P networks to support complex query processing. To our knowledge, there is no reported work, which provides such a framework. Instead, solutions have been contributed which focus on supporting one specific query type, such as range, or join/aggregation queries.

The approach proposed in Gupta et. al [9] assumes that users ask broad queries provides thus only approximate answers for range queries, by looking for data in peers that store similar ranges with high probability (i.e. based on similarity). In their experimental results, they report a 50% success in matching partitions with similarity between 0.9 and 1.0, using min-wise independent permutations, and "good" matches for only about 35% of the queries, when using approximate min-wise independent permutations for faster results.

Sahin et al. [11] propose a solution that uses a method to process range queries over the CAN DHT system with d=2. The proposed technique ensures that a range lookup will always yield a range partition that is a superset of the query range, if it exists. However, their approach is not efficient, when compared with solutions based on Chord since for d=2, CAN lookups require $O(2N^{1/2})$ hops,.

Andrzejak and Xu ([12]), deal with ineffiency and load communication overhead in range querying and updating by proposing directed controlled flooding based on the proximity preservation properties of the Hilbert function. However, their solution is also based on CAN and thus has the abovementioned drawbacks associated with it.

With respect to multi-attribute queries, there is no specific work addressing their efficient processing. We have moved forward by proposing techniques to reduce data storage overheads (by storing pointers to data tuples), and/or storing tuples using indices based on more than one attribute.

With respect to join and other complex operations (such as group by), there is only one work (to our knowledge) that supports them in P2P systems, the PIER system ([15], [16]). However, this approach does not support range queries. Furthermore, employing multicasting to perform joins is not efficient, since all peers must be involved in performing a join, which may create scalability problems. Our proposal involving range guards in conjunction with an order preserving hash function may help in avoiding these costs, by executing joins at only select subsets of the peers.

7   Concluding Remarks

With this work we make a first step towards developing a unifying framework for complex query processing in peer-to-peer data networks. Such a framework is very much lacking: related work has so far focused on supporting only a single query type (typically, range queries or join/aggregate queries). To our knowledge our proposal is the only one that addresses range queries, multi-attribute queries, and queries involving joins.

Our proposal supporting range queries enjoys advantages compared to related work. We have also proposed more efficient methods to process multi-attribute queries. Finally, the proposed architecture and data placement along with the notion of range guards, can significantly improve the performance of range and join queries.

A large number of issues remain open; here we name only a few. The efficiency of query processing depends on avoiding data [22] and routing hotspots, which are currently a problem for all known approaches. We are currently building appropriate hash functions to deal with load balancing problems due to skewed value distributions, and evaluating optimization query processing techniques. With respect to range guards, we are developing methods to identify them efficiently, and form efficient architectures [23].

References

1.   Gnutella: http://gnutella.wego.com
2.   Wilcox, B., Hearn, O.: Experiences Deploying a Large-Scale Emergent Network. In the 1st International Workshop on Peer-to-Peer Systems, IPTPS'02 (2002)

3. Stoica, I., Morris, R., Karger, D., Kaashoek, K. F., Balakrishnan, H.: Chord: A scalable peer-to-peer lookup service for internet applications. In Proceedings of the 2001 conference on applications, technologies, architectures, and protocols for computer communications. ACM Press (2001) 149–160

4. Ratnasamy, S., Francis, P., Handley, M., Karp, R., Shenker, S.: A scalable Content-Addressable Network. ACM SIGCOMM '01 (2001)

5. Rowstron, A., Druschel, P.: Pastry: Scalable, decentralized object location and routing for larg-scale peer-to-peer systems. In Middleware, vol. 2218 of Lecture Notes in Computer Science. Springer (2001) 329–350

6. Zhao, Y. B., Kubiatowitcz, J., Joseph, A.: Tapestry: An infrastructure for fault-tolerant wide-area location and routing. Tech. Rep. UCB/CSD-01-1141, University of California at Berkley, Computer Science Department (2001)

7. Aberer, K.: P-Grid: A self-organizing access structure for P2P information systems. In Proc. of the 6th International Conference on Cooperative Information Systems (CoopIS 2001), Trento, Italy (2001)

8. Gribble, S., Halevy, A., Ives, Z., Rodrig, M, Suciu, D.: What Can Databases Do for Peer-to-Peer? In Proc. of the WebDB Workshop on Databases and the Web (2001)

9. Gupta, A., Agrawal, D., Abbadi, A. E.: Approximate Range Selection Queries in Peer-to-Peer Systems. In Proc. of the 2003 CIDR Conference (2003)

10. Broder, A., Charikar, M., Frieze, A., Mitzenmacher M.: Min-wise independent permutations (extended abstract). In Proc. of the thirtieth annual ACM symposium on Theory of computing. ACM Press (1998) 327–336

11. Sahin, O. D., Gupta, A., Agrawal, D., Abbadi, A. E.: Query Processing Over Peer-to-Peer Data Sharing Systems. Technical Report UCSB/CSD-2002-28, University of California at Santa Barbara (2002)

12. Andrzejak, A., Xu, Z.: Scalable, Efficient Range Queries for Grid Information Services. In Proc. of the 2nd IEEE International Conference on Peer-to-Peer (2002)

13. Asano, T., Ranjan, D., Roos, T., Welzl, E., Widmaier, P.: Space Filling Curves and their use in Geometric Data Structures. Theoretical Computer Science, 181, (1997) 3–15

14. Felber, P.A., Biersack, E. W., Garces-Erice, L., Ross, K.W., Urvoy-Keller, G.: Data Indexing and querying in DHT Peer-to-Peer Networks. Working paper.

15. Harren, M., Hellerstein, J., Huebch, R., Loo, B. T., Shenker, S., Stoica, I.: Complex Queries in DHT-based Peer-to-Peer Networks. In the 1st International Workshop on Peer-to-Peer Systems, IPTPS'02 (2002)

16. Huebsch, R., Hellerstein, J., Lanham, N., Loo, B. T., Shenker, S.: Querying the Internet with PIER. In the Proc. of the 29th VLDB Conference, Berlin, Germany (2003)

17. FIPS180-1. Secure hash Standard. U.S. Department of Commerce/NIST, National Technical Information Service, Springield, VA (1995)

18. Ratnasamy, S., Shenker, S., Stoica, I.: Routing Algorithms for DHTs: Some Open Questions. In the 1st International Workshop on Peer-to-Peer Systems, IPTPS'02 (2002)

19. Mishra, P., Eich, M.: Join Processing in Relational Databases. ACM Computing Surveys, Vol. 24, No. 1 (1992)

20. Kossman, D.: The State of the Art in Distributed Query Processing. ACM Computing Surveys (2000)

21. Clarke, I., et al: Freenet: A Distributed, Anonymous Information Storage and Retrieval System. In Proc. ICSI Works. on Design Issues in Anonymity and Unobservability (2000)

22. Triantafillou, P. et al: Towards High Performance Peer-to-Peer Content and Resource Sharing Systems. In Proc. CIDR Conf. on Innovative Data Systems Research (2003).

23. Triantafillou, P.: Peer-to-Peer Network Architectures: The Next Step. Invited presentation at SIGCOMM'03 / FDNA'03 (www.ceid.upatras.gr/faculty/peter/papers/fdna03.pdf).

Distributed Queries and Query Optimization in Schema-Based P2P-Systems

Ingo Brunkhorst[1], Hadhami Dhraief[2], Alfons Kemper[3], Wolfgang Nejdl[1,2], and Christian Wiesner[3]

[1] Learning Lab Lower Saxony, University of Hannover, Germany,
{brunkhor,nejdl}@learninglab.de
[2] Information Systems Institute, University of Hannover, Germany,
{hdhraief,nejdl}@kbs.uni-hannover.de
[3] Computer Science Department, University of Passau, Germany,
{wiesner,kemper}@db.fmi.uni-passau.de

Abstract. Databases have employed a schema-based approach to store and retrieve structured data for decades. For peer-to-peer (P2P) networks, similar approaches are just beginning to emerge, also motivated by the fact, that sending (atomic) queries to the appropriate peers clearly fails for queries which need data from more than one peer to be executed. While quite a few database techniques can be re-used in this new context, a P2P data management infrastructure poses additional challenges which have to be solved before schema-based P2P networks become as common as schema-based databases. Because of the dynamic nature of P2P networks, we can neither assume global knowledge about data distribution, nor are static topologies and static query plans suitable for these networks. Unlike in traditional distributed database systems, we cannot assume a complete schema instance but rather work with a distributed schema which directs query processing tasks from one node to one or more neighboring nodes.

In this paper, we will first discuss a suitable topology for schema-based P2P networks and how distributed knowledge about data distribution can be stored, accessed and updated based on that topology. Second we will describe how this knowledge can be used to distribute abstract query plans through the P2P network and expand them on the fly such that we can place query operators next to data sources and utilize distributed computing resources more effectively.

1 Introduction

P2P applications have been quite successful, e.g., for exchanging music files, where networks use simple attributes to describe these resources. A lot of effort has been put into refining topologies and query routing functionalities of these networks, and simple systems like Napster and Gnutella have inspired more efficient infrastructures such as the ones based on distributed hash tables (e.g., CAN and CHORD [28,31]). Less effort has been put into extending the representation and query functionalities offered by such networks, and projects exploring more expressive P2P infrastructures [24,2,1,14] have only slowly started the move toward schema-based P2P networks.

At the same time, database systems have evolved toward a higher degree of distribution. While it has been a long way from central databases to truly distributed databases, we currently see first explorations toward true peer-to-peer data management infrastructures

K. Aberer et al. (Eds.): VLDB 2003 Ws DBISP2P, LNCS 2944, pp. 184–199, 2004.
© Springer-Verlag Berlin Heidelberg 2004

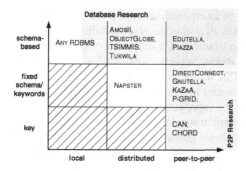

Fig. 1. Schema Capabilities and Distribution

which will have all characteristics of P2P systems, i.e., *local control of data, dynamic addition and removal of peers, only local knowledge of available data and schemas* and *self-organization and -optimization*. In this view, schema-based P2P systems are the point where these two directions of research meet [12] (see Figure 1).

In the Edutella project [8,24,26] we have been exploring some issues arising in that context, with the goal of designing and implementing a schema-based P2P infrastructure for the Semantic Web. Edutella relies on the W3C metadata standards RDF and RDF Schema (RDFS) [21,5] to describe distributed resources, and uses basic P2P primitives provided as part of the JXTA framework [10]. In the ObjectGlobe project [4,19,20] we have designed and implemented a distributed data network consisting of three kinds of suppliers: *data-providers* supply data, *function-providers* offer query operators to process data, and *cycle-providers* are contracted to execute query operators. ObjectGlobe enables applications to execute complex queries which involve the execution of operators from multiple function providers at different sites (cycle providers) and the retrieval of data and documents from multiple data sources.

In this paper, we discuss in Section 2, how a super-peer based topology and "schema-aware" routing indices allow us to efficiently route queries only to appropriate peers, and how these indices are built and updated, when new peers enter or leave the network. In Sections 3 and 4 we describe how these indices facilitate the distribution and dynamic expansion of query plans, and will explore different strategies for optimizing query plans in this environment. Section 5 gives an overview of two prototypes implementing the proposed techniques and Section 6 concludes with further ideas.

2 Routing in Schema-Based P2P-Systems

Efficient query routing is one of the corner stones of advanced P2P systems. By relying on a super-peer topology with "schema-aware" routing indices we show how to advance the efficiency of recent P2P systems. We will start from super-peer networks as a particularly appropriate topology for our schema-based P2P topologies, and discuss topology and routing indices in such a network.

2.1 Super-Peer Networks

Each peer in a P2P network usually has varying resources available, e.g., regarding bandwidth or processing power. As discussed in [33], exploiting the different capabilities in a

P2P network can lead to an efficient network architecture, where a small subset of peers, called super-peers, takes over specific responsibilities for peer aggregation, query routing, and mediation. An example of a simple super-peer based architecture is the KaZaA network [16], more elaborate versions are described in [6] and [25].

Super-peer based P2P infrastructures are usually based on a two-phase routing architecture, which routes queries first in the super-peer backbone, and then distributes them to the peers connected to the super-peers. Caching of the peers data at the super-peers avoids the second query distribution step but requires considerable amount of storage space. Furthermore, data integrity is not guaranteed. Super-peer routing is usually based on different kinds of indexing and routing tables, as discussed in [6] and [25]. Here, we will discuss a routing mechanism based on two indices storing information to route within the P2P backbone and between super-peers and their respective peers.

2.2 Routing Indices

The Edutella Super-Peer Topology. Edutella super-peers [25] employ routing indices which explicitly acknowledge the semantic heterogeneity of schema-based P2P networks, and therefore include schema information as well as other possible index information. Network connections among the super-peers form the super-peer backbone that is responsible for message routing and integration/mediation of metadata.

Super-peers in the Edutella network are arranged in the HyperCuP topology. The HyperCuP algorithm described in [29] is capable of organizing super-peers of a P2P network into a recursive graph structure called a hypercube that stems from the family of Cayley graphs. Super-peers join the HyperCuP based super-peer topology by asking any of the already integrated super-peers which then carries out the super-peer integration protocol. No central maintenance is necessary for changing the HyperCuP structure.

HyperCuP enables efficient and non-redundant query broadcasts. For broadcasts, each node can be seen as the root of a specific spanning tree through the P2P network. The topology allows for $\log_2 N$ path length and $\log_2 N$ number of neighbors, where N is the total number of nodes in the network (i.e., the number of super-peers in our case). Peers connect to the super-peers in a star-like fashion, providing content and content metadata. Alternatives to this topology are possible provided that they guarantee the spanning tree characteristic of the super-peer backbone, which we exploit for maintaining our routing indices and distributed query plans.

Super-Peer/Peer Routing Indices. The super-peer/peer routing indices (SP/P indices for short) contain information about metadata usage at each peer, i.e., which schema and attributes are used to describe the content stored at the peers. On registration the peer provides this information to its super-peer.

In contrast to other approaches (Gnutella [9], CAN [28]), our indices do not refer to individual content elements but to peers (as in CHORD [31]). The indices can contain information about peers at different granularities: schemas, schema properties, property value ranges and individual property values:

Schema Index. We assume that different peers will support different schemas and that these schemas are uniquely identified (by a URI). The routing index contains the schema identifier as well as the peers supporting this schema.

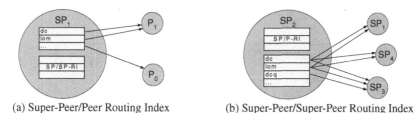

(a) Super-Peer/Peer Routing Index   (b) Super-Peer/Super-Peer Routing Index

Fig. 2. SP/P and SP/SP Routing Indices

Property/Sets of Properties Index. Peers might choose to use only a selection of properties from (one or more) schemas to describe their content. While this is unusual in conventional database systems, it is more often used for data stores using semi-structured data, and very common for RDF-based [5] systems. In this kind of index, super-peers use the properties (uniquely identified by schema ID plus property name) or sets of properties to describe their peers.

Property Value Range Index. For properties which contain values from a predefined hierarchical vocabulary we can use an index which specifies taxonomies or part of a taxonomy for properties.

Property Value Index. For some properties it may also be advantageous to create value indices to reduce network traffic. This case is identical to a classical database index with the exception that the index entries do not refer to the resource, but the peer providing it. This index contains only properties that are used very often compared to the rest of the data stored at the peers.

Using indices with different granularities enables us to state queries at different levels of accuracy. Figure 2(a) gives an example of an SP/P index at the schema granularity. Peer P_1 uses two schema standards for describing its content, the Dublin Core standard [7] (dc for short) and the Learning Object Metadata standard [23] (lom for short).

Super-Peer/Super-Peer Routing Indices. In order to avoid query broadcasting (flooding) in the super-peer backbone we introduce super-peer/super-peer routing indices (SP/SP indices) to forward queries among the super-peers. These SP/SP indices are essentially extracts and summaries from all super-peer local SP/P indices. Similar to the SP/P indices they contain schema information at different granularities, but refer to the super-peers' neighbors in the super-peer backbone (as shown in Figure 2(b)). Queries are forwarded to super-peer neighbors based on the SP/SP indices, and sent to connected peers based on the SP/P indices. For instance, Table 1 states the SP/SP routing index of the super-peer SP_2 at different granularities.

For constructing the SP/SP index a super-peer can be seen as the root of a spanning tree. The SP/SP index is built dynamically based on the SP/P indices of all the super-peers on this spanning tree, by backward propagation and aggregation of the SP/P information. The other super-peers update their SP/SP indices accordingly.

For example, the SP/SP routing index of SP_2 states at the schema level that all neighbors (SP_1, SP_3, SP_4) support the Dublin Core Schema dc and the Learning Object Metadata schema lom, but only SP_3 contains information described by the Qualified Dublin Core Element Set dcq). Thus, a query requiring both dcq and lom will not be routed to SP_1 and SP_4 but to SP_3. The same routing mechanism applies for queries on the other levels of

Table 1. SP/SP Index of SP_2 at Different Granularities

Granularity	Index of SP_2		
Schema	dc		SP_1, SP_3, SP_4
	lom		SP_1, SP_3, SP_4
	dcq		SP_3
Property	dc:subject		SP_1, SP_3, SP_4
	lom:type		SP_1, SP_3, SP_4
	dc:format		SP_3, SP_4
Property Value Range	dc:subject	ccs:dbms	SP_1, SP_2, SP_3
Property	lom:type	"exercise"	SP_3
Value	dc:language	"de"	SP_3, SP_4

granularity. A special case is the *Property Value Range* level which gives specific properties in combination with classification hierarchies (like the ACM Computing Classification System, ACM CCS[1]). Making use of the topic hierarchy, the routing index can contain aggregate information in order to reduce the index size.

2.3 Peers Registering at Super-Peers

Peers connecting to a super-peer have to register their metadata information at this super-peer thus providing the necessary schema information for constructing the SP/P and SP/SP routing indices. For registration an XML registration message encapsulates a metadata-based description of the peer properties. A peer must register at least one schema (e.g., the DC or the LOM element set) with a set of properties (possibly with additional information), or with information about specific property values. A complete registration example in the RDF-syntax can be found at [15].

The behavior of (super-)peers is rather unpredictable in a P2P network. Thus, these registration messages are valid for a certain period only, and peers have to re-register periodically. By invalidating the peers' registrations periodically we chose a behavior similar to other protocols for dynamic settings (like DHCP) since peers may leave the network without any notice. If a super-peer fails, its formerly connected peers must re-register with another super-peer. We are currently investigating deterministic reconnection strategies using testaments which specify alternative super-peers, and clustering strategies, grouping similar peers (in terms of supported schema) together.

2.4 Update of Routing Indices

Update of the SP/P Index. An update of the SP/P index of a given super-peer occurs, when a peer leaves the super-peer, a new peer registers, or the metadata information of a registered peer changes (e.g., new attributes are added or deleted).

If a peer leaves the super-peer all references to this peer have to be removed from the SP/P index of the respective super-peer. The same applies if a peer fails to re-register periodically. In the case of a peer joining the network or re-registering, its respective metadata/schema information are matched against the SP/P entries of the respective super-peer. If the SP/P routing index already contains the peers' metadata only a reference to the

---

[1] Note that ccs:networks is a common super concept of ccs:ethernet and ccs:clientserver in the ACM CCS taxonomy

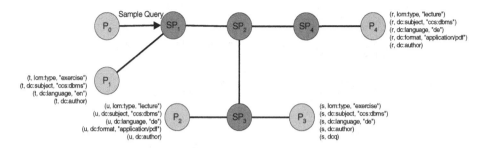

Fig. 3. Routing Example Network

peer is stored in the index otherwise the respective metadata with references to the peer are added to the index. The following algorithm formalize this procedure:

We define S as a set of schema elements[2]: $S = \{s_i \| i = 1...n\}$. The super-peer SP_x already stores a set S_x of schema elements in its SP/P index. The SP/P index of a super peer SP_x can be considered as a mapping $s_i \mapsto \{P_j \| j = 1...m\}$. A new peer P_y registers to the super peer SP_x with a set S_y of schema elements.

1. If $S_y \subseteq S_x$, then add P_y to the list of peers at each $s_i \in S_y$
2. Else if $S_y \setminus S_x = \{s_n, ..., s_m\} \neq \emptyset$, then update the SP/P index by adding new rows $s_n \mapsto P_y, ..., s_m \mapsto P_y$.

Update of the SP/SP Index. Let us first consider how to update the SP/SP indices in the backbone, when one of them has been modified as described before. We assume here, that each SP/P modification triggers the update process for SP/SP indices, though we can also collect the modifications for a given period and trigger the SP/SP update process then.

We further assume that the super-peers cluster peers according to their schema characteristics, so that peers connected to a super-peer usually have similar characteristics, and SP/P modifications trigger SP/SP index updates less frequently. If we take for example the network in Figure 3 and the example SP/SP index of SP_2 shown in Table 1, a new peer P_x registering at super-peer SP_1 with the property *dc:language* does not trigger the update process since this metadata information already exists in the SP/P index. If a new peer P_y registers at SP_1 with the property *dcq:created*, the SP/SP update process starts, as this property was not included in the index before.

SP/SP Update Process. Remember that super-peers in the network are organized into a HyperCuP topology, which implicitly defines each super-peer as root of a spanning tree. Query routing takes place along the spanning trees (restricted by the SP/SP indices), so the update of SP/SP indices has to be done in the reverse direction. For these updates, again each super-peer acts as the root of a spanning tree (in the "backward direction"), as shown in Figure 4 for the super-peer G. In this example we have a simple (complete) cube, which has three dimensions (0,1,2), such that every node has 3 neighbors.

In order to update the SP/SP indices after an update of the SP/P index of the super-peer SP_x we build the spanning tree of the super-peer SP_x as follows: SP_x sends the update message to all its neighbors, tagging it with the edge label (dimension) on which the message was sent. Super-peers receiving the message update their SP/SP index accordingly

---

[2] A complete schema, e.g., *dc* is also considered as schema element

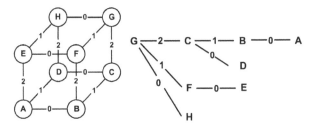

Fig. 4. HyperCup Topology and Spanning Tree Example

and forward the update message, but only to those super-peers tagged with lower edge labels. Furthermore, whenever a message does not change the SP/SP index at a receiving super-peer SP_y, forwarding stops. The update is done as follows:

- For all $s_i \in S_x \cap S_y$ add dimension of SP_x to the list of dimensions at row s_i if this dimension does not exist.
- For all $s_i \in S_x \setminus S_y$ add a new row $s_i \mapsto dimension(SP_x)$

Adding new Super-Peers. Adding a new super-peer is a bit more complicated. For a new super-peer, the HyperCuP protocol takes care of identifying new neighbors as discussed in [29]. In this process one of the super-peers is "responsible" for integrating the new super-peer. In most cases the new super-peer will fill a "vacant" position in the hypercube, which has temporarily been administered by the responsible super-peer. In this process, this super-peer, who has been holding an additional SP/SP and SP/P index for the vacant position, transfers these indices to the new super-peer. If the new super-peer opens a new dimension, it has to take over some peers from the old super-peer, and the SP/SP index has to be split into two indices. The neighboring super-peers have to update their indices accordingly, by exchanging the responsible super-peer with the new super-peer on the appropriate dimension. Beyond the immediate neighbors, no further update is necessary.

Removing Super-Peers. The HyperCuP protocol also takes care of super-peers leaving the backbone. We usually assume that the leaving super-peer coordinates this operation, and specifically asks appropriate super-peer(s) (more than one if the leaving super-peer temporarily fills several positions) that will administer its position afterwards. In this process the administering super-peers take over the SP/SP and SP/P indices of the leaving super-peer, and the neighbors of the leaving super-peer as well as of the administering ones have to update their SP/SP indices. Again, no update is required beyond the immediate neighbors. Peers of the leaving super-peer reconnect to the super-peer which administers the vacant position.

In the case of unexpected link failure its neighbors determine the "closest" (regarding smallest hop distance) super-peer. This super-peer then coordinates the administration of the open position with the same procedure as described above. Peers of the failing super-peer have to reconnect at some other super-peer, possibly triggering further SP/SP update messages.

3 Query Processing in P2P Networks

As described before, P2P networks can be divided into the two classes: pure P2P networks and schema-based P2P networks. In this section we demonstrate at first the deficiencies of traditional query processing in both classes as they rely on data shipping. Then we propose our approach on dynamic, extensible, and distributed query processing in schema-based P2P networks. We illustrate query processing by Figures 5 and 6 where a client peer states a query to search for some information and uses its own filter predicates (the two stars) to select the relevant information.

Although distributed query optimization and execution are well known problems in databases, distributed query processing on distributed metadata is novel. Middleware systems, e.g., Garlic [17], have been used to overcome the heterogeneity faced when data is dispersed across different data sources. In [22] a central mapping information of all participating, distributed data sources is queried. [27] introduces so called mutant query plans which encapsulate partially evaluated query plans and data. Their approach is not capable of supporting user-defined operators. Furthermore, loss of pipelining during execution limits the general applicability for distributed query processing. [3] presents a query processing architecture for execution SQL queries over an P2P network. Their approach is based on distributed hashtables and does not take into account user-defined operators. PIER ([18]) constitutes a P2P information exchange and retrieval system which is also based on distributed hashtables.

3.1 Pure P2P Query Processing: Flooding Requests

In pure P2P systems like Gnutella query processing takes place entirely at the client. Therefore, all required data has to be shipped to the client whereby the network is flooded with requests for resources which are propagated to all neighbors through the network up to a particular horizon. Usually the majority of these peers host none of the desired information. On the other side, due to the horizon, some information is never discovered. The URIs of the results are returned to the client and another round-trip is necessary to obtain the data itself. The results of this initial data shipping phase are processed centrally at the client, i.e., only at the client the user-defined filtering (execution of special-purpose code) can take place and possibly large volumes of data are shipped to the client.

3.2 Schema-Based P2P Query Processing: Routing Requests

In schema-based P2P networks a distributed index systematically guides the search to the appropriate (super-)peers. Whenever a new participant joins the P2P network the index is updated with the metadata of the resources by the new peers as described in the previous section. Figure 5 shows on the left hand side that the search of information usually involves only a small part (depending on the clustering) of the network. The right hand side of Figure 5 illustrates that the local indices are consulted to selectively propagate the search. The routing of requests constitutes an enormous improvement compared to flooding requests in pure P2P networks. All relevant information is found and must be shipped to the client to make the user-defined filters applicable. Search in schema-based P2P networks is much more efficient, as only the necessary peers are contacted and flooding the network with requests is avoided. Nevertheless, entire query processing still takes place only at the client and user-defined filters and complex operators can only be applied after the data has already been shipped to the client.

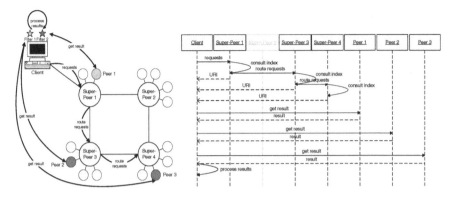

Fig. 5. Traditional Query Processing in Schema-Based P2P Networks (Routing Requests)

3.3 Extensible Distributed Query Processing: Pushing Code-Carrying QEPs

To enable dynamic, extensible, and distributed query processing in schema-based P2P networks, where both standard query operators and user-defined code can be executed nearby the data, we distribute query processing to the (super-)peers. Therefore, super-peers provide functionality for the management of the index structures, query optimization, and query processing capabilities. Additionally, we expect that peers provide query processing capabilities to be a full member of the P2P network. [3] These query processors can be dynamically extended by special-purpose query operators that are shipped to the query processor as part of the query plan. This way, query evaluation plans (QEPs) with user-defined code, e.g., selection predicates, compression functions, join predicates, etc., can be pushed from the client to the (super-)peers where they are executed. Furthermore, super-peers have to provide an optimizer for generating good query plans from the queries they receive. We utilize these distributed query processing capabilities at the super-peers and distribute the query stated by the user to the corresponding super-peers. This distribution process is guided by the index which is dynamic and corresponds to the data allocation schema in traditional distributed DBMSs. However, as the index is dynamic and dispersed, static query optimization is not possible. Thus, query optimization must also be dynamic and based on the allocation schema of the data known at the super-peer.

Figure 6 illustrates schema-based P2P networks with extensible distributed query processing capabilities. We assume for our example, that the (super-)peers install a fully functional optimizer and an extensible query processor as mentioned above. The left hand side of Figure 6 shows the architecture and the flow of messages in our approach where queries and code are pushed through the network. The client sends the query including user-defined operators to the first super-peer where the local indices are consulted and the query is split into two parts. The local optimizer determines the parts to be sent to the next (super-)peers and the operators to be executed locally to combine the results. Section 4 discusses three basic alternative optimization strategies. The first part including Filter 1 is shipped to Peer 1, where the filter can be applied directly on the data before shipping the results to Super-Peer 1. The later part of the original query including Filter 2 is pushed

---

[3] This assumtion is no necessity for our approach, e.g., thin clients such as mobile devices presumably would provide no query processing capabilities. In this case the next super-peer takes over query processing.

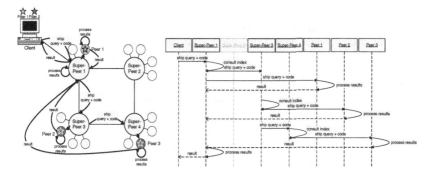

Fig. 6. Pushing Code-Carrying Query Evaluation Plans (QEPs)

to Super-Peer 3, where the same process is repeated. Again, a part of the query is sent to Super-Peer 4 and the results are sent to Super-Peer 1, where they are processed further and finally returned to the client. The client just needs to display the results, and very limited resources suffice for clients. Less data shipping enables thin clients and even mobile devices, e.g., cellular telephones and PDAs, to query the P2P network. The right hand side of Figure 6 shows the sequence of index lookups, shipping of queries and code, and local query processing at the (super-)peers. The query plan is decentrally optimized, whereby each super-peer optimizes just the piece of the query it receives. The remaining parts are pushed further. This way, user-defined code such as filter predicates are pushed to the data sources.

3.4   Summary and Classification of P2P Networks

The following table classifies P2P networks summarizing the most important characteristics regarding query processing facilities and usage of index structures:

		Flooding Code-Carrying QEPs	**Pushing Code-Carrying QEPs**
with extensible, distributed	query processor	+ user-defined operators + query processing at (super-)peers + pushing QEPs & code to the data + low transfer volumes (only results) − inefficient search by flooding − many peers are queried	+ user-defined operators + query processing at (super-)peers + pushing QEPs & code to the data + low transfer volumes (only results) + efficient search by routing + only necessary peers are queried
		Flooding Requests	**Routing Requests**
without extensible, distributed	query processor	− fixed set of query operators − query processing at client − data shipping to client − huge transfer volumes − inefficient search by flooding − many peers are queried	− fixed set of query operators − query processing at client − data shipping to client − huge transfer volumes + efficient search by routing + only necessary peers are queried
		without index	with index

select r_1.data, r_2.data, r_3.data

from   Resources r_1, Resources r_2, Resources r_3

where r_1.lom_type = "lecture" **and** r_1.dc_subject = "ccs:dbms" **and** r_1.dc_language = "de" **and**
      r_1.dc_format = "application/pdf" **and** occur(r_1.data, "transaction processing") $>= 2$ **and**
      r_2.lom_type = "exercise" **and** r_2.dc_subject = "ccs:dbms" **and** r_2.dc_language = "de" **and**
      r_3.lom_type = "exercise" **and** r_3.dc_subject = "ccs:dbms" **and** r_3.dc_language = "en" **and**
      r_1.dc_author = r_2.dc_author **and** r_1.dc_author = r_3.dc_author

Fig. 7. SQL Formulation of the Example Query

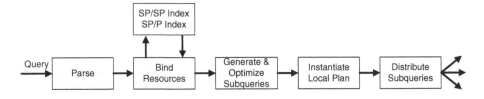

Fig. 8. Plan Generation at a Super-Peer

4 Plan Generation and Distribution

In this section we describe the generation of a query evaluation plan at one super-peer using the allocation schema provided by the index structures. For illustration let us consider the following example query: "Retrieve the data of resources r_1, r_2, and r_3 where r_1 is a lecture about *ccs:dbms*, and the language is *de*; furthermore, resource r_1 should be a PDF file containing at least twice the phrase "transaction processing"; r_2 is an exercise about *ccs:dbms*, the language is *de*; r_3 is an exercise about *ccs:dbms*, the language is *en*; the resources should be written by the same *author*." The corresponding SQL formulation of this query is shown in Figure 7. The query accesses "Resources", which represents the collection of all resources registered in the P2P network. The attribute *data* represents all the data belonging to the registered resource, i.e., in our example the PDF file. The user-defined filter occur(r_1.data, ''transaction processing'') $>= 2$ counts the number of appearances of the string in the PDF file. This is operation has to be executed nearby the data sources to reduce the network traffic.

4.1 Details of the Plan Generation and Distribution

In contrast to traditional distributed query optimization, the plan is not generated statically at one single host. In our approach, super-peers generate partial query plans which are executed locally and the remainders of the query are pushed to the neighbors. Thereby, plan generation involves five major steps as depicted in Figure 8:

Parse. The received SQL query is parsed and transformed into an internal representation which is a decomposition of the query into its building blocks. The succeeding steps are prepared, i.e., properties, property-values, and user-defined operators are identified.

Bind Resources. The local indices are consulted to determine the location of the required resources. For this purpose we introduce resource directions (*RD*), physical resources (*PR*), and logical resources (*LR*): Users specify the desired information by giving properties and property-values which restrict LRs. These LRs are bound to RDs, if a corresponding data source is found in the SP/SP index. Using the SP/P index, LRs are bound to PRs, i.e., the URIs of registered resources. Binding the LRs to PRs and RDs, all levels of granularity of the indices have to be considered. In our example scenario we obtain the following bindings at SP_1: $r_1 = RD_1^1 @SP_2$, $r_2 = RD_2^1 @SP_2$, and $r_3 = PR_3^1 @P_1 = t$, where, e.g., $RD_2^1 @SP_2$ denotes the first resource direction for the logical resource r_2 and references super-peer SP_2. Multiple RDs and PRs can contribute data for the same LR.

Generate & Optimize Subqueries. Based on the bindings, a local query plan is generated. For the remaining parts subqueries are generated. As super-peers have a very limited view of the whole P2P network (only the neighbors are known), it is obvious that no comprehensive static plan in the traditional sense can be produced. Furthermore, we determine which subplans are executed at the neighboring (super-)peers.

As only partial information is available to the query optimizer this is a non-standard query optimization problem where only a part of the query plan is generated. The remainder of the query which could not be executed locally is identified and grouped by host. These remaining parts constitute the inputs to the local plan. To perform cost based optimization, the optimizer uses statistics of the input data, the network topology, and the hosts. When LRs are bound at least the number of referenced resources should be provided by the index structures. This forms the basis of the cost estimation. Furthermore, the optimizer may learn response times, transfer rates, and even result sizes from previous query executions whereby the techniques presented by [13] can be adopted for P2P query processing to obtain fine-grained and up-to-date statistics.

During plan generation, each query operator is annotated with the host where it is executed. This is done bottom up from the leaves of the operator tree, which constitute PRs and RDs. The annotations of the leaves are given by the binding phase. Now, an operator can be executed on a host H, if all its input operators are executed at H, too. This means, that a join must be executed at a host, if both inputs stem from different hosts. For instance, the following query plan could be generated at SP_1:

$$\bowtie_{author} @SP_1$$
$$\diagup \qquad \diagdown$$
$$\bowtie_{author} @SP_2 \qquad PR_3^1 @P_1 = t$$
$$\diagup \qquad \diagdown$$
$$\sigma_{occur(u.data,...)>=2} @SP_2 \qquad RD_2^1 @SP_2$$
$$\mid$$
$$RD_1^1 @SP_2$$

The left-hand subtree can be executed at SP_2, a subquery is pushed to SP_2 which will be optimized analogously (based on the bindings $r_1 = RD_1^1 @SP_3 \cup RD_1^2 @SP_4$ and $r_2 = RD_2^1 @SP_3$). The following query plan could be generated at SP_2 for the subquery, where again the individual subtrees can be pushed to SP_3 and SP_4:

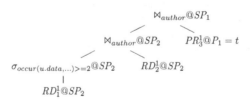

Instantiate Local Plan. The local query plan is instantiated at the super-peer, all user-defined code is loaded and the communication path to the super-peer which uses this part of the query plan as input is established. The execution of the local query plan is not started until the distributed subqueries have established their communication paths. When the subqueries are instantiated the plan is executed following the iterator model [11].

Distribute Subqueries. The remaining subqueries are distributed to the corresponding super-peers, where they are processed further.

4.2 Optimization Strategies

As shown above, several PRs and RDs can contribute data for the same LRs. The simplest way for incorporating the data for such an LR would be to union all the affected physical resources before any other operation is considered for that LR. First, this naive strategy would produce good plans in some cases, but usually leads to an increase of the transmitted data. Second, query optimization would be limited, however, and possibly better plans might not be considered. Thus, several alternatives for the naive query plan must be considered by applying equivalence transformations. Unfortunately, the number of plans which has to be considered during query optimization when all possible equivalence transformations should be taken into account, is rather large. The naive strategy is acceptable, if the bound resources are spread widely over multiple hosts. To increase the degree of distribution, this query plan can be transformed using an equivalence transformation which turns the join of unions into a union of joins, e.g., $(R_1 \cup R_2) \bowtie S = (R_1 \bowtie S) \cup (R_2 \bowtie S)$. The joins may then be distributed to the neighboring super-peers. This plan may have a huge number of subqueries, however, which may not be efficient.

The most promising strategy in such a distributed environment is to collect as many bindings of one LR as possible at one host. Utilizing statistics the optimizer determines one "collecting host" to collect all data of one logical resource and the other hosts are informed to send all data to the collecting host. This designated collecting host may change during the plan generation. Furthermore, the selection of the collecting host can take into account the current load situation to balance the load among all participanting (super-)peers. Figure 9 shows the mapping of the query plan onto the network, in which this strategy is used. In this plan all resources for r_1 are collected at first at P_2 (where the union is executed), then the join of resources r_1 with r_2 is done at SP_3.

5   Implementation

5.1 The QueryFlow System as a Basis for P2P Query Processing

One of our platforms for implementing the ideas described above is the QueryFlow system ([19,20]) which is based on ObjectGlobe ([4]). The idea of ObjectGlobe is to create an open market place for three kinds of suppliers: *data-providers* supply data, *function-providers* offer query operators to process data, and *cycle-providers* are contracted to execute query operators. A single site (even a single machine) may comprise all three services. Object-Globe enables applications to execute complex queries which involve the execution of operators from multiple function providers at different sites (cycle providers) and the retrieval of data and documents from multiple data sources. The system is written in Java, as are user-defined query operators which are loaded on demand and executed at the cycle

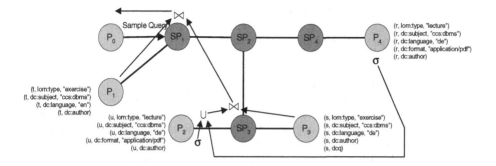

Fig. 9. Query Plan Mapped onto the P2P Network (The Arrows Indicate the Flow of Results)

provider in their own Java sandbox. User-defined query operators, e.g., filters or joins using complex predicates, must implement the iterator model of [11].

The QueryFlow system extends the idea of dynamic query execution by introducing incomplete query plans. Hyperlinks reference single query plans (HyperQueries), which are embedded as virtual attributes into the database of one host. The HyperQueries reside on hosts in the Internet and are accessed dynamically. Whenever a virtual attribute is accessed during execution, the referenced HyperQuery is executed at the remote host and the result is returned to the caller. In our prototypical implementation, we assume that each super-peer is a fully functional cycle-provider, i.e., HyperQueries and operations such as joins, selection, projections, and user-defined operators can be executed by them.

Code-carrying QEPs do not really transmit the Java code of the operators but the query plan is annotated with information which indicates the function-provider the user-defined operator is loaded from. A class loader loads the bytecode of the operator on demand into memory, whereby access to safety critical system resources is controlled by Java's security manager. Therby, a so-called *sandbox* is created in which untrusted code is safely executed. Details of security, trust, and resource consumption are discussed in [30].

5.2   The Edutella P2P Infrastructure

The Open Source Edutella project [8,24,26] has the goal to design and implement a schema-based P2P infrastructure for the Semantic Web. Edutella relies on the W3C metadata standards RDF and RDF Schema (RDFS) [21,5] to describe distributed resources. It connects heterogeneous RDF (and also XML) repositories describing the resources available in the network. Provider peers integrate heterogeneous data sources into the network, by allowing local translation (wrapping) from the common data and query model (ECDM) [24], to backend databases using either memory-based RDF models, database systems using SQL, or systems based on logic (e.g., Prolog). The ECDM and the corresponding query exchange language RDF-QEL is based on Datalog semantics and is represented in RDF. Edutella is written in Java, and uses the JXTA architecture [10] developed by Sun for basic P2P functionality, like initial peer discovery, network groups and pipe-based communication between peers.

The Edutella super-peers [25] include schema information as well as other possible index information in the corresponding routing indices. The current implementation uses the routing indices to select (super-)peers who can answer a given query using the index information and the query characteristics. We are currently implementing distributed query processing and query plans as discussed in Section 3.

6 Conclusions and Future Work

In this paper we have discussed additional challenges for P2P data management regarding query routing and query planning, based on the specific characteristics of schema-based P2P systems, which make straightforward adoptions of distributed database techniques impossible. We have discussed an innovative query routing and planning architecture based on distributed routing indices, which allows us to place query operators next to data sources and utilize distributed computing resources more effectively. In the future we try to merge both systems by processing code-carrying query plans in Edutella and supporting more schema-based features by the QueryFlow system.

For further optimization, we want to investigate the inclusion of additional statistical information in the indices, e.g., average response time, amount of registered data regarding schematas, properties, etc. Furthermore, top-down query optimization seems to be an interesting strategy especially as query optimization can be interrupted at any time and a query plan is provided. At last, studying other strategies for the plan generation and a more dynamic placement of operators would offer new possibilities. A demonstration of the QueryFlow-based implementation will be given in [32].

References

1. K. Aberer and M. Hauswirth. Semantic gossiping. In *Database and Information Systems Research for Semantic Web and Enterprises, Invitational Workshop*, 2002.
2. P. A. Bernstein, F. Giunchiglia, A. Kementsietsidis, J. Mylopoulos, L. Serafini, and I. Zaihrayeu. Data management for peer-to-peer computing: A vision. In *Proc. of the 5th Intl. Workshop on the Web and Databases*, 2002.
3. P. Boncz and C. Treijtel. AmbientDB: Relational Query Processing over P2P Network. In *Intl. Workshop on Databases, Information Systems and Peer-to-Peer Computing*, 2003.
4. R. Braumandl, M. Keidl, A. Kemper, D. Kossmann, A. Kreutz, S. Seltzsam, and K. Stocker. ObjectGlobe: Ubiquitous query processing on the Internet. *The VLDB Journal: Special Issue on E-Services*, 10(3), 2001.
5. D. Brickley and R. V. Guha. RDF vocabulary description language 1.0: RDF Schema, 2003. http://www.w3.org/TR/rdf-schema/.
6. A. Crespo and H. Garcia-Molina. Routing indices for peer-to-peer systems. In *Proc. Intl. Conf. on Distributed Computing Systems*, 2002.
7. Dublin core metadata initiative.
8. The Edutella Project. http://edutella.jxta.org/, 2002.
9. J. Frankel. Gnutella. www.gnutella.com, March 1999. Information portal with community, development information and downloads.
10. L. Gong. Project JXTA: A technology overview. Technical report, SUN Microsystems, 2001. http://www.jxta.org/project/www/docs/TechOverview.pdf.
11. G. Graefe. Query Evaluation Techniques for Large Databases. *ACM Computing Surveys*, 25(2), 1993.
12. S. Gribble, A. Y. Halevy, Z. G. Ives, M. Rodrig, and D. Suciu. What can databases do for peer-to-peer. In *Proc. of the 4th Intl. Workshop on the Web and Databases.*, 2001.

13. J. R. Gruser, L. Raschid, V. Zadorozhny, and T. Zhan. Learning response time for websources using query feedback and application in query optimization. *The VLDB Journal*, 9(1), 2000.

14. A. Y. Halevy, Z. G. Ives, P. Mork, and I. Tatarinov. Piazza: Data management infrastructure for semantic web applications. In *Proc. of the 12th Intl. World Wide Web Conf.*, 2003.

15. H.Dhraief. Peer Registration RDF Document.
    http://www.kbs.uni-hannover.de/~hdhraief/edutella/.

16. N. Hemming. KaZaA. www.kazaa.com.

17. V. Josifovski, P. Schwarz, L. Haas, and E. Lin. Garlic: A New Flavor of Federated Query Processing for DB2. In *Proc. of the ACM SIGMOD Conf. on Management of Data*, 2002.

18. R. Huebsch, J. M. Hellerstein, N. Lanham, B. T. Loo, S. Shenker, and I. Stoica. Querying the Internet with PIER. In *Proc. of the Conf. on Very Large Data Bases*, 2003.

19. A. Kemper and C. Wiesner. HyperQueries: Dynamic Distributed Query Processing on the Internet. In *Proc. of the Conf. on Very Large Data Bases*, 2001.

20. A. Kemper, C. Wiesner, and P. Winklhofer. Building dynamic market places using hyperqueries. In *Proc. of the Intl. Conf. on Extending Database Technology*, 2002.

21. O. Lassila and R.R. Swick. W3C Resource Description Framework model and syntax specification, 1999. http://www.w3.org/TR/REC-rdf-syntax/.

22. A. Y. Levy, D. Srivastava, and T. Kirk. Data Model and Query Evaluation in Global Information Systems. *Journal of Intelligent Information Systems*, 5(2), 1995.

23. IEEE Learning Technology Standards Committee, IEEE P1484.12 Learning Object Metadata Working Group.

24. W. Nejdl, B. Wolf, C. Qu, S. Decker, M. Sintek, A. Naeve, M. Nilsson, M. Palmér, and T. Risch. EDUTELLA: a P2P Networking Infrastructure based on RDF. In *Proc. of the 11th Intl. World Wide Web Conf.*, 2002.

25. W. Nejdl, M. Wolpers, W. Siberski, C. Schmitz, M. Schlosser, I. Brunkhorst, and A. Loser. Super-peer-based routing and clustering strategies for RDF-based peer-to-peer networks. In *Proc. of the Intl. World Wide Web Conf.*, 2003.

26. W. Nejdl, B. Wolf, S. Staab, and J. Tane. Edutella: Searching and annotating resources within an RDF-based P2P network. In *Proc. of the Semantic Web Workshop, 11th Intl. World Wide Web Conf.*, 2002.

27. V. Papadimos and D. Maier. Distributed Query Processing and Catalogs for Peer-to-Peer Systems. 2003.

28. S. Ratnasamy, P. Francis, M. Handley, R. Karp, and S. Shenker. A scalable content addressable network. In *Proc. of the 2001 Conf. on applications, technologies, architectures, and protocols for computer communications*, 2001.

29. M. Schlosser, M. Sintek, S. Decker, and W. Nejdl. HyperCuP—Hypercubes, Ontologies and Efficient Search on P2P Networks. In *Intl. Workshop on Agents and P2P Computing*, 2002.

30. S. Seltzsam and S. Börzsönyi and A. Kemper. Security for Distributed E-Service Composition. In *Proc. of the 2nd Intl. Workshop on Technologies for E-Services*, 2001.

31. I. Stoica, R. Morris, D. Karger, M. F. Kaashoek, and H. Balakrishnan. Chord: A scalable peer-to-peer lookup service for internet applications. In *Proc. of the 2001 Conf. on applications, technologies, architectures, and protocols for computer communications*, 2001.

32. C. Wiesner, A. Kemper, and S. Brandl. Dynamic, Extendible Query Processing in Super-Peer Based P2P Systems (Demonstration). In *Proc. IEEE Conf. on Data Engineering*, 2004.

33. B. Yang and H. Garcia-Molina. Improving search in peer-to-peer systems. In *Proc. of the 22nd Intl. Conf. on Distributed Computing Systems*, 2002.

PePeR: A Distributed Range Addressing Space for Peer-to-Peer Systems[*]

Antonios Daskos, Shahram Ghandeharizadeh, and Xinghua An

Department of Computer Science, University of Southern California,
Los Angeles, California 90089
{daskos,shahram,anx}@usc.edu

Abstract. This paper describes a **P**eer-to-**P**eer **R**ange (PePeR) addressing space to process the "select" relational algebra operator. PePeR consists of several novel design decisions to support both exact-match and range selection predicates. First, it constructs Z ranges per node in order to efficiently route predicates in a decentralized manner. Second, it employs interleaved range declustering to minimize mean time to data loss in the presence of node removal(s). Third, it uses innovative techniques to adjust its addressing space in the presence of node insertion. The insertion of nodes is done in a distributed manner and we present a technique that approximates a uniform distribution of records across the nodes. In addition, we present performance numbers from PePeR and compare it with a distributed hash table (DHT). The obtained results show the following. If the workload of a relation is dominated by range predicates then PePeR is a superior alternative. On the other hand, if the workload of a relation is primarily exact-match retrievals (selection predicates using the equality comparison operator), then a DHT provides better performance. Both PePeR and DHT may co-exist in a peer-to-peer system simultaneously, enabling a database specialist to employ DHT with one relation and PePeR with another.

1 Introduction

A key characteristic of peer-to-peer (P2P) systems is their flexibility to enable a node to join and leave without impacting the overall system. These systems are taxonomized [LCC+02,CS02] into: 1) Centralized systems that employ a central directory server for processing queries, e.g., Napster, 2) Decentralized systems that route queries using their peers. The decentralized systems are further categorized into addressable and ad-hoc addressing. The addressable systems maintain a logical mapping between the location of data and network topology, e.g., OceanStore [KBC+00], CAN [RFH+01], Chord [SMK+01], etc. The ad-hoc addressing systems maintain no mapping and employ flooding of queries to retrieve relevant data, e.g., KaZaA, Gnutella, etc. The focus of this study is on

---

[*] This research was supported in part by an unrestricted cash gift from Microsoft Research.

K. Aberer et al. (Eds.): VLDB 2003 Ws DBISP2P, LNCS 2944, pp. 200–218, 2004.

decentralized, addressable P2P systems. To simplify discussion, for the rest of this paper, the term P2P refers to this specific category.

P2P systems may employ a Distributed Hash Table (DHT) [LNS96,PRR97, RFH+01,TJ02,KBC+00] to control placement of data across nodes for efficient retrieval. This is specially true for comparison operators that employ an equality predicate, termed exact-match selection predicates. For example, with a P2P network consisting of thousands of nodes, one may apply a DHT to the name of audio and video clips to assign each to a node. Subsequently, when a user requests a clip by referencing its name, the peers employ the DHT to route the request to the peer containing the referenced clip. This distributed routing is important because it minimizes the amount of state information maintained by a peer, enabling one or more nodes to join and leave without centralized control.

One may employ a DHT with relational databases to control placement of records and processing of exact-match selection predicates. In its simplest form, given a table $S(a_1,a_2, ..., a_n)$, a hash function is applied to the partitioning attribute of each record of S, say $S.a_1$, to map this record to a d dimensional order-preserving Cartesian space. The address space is mapped to the peers in the network, dictating the placement of S's records. An exact-match selection predicate referencing $S.a_1$ such as $S.a_1=C$ (C is a constant) might be initiated at one of the peers, say N_i. N_i applies the hash function to C to compute its hash function value, $V=h(C)$. If V is contained by the range of Cartesian space assigned to N_i then N_i processes the predicate. Otherwise, N_i compares V with the ranges assigned to its neighbors and routes the predicate to the neighbor with the minimum numerical distance to V. This process repeats until the predicate arrives at the node containing the relevant data (distance = 0).

A limitation of DHT is its lack of support for range predicates that reference $S.a_1$. While a system may query each discrete value in a range using DHT, this approach is perceived as infeasible in most cases. Typically, these predicates must be directed to all those nodes containing a fragment of S. This is undesirable for those predicates that retrieve only a few records because many (potentially millions of) nodes will search their repository only to find no relevant data. In addition to wasting resources, this results in a high response time because the underlying overlay network must route this predicate to every single node.

The primary contribution of this paper is PePeR, a distributed addressing space in support of range predicates. PePeR assigns Z ranges of the partitioning attribute of S, $S.a_1$, to each node. It supports distributed routing of both exact-match and range predicates that reference $S.a_1$, along with insertion and removal of nodes in a decentralized manner. In order to enhance availability of data in the presence of node removals, PePeR employs interleaved placement to construct sub-ranges of each range. The placement of these sub-ranges is a natural consequence of how PePeR defines the neighbor relationship between nodes, see Section 3.

PePeR shares its roots with our prior work on placement of data in multi-processor DataBase Management Systems (DBMSs), MAGIC [GDQ92,MS98]. PePeR is novel and different because data placement algorithms in multiprocessor DBMSs are centralized in nature. In addition, they lack concepts such as distributed routing of a predicate from one node to another. This concept is fundamental to PePeR (and P2P systems in general).

P2P systems have been the focus of recent study by the database community. For example, processing of complex queries is described in [HHH+02]. Techniques to compute approximate results for complex queries by finding data ranges that are approximate answers are the focus of [GAE03]. Both studies are different because they assume a DHT as their underlying data placement and routing strategy. Hybrid systems, where some functionality is still centralized constitutes the focus of [YGM01]. A similar approach for management of documents is described in [TXKN03].

Most relevant studies are [AS03,AX02,CFCS03]. Skip graphs [AS03] extend an alternative to a balanced tree, skip lists [Pug90], to provide an order-preserving address space on a collection of nodes. When compared with PePeR, skip graphs are different for several reasons. First, PePeR constructs Z ranges per peer (in a distributed manner), in order to facilitate intelligent routing. Skip graphs, on the other hand, construct pointers from one range to several other ranges to accomplish the same. Second, skip graphs construct a hierarchical data structure that might require a node removal to include the participation of many more nodes than its neighboring nodes. With PePeR a node removal impacts $4Z$ nodes. Note that PePeR and skip graphs are complementary and can be combined into a hybrid approach. For example, our interleaved declustering scheme can be used with skip graphs to increase the availability of data. (Availability of data is not considered in [AS03].)

With [AX02], all peers agree on a d-dimensional Hilbert curve that maps a range of $S.a_1$ to CAN's d-dimensional Cartesian coordinate space. Given a query, a peer employs the space filling curve to identify those coordinates of a CAN's Cartesian space containing the relevant data. Next, it employs CAN's routing mechanism to direct the predicate to these nodes. Similarly, MAAN [CFCS03] supports range queries by mapping neumerical attribute values to Chord [SMK+01] DHT. MAAN relies on Chord's SHA1 hashing to assign an identifier consisting of m bits to each participating node. However, when mapping objects using a numerial attribute value, MAAN employs a locality preserving hashing function to assign an object in the m-bit space. PePeR is novel because it is an alternative to a DHT and independent of either CAN or Chord (as such, it is more comparable with skip graphs [AS03]). We intend to quantify the tradeoff associated with these alternatives when compared with PePeR in the near future.

The rest of this paper is organized as follows. Section 2 illustrates the key elements of PePeR using an example. Section 3 presents the terminology required to present PePeR. Section 4 presents a class of decentralized techniques to insert a node into an existing PePeR configuration. In Section 5, we present a performance study of PePeR and its parameters. We also compare PePeR with a flooding environment that directs a predicate to all nodes of P2P system. We conclude with brief remarks in Section 6.

2   Overview of PePeR

PePeR constructs a range addressing space for a table $S(a_1, a_2, ..., a_n)$ using one of its attributes, say a_1. This attribute is termed S's partitioning attribute. As an example, Figure 1 shows PePeR with a nine node P2P configuration. This figure assumes $S.a_1$ is an integer attribute with values ranging from 0 to 180. Each node N_i is assigned a range R_i, defined as $[l_i, u_i)$. This notation implies $S.a_1$ value of those rows assigned to node N_i is equal to or greater than l_i and less than u_i. A collection of records corresponding to range R_i is termed a fragment. For example, in Figure 1.a, the fragment assigned to node 1 contains those rows with $S.a_1$ values greater than or equal to 20 and less than 40. With PePeR, a node employs a range to route a predicate and a fragment to process a predicate. We start this overview by describing how the system performs routing in a distributed manner. Next, we explain node removal and data availability. Subsequently, we describe how a new node is inserted into PePeR. This discussion uses terms neighbor, containment, partial containment, and distance by defining them informally. The precise definition of these terms is provided in Section 3.

Distributed predicate routing:

To route a predicate in a distributed manner, PePeR requires a node to maintain the Z ranges assigned to each of its neighbors. The neighbors of a node are defined as those with consecutive ranges (see Section 3 for a formal definition of neighbors). For example, in Figure 1.a, node 4's (N_4) neighbors are N_3 and N_5. N_4 stores the ranges assigned to N_3 and N_5. Figure 2.a shows this neighbor relationship using a double arrow. The two edges of an arrow point to identical values that indicate the consecutiveness of two ranges. (The dashed arrow is an exception and described in the following paragraphs.) The range of a selection predicate P, i.e., $\sigma_{S.a_1 \geq l_P \wedge S.a_1 < u_P}(S)$, is defined as $[l_P, u_P)$. Assume P's range is $[10,15)$ and is initiated at N_4 of Figure 1.a. N_4 routes this predicate towards N_0 by routing it to the neighbor with smallest distance to P, i.e., N_3. N_3 repeats

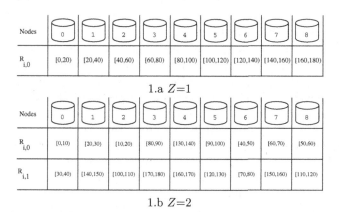

Fig. 1. PePeR with nine nodes and two different Z values.

this process by computing the distance between P and its neighbors in order to route P to N_2. This process terminates when P arrives at N_0 because N_0's range contains P. At this point, N_0 processes the predicate using its fragment to produce results.

It is important to distinguish between routing and processing of a predicate P. In our example, P was routed using four different nodes (N_4, N_3, N_2, and N_1) to arrive at N_0 for processing. A node routes P by comparing its distance with the ranges assigned to its neighbors. N_0 processed P by searching its assigned fragment for those records with a value greater than or equal to 10 and less than 15. A node may both process and route a predicate when P partially overlaps its range. For example, if P's range is [15,22) then N_1 both processes P and routes P to N_0 (assuming P was initiated at N_4).

PePeR may assign Z ranges to each node where Z is a positive integer. In Figure 1.a, Z is equal to one. Figure 1.b shows a partitioning of S with 2 ranges assigned to each node, $Z=2$. We denote the Z ranges assigned to a node i as: $R_{i,0}$, $R_{i,1}$, ..., $R_{i,Z-1}$. For example, N_0 is assigned two ranges: $R_{0,0}=[0,10)$, and $R_{0,1}=[30,40)$. This results in a Z dimensional space that dictates $2Z$ neighbors for each node, see Figure 2.b. For example, in Figure 2.b, N_4's neighbors are N_1, N_3, N_5, and N_7. The assignment of ranges to nodes is paramount because it impacts the average number of hops. A naive assignment such as round-robin results on an average of $\frac{N}{4}$ hops to process a predicate (independent of Z's value).

Figure 2.b shows the logical neighbor relationship obtained from the assignment of Figure 1.b. Note that consecutive ranges are neighbors. We have intentionally directed each edge of an arrow to a specific value in each node to show this relationship. Once again, consider the routing of the range predicate P [10,15) when initiated at N_4. PePeR's routing mechanism employs distance to guide the predicate towards peer with relevant data. It employs the distance between P's range and the ranges assigned to N_4's neighbors and forwards P to the node with closest range. In our example, the range [20,30) assigned to node N_1 is closest and P is routed to this node. N_1 repeats this process to route P to N_2. N_2 processes P because its range [10,20) contains P.

If each node maintains the minimum and maximum values for $S.a_1$ then PePeR realizes a torus (i.e., the dashed line of Figure 2). This might be used for routing a predicate. To illustrate, in Figure 1.a, if the system maintains 180 and 0 as $S.a_1$'s maximum and minimum value, respectively, then it may process a predicate by visiting nodes in the reverse order of range values. For example, if a range predicate P is interested in those rows that satisfy the range [175,177), and is directed to node N_2, then it is routed through N_0 to arrive at node N_3 in two hops. In the absence of $S.a_1$'s minimum and maximum value at each node, P is routed to N_1, followed by N_4 to arrive at N_3. In this example, the presence of torus saved one hop. However, this is not true at all times.

Maintaining the minimum and maximum $S.a_1$ values at each node requires the propagation of these values to all nodes every time they change. If the value of minimum and maximum values becomes inconsistent due to their overlapped

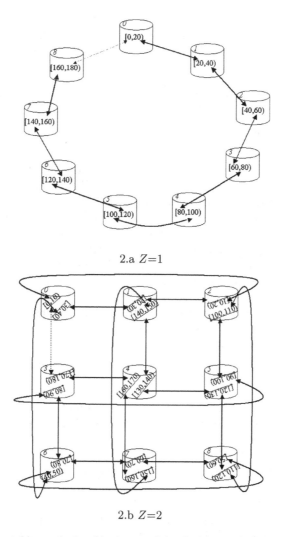

2.a $Z=1$

2.b $Z=2$

Fig. 2. Logical neighbor relationship imposed by PePeR with different Z values on the nine nodes using assignment of Figure 1. Each disk represents a node. The dashed arrow corresponds to a logical neighbor relationship that exists if and only if all nodes are provided with the minimum and maximum values for the partitioning attribute.

propagation while routing predicates, the correctness of routing is **not** impacted. This impacts the number of hops required to route P to the node containing the relevant data.

The distributed nature of PePeR prevents it from computing the shortest path for a predicate P even with a smart assignment and a torus. This is because our routing looks only one step ahead to choose its next hop. This local decision making might route P to more nodes than necessary. As an example, consider the assignment of Figure 1.b and an exact-match predicate P that retrieves $S.a_1{=}40$. Moreover, assume P is initiated at node N_4. Our routing algorithm must route P to N_6 containing the relevant data. Looking at the logical graph of Figure 2.b, the shortest route consists of two hops: either (1) $N_4 \rightarrow N_3 \rightarrow N_6$, or (1) $N_4 \rightarrow N_7 \rightarrow N_6$. However, using the concept of distance, our greedy routing algorithm is misled with the local optimal distance and routes P from N_4 to N_1 because its distance is closer. This causes P to incur 3 hops: $N_4 \rightarrow N_1 \rightarrow N_0 \rightarrow N_6$.

With PePeR, a node maintains $2Z^2$ ranges assigned to its $2Z$ neighbors. (These ranges are used for routing predicates.) For example, in Figure 2.a, a node maintains the two ranges assigned to its two neighbors. In Figure 2.b, each node maintains the 8 ranges assigned to its four neighbors. As one increases Z's value, the number of ranges known by a node increases (see Figure 3.a), reducing the number of hops incurred by a predicate. The percentage reduction in hops as a function of Z's value levels off with larger Z values. This is because the incremental percentage increase in the number of ranges stored at a node diminishes as a function of Z, see Figure 3.b. For example, when one increases the value of Z from 1 to 2, there is a 300% increase in the number of neighbor-ranges known by a node. When we increase Z from 2 to 3, the number of ranges known by a node increases by another 125%. When we increase Z from 5 to 6, this percentage increase is only 44%.

Node removal:

In order to prevent loss of data in the presence of node removals and/or failures, we employ interleaved declustering. The basic idea here is to construct additional replicas of a fragment and partition it across multiple nodes. This enables PePeR to distribute the workload of a failed node across multiple nodes, enhancing the overall scalability of the framework. Interleaved declustering partitions a range assigned to a node into 2 fragments and assigns it to those 2 neighbors (out of $2Z$ neighbors) that are the logical neighbors of this range. This assignment is performed in a manner that preserves the logical neighbor relationship in presence of node removals. To illustrate, with the logical assignment of Figure 2.b, the range 130-140 assigned to node 4 is range partitioned into [130,135) and [135,140). The first, [130,135), is assigned to N_5 because it is the logical neighbor of the range [120,130) assigned to N_5. The second, [135,140), is assigned to N_1 because it is the logical neighbor of the range [140,150). Similarly, the range [160,170) assigned to N_4 is partitioned into [160,165) and [165,170), and assigned to nodes N_7 and N_3, respectively. Once N_4 is removed, its load is imposed onto four different nodes: N_1, N_3, N_5, and N_7, see Figure 4.b

With PePeR, a node monitors the presence of its neighbors using a heart-beat message. When one or more nodes detect the absence of a neighbor, they enter the process of range-merging. For example, when node N_4 is removed from Figure 1.a, one or more of its neighboring nodes (one of N_5, N_1, N_3, N_7) enters range-merging. During this process, they elevate their backup fragments to a

Total number of neighbor ranges per node

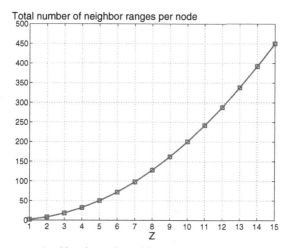

3.a Number of neighbor ranges per node

% incremental increase

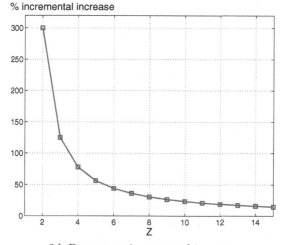

3.b Percentage incremental increase

Fig. 3. While the number of neighbor ranges per node increases dramatically as a function of Z, the percentage incremental increase in the number of ranges per node starts to level off. Percentage incremental increase with Z=i is defined as $\frac{i^2-(i-1)^2}{i^2}*100$ where $i > 1$.

primary status, extending their logical range to cover N_4's range. This in turn changes the logical neighbor relationship to that of Figure 4.b.

Node insertion:

PePeR may insert a node N_{new} into its existing address space in a variety of distributed ways. One approach is for the new node to insert P probes into the system to sample the existing ranges of a table. Each probe visits W nodes by

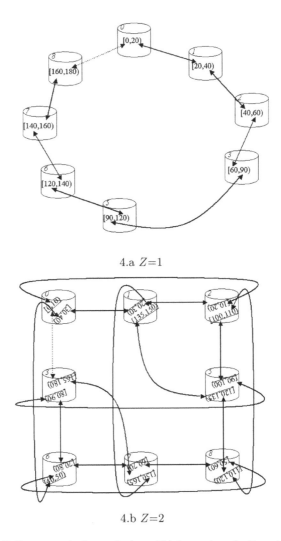

4.a $Z=1$

4.b $Z=2$

Fig. 4. With PePeR, removal of a node (say N_4) impacts only its neighbors and their logical relationship.

performing random walks. Upon visiting a node, a probe collects the ranges assigned to that node and its neighbors along with other relevant statistics such as the cardinality of a range. N_{new} uses this information to choose Z ranges. Next, N_{new} contacts the owner of each range to break its range into two and assign one of the new ranges and the records belonging to that range to N_{new}. N_{new} may employ different policies when choosing the Z ranges. Section 4 presents three alternative policies and their performance tradeoffs.

3   Definitions and Terminology

This section presents two formal concepts essential to PePeR, namely: (a) neighbor relationship, and (b) the quantification of distance between a node's range and a predicate's range. We use the examples of Section 2 for illustration purposes. PePeR assumes ranges are consecutive. Thus, given a range $[l_i, u_i)$, there must exist (1) an l_k equal to u_i unless u_i is the maximum value for the partitioning attribute, and (2) a u_k equal to l_i unless l_i is the minimum value for the partitioning attribute. To illustrate, in Figure 1.a, there might exist no records with l_i value equal to 40, however, the system continues to maintain the range $[40, 60)$ for node 2 in order to prevent holes and ensure consecutive nature of the ranges. Node 0 (8) satisfies this constraint because its l_0 (u_8) is the minimum (maximum) value for the partitioning attribute.

Two nodes N_i and N_k are neighbors iff one of these four conditions hold true: either (a) $u_i = l_k$, (b) $u_k = l_i$, (c) u_k and l_i are the the maximum and minimum value for the partitioning attribute, respectively, or (d) reverse of (c) where u_i and l_k are the maximum and minimum value for the partitioning attribute, respectively. For example, in Figure 2.a, neighbors of node 2 are nodes 1 and 3 because $u_2 = l_3$ and $l_2 = u_1$. Similarly, neighbors of node 8 are nodes 7 and 0 because $u_7 = l_8$ and u_8 is the maximum partitioning value and l_0 is the minimum partitioning value. In essence, our definition of neighbors forms a torus when the minimum and maximum value of $S.a_1$ is known by all nodes (see the following paragraphs).

Given a range selection predicate P, its range is defined as $[l_P, u_P)$, i.e., $\sigma_{S.a_1 \geq l_P \wedge S.a_1 < u_P}(S)$. The range of a node N_i **contains** this predicate iff $l_i \leq l_P$ and $u_P \leq u_i$. For example, given a predicate $[40, 50)$, N_2's range (see Figure 1.a) contains this predicate. N_i's range **partially-contains** this predicate if either: (a) $l_i < u_P$ and $u_i < u_P$, or (a) $l_P \leq l_i$ and $l_i < u_P$. To illustrate, given a predicate $[150, 170)$, the range assigned to node 7 (see Figure 1.a) partially contains this predicate. The reverse of these definitions also apply where a predicate P may either contain or partially-contain the range assigned to a node N_i.

Given a predicate P and node N_i's range $R_{i,j}$, we define their **distance**, denoted $\Delta(P, R_{i,j})$, to be zero if $R_{i,j}$ either contains or partially contains P, or vice versa. Otherwise, the distance between P and $R_{i,j}$ is computed as follows. Assume $S.a_1$'s maximum and minimum values, denoted as $a_{1,min}$ and $a_{1,max}$, respectively, are known by all nodes. First, we compute the length as $Length = a_{1,max} - a_{1,min}$. Next, we compute the expected median M_P of the range specified by P, $M_P = \frac{l_P + u_P}{2}$. Next, we compute $\delta_1 = M_P - l_j$, $\delta_2 = M_P - u_j$, $\delta_3 = Length - \delta_1$, and $\delta_4 = Length - \delta_2$. Distance of P and R_i is defined as the minimum of these deltas, $\Delta(P, R_i) = min(\delta_1, \delta_2, \delta_3, \delta_4)$. To illustrate, in Figure 2.a, assuming a range predicate $[160, 170)$, distance of M_P (165) relative to N_0's range, $R_0 = [0, 20)$, is 15. This is because Length=180, resulting in: 1) $\delta_1 = 165$, 2) $\delta_2 = 145$, 3) $\delta_3 = 15$, 4) $\delta_4 = 35$, and 5) $\Delta(P, R_{1,0}) = min(165, 145, 15, 35) = 15$. The distance of this predicate relative to N_2's range is 55: 1) $\delta_1 = 125$, 2) $\delta_2 = 105$, 3) $\delta_3 = 55$, 4) $\delta_4 = 75$, 5) $\Delta(P, R_{2,0}) = min(125, 105, 55, 75) = 55$.

If $S.a_1$'s maximum and minimum values are unknown, a node may employ the theoretical positive and negative values of an attribute domain to compute Length in the above methodology. For example, if the age attribute of a table is an unsigned short (16 bit integer), then PePeR may assume 0 and $2^{16} - 1$ as the minimum and maximum values of this attribute.

4 Insertion of Nodes

This section describes a decentralized class of techniques, termed probe-based, to insert a new node (say N_{new}) into an existing PePeR configuration. As implied by its name, the primary characteristic of this approach is its use of P probes to identify the Z candidate ranges along with their fragments that will be assigned to N_{new}. A probe performs W random walks from a randomly chosen node, N_{Start}, of the existing configuration. The walks are performed by choosing a random neighbor of the current node, starting with N_{Start}. The termination condition of a probe is satisfied when it either (1) performs W walks, or (2) encounters a node whose neighbors have already been visited by this probe. When a probe encounters one of these termination conditions, it transmits all its accumulated ranges to N_{new}. Once N_{new} has received these ranges, it chooses Z ranges among them. Next, it requests the owner of each chosen range to split its range into two parts and assign one to N_{new}. A simple approach to split a range might be to choose the median that divides that range into two equi-sized fragments. How N_{new} chooses the Z ranges from the accumulated ranges differentiates the alternative probe-based approaches. Here we describe three alternative policies: Random, Uniform and Elastic. All three strive to minimize the likelihood of N_{new} neighboring the same node multiple times unless it is impossible for the current configuration to satisfy this constraint, e.g., current configuration consists of fewer than Z nodes. In order to achieve this goal, a policy must be aware of the neighbors of each node. Thus, a probe gathers two sets of ranges: set $\{p_1\}$ consisting of the ranges assigned to the visited nodes, and set $\{p_2\}$ consisting of the ranges assigned to the neighbors of visited nodes. If a probe visits W unique nodes, set $\{p_1\}$ will consist of ZW ranges, while set $\{p_2\}$ will consist of a maximum of $2Z^2W - 2Z(W - 1)$ ranges, depending on the number of distinct nodes that are neighbors to the W visited nodes. This maximum value is realized when there exists W total common neighbors between any two nodes visited by the W walks of a probe. In most cases the cardinality of $\{p_2\}$ will be less than this maximum.

Random, the simplest policy, computes the union of sets $\{p_1\}$ and $\{p_2\}$. Let set $\{p\}$ denote this union, i.e., $\{p\}=\{p_1\}\cup\{p_2\}$. As implied by its name, Random chooses Z ranges from $\{p\}$ randomly. If it selects two or more ranges that belong to the same node then one is kept and the remaining ones are discarded. The discarded ones are replaced by re-applying random to the remaining elements of $\{p\}$. This process may repeat several times until all Z chosen ranges belong to different nodes. If $\{p\}$ becomes empty then new probes are generated to accumulate additional ranges. The new probes might be tagged with the identity of the already known nodes in order to prevent a probe from visiting them again. If this fails ω attempts, a technique proceeds to choose the remaining ranges from the available list (causing N_{new} to neighbor a single node multiple times).

Uniform, the second policy, strives to construct equi-sized fragments. It requires the original probe to gather the cardinality of a fragment for each range in $\{p_1\}$ and $\{p_2\}$. Uniform computes the union of sets $\{p_1\}$ and $\{p_2\}$, $\{p\}=\{p_1\} \cup \{p_2\}$. It sorts $\{p\}$ in descending order based on the cardinality of each range. Next, it selects the first Z ranges with highest cardinality that belong to different nodes. If this fails, Uniform selects the first Z ranges from set $\{p\}$ (those with highest cardinality), causing N_{new} to neighbor the same node multiple times. An obvious variation of Uniform might generate new probes in case of failures to accumulate new ranges (similar to Random). An investigation of this variations is a future research direction.

Elastic is an adaptable technique with tunable parameters that controls both the fragment size and the numerical distance between the Z ranges assigned to a node. It is designed to strike a compromise between the following two objectives: (1) construction of equi-sized fragments that have at least $\lceil \frac{RS}{2} \rceil$ records, and (2) minimization of the number of hops when routing a predicate. Consider each objective in turn. The first is similar to Uniform with two differences: First is the parameter RS that requires Elastic to choose Z ranges each with more than RS records. Second, Elastic chooses Z ranges only from set $\{p_1\}$.

To realize the second objective, Elastic uses γ to control the variation in the distance covered by the Z chosen ranges. Its details are as follows. First, from set $\{p_1\}$, it identifies the range with the highest number of records, R_h. With multiple candidates, it chooses one randomly. Next, it identifies each range R_i by its mean, $m_i=\frac{l_i+u_i}{2}$, and computes its distance d_i from R_h, $d_i = |m_i - m_h|$. Let A denote the maximum d_i. Elastic chooses z distances from N_h, each denoted as D_i such that:

$$D_i = \begin{cases} 0, \; if \; i = 0 \\ D_{i-1} + \gamma^{a_i} d, \; 1 \leq i \leq z-1, \; 0 \leq a_i \leq z-2, \; a_i \neq a_j \; for \; i \neq j \end{cases} \quad (1)$$

where $d = A\frac{\gamma-1}{\gamma^{z-1}-1}$. This ensures $D_{z-1} = A$. At the same time, Elastic requires the Z identified ranges are chosen such that N_{new} does not neighbor the same node multiple times. It employs both sets $\{p_1\}$ and $\{p_2\}$ for this purpose. To achieve this, the algorithm evaluates all possible combinations of Z ranges from Z different nodes and choose the best one. An obvious variation of Elastic is to choose the first Z elements from the union of $\{p_1\}$ and $\{p_2\}$. An investigation of this alternative is a future research direction.

We illustrate Elastic with an example. Consider a tenth node joining the PePeR network of Figure 2.b. Assume its probe visits nodes N_4, N_5 and N_8, constructing set $\{p_1\}$ with six elements: $p_{1,0}=R_{8,0}=[50,60)$, $p_{1,1}=R_{5,0}=[90,100)$, $p_{1,2}=R_{8,1}=[110,120)$, $p_{1,3}=R_{5,1}=[120,130)$, $p_{1,4}=R_{4,0}=[130,140)$ and $p_{1,5}=R_{4,1}=[160,170)$. Elastic picks the range with the highest number of records, say $p_{1,4}$, i.e., $R_h=p_{1,4}=[130,140)$. The mean of this range is 135, $m_h=135$. Next, it computes the mean for each range in set $\{p_1\}$ and their distances d_i from m_h, resulting in the following: $\{m_0=55, d_0=80\}$, $\{m_1=95, d_1=40\}$, $\{m_2=115, d_2=20\}$, $\{m_3=125, d_3=10\}$, $\{m_4=135, d_4=0\}$, $\{m_5=165, d_5=30\}$. A equals the maximum d_i value, in this case, $d_0=80$. Assuming the value of γ is 10, Elastic computes D_i as follows: $d = 80\frac{10-1}{10^2-1-1}=80$, $a_0 = 0$, $D_0=0$ and $D_1 = 80$. This leads the new node to target ranges $R_{4,0}=[130,140)$ and $R_{8,0}=[50,60)$ because $|d_4 - D_0| + |d_0 - D_1|$ is smaller than any other choice of ranges and they belong to different nodes. Next, the new node sends a request to nodes 4 and 8 to: (a) split each identified range into two, and (b) assign each new range and its appropriate fragment to the new node.

In this example, with $Z = 2$, the computation of D_0 and D_1 is independent of γ because it is raised to power of 0 in Equation 1. For $Z \geq 3$ the value of γ impacts the choice of ranges assigned to the new node. Consider what happens when $Z=3$ and the probe gathers the same ranges as before. Now, $A = d_{max} = 80$, resulting in $d = 7.273$ and $D_0 = 0$, $D_1=7.273$ and $D_2= 80$, assuming $a_0=0$ and $a_1=1$. We can see that $D_2=A$, thus ensuring that the last of the chosen ranges is as far as possible from the first one, which is either R_h or one close to R_h. The γ value will guide the algorithm into choosing the middle (second) range. Depending on its value, that choice will be closer to either the first or the third one. Based on the three calculated values, the chosen ranges would then be $R_{4,0}$, $R_{5,1}$ and $R_{8,0}$ because they minimize $|d_4 - D_0| + |d_3 - D_1| + |d_0 - D_2|$ and belong to different nodes.

4.1   A Comparison

We compared these alternative insertion techniques in a simulation study. Our implementation is flexible enough to support different numerical data types. Other data types such as string can be supported by mapping alphabets to a numerical data type. In our experiments, the partitioning attribute of a table is a real number uniformly distributed between 0.0 and 1.0. We start by placing this table on one node. Next, we increase the number of nodes from 1 to 4000 by inserting nodes one at a time. In all experiments the number of probes (P) equals Z, and W equals 10. Every time the number of nodes in our configuration becomes a multiple of hundred, we measure the average number of hops required to route 100,000 randomly generated range predicates.

Figure 5 shows the number of hops with Random, Uniform, and Elastic with two different Z parameter values, 3 and 4. This figure shows the average number of hops as a function of the number of nodes for a table consisting of one million records. Elastic was configured with $\gamma=15$. These results show Uniform and Random perform approximately the same number of hops. Elastic results in fewer hops. This is because Elastic controls the distance between the ranges assigned to a newly inserted node. With smaller γ values (less than 5), Elastic results in the same average number of hops as Uniform and Random.

The theoretical lower bound on the number of hops with PePeR is $\frac{d}{4}\sqrt[d]{\mathcal{N}}$ (similar to CAN [RFH+01]). Figure 6 shows the percentage difference between the number of hops observed with Uniform and Elastic relative to this theoretical

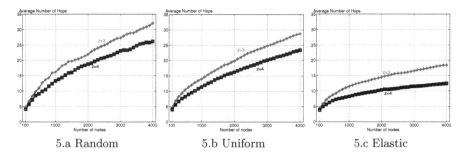

5.a Random   5.b Uniform   5.c Elastic

Fig. 5. Average number of hops with the alternative insertion strategies.

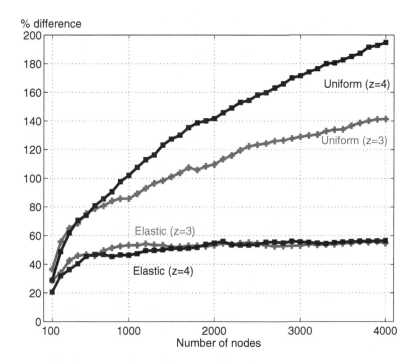

Fig. 6. Percentage difference in number of hops relative to the theoretical lower bound. If h_e and h_t denote the number of hops with Elastic and the theoretical lower bound, respectively, then percentage difference is defined as $100 \times \frac{h_e - h_t}{h_t}$.

lower bound. The results show that Elastic remains a fixed distance away from the theoretical lower bound with an increasing number of nodes. This stable characteristic of Elastic is a desirable advantage.

Figure 7.a shows the number of records for the partition corresponding to each range with $Z=4$. (The obtained results for $Z=3$ is similar and eliminated from this presentation.) Uniform constructs ranges with six different sizes: 30,

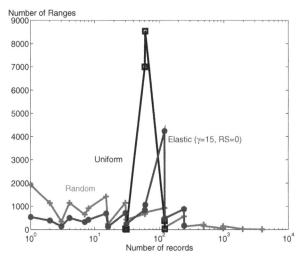

7.a Alternative insertion techniques

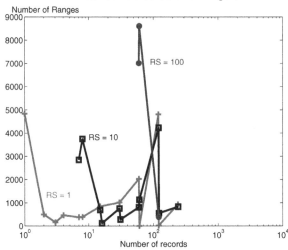

7.b Elastic with different RS values

Fig. 7. Distribution of records across the ranges. This is shown as the number of ranges for each unique range cardinality.

31, 60, 61, 121, and 122 records. More than 95% of the ranges contain either 60 or 61 records. Random results in non-equi sized ranges that vary from 0 to 3875 records. Elastic reduces this variability by limiting the cardinality of the largest range to 243 records. (Elastic continues to construct ranges with zero records.)

With Elastic, the variability in the range sizes can be controlled by manipulating the value of RS. Figure 7.b shows the distribution of records across the ranges with different RS values. Note that with RS=100, Elastic constructs ranges that behave the same as Uniform. With RS=1, Elastic avoids ranges with zero records. However, it does construct many ranges with one record. Different RS values have marginal impact on the average number of hops observed with Elastic. Figure 8 shows the percentage difference between RS=0 and three different RS values: 1, 10, and 100. The percentage difference is almost always lower than 10%.

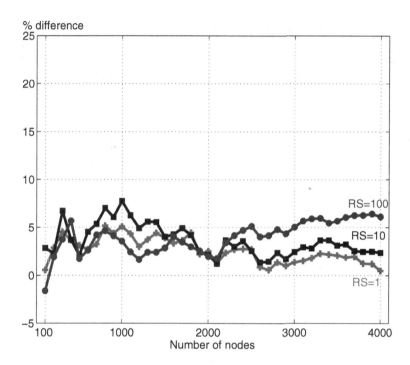

Fig. 8. Percentage difference in the number of hops with Elastic and RS=0 when compared with three different RS values 1, 10 and 100. Assuming h_i denotes the number of hops with a given RS=i value, percentage difference between RS=0 and RS=100 is defined as $100 \times \frac{h_0 - h_{100}}{h_0}$.

5   A Comparison with DHT

When compared with a DHT, the primary benefit of PePeR is its ability to direct range predicates to the node(s) containing relevant data. A DHT, on the other hand, must direct these predicates to all nodes containing a fragment of a relation. For those predicates that retrieve only a few rows, this forces many nodes to search their fragments only to find no relevant data, reducing the overall processing capability of the nodes. Figure 9 shows the response time (RT) as a function of arrival rate for an open simulation model consisting of 256 nodes. It shows PePeR with two different Z values, 2 and 4. It also includes the scenario where a predicate is routed to all nodes when CAN is configured with $d = 4$. Note that CAN is not designed to do flooding; we performed the flooding to simulate a CAN when processing a range predicate. We term this configuration All-Nodes. In this model, the network time required to route a message is 5 milli-seconds (msec). The time required by a peer to process a predicate is 20 msec. With a small arrival rate ($\lambda=2$), the average response time when the query is routed to all nodes is 221 msec. With PePeR when $Z=2$ ($Z=4$), the average response time is 257 (140) msec. The response time with All-Nodes is better than PePeR with $Z=2$ because PePeR must perform 9 hops as compare to a maximum of 8 hops with All-Nodes. (PePeR performs 9 hops because of the local optimal routing decision discussed in Section 2.) When $Z=4$, PePeR performs 4.6 hops, outperforming All-Nodes.

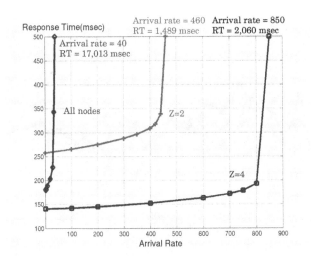

Fig. 9. Response time as a function of arrival rate for a 256 node configuration.

With a high arrival rate, All-Nodes becomes fully utilized with an arrival rate of 40 predicates per millisecond because all 256 nodes must process each predicate. With PePeR only the nodes containing relevant data search for data, freeing other nodes to perform useful work. With $Z=2$, the system starts to observe hot spots and bottlenecks with arrival rates between 440 and 460 predicates per millisecond. With $Z=4$, the number of hops is smaller, relieving additional nodes from the overhead of routing to process predicates. This enables the system to process additional predicates to support a higher arrival rate ranging 800 and 850. These results make a convincing case for the use of PePeR with range predicates.

6 Conclusion and Future Research Directions

This paper describes PePeR in support of range queries in a decentralized, addressable P2P system. We outlined Random, Uniform and Elastic as decentralized techniques to enable a new node to join an existing PePeR address space. The obtained results demonstrate both the flexibility and superiority of Elastic. Results from an open simulation model show the superiority of PePeR over a DHT for a workload dominated by range predicates.

Our short term research directions are three folds. First, we intend to study techniques to publish a relation with an existing PePeR configuration. Second, we plan to qualitatively evaluate whether minimizing the number of hops is the right criterion for database applications. For example, when inserting nodes, our design objective is to maintain a reasonable number of hops. It is not clear whether this objective would enhance response time (or throughput) of a P2P system. An alternative objective might be to distribute the workload of a relation more evenly across the nodes based on resource heterogeneity [ZG00,VBW98, GGGK03]. We intend to study extensions of PePeR with this alternative. Third, we hypothesize PePeR and Skip Graphs [AS03] to be members of a more general framework. We intend to investigate this framework and its hybrid instances of PePeR and Skip Graphs.

References

[AS03]   J. Aspnes and G. Shah. Skip Graphs. In *Proceedings of the Fourteenth Annual ACM-SIAM Symposium on Discrete Algorithms (SODA)*, January 2003.

[AX02]   A. Andrzejak and Z. Xu. Scalable, Efficient Range Queries for Grid Information Services. In *Proceedings of the Second IEEE International Conference on Peer-to-Peer Computing (P2P2002)*. Linköping University, Sweden, September 2002.

[CFCS03] M. Cai, M. Frank, J. Chen, and P. Szekely. MAAN: A Multi-Attribute Addressable Network for Grid Information Services. In *Proceedings of the Fourth International Workshop on Grid Computing (Grid 2003)*. Phoenix, Arizona, November 2003.

[CS02]   E. Cohen and S. Shenker. Replication Strategies in Unstructured Peer-to-Peer Networks. In *Proceedings of the ACM SIGCOMM*, August 2002.

[GAE03]   A. Gupta, D. Agrawal, and A. El Abbadi. Approximate Range Selection Queries In Peer-to-Peer Systems. In *Proceedings of the First Biennial Conference on Innovative Data Systems Research*, Asilomar, California, United States, January 2003.

[GDQ92]   S. Ghandeharizadeh, D. DeWitt, and W. Qureshi. A Performance Analysis of Alternative Multi-Attribute Declustering Strategies. In *Proceedings of the 1992 ACM-SIGMOD Conference*, May 1992.

[GGGK03] S. Ghandeharizadeh, S. Gao, C. Gahagan, and R. Krauss. High Performance Parallel Database Management Systems. In J. Blazewicz, W. Kubiak, T. Morzy, and M. Rusinkiewicz, editors, *Handbook on Data Management and Information Systems*. Springer, 2003.

[HHH+02] M. Harren, J. M. Hellerstein, R. Huebsch, B. T. Loo, S. Shenker, and I. Stoica. Complex Queries in DHT-based Peer-to-Peer Networks. In *Proceedings of First International Workshop on Peer-to-Peer Systems*, March 2002.

[KBC+00] J. Kubiatowicz, D. Bindel, Y. Chen, S. Czerwinski, P. Eaton, D. Geels, R. Gummadi, S. Rhea, H. Weatherspoon, W. Weimer, C. Wells, and B. Zhao. OceanStore: An Architecture for Global-scale Persistent Storage. In *Proceedings of ACM ASPLOS*. ACM, November 2000.

[LCC+02] Q. Lv, P. Cao, E. Cohen, K. Li, and S. Shenker. Search and Replication in Unstructured Peer-to-Peer Networks. In *Proceedings of the $16^{t}h$ Annual ACM International Conference on Supercomputing*, 2002.

[LNS96]   W. Litwin, M.-A. Neimat, and D. A. Schneider. LH* - A Scalable, Distributed Data Structure. *TODS*, 21(4):480–525, 1996.

[MS98]   B. Moon and J. Saltz. Scalability Analysis of Declustering Methods for Multidimensional Range Queries. *IEEE Transactions on Knowledge and Data Engineering*, 10(2):310–327, March 1998.

[PRR97]   C. Plaxton, R. Rajaram, and A. W. Richa. Accessing Nearby Copies of Replicated Objects in a Distributed Environment. In *Ninth Annual ACM Symposium on Parallel Algorithms and Architectures (SPAA)*, June 1997.

[Pug90]   W. Pugh. Skip Lists: A Probabilistic Alternative to Balanced Trees. *Communications of the ACM*, 33(6):668–676, June 1990.

[RFH+01] S. Ratnasamy, P. Francis, M. Handley, R. Karp, and S. Shenker. A Scalable Content Addressable Network. In *ACM SIGCOMM*, 2001.

[SMK+01] I. Stoica, R. Morris, D. Karger, M. F. Kaashoek, and H. Balakrishnan. Chord: A Scalable Peer-to-Peer Lookup Service for Internet Applications. In *ACM SIGCOMM*, 2001.

[TJ02]   M. Theimer and M. Jones. Overlook: Scalable Name Service on an Overlay Network. In *The 22nd International Conference on Distributed Computing Systems*, July 2002.

[TXKN03] P. Triantafillou, C. Xiruhaki, M. Koubarakis, and Nikolaos Ntarmos. Towards High Performance Peer-to-Peer Content and Resource Sharing Systems. In *Proceedings of the First Biennial Conference on Innovative Data Systems Research*, Asilomar, California, United States, January 2003.

[VBW98]   R. Vingralek, Y. Breitbart, and G. Weikum. Snowball: Scalable Storage on Networks of Workstations with Balanced Load. *Distributed and Parallel Databases*, 6(2):117–156, 1998.

[YGM01]   B. Yang and H. Garcia-Molina. Comparing Hybrid Peer-to-Peer Systems. In *The VLDB Journal*, pages 561–570, sep 2001.

[ZG00]   R. Zimmermann and S. Ghandeharizadeh. HERA: Heterogeneous Extension of RAID. In *In Proceedings of the International Conference on Parallel and Distributed Processing Techniques and Applications (PDPTA 2000)*, June 2000.

Efficient Search in Structured Peer-to-Peer Systems: Binary v.s. K-Ary Unbalanced Tree Structures

Magdalena Punceva and Karl Aberer

Department of Communication Systems,
Swiss Federal Institute of Technology (EPFL),
1015 Lausanne, Switzerland
{magdalena.punceva, karl.aberer}@epfl.ch

Abstract. We investigate the search cost in terms of number of messages generated for routing queries in tree-based P2P structured systems including binary and k-ary tree structures with different arities and different degrees of imbalance in the tree shape. This work is motivated by the fact that k-ary balanced tree access structures can greatly reduce the number of hops for searching compared to the binary trees. We study to what extent the same fact is true when the tree-like structures for access in P2P environments are unbalanced. Another important issue related to P2P environments is how to build these structures in a self-organizing way. We propose a mechanism for constructing k-ary tree based decentralized access structure in a self-organizing way and based on local interactions only. The ability to search efficiently also on unbalanced k-ary trees opens interesting opportunities for load balancing as has been shown in earlier work on P-Grid, our approach to structured P2P systems.

1 Introduction

Peer-to-peer applications attracted a lot of attention within the last few years. The reason for this fast growing interest lies in the fact that they seem to be an attractive solution for creating a network with millions of users and providing a lots of desirable properties like decentralization, self-organization, robustness, scalability, autonomy etc. A variety of approaches both from research communities and companies have been proposed. Although these approaches can have different properties and also their goals can be different to some extent, they can be classified in two main categories: unstructured and structured. In unstructured systems, for which example is Gnutella [8,10], in principle peers are unaware of the local storages that other peers in the overlay network maintain. The search is simply flooding queries to all neighboring peers all the time without acquiring any knowledge about the others peers' storages. As a consequence, they generate a large amount of messages per query which makes the approach poorly scalable in terms of communication cost when the number of peers grows. Also, despite the large number of messages generated, there is no guarantee on the search

K. Aberer et al. (Eds.): VLDB 2003 Ws DBISP2P, LNCS 2944, pp. 219–231, 2004.

success. It is especially difficult to find rare data objects in an unstructured P2P system. However, unstructured P2P systems have generated substantial interest because of emergent global-scale phenomena. Gnutella overlay network exhibits properties like: small diameter and power-law distribution of node's degrees, which ensures that the time-to-live for search is relatively low. Such properties have been discovered in other systems and are result of a "preferential attachment". Gnutella is completely decentralized but also self-organizing: from local interactions of peers global structure emerge.

Structured P2P systems, for which among many others examples are FreeNet [7], Chord [9], CAN [12], Pastry [14], Tapestry [13], Kademlia [11] and P-Grid [1,5] usually assume existence of a distributed hash table (DHT). Thus, in contrast to unstructured systems, in structured systems peers maintain information about resources stored by other peers. The DHT implementation can be done in different ways: tree-like structures, multidimensional space, XOR metric etc. All these mechanisms provide possibilities to direct queries and guarantees for locating data objects within small number of messages compared to the total population size (example: $O(logN)$ for tree-like structures). However, this relatively small search cost may increase due to unreliable peers, so the search cost is still an important issue in structured systems as well. In this paper we focus on tree-based P2P structured systems. We are interested in studying what is the search cost in terms of messages that is associated to tree-like structures with different shapes and outdegrees i.e arities. We study this problem for P-Grid a tree-based structured DHT that allows adaptation of the structure to different data distributions, and is thus particularly suitable for data management-oriented P2P architectures.

2   Problem Statement

The motivation for this study is the intuitive fact that the k-ary tree structures can substantially reduce the number of hops when searching, as k-arity increases, if trees are balanced. For balanced trees the search process requires $O(log_k N)$ hops, where k is the arity of the tree and N corresponds to the number of leaves in the tree. This is relevant for P2P systems, that are based on tree-like structures for accessing data, since larger arities k may reduce the number of messages required for routing the query. Here, we provide theoretical and experimental results regarding the search cost, for the case with balanced trees. These results for the balanced case are also generalizable to the other tree-based DHT approaches, mentioned above. Further we extend our study to unbalanced tree structures. Unbalanced trees are of particular interest for our P-Grid. They are very likely to occur in P-Grid with non-uniform data distribution due to the constructing and storage load balancing mechanism which is explained bellow. Although intuitively it seems reasonable to expect that using k-ary tree structure with greater k will reduce the number of generated messages it is not clear how much in terms of communication cost will be saved.

P-Grid [1,5] is our version of DHT for P2P Systems. The original version of P-Grid uses binary tree-like access structure for routing queries. Its salient features, distinguishing it from other DHT approaches are:

1. Peers do not use pre-assigned identities in order to determine the search space and thus the data items they are responsible for.
2. Peers acquire in a decentralized, self-organizing process by means of bilateral interactions the search space (or search path) they support. While doing this they aim at balancing load (more precisely storage load) among peers. During bilateral interactions peers can dynamically decide to split or join subspaces, by adding or removing a bit from the search path they support. Thus the P-Grid construction and maintenance relies on the binary structure of the tree.
3. As a result of load balancing the search paths (resp. tree structure underlying P-Grid) may be heavily unbalanced since data distribution and tree shape are tightly coupled. Realistic data distributions are frequently non-uniformly distributed, e.g. following a Zipf-like distribution. In principle, this might compromise search efficiency. However, a fundamental theoretical result [3] shows that the search cost in number of messages on average remains logarithmic, more precisely strictly bounded by $log_e N$, where N is the number of tree leaves, due to the probabilistic nature of the approach.

Though being very desirable Feature 2 and 3 appear to be tightly connected to the binary nature of the search structure underlying a P-Grid. Our goal in this paper is to verify that it is possible to maintain the salient features of P-Grid while extending the underlying data structure to k-ary tree structures.

In this paper we propose a model for constructing k-ary tree-like access structure whose construction process is based on local bilateral interactions only, similarly as in the original P-Grid. The k-ary routing structure will be compatible to the original binary P-Grid structure. The only constraint is that the arity k, in our approach, can have values that are powers of 2. The algorithm for constructing allows both the binary and the k-ary structure to be constructed simultaneously. Thus it is possible for a peer to maintain also the binary structure in addition to the k-ary, which is necessary to ensure successful termination of the search algorithm. Also, having the two structures can lead possibly to increased robustness of the system or better load balancing of the query load per peer.

We first, show analytically what is the expected number of routing messages when using balanced k-ary tree structures. Then simulation results are provided to analyze search performance when k-ary trees are used with skewed data distributions.

3   P-Grid: Binary Tree Like Structure

3.1   Data Structure

As any DHT approach P-Grid is based on the idea of associating peers with data keys from a key space $\mathcal{K}$. Without constraining general applicability we will only consider binary keys in the following. In contrast to other DHT approaches we do not impose a fixed or maximal length on the keys, i.e., we assume $\mathcal{K} = \{0, 1\}^*$.

In the P-Grid structure each peer $p \in Peers$ is associated with a binary key from $\mathcal{K}$. We denote this key by $path(p)$ and will call it the path of the peer.

This key determines which data keys the peer has to manage, i.e., the keys in $\mathcal{K}$ that have $path(p)$ as prefix. In particular the peer has to store them. In order to ensure that the complete search space is covered by peers we require that the set of peers' keys is *complete*. The set of peers' keys is complete if for every prefix s_{pre} of the path of a peer p there exists a peer p' such that $path(p') = s_{pre}$ or there exist peers p_0 and p_1 such that $s_{pre}0$ is a prefix of $path(p_0)$ and $s_{pre}1$ is a prefix of $path(p_1)$. Naturally one of the two peers p_0 and p_1 will be p itself in that case. Completeness needs to be guaranteed by the algorithms that construct and maintain the P-Grid data structure.

We do not exclude the situation where the path of one peer is a prefix of the path of another peer. This situation will occur during the construction and reorganization of a P-Grid. However, ideally this situation is avoided and any algorithm for maintaining a P-Grid should eventually converge to a state where the P-Grid is *prefix-free*, i.e., for peers p_0 and p_1 we have $path(p_0) \not\subseteq path(p_1) \wedge path(p_1) \not\subseteq path(p_0)$, where $s \subseteq s'$ denotes the prefix relationship among strings s and s'.

We also allow multiple peers to share the same paths, in that case we call the peers replicas. The number of peers that share the same path is called the *replication factor* of the path. Replication is important to support redundancy and thus robustness of a P-Grid in case of failures and to distribute workload when searching in a P-Grid.

For enabling searches peers maintain *routing tables* which are an essential constituent of the P-Grid structure. The routing tables are defined as (partial) functions $ref : Peers \times N \rightarrow \{Peers\}$ with the properties

1. $ref(p, l)$ is defined for all $p \in Peers$ and $l \in N$ with $1 \leq l \leq |path(p)|$
2. $ref(p, l) \subseteq Peers_{s_1 s_2 \ldots s_{l-1}(1-s_l)}$ with $path(p) = s_1 s_2 \ldots s_{l-1} s_l \ldots s_k, k \geq l$

where $Peers_t = \{p \in Peers | t \subseteq path(p)\}$ for $t \in \mathcal{K}$.

The definition of P-Grid does not exclude the case where the length of the paths is up to linear in the number of peers. Therefore searches can require a linear number of messages in the worst case which would make the access structure non-scalable. The following theorem that applies to P-Grids of any shape, shows that the expected average search cost is logarithmic, however.

Theorem 1. The expected search cost for the search of a specific key t using a P-Grid P, where routing tables are randomly selected among all possible candidates, starting at a randomly selected peer s is less than $\log(|Peers|)$.

A formal proof for prefix-free P-Grids without replication of paths and of references is given in [2]. For general P-Grids with replication and which are not prefix-free simulation results have shown that the property continues to hold [4].

3.2   Construction

The original P-Grid is a binary search tree that is distributed among the participating peers. In order to construct such a tree without global coordination, the construction process depends on random bilateral peer interactions. During the interactions peers decide whether to modify the distributed tree data structure by changing their paths. All decisions are made locally based on mutual information exchange. Peers decide to change their paths depending on the data they store, aiming at more balanced data distribution after the change. A peer's path change is performed as a path extension or path retraction by one bit, which corresponds to splitting the search space in two and taking over responsibility of one of the both parts by each peer or joining two parts that have been split earlier. We refer to the path extension as a peer's "specialization", since the peer who extends its path for one bit takes over the responsibility i.e "specializes" for the data whose keys in $\mathcal{K}$ have $path(p)$ as prefix. In addition the peer p adds a reference to the other peer in its binary routing table to cover the other part of the data space. Apparently this method relies on the fact that one uses binary trees. A more detailed description of the algorithm can be found in [4].

3.3   Search

The search algorithm for locating data keys indexed by a P-Grid is defined as follows: Each peer $p \in Peers$ is associated with a location $loc(p)$ (in the network). Searches can start at any peer. Peer p knows the locations of the peers referenced by $ref(p, l)$, but not of other peers. Thus the function $ref(p, l)$ provides the necessary routing information to forward search requests to other peers in case the searched key does not match the peer identifier. Let $t \in \mathcal{K}$ be the searched data key and let the search start at $p \in P$. Then the following recursive algorithm performs the basic search.

$search(t, loc(p)) :=$

if $path(p) \subseteq t$ **then** $return(loc(p))$

else

       determine maximal l such that $t_1 \ldots t_{l-1}(1 - t_l) \subseteq path(p)$;

       $r =$ randomly selected element from $ref(p, l)$; $search(t, loc(r))$;

The algorithm $search(t, loc(p))$ always terminates successfully: due to the definition of ref the function $search$ will always find the location of a peer at which the search can continue (use of completeness). With each invocation of $search(t, loc(p))$ the length of the common prefix of $path(p)$ and t increases at least by one. Therefore the algorithm always terminates.

In case of an unreliable network it may occur that a search cannot continue since the peer r selected from the routing table is not available. Then alternative peers can be selected from the routing table to continue the search.

4   Extending P-Grid: From Binary to K-Ary Tree-Like Structure

We propose an extension of the binary tree-based DHTs to k-ary tree-based ones. The arity is determined by the parameter d which corresponds to the minimal number of query bits that can be resolved by generating one message. Generating one message here means choosing a peer from a k-ary routing table and forwarding the message to it while searching. Thus the arity is $k = 2^d$ including the peer's own path. In the binary case $d = 1$ which results in $k = 2$, while for the $d \geq 2$ the possible values of k are 4,8,16...

4.1   K-Ary Data Structure

The description of the k-ary data structure is given using notations analogous to the previous binary case. As in the previous case, each peer $p \in Peers$ is associated with a binary key from $\mathcal{K} = \{0,1\}^*$, and is denoted by $path(p)$. Assuming that $\mathcal{B} = \{0,1\}$, the k-ary routing tables are defined as (partial) functions: $kref : Peers \times N \times N \times \mathcal{B}^d \rightarrow \{Peers\}$ with the properties:

1. $kref(p,d,c,r)$ is defined for all $p \in Peers$, $d \in N$ such that $d < |path(p)|$, for all $c \in N$ such that $1 \leq c \leq \lfloor \frac{|path(p)|}{d} \rfloor$, for all $r \in \mathcal{B}^d$
2. $kref(p,d,c,r) \in Peers_{s_1...s_{(c-1)*d}r_1...r_d}$ where $r = r_1...r_d$ and $path(p) = s_1 s_2 \ldots s_{(c-1)*d} \ldots s_k$, $k \geq c * d$

The parameter d determines the arity as mentioned above. Parameters c and r correspond to the levels in the routing table.

In order to retain searchability we decide that each peer in addition to the k-ary routing table also maintains the binary routing table because:

- The k-ary structure is not guaranteed to be complete and thus it doesn't guarantee to cover the whole search space. For example assume that a peer has a path 0000 and builds a k-ary structure with $d = 2$ and a binary one. Since the binary structure has the completeness property there must be a peer with path 001. If the peer maintains only the k-ary structure he is supposed to have references to the peers with paths 0010 and 0011 whose existence is not guaranteed.
- The k-ary structure doesn't guarantee to address the highest granularity of the search space. In that case, it is not possible to address a query with a key larger than the largest existing k-ary reference. For example assume a peer has a path 00000 and maintains a k-ary structure with $d = 2$, thus the query 00001 cannot be addressed with the k-ary structure. This means, if the length of the peer's path is not a power of 2, in addition to the k-ary routing table each peer also must maintain a routing table as in the binary case that corresponds to at least the last remaining bits $\lfloor \frac{|path(p)|}{d} \rfloor * d \leq l \leq |path(p)|$.

4.2   Construction Algorithm

This method is a natural extension of the P-Grid approach that uses a binary tree structure. The construction process assumes that exchanges between random peers occur. Exchanges always happen between two peers as in the previous version with binary tree.

In order to highlight the difference to the original construction process we discuss here only the mechanism used to construct the k-ary routing table entries. To that end we assume that a binary P-Grid is already constructed, but the k-ary routing tables are empty.

We observe that actually the k-ary routing tables will not be able to completely cover the search space when the P-Grid is unbalanced, a situation that
results naturally from the P-Grid construction when the data distributions are
skewed. In the extreme case, when the tree underlying the P-Grid is a linear
tree, it is not possible to construct a k-ary routing table at all.

In Figure 1 we see an example. Assume the tree associated with peer $P1$
also corresponds to the tree underlying the construction of the P-Grid, i.e. there
exist only peers with paths 00000, 00001, 0001, 001, 01, 10, and 11 and the tree
is unbalanced. Then peer $P1$ can maintain a 2-ary routing table at the top level
only as illustrated. For all other levels it maintains only binary routing tables.
The second peer $P2$ is associated with path 11.

For filling the k-ary routing tables peers exchange information during bilateral interactions. With a passive strategy they exchange information on their
own path and on their routing table entries in order to obtain new entries for
their k-ary routing tables. An example of some actions taken in such a step is
illustrated in Figure 1 when peer $P1$ encounters peer $P2$. $P1$ can enter immediately the address of peer $P2$ into its 2-ary routing table. In addition it can copy
an entry $P3$ from $P2$'s (binary) routing table.

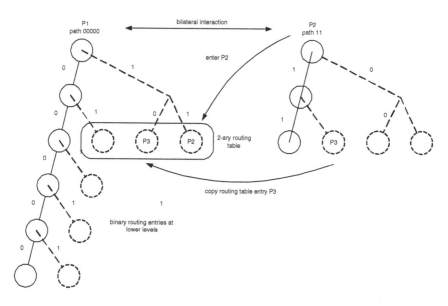

Fig. 1. P-Grid data structure example

We also considered a proactive construction method which takes place in addition to the passive construction. When a peer reaches certain level determined
by d, it sends information about the newly obtained references up the hierarchy
till the level just after previous level for which k-ary level was constructed. This

speeds up the construction of k-ary routing tables at the expense of additional messages.

Regarding the maintenance of the entries in the routing tables, the correcting of the entries in the routing tables both k-ary and binary can be made as a result of the querying process. The query message contains the searched key t and the number of already resolved bits. Thus the peer who receives the message can immediately determine whether the peer who sends the message has the correct routing entry. A similar mechanism was proposed for a k-ary extension of the Chord-based P2P system [6]. The efficiency of such an approach will depend on the frequencies of queries and updates and is yet to be evaluated.

4.3   Search Using the K-Ary and the Binary Routing Tables

The search algorithm presented here uses a combination of both the k-ary and binary routing tables. The idea is to guarantee searchability which is not possible by using the k-ary routing tables only, as discussed above. The search algorithm tries first to find an appropriate reference in the k-ary routing table if such a reference exist. In case it doesn't exist a reference from the binary routing table is selected. The function $prefix(t, d_1, d_2)$ extracts from string t the bits from position d_1 to d_2.

$ksearch(t, loc(p)) :=$

if $path(p) \subseteq t$ **then** $return(loc(p))$

   else

        determine maximal l such that $t_1 \ldots t_{l-1}(1 - t_l) \subseteq path(p)$;

        $r_k = kref(p, d, \lceil l/d \rceil, prefix(t, d * (\lceil l/d \rceil - 1), d * \lceil l/d \rceil))$;

        if r_k is not empty **then** $r =$ randomly selected element from r_k

        $ksearch(t, loc(r))$

          else

             $r =$ randomly selected element from $ref(p, l)$

             $search(t, loc(r))$;

In the following we give a result on the expected number of messages generated by using this algorithm for the balanced case. Whether this result generalizes to the unbalanced case, as it has been shown for binary P-Grids by Theorem 1, is the question we will evaluate experimentally in the succeeding section.

Theorem 2. The expected number of messages for a balanced P-Grid, generated by the search algorithm that uses both k-ary and binary routing tables, when peers have paths of lengths l_p and the k-ary routing tables, defined by the parameter d, are complete is : $Div(l_p, d) * (1 - (\frac{1}{2})^d) + Mod(l_p, d) * \frac{1}{2}$

Proof: For showing the claim we first show that in a k-ary tree based P2P system that consists of N peers with different paths and each has complete k-ary routing tables and paths and queries are uniformly distributed the expected number of messages per query is $log_k N * (1 - \frac{1}{k})$. It is assumed that the keys for both the peer's paths and queries are based on a set consisting of k different symbols. When a query arrives at a peer the probability that the peer itself has the answer is $\frac{1}{k}$ and thus the probability that the message is needed is $(1 - \frac{1}{k})$. Since the depth of the tree is $log_k N$ the expected number of messages per query is $log_k N * (1 - \frac{1}{k})$. Now, the first part of the claim regarding the combined search method corresponds to search using the k-ary routing tables. $Div(l_p, d)$ is the depth of the k-ary tree routing table. The probability that peer who receives the query has the answer itself means that d bits from the query should match the corresponding d bits from the peer's path which is $(\frac{1}{2})^d$. The second part corresponds to searching for the remaining bits of the query using the binary tree structure.

5   Experiments

In order to gain a better understanding on how much communication cost in terms of messages can be saved by using the proposed approach with routing tables of higher arities, we made a simulation of the algorithms in Mathematica 4.2. Many experiments were conducted to evaluate the search performances under different conditions.

The following list of parameters and settings are considered to have an influence on the final results in terms of communication cost savings:

- Initial data distribution: we examine uniform and non-uniform distributions including Zipf-like distribution.
- Parameter d: defines the arity of the k-ary routing table
- Query distribution: we assume that the query distribution is coupled to the data distribution, i.e. all data items are queried with the same probability.

For each experiment, we present the following values:

- Number of messages generated per query using the binary routing tables only.
- Number of messages generated per query using both the k-ary and the binary routing tables.
- Expected number of messages generated per query using both the k-ary and the binary routing tables, calculated as an average value of expected values for all peers according to Theorem 2.
- The imbalance of the tree that represents the peer's paths distribution.

Regarding the imbalance measure, we give a definition that is used in presenting the results:

Definition. The *imbalance measure of a node* is defined as the absolute difference between the numbers of leaves in its left and right subtrees. The *imbalance measure of a tree* is the sum of imbalance measures of all its nodes.

For examining the impact of the data distribution, we performed experiments with three different data distributions: uniform and two types of Zipf-like distributions. For the Zipf-like distributions, in the first case, the parameter Θ was chosen to be 0.8614 which is very frequently observed value in many situations. In the second case, higher value for Θ was used to produce more skewed data distribution. In the first case the data distribution is uniform. The size of the peer's population was set to 256 and the number of peer interactions required for constructing the P-Grid with all k-ary routing tables. The stable state was determined by performing a large set of experiments and observing the changes in the k-ary routing structures. The system is considered to be in a stable state when no more changes occur. For each type of data distribution, the parameter d received values of 2, 3, 4 and 5 which corresponds to arities: 4, 8, 16 and 32 respectively. Using higher values of d doesn't make sense as in that case each peer will have to store routing information about a large fraction of peers compared to the size of the peer's population. The number of different inserted data objects was 4096. Each experiment consisted of 1000 queries with the query distribution that matches the initial data distribution. Queries were sent to randomly chosen peers.

As can be observed from the results, each data distribution results in a different imbalance of the tree of the path's distribution. While for the uniform data distribution this value is pretty low, less than 10, for the Zipf-like distributions is much higher.

Table 1 shows the results obtained by using the uniform data distribution. It can be observed that the number of messages generated per query with the combination search method matches very well the expected number of messages calculated according to the Theorem 1. It can be observed that it drops with increasing d(arity) and reaches its minimum value for $d = 4$. However, when d is increased to 5 both the expected and the observed from the simulation values for generated messages increase. This is due to the fact that most of the peers reach path lengths of 8 in this experiment. Thus, when $d = 4$ they are able to construct 2 levels in their k-ary routing tables, while for $d = 5$ at most 1 level can be constructed. When using $d = 4$ approximately 43% of communication cost can be saved compared to the case when only binary routing tables are used for search.

Table 2 and Table 3 show the results obtained by using Zipf-like data distributions. In this case we have no theoretical result to predict the message cost. From the binary case we know that the expected cost should remain logarithmic. With this experiment we determine how this result generalizes when using k-ary routing tables.

Since the tree structure is unbalanced the k-ary routing tables are incomplete in these experiments. The number of levels constructed in a peer's k-ary routing table and its presence in other peers' k-ary routing tables depends on its path length. The k-ary references can be constructed only by peers with longer paths and only those can be stored as k-ary references by other peers. However, the simulation results show that the resulting number of messages generated by using both types of routing tables is pretty close to the number of messages generated with the uniform data distribution. This means that it is enough to construct

Table 1. Influence of changing the initial data distribution

$\Theta_d{}^a$	n^b	cycles^c	delta^d	im^e	mb^f	mk^g	e^h
0	256	15000	2	7	3.441	2.667	2.649
0	256	15000	3	3	3.318	2.269	2.252
0	256	25000	4	8	3.495	1.992	1.938
0	256	25000	5	2	3.502	2.046	2.099

^{a} Zipf distribution parameter for data
^{b} total number of peers
^{c} number of random exchanges
^{d} determines k-ary fanout
^{e} imbalance tree measure
^{f} number of messages generated using the binary routing tables
^{g} number of messages generated using the k-ary and binary routing tables
^{h} expected number of messages generated using the k-ary and binary routing tables

k-ary routing tables only for longer paths. The saved cost, when using k-ary routing tables, is for $d = 4$ approximately 39%.

Table 2. Influence of changing the initial data distribution

Θ_d	n	cycles	delta	im	mb	mk
0.8614	256	15000	2	42	2.893	2.375
0.8614	256	15000	3	33	2.861	2.122
0.8614	256	25000	4	41	2.922	1.776
0.8614	256	25000	5	38	2.903	1.885

These experiments show that the amount of saved messages is in line with the results obtained for uniform data distributions with balanced search structures. Thus the result from Theorem 1 is most likely also to generalize when using k-ary routing structures. It is worth to note that the saving in communication cost in the experiments appears to be not very substantial. However, we performed the experiments with relatively short paths, just sufficient to study the effects of using k-ary routing tables. From Theorem 2 it is clear that for longer paths the savings will be substantial with increasing values of d.

6   Conclusions and Future Work

We have proposed algorithms for constructing a k-ary access structure for P2P system in a self-organizing way and based on local bilateral interactions. We show analytically what is the expected communication cost when query distribution is

Table 3. Influence of changing the initial data distribution

Θ_d	n	cycles	delta	im	mb	mk
0.9614	256	15000	2	55	2.838	2.313
0.9614	256	15000	3	76	2.809	2.078
0.9614	256	25000	4	62	2.812	1.709
0.9614	256	25000	5	56	2.819	1.917

uniform and the k-ary tree structure for routing is complete. Due to the skewed data distribution and our construction mechanism the k-ary structures can be incomplete. We performed a set of experiments that justify the expected cost with the complete k-ary structures. The simulations show only minor degradation in searching performances when Zipf-like data and query distributions are used. The simulated and the expected numbers of messages generated show that the increasing arity doesn't always lead to improving performances. Thus taking into account other parameters like maintenance cost it will be possible to find an optimal value for the arity of the access structure. Here we give a simulation with the P-Grid system. However, the results with the balanced tree structures are generic and applicable to other structured P2P systems.

References

1. Aberer, K.: P-Grid: A Self-organizing Access Structure for P2P Information Systems. Sixth International Conference on Cooperative Information Systems (CoopIS 2001), Trento, Italy (2001)
2. Aberer, K.: Efficient Search in Unbalanced, Randomized Peer-To-Peer Search Trees. Techical Report IC/2002/79, Ecole Polytechnique Fédérale de Lausanne (EPFL), (2002). http://www.p-grid.org/Papers/TR-IC-2002-79.pdf
3. Aberer, K.: Scalable Data Access in P2P Systems Using Unbalanced Search Trees.Workshop on Distributed Data and Structures (WDAS 2002), Paris, France (2002).
4. Aberer, K., Datta, A., Hauswirth, M.: The Quest for Balncing Peer Load in Structured Peer-to-Peer Systems. Technical Report IC/2003/32, Ecole Polytechnique Fédérale de Lausanne (EPFL), (2003). http://www.p-grid.org/Papers/TR-IC-2003-32.pdf
5. Aberer, K., Hauswirth, M., Punceva, M., Schmidt, R.: Improving Data Access in P2P Systems. IEEE Internet Computing, 6(1), Jan/Feb. (2002)
6. Alima, L.O., El-Ansary, S., Brand, P., Haridi, S.: A Framework for Peer-to-Peer Lookup Services Based on k-ary Search. SICS Technical Report T2002-06 (2002). http://www.sics.se/~ seif/Publications/SICS-T–2002-06–SE.pdf.
7. Clarke, I., Sandberg, O., Wiley, B., Hong, W.T.: Freenet: A Distributed Anonymous Information Storage and Retrieval System. Designing Privacy Enhancing Technologies: International Workshop on Design Issues in Anonymity and Unobservability, number 2009 in LNCS (2001). http://freenetproject.org/cgi-bin/twiki/view/Main/ICSI.

8. Clip2. The Gnutella Protocol Specification v0.4. Document Revision 1.2, Jun (2001). http://www9.limewire.com/developer/gnutella_protocol_0.4.pdf.

9. Dabek, F., Brunskill, E., Kaashoek, F.M., Karger, D., Morris, R., Stoica, I., Balakrishnan, H.: Building Peer-to-Peer Systems with Chord, a Distributed LookupService. Eighth Workshop on Hot Topics in Operating Systems (HotOS), (2001).

10. Lv, Q., Cao, P., Cohen, E., Li, K., Shenker, S.: Search and Replication In Unstructured Peer-to-Peer Networks. International Conference on Supercomputing (2002).

11. Maymounkov, P., Mazieres, P.: Kademlia: a Peer-to-Peer Information System based on XOR Metric. First International Workshop on Peer-to-Peer Systems (IPTPS)(2002).

12. Ratnasamy, S., Francis, P., Handley, M., Karp, R., Shenker, S.: A Scalable Content Addressable Network. (ACM SIGCOMM)(2001).

13. Rhea, S., Wells, C., Eaton, P., Geels, D., Zhao, B., Wearherspoon, H., Kubiatowitcz, J.: Maintenance-Free Global Data Storage. IEEE Inetrenet Computing, 5(5), (2001).

14. Rowstron, A., Druschel, P.: Pastry: Scalable, Distributed Object Location and Routing for Large-Scale Peer-to-Peer Systems.ACM INternational Conference on Distributed Systems Platforms (Middleware), (2001).

Content-Based Overlay Networks for XML Peers Based on Multi-level Bloom Filters[1]

Georgia Koloniari, Yannis Petrakis, and Evaggelia Pitoura

Department of Computer Science
University of Ioannina, Greece
{kgeorgia, pgiannis, pitoura}@cs.uoi.gr

Abstract. Peer-to-peer systems are gaining popularity as a means to effectively share huge, massively distributed data collections. In this paper, we consider XML peers, that is, peers that store XML documents. We show how an extension of traditional Bloom filters, called multi-level Bloom filters, can be used to route path queries in such a system. In addition, we propose building content-based overlay networks by linking together peers with similar content. The similarity of the content (i.e., the local documents) of two peers is defined based on the similarity of their filters. Our experimental results show that overlay networks built based on filter similarity are very effective in retrieving a large number of relevant documents, since peers with similar content tend to be clustered together.

1 Introduction

Peer-to-peer (p2p) computing refers to a new form of distributed computing that involves a large number of autonomous computing nodes (the peers) that cooperate to share resources and services [17]. P2p systems are gaining popularity as a way to effectively share huge, massively distributed data collections.

In this paper, motivated by the fact that XML has evolved as the new standard for data representation and exchange on the Internet, we assume that peers store XML documents: either XML files that they want to share or XML-based descriptions of the resources and services that they offer. We extend search in p2p, by considering path queries that explore the structure of such hierarchical documents.

Bloom filters have been proposed for summarizing documents (e.g., in [3]). Bloom filters are compact data structures that can be used to support membership queries, i.e., whether an element belongs to a set. In [9], we have introduced multi-level Bloom filters that extend traditional simple Bloom filters for answering path queries.

We show how multi-level Bloom filters can be used to route queries in a p2p system. Each peer maintains a summary of its content (i.e., local documents) in the

---

[1] This work was partially funded by the Information Society Technologies programme of the European Commission, Future and Emerging Technologies under the IST-2001-32645 DBGlobe project and by a Greek Ministry of Education program for Supporting Graduate Studies in Computer Science (EPEAEK II).

K. Aberer et al. (Eds.): VLDB 2003 Ws DBISP2P, LNCS 2944, pp. 232–247, 2004.

form of a multi-level Bloom filter. It also maintains one merged multi-level Bloom filter for each of its links summarizing the content of all peers that can be reached through this link. Using such merged filters, each peer decides to direct a query only through links that may lead to peers with documents that match the query. For scalability reasons, we limit the number of peers that are summarized through the concept of horizons. We also propose a heuristic for choosing through which among more than one qualifying link to route the query.

Furthermore, we show how Bloom filters can be used to build content-based overlay networks, that is, to link together peers with similar content. The similarity of the content (i.e., the local documents) of two peers is defined based on the similarity of their filters. This is cost effective, since a filter for a set of documents is much smaller than the documents themselves. Furthermore, the filter comparison operation is more efficient than a direct comparison between sets of documents. Our experimental results show that overlay networks built based on filter similarity are very effective in retrieving a large number of relevant documents, since relevant peers tend to be clustered together.

In summary, this paper makes the following contributions:

- Extends keyword queries in p2p to path queries by proposing multi-level Bloom-based filters,
- Shows how traditional and multi-level Bloom filters can be used to search in a horizon-based distribution and proposes a search heuristic based on the characteristics of Bloom filters,
- Proposes building content-based overlay network, where a peer connects to peers with similar content where similarity is based on the similarity of their filters. Such networks are shown to be very effective in retrieving a large number of relevant documents.

The remainder of this paper is structured as follows. Section 2 describes the system model, our multi-level Bloom filters and filter distribution using horizons. Section 3 introduces an overlay network organization based on content-similarity criteria and our similarity metric. Section 4 presents our experimental results. In Section 5, we compare our work with related research and we conclude in Section 6 with directions for future work.

2   Multi-level Blooms as P2P Routers

2.1   System Model

We consider a system of peers where each peer n_i maintains a set of documents D_i (a particular document may be stored in more than one peer). Each peer is logically linked to a relatively small set of other peers called its *neighbors*. Motivated by the fact that XML has evolved as the new standard for data representation and exchange on the Internet, we assume that peers store XML files: XML documents that they want to share or XML-based descriptions of the available local services and resources.

In our data model, an XML document is represented by an unordered-labeled tree, where tree nodes correspond to document elements, while edges represent direct element-subelement relationships. Although, most p2p systems support only queries for documents that contain one or more *keywords*, we want also to query the structure of documents. Thus, we consider *path queries* that are simple path expressions in an XPath-like query language.

Definition 1 (path query): A simple path expression query of length k has the form "$s_1 \, l_1 \, s_2 \, l_2 \, \ldots \, s_k \, l_k$" where each l_i is an element name, and each s_i is either / or // denoting respectively parent-child and ancestor-descendant traversal.

A keyword query searching for documents containing keyword k is just the path query //k. For a query q and a document d, we say that q is satisfied by d, or *match(d, q)* is true, if the path expression forming the query exists in the document. Otherwise we have a *miss*.

A given query may be matched by documents at various peers. To locate peers with matching documents, we maintain at each peer specialized data structures called *filters* that summarize large collections of documents reachable from this peer. The aim is to be able to deduce whether there is a matching document along a particular link by just looking at the filter. To this end, each filter $F(D)$ summarizing a set of documents D should support an efficient *filter-match* operation, *filter-match(F(D), q)*, that for each query q, if there is a document $d \in D$ such that *match(d, q)* is true then *filter-match(F(D), q)* is also true. If the filter-match returns false, then we have a *miss* and we can conclude that there is no matching document in D. The reverse does not necessarily hold. That is, *filter-match(F(D), q)* may be true but there may be no document $d \in D$ for which *match(d, q)* is true. This is called a *false positive* and may lead to following paths to peers with no matching documents. However, no matching documents are lost. We are looking for filters for which the probability of false positive is low.

Bloom filters are appropriate as summarizing filters in this context in terms of scalability, extensibility and distribution. However, they do not support path queries. To this end, we have proposed an extension called multi-level Bloom filters [9].

2.2 Multi-level Bloom Filters

Bloom filters are compact data structures for probabilistic representation of a set that supports membership queries ("Is element a in set A?"). Since their introduction [1], Bloom filters have been used in many contexts including web cache sharing [2], query filtering and routing [3, 4] and free text searching [5].

Consider a set $A = \{a_1, a_2, \ldots, a_n\}$ of n elements. The idea (Figure 1) is to allocate a vector v of m bits, initially all set to 0, and then choose k independent hash functions, $h_1, h_2, \ldots, h_k$, each with range 1 to m. For each element $a \in A$, the bits at positions $h_1(a), h_2(a), \ldots, h_k(a)$ in v are set to 1. A particular bit may be set to 1 many times. Given a query for b, we check the bits at positions $h_1(b), h_2(b), \ldots, h_k(b)$. If any of them is 0, then certainly b is not in the set A. Otherwise we conjecture that b is in the set although there is a certain probability that we are wrong, i.e., we may have a false positive. This is the payoff for Bloom filters compactness. The parameters k and m should be chosen such that the probability P of a false positive is acceptable. It has been shown [1] that: $P = (1 - e^{-kn/m})^k$.

To support updates of the set A, we maintain for each location l in the bit array a count $c(l)$ of the number of times that the bit is set to 1 (the number of elements that hashed to l under any of the hash functions). All counters are initially set to 0. When a key a is inserted or deleted, the counters $c(h_1(a))$, $c(h_2(a))$, ..., $c(h_k(a))$ are incremented or decremented accordingly. When a counter changes from 0 to 1, the corresponding bit is turned on. When a counter changes from 1 to 0, the corresponding bit is turned off.

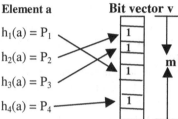

Fig. 1. A Bloom Filter with $k = 4$ Hash Functions

For processing a path query, we check whether each element of the path is matched by the filter. If there is a match for every element of the query, then we conjecture that the path may exist in the filter without taking structure into account.

We consider two ways of extending Bloom filters for hierarchical documents. Let an XML tree T with j levels, and let the level of the root be level 1. The *Breadth Bloom Filter* (BBF) for an XML tree T with j levels is a set of $i + 1$ Bloom filters $\{BBF_0, BBF_1, BBF_2, ..., BBF_i\}$, $i \leq j$. In BBF_0, we insert all elements that appear in any level of the tree. Then, there is one Bloom filter, denoted BBF_i, for the level i of the XML tree, in which we insert the elements of all nodes at level i. Depth Bloom filters provide an alternative way to summarize XML trees. We use different Bloom filters to hash paths of different lengths. The *Depth Bloom Filter* (DBF) for an XML tree T with j levels is a set of i Bloom filters $\{DBF_0, DBF_1, DBF_2, ..., DBF_{i-1}\}$, $i \leq j$. There is one Bloom filter, denoted DBF_i, corresponding to the paths of the tree of length i, (i.e., having $i + 1$ nodes), where we insert all paths of length i. Note that we insert paths as a whole, we do not hash each element of the path separately; instead, we hash their concatenation.

To implement the filter match for a path query, in the case of BBFs, we first check, whether all elements in the path expression appear in BBF_0. Then, the first element of the path query is checked at BBF_1. If there is a match, the next element is checked at the next level of the filter and the procedure continues until either the whole path is matched or there is a miss. For paths with the ancestor-descendant axis //, the path is split at the //, and the sub-paths are processed at all the appropriate levels. All matches are stored and compared to determine whether there is a match for the whole path.

The procedure that checks whether a DBF matches a path query, first checks whether all elements in the path expression appear in DBF_0. If this is the case, for a query of length p, every sub-path of the query from length 2 to p is checked at the filter of the corresponding level. If any of the sub-paths does not exist then the algorithm returns a miss. For paths that include the ancestor-descendant axis //, the path is split at the // and the resulting sub-paths are checked. If we have a match for all sub-paths the algorithm succeeds, else we have a miss.

2.3 Filter Distribution Based on Horizons

A query may originate at any peer of the network, whereas documents matching the query may reside in numerous other peers. To direct the query to the appropriate peers, each peer maintains a number of filters. In particular, each peer n_i maintains a *local filter* $F(D_i)$ that summarizes all documents D_i stored locally at n_i and one filter, called *merged filter*, for each of its links. The merged filter for a link e of n_i summarizes the documents that reside at peers reachable from n_i through any path starting from link e. Merged filters are used to direct the query only to peers that have a large probability to contain documents matching the query.

Ideally, the merged filter for each link should summarize the documents of *all* reachable peers. However, this introduces scalability problems. In this case, an update of the content of a peer must be propagated to a huge number of other peers. The same holds for the filters of peers joining or leaving the network. By introducing *horizons*, a peer bounds the number of neighbors whose documents it summarizes. The horizon of a peer n_i includes all peers that can be reached with at most R hops starting from n_i. We call R the *radius* of the horizon.

Definition 2 (Distance): *The distance between two peers n_i and n_j, $d(n_i , n_j)$ is the number of hops on the shortest path from n_i to n_j in the overlay network.*
Definition 3 (Horizon): *A peer n_i has a horizon of R, if it stores summaries for all peers n_j for which the distance $d(n_i, n_j) \leq R$, where R is the radius of the horizon.*

In horizon-based distribution, the merged filter for a link e of n_i summarizes (i.e., merges the local filters) of all peers that are reachable from n_i by a path of length R or smaller starting from e. Figure 2 shows for each link of peer 5, the local filters of which peers are merged at the corresponding merged filter, when $R = 2$. In the case of cycles, the documents of some peers (peer 8 in this example) may be included in more than one merged filter. We describe later, why and how this may be avoided.

In order to calculate the merged Bloom filter of a set of Bloom filters we take the bitwise OR of these Bloom filters. In particular, the merged Bloom filter BF_m of a set $\{BF_1, BF_2,..., BF_n\}$ of Bloom filters is equal to BF_1 *OR* BF_2 *OR* ...*OR* BF_n. Similarly, for multi-level Blooms, we take the bitwise OR for each of their levels. Apart from the merged filter, merged counters are also stored, to support updates. Merged counters are produced by adding together the corresponding counters of the set of Bloom filters.

2.4 Join and Update

When a new peer n_k joins the system, it must inform the other peers at distance R about its documents. To this end, n_k sends a message *New(F(D_k), Counter)* to all its neighbors, where $F(D_k)$ is its local filter (ie., the filter summarizing its documents) and *Counter* is set to R. Upon receipt of a *New* message, each peer n_i merges the received $F(D_k)$ filter with the merged filter of the corresponding link. Then, it reduces *Counter* by one, and if *Counter* is nonzero, it sends a *New(F(D_k), Counter-1)* message to all other of its neighbors. This way, the summary of the documents of the new node is propagated to the existing peers.

In addition, the new node must construct its own merged filters. This is achieved through a sequence of *FW(Filter, Counter, flag)* messages. In particular, each node n_i upon receipt of a *New* message from a node n_j, it replies to n_j with a *FW(F(D_i), R, False)* message where $F(D_i)$ is n_i's local filter and *Counter* is set to R. The use of the *flag* parameter will be explained shortly. Upon receipt of a *FW(F(D_i), Counter, False)* message, each peer n_j, decrements the Counter by one, and if Counter is nonzero, it sends a *FW(F(D_i), Counter-1, False)* message back to the peer that has sent the *New* message to it. This way, the local summaries reach the new peer n_k. Peer n_k creates its merged filters by merging the corresponding local filters received by the various *FW* messages.

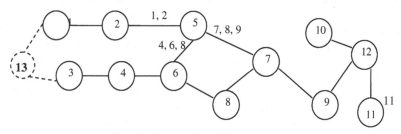

Fig. 2. Horizon-Based Distribution

We now explain the use of the flag parameter. *Flag* is used because the insertion of a new peer may change further the horizons of existing peers. Take for example the network of Figure 2 with $R = 2$. Say a new peer, peer 13, enters the network and links to both peers 1 and 3. The local filter of 13 must be propagated to 1, 2 and 3, 4; this is achieved through the *New* messages. Peer 13 must also construct its own merged filters; this is achieved through the *FW* messages with flag equal to False. However, note that the insertion of 13 has changed the relative distance of some peers. In particular, now peer 3 (1) belongs to the horizon of 1 (3) since their distance (through the new peer 13) is now 2. Thus, the local filter of 3 (1) must now be merged with the corresponding filter of 1 (3).

Flag is used as follows. *Flag* is initially set to False. When the new node n_k receives a *FW(Filter, Counter, False)* message, it changes *Flag* to *True*, decrements Counter by one, and if *Counter* is nonzero, it propagates a message *FW(Filter, Counter-1, True)* to all of its other neighbors. Upon receipt of a *FW(Filter, Counter, True)* message, each peer merges the *Filter* with its corresponding merged filter, decrements *Counter* by one, and if *Counter* is nonzero, it sends a *FW(Filter, Counter-*

1, True) message to its neighbors. This way, summaries of peers whose horizons change by the introduction of the new peer are propagated to each other.

When a peer wishes to leave the system, it sends an update message to all its neighbours with a counter set to the radius R. When the message reaches a peer, the peer performs the update at its merged filter and propagates the message further until the counter reaches 0. Furthermore, it sends it own local filter through the same link with a counter set to R to inform the peers that are now included in its horizon, since the departure of the peer has resulted in the decrease of its distance with other peers.

Note that, as indicated in Figure 2, it is possible that the local filter of a peer n_i is included in more than one merged filter of some other peer n_j. However, we may want to avoid this, because during search, two different paths will lead us to the same peer. This problem can be overcome by using peer identifiers. Each peer stores the identifiers of the peers that are included in each of its merged filters. When a local filter reaches a peer during the join procedure, the peer first checks whether it has already stored this filter at the merged filter of some other link.

2.5 Query Routing

We now discuss in detail how a query q posed at a peer n is processed. Our goal is to locate all peers that contain documents matching the query.

Peer n first checks it own local filter to see whether it matches the query. Then, it propagates the query only through one or more of those links whose merged filters match the query. Analogously, each peer that receives the query first check its own local filter and propagates the query only to links whose merged filters match the query. This procedure ends when a maximum number of peers has been visited or when the desired number of matching documents (results) has been attained.

When a query reaches a peer that has no outgoing edges that match the query, backtracking is used. This state can be reached either by a false positive or when we are interested in locating more than one matching document. In this case, the query is returned to the previous visited peer that checks whether there are any other links that match the query that have not been followed yet, and propagates it through one or more of them. If there are no such matching links, it sends the query to its previous peer and so on. Thus, each peer should store the peer that propagated the query to it. In addition, we may store an identifier for each query to avoid cycles.

We now describe a heuristic that can be used to choose which of the links that match a query to follow. The heuristic uses the counters of the matching merged filters to select the link through which we expect to find more matching documents. We describe first the idea for simple (single-level) Bloom filters.

Assume we have a query q with s element names: $\alpha_1, \alpha_2, ..., \alpha_s$. For each matching merged filter, we compute a value, called MIN, as follows. For each element α_i, the counters at the corresponding positions are checked and the minimum value $min(\alpha_i) = min(c(h_1(\alpha_i)),..., c(h_k(\alpha_i)))$ is stored. Then, we take the overall minimum for all element names: $MIN = min\{min_i(\alpha_i)\}$, for $i = 1,..., s$. This is the maximum number of results (matching documents) for q that can be found following the link of this merged filter. The query is propagated through the link whose merged filter has the largest value for MIN, because it is expected that the peers who can be reached through this link maintain the most results.

For multi-level filters the procedure is slightly altered. For every element in the query, the counters of the corresponding level that gave a match are checked and the minimum value is selected. The minimum values of every element are added together (SUM = $\min(a_i)$ + .. + $\min(a_s)$) and the link chosen is the link whose filter gave the largest sum. If a path matches more times in a single filter (the path exists at different levels), the largest of the SUMs produced is chosen to be compared with the SUMs of the other filters.

3   Content-Based Overlay Networks

In this section, we discuss how the overlay network is created. The approaches refer to the way a peer chooses its neighbors in the overlay network when it joins the system.

3.1 Content-Based Organization

In most unstructured peer-to-peer systems, whenever a new peer wishes to join the system, it connects to an existing peer randomly selected from a list of known peers. This approach has the drawback that it does not take into account the content of the peers and thus, the topology of the network is created randomly.

In order to achieve a network topology that depends on the content of the peers, we propose a *content-based organization* in which peers select their neighbors based on the similarity of their content, that is, based on the similarity of their local documents. This approach attempts to group relevant peers together. The motivation for such a content-based organization is to minimize the number of irrelevant peers that are visited when processing a query.

Instead of checking the similarity of documents, we rely on the similarity of their filters. This is more cost effective, since a filter for a set of documents is much smaller than the documents themselves. Furthermore, the filter comparison operation is more efficient than a direct comparison between two sets of documents. Documents with similar filters are expected to match similar queries.

In this organization, a peer n_i that joins the system propagates its local filter $F(D_i)$ to the existing peers. A peer n_j receiving the message replies with the distance of its own local filter from n_i's filter, $distance(F(D_i), F(D_j))$. Peer n_i chooses to attach to the peers that returned the smallest distances, i.e., the most similar ones.

This way peers with relevant content are expected to be grouped together so as to form content-based clusters of peers. With this organization, once a query enters the relevant cluster, peers with matching documents are expected to be within reach.

3.2 Filter-Based Similarity Metric

For Bloom-based filters the distance function used to evaluate the degree of similarity between two filters BF_1 and BF_2, $distance(BF_1, BF_2)$, is computed using the Hamming distance. This distance corresponds to the number of bits at which the two Bloom filters differ. The more similar the two documents are, the smaller their Hamming distance is. An example is shown in Figure 3(a). For multi-level Blooms, to compute their distance, the distance of each level is calculated the same way as for a simple Bloom, and the results are added together.

Figure 3(b) illustrates an experiment that confirms the validity of the metric. We used different percentage of elements repetition between documents and measured their distance. The distance decreases linearly with the increase of the repetition between the documents. The same holds for the similarity between multi-level Blooms, although in this case, the metric depends on the structure of the documents as well.

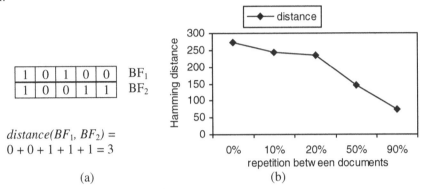

(a)   (b)

Fig. 3. (a) Similarity Metric (b) Document and Filter Similarity

4   Performance Evaluation

4.1 Simulation Model

We simulated the peer-to-peer network as a graph where each node corresponds to a peer. A number of XML documents are associated with each node. We simulated the organization of the peers using horizons both with and without the use of filters and compared both the content-based and the random (non content-based) organizations. For the first two experiments we used simple Bloom filters as summaries and queries of length 1. In the last two experiments, we show how multi-level filters outperform simple ones in this distributed setting when evaluating queries with length greater than 1. We used only Breadth Bloom filters in our experiments; Depth Bloom filters are expected to perform similarly with Breadth Bloom filters [9].

For the hash functions, we used MD5 [13] that is a cryptographic message digest algorithm that hashes arbitrarily length strings to 128 bits. The k hash functions are built by first calculating the MD5 signature of the input string, which yields 128 bits, and then taking k groups of $128/k$ bits from it. We select MD5 because of its well-known properties and relatively fast implementation. For the generation of the XML documents, we used the Niagara generator [14] that generates tree-structured XML documents of arbitrary complexity. It allows the user to specify a wide range of characteristics for the generated data by varying a number of simple and intuitive input parameters, which control the structure of the documents and the repetition between the element names.

The structure of the network depends on: the diameter of the graph (the maximum distance between any two nodes through the shortest available path), the number of nodes (peers), the number of edges (links), the maximum fanout for a peer and the radius of the horizon. In our experiments, the size of the network was set to 100 peers and its diameter to 30 hops, the filter size was fixed to 2000bits with 4 hash functions. XML documents have 5 levels and 80 elements, but follow different structures. Every 10% of the documents are 50% similar to each other in terms of element names. The search stops when a maximum number of 30 hops are traversed. The selection of the maximum hops was random and large enough to cover a sufficient proportion of the network without producing excessive delays to a query. Our performance metrics are the percentage of successful queries (i.e., queries that found at least one matching node) and recall (i.e., the percentage of results found).

Table 1. Summary of Performance Parameters

Parameter	Default Value	Range
Filter size	2000 bits	
Number of hash functions	4	
Number of queries	200	
Number of elements per document	80	
Number of levels per document	5	
Length of query	1	1-3
Number of nodes	100	
Percentage of hits (matching nodes per query) in the network	7%	
Radius of horizon	5	3-11
Diameter	30	
Max fanout	5	
Max number of hops	30	
Number of hits per node	1	1-50

4.2 Experimental Results

Experiment 1: Radius (R)

At this first experiment, we examine the influence of the radius. The network structure was fixed to 100 nodes with diameter 30 and we varied the radius from 3 to 11. We measured the percentage of successful queries and the percentage of results found (recall), with and without the use of Bloom Filters.

Bloom filters improve the performance of search for any value of the Radius (R). Radius 3 gives the smallest number of results and the smallest percentage of successful queries. This is expected because search for matching documents is limited to peers within distance 3 from the peer issuing the query, thus matching peers furthest away are never visited. Radius 5 gives the most results and the best percentage of successful queries. Increasing the Radius further does not improve the performance. There are two reasons for this. First, as the radius increases, the number of peers that correspond to each merged Bloom filter also increases. This leads to more false positives for a same size filter. Second, when the radius becomes relatively large, the merged filter of each link summarizes the content of a very large number of peers reached through this link. Thus, a path may be followed to a matching peer located very far away from the peer issuing the query instead of a path to a near-by matching peer. In the rest of our experiments we set $R = 5$.

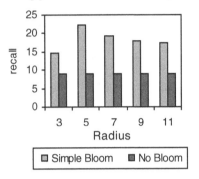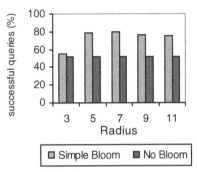

Fig. 4. Influence of the Radius

Experiment 2: Benefits of the Content-Based Organization

At the second set of experiments, we study content-based distribution. The performance of content-based distribution depends on whether, for a given query, we are able to locate the cluster with peers that have results similar to it. Once in the right cluster, we are able to find all results nearby, since the matching nodes are linked together. To model this, we varied the percentage of queries issued from a node that matches the query from 0 to 100% (that is, the percentage of queries that start from the correct cluster). As shown in Figure 5(left), once in the right cluster (100% query distribution), we are able to locate all matching documents, whereas with the non content-based distribution less than 30% of the matching nodes are identified. On the other hand, non content-based organization has a larger percentage of successful queries, since the matching peers for each query are distributed randomly across the network. On the contrary, in the content-based organization, all peers with similar documents are clustered together. Thus, if the requesting peer is far from the correct cluster, it may not be able to find any matching node in its cluster.

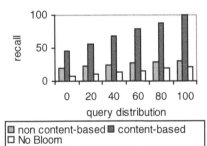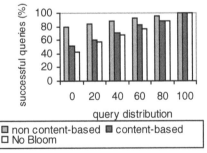

Fig. 5. Varying Query Distribution

Figure 6 shows the effectiveness of our content-based join procedure. It depicts for a query and a matching node *n*, the percentage of matching nodes within distance *R* from *n*. For *R* larger than 5, all matching nodes are within the horizon, that is, they are within this distance and thus they can be located efficiently.

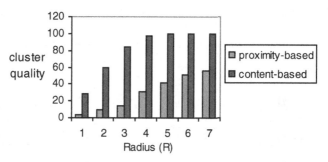

Fig. 6. Quality of Clustering (Percentage of matching nodes with R)

Experiment 3: Breadth vs Simple Bloom Filters

In this set of experiments, we used Simple and Breadth Blooms to demonstrate that our distribution mechanisms can also be used with multi-level filters. Our queries in this example are path queries of length 3. We denote with *P* the percentage of documents that contain the element names that appear in the path query but without them forming the actual path. In the first experiment (Figure 7 (left)), we vary the radius *R* setting P = 75%, while in the second experiment (Figure 7(right), we vary *P* setting *R* = 5. The results of the first experiment for the multi-level are analogous to these of Experiment 1 (Figure 4(left)), but the percentage of results for the simple Bloom Filter is nearly constant. This happens because the number of false positives is very large for any value of the radius for path queries. Figure 7(right) shows that for *P* = 0 both filters perform nearly the same, but as *P* increases the performance of the simple Bloom Filter reduces due to the increase of false positives.

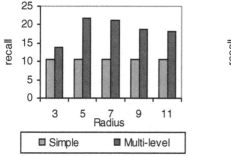 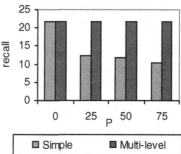

Fig. 7. Simple and Multi-level Blooms

Experiment 4: Use of Counters

At this last experiment, we examine how the use of the counters heuristic improves performance, both for Simple and Breadth Blooms. We varied the number of hits (matching documents) per node and measured the percentage of results found and the percentage of successful queries. The variance of the results is a value that shows the average difference between the number of hits to each peer (that maintains results) and the average number of hits of all that peers at square power. More specifically, variance $= \sum_{i=1,...,k}(x_i-\mu)^2/k$, where k is the number of peers that have results, x_i is the number of hits for peer n_i and $\mu = (\sum_{i=1,...,k} x_i) / k$ (average hits per peer that has results).

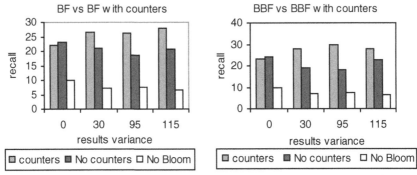

Fig. 8. Use of Counters

Figure 8 shows that in both cases (multi-level and simple Bloom filters) for zero variance (which means that all peers have the same number of results) using or not counters has approximately the same performance. For non-zero variance, the use of counters gives better performance since the query is propagated to edges through which we expect more results to be found.

5   Related Work

In the context of peer-to-peer computing, many methods for resource discovery have been proposed. These methods construct indexes that store summaries of other nodes and additionally provide routing protocols to propagate the query to the relevant nodes.

Bloom filters have been used as summaries in such a context. The resource discovery protocol in [4] uses simple Bloom filters as summaries. Servers are organized into a hierarchy modified based on the query workload to achieve load balance. Each server stores summaries, which are used for query routing. Summaries are a single filter with all the subset hashes of the XML documents up to a certain threshold. To evaluate a query, the query is split to all possible subsets and each one is checked in the index. Another method based on Bloom filters for routing of queries in peer-to-peer networks is presented in [7]. It is based on a new structure, called attenuated Bloom filter, residing in every node of the system. The filter stores information about nodes within a range of the local node and uses a probabilistic algorithm in order to direct a query. The algorithm either finds results quickly, or fails quickly and exhaustive searching is then deployed. Another use of Bloom filters as routing mechanisms is proposed in [11]. Local and Merged Blooms are used, but there is no horizon to limit the information a node stores about other nodes, and thus scalability is an issue. Also the filters are constructed based on file names and not on file content. A similar approach is followed in [6], where routing indices (other than Blooms), placed at each node, are used for efficient routing of queries. By keeping such an index for each outgoing edge, a node can choose the best neighbor for forwarding the query. The choice is based on summarized information about the documents along that path, which is stored in the index.

However, all these methods do not provide any grouping of the nodes according to their content, and use summaries only for routing and not for building the overlay network. Also they are limited in answering membership queries and not path queries.

Content-based distribution was recently proposed in [8] which introduced Semantic Overlay Networks (SONs) [8]. With SONs, nodes with semantically similar content are "clustered" together, based on a classification hierarchy of their documents. Queries are processed by identifying which SONs are better suited to answer it. However, there is no description of how queries are routed or how the clusters are created and no use of filter or indexes to efficiently locate the node that stores a particular data item. Schema-based peer-to-peer networks, is an approach that supports more complex metadata clustering than previous work and thus can support more complex queries. An RDF-based peer-to-peer network is presented in [15]. The system can support heterogeneous metadata schemes and ontologies, but it requires a strict topology with hypercubes and the use of super-peers, limiting the dynamic nature of the network. In [16], attribute-based communities are introduced. Each peer is described by attributes representing its interests, and the emphasis is on the formation and discovery of communities and not searching within them. Since the communities are attribute-based they are less expressive than schema-based or content-based networks and support less complex queries. In [10], documents are classified into categories based on keywords and metadata. Nodes are then clustered based on these categories. Focus is given on load-balancing.

Chord [12] is a representative of structured p2p networks that uses a distributed lookup protocol designed so that documents can be found with a very small number of messages. It maps keys and nodes together to improve search efficiency. However, this approach lacks node autonomy and provides no grouping between nodes with similar content.

Our work relates also to distributed processing of XML queries. There is not much work on the topic. Recent work is presented in [18], where a cost-model for a p2p-context is designed and used for efficient collaborative query processing. Also a query decomposition technique is presented for querying XML data that may be distributed and (partially) replicated.

6 Conclusions

In this paper, we have presented multi-level Bloom filters that are hash-based indexing structures that can be used for the representation of hierarchical data and support the evaluation of path queries. We showed how such filters can be distributed using a horizon-based organization to support the efficient routing of queries in a p2p network. In addition, we described how content-based overlay networks can be built using a procedure that clusters together peers with similar content. Similarity of peer content is based on the similarity of their filters. Our performance results show that content-based overlay networks built by this procedure are very efficient in locating a large number of peers with matching documents.

Future work includes the development of an efficient approach of "linking" clusters together so that the appropriate cluster for a query is identified efficiently. In addition, we plan to experiment with p2p networks with properties that match those of popular p2p networks as indicated by current measurement studies (e.g. [19], [20]).

References

1. B. Bloom. Space/time trade-offs in hash coding with allowable errors. Communications of the ACM, pages 13(7): 422–426, July 1970.
2. L. Fan, P. Cao, J. Almeida, A. Broder. Summary cache: A scalable wide-area Web cache sharing   protocol. In Procs of ACM SIGCOMM Conference, pages 254–265, Sept. 1998.
3. S.D. Gribble, E.A. Brewer, J.M. Hellerstein, D. Culler. Scalable Distributed Data Structures for   Internet Service Construction. In Procs of the Fourth Symposium on Operating Systems Design and Implementation, 2000.
4. T.D. Hodes, S.E. Czerwinski, B.Y. Zhao, A.D. Joseph, R.H. Katz. Architecture for Secure Wide-Area Service Discovery. Mobicom '99.
5. M.V. Ramakrishna. Practical performance of Bloom Filters and parallel free-text searching. Communications of the ACM, 32 (10). 1237–1239.
6. A. Crespo and H. Garcia-Molina. Routing Indices for Peer-to-peer Systems. In ICDCS, 2002.
7. S. C. Rhea, J. Kubiatowicz. Probabilistic Location and Routing. In INFOCOM, 2002.
8. A. Crespo and H. Garcia-Molina. Semantic Overlay Networks for P2P Systems. Submitted for publication.
9. G. Koloniari and E. Pitoura. Bloom-Based Filters for Hierarchical Data. WDAS 2003.
10. P. Triantafillou, C. Xiruhaki, M. Koubarakis, N. Ntarmos. Towards High Performance Peer-to-Peer Content and Resource Sharing Systems. CIDR 2003.
11. A. Mohan and V. Kalogeraki. Speculative Routing and Update Propagation: A Kundali Centric Approach. IEEE International Conference on Communications (ICC'03), May 2003.
12. I.Stoica, R. Morris, D. Karger, M.F. Kaashoek, and H. Balakrishnan. Chord: A Scalable Peer-to-Peer Lookup Service for Internet Applications. Procs. of the 2001 ACM SIGCOMM Conference.
13. The MD5 Message-Digest Algorithm. RFC1321.
14. The Niagara generator, http://www.cs.wisc.edu/niagara
15. W. Nejdl, M. Wolpers, W. Siberski, C. Schmitz, M. Schlosser, I. Brunkhorst, A. Loser. Super-Peer-Based Routing and Clustering Strategies for RDF-Based Peer-To-Peer Networks. WWW 2003, May 2003, Budapest, Hungary. ACM 1-58113-680-3/03/0005.
16. M. Khambatti, K. Ryu, P. Dasgupta. Peer-to-Peer Communities: Formation and Discovery. Fourteenth IASTED International Conference on Parallel and Distributed Computing and Systems, Cambridge, 2002.
17. D. S. Milojicic, V. Kalogeraki, R. Lukose, K. Nagaraja, J. Pruyne, B. Richard, S. Rollins, and Z. Xu. "Peer-to-Peer Computing", HP Technical Report, HPL-2002-57
18. S. Abiteboul, A. Bonifati, G. Cobéna, I. Manolescu, T. Milo. Dynamic XML Documents with Distribution and Replication. SIGMOD 2003.June 2003, San Diego, CA.

19. S. Saroiu,K. Gummadi and S. Gribble. A measurement study of peer-to-peer file sharing systems. Proceedings of Multimedia Conferencing and Networking 2002.
20. F. S. Annexstein, K. A. Berman and M. A. Jovanovic. Latency Effects on Reachability in Large-scale Peer-to-Peer Networks. Procs of the 13th annual ACM symposium on Parallel algorithms and architectures, Crete, Greece 2001.

Author Index

c